9-1-15

A Jubilee for All Time

A Jubilee for All Time

The Copernican Revolution in
Jewish-Christian Relations

EDITED BY

GILBERT S. ROSENTHAL

PICKWICK *Publications* · Eugene, Oregon

A JUBILEE FOR ALL TIME
The Copernican Revolution in Jewish-Christian Relations

Pickwick Publications
An Imprint of Wipf and Stock Publishers
199 W. 8th Ave., Suite 3
Eugene, OR 97401

www.wipfandstock.com

ISBN 13: 978-1-62564-597-5

Cataloguing-in-Publication data:
_____

A jubilee for all time: the Copernican revolution in Christian-Jewish relations / edited by Gilbert S. Rosenthal.

xxxii + 330 p. ; 23 cm. Includes bibliographical references.

ISBN 13: 978-1-62564-597-5

1. Vatican Council (2nd: 1962–1965: Basilica di San Pietro in Vaticano). Declaratio de ecclesiae habitudine ad religiones non-Christianas. 2. Religions—Relations. I. Rosenthal, Gilbert S. II. Title.

BM535 J75 2014
_____

Manufactured in the U.S.A.   04/23/2015

Nostra Aetate and *Evangelii Gaudium* © LIBRERIA EDITRICE VATICANA.

In Honor of Charles Dimston

"And you will find favor and approbation
in the eyes of God and humanity."

Proverbs 3:4

Contents

Preface

GRATITUDE IS A LOVELY quality of character; ingratitude is repugnant. Consequently, it is appropriate to offer appreciation to those people who made this volume possible. Father Professor John Pawlikowski and Professor Eugene Fisher have been extremely helpful in advising me about candidates to write chapters in the book and in other details. Professor Philip Cunningham has offered his unfailingly good advice and suggestions and has pointed me to relevant Catholic sources and texts. I am grateful to them and cherish their friendship.

The editorial staff at Wipf and Stock Publishers and Pickwick Publications has been most cooperative and valuable, and I must thank their editor-in-chief, Dr. K. C. Hanson, as well as Christian Amondson, Matthew Wimer, Calvin Jaffarian and Jeremy Funk. It has been my pleasure to work with Pickwick Publications, as it was when I produced my earlier volume, *What Can a Modern Jew Believe?*

My son-in-law, Nelson Stacks, helped me with many of the technical issues in producing the manuscript. Candace Johnson offered invaluable help in preparing the files for the publisher and I owe her much.

The Library of the Hebrew College in Newton, Massachusetts, was, as usual, at my service at all times. I am deeply grateful to Harvey Sukenic and his staff for all their readiness to help me even at great distance. Without their assistance, I could not have realized my hope to produce this complex volume. And, of course, I am truly happy and gratified that so many wonderful contributors in five nations and of diverse religious traditions eagerly signed aboard in offering their views on the meaning of the Second Vatican Ecumenical Council and *Nostra Aetate*. They have produced, in my judgment, a worthy tribute to that landmark document.

I cannot sufficiently express my deep appreciation to my dear friend, Mr. Charles Dimston of Kings Point, New York, whose financial support made this volume possible. Mr. Dimston is a true philanthropist, who supports educational and religious institutions in America and in Israel, and whose sponsorship of literary projects is admirable.

Additionally, I thank my life's partner, Ann T. Rosenthal, my love and wife for over fifty-six years, for reading all the texts, offering suggestions, and urging me to undertake this complex project. Her encouragement and assistance have been unfailingly vital these many years.

Finally, I offer thanks to the Master of all, whose often fractious and truculent children exhibited in the documents produced at Vatican II a glimmer of what the messianic era must look like: love and justice for all; compassion and understanding that differences are a blessing and not a curse; that God has willed it so until the end of days.

Introduction

Gilbert S. Rosenthal

I WAS A YOUNG and callow rabbi serving a congregation in New Jersey about forty miles from New York City. The year was 1960, and Thanksgiving was approaching. I had an inspirational idea: My synagogue was literally across the road from a Roman Catholic church. Why not invite the priest and his flock to join my congregation in a program—not a worship service—of thanksgiving for the blessings of freedom in this blessed land? So I called the priest whom I had never met and enthusiastically told him of my idea, stressing that this would be a program without any liturgical content, confident that he would accept my invitation. I was quite wrong: The priest responded, "Rabbi, I should very much like to take you up on your offer but I cannot. You see, my bishop, Bishop Ahr of Trenton, prohibits his priests from ever entering a synagogue." I was amazed and crushed. The fact that I vividly remember that conversation after over fifty years have elapsed underscores my sense of despair and the lasting impression it made on me. Imagine that a scant fifteen years after the *Shoah*—the Holocaust that destroyed six million Jews in Christian Europe—and the Catholic Church would not even talk to Jews or enter their houses of worship! We were just across the road from each other, but we might as well have been on other sides of the world. Perhaps that episode was the catalyst of my commitment to interreligious dialogue throughout my long rabbinic career.

That was in 1960. In 1986, the Holy Father himself, Pope John Paul II, of blessed memory, went to the Great Synagogue of Rome (the first pope ever to do so): he embraced Chief Rabbi Elio Toaff, sat with him before the Holy Ark containing the Torah scrolls, and chatted amiably and amicably with him, younger brother with his beloved older brother, as the pope put it so warmly, stating that Judaism is intrinsically bound up with Christianity. And then his successor, Pope Benedict XVI, visited synagogues in Cologne, Germany; New York City; and Rome. Moreover, I met Pope John Paul II at a small gathering in the office of the late Cardinal John O'Connor of New York in 1995. And I was an official Jewish greeter to Pope Benedict XVI in 2008 when he met with a delegation of religious leaders of various faiths at the Pope John Paul II Center in Washington DC. Frankly, I never dreamed that I would meet and greet a pope!

What had happened to bring about such a sea change in Catholic-Jewish relations? What occurred since my youthful rebuff of 1960? The answer is Pope John XXIII, of blessed memory, the Second Vatican Ecumenical Council, and a document known as *Nostra Aetate* (*In Our Time*). Nothing less than a Copernican revolution in Catholic-Jewish relations had taken place in the wake of that historic Ecumenical Council that lasted from 1962 to 1965 and that produced a number of earth-shaking documents, most notably *Nostra Aetate*, especially section 4.

Pope John XXIII had served as Nuncio Roncalli in the Balkans and Turkey during World War II. He had seen firsthand what was happening to European Jewry, and his conscience was deeply affected. He was responsible for issuing fake documents including "Certificates of Immigration to Palestine" for Slovak and Bulgarian Jews that enabled numerous Jews to escape the Nazi killing machine, and he tried in vain to prompt the Vatican to take more vigorous action. When he was elected pope, he determined that he would set the course for the Catholic Church towards *aggiornamento*—updating its teachings and doctrines, and revising the Church's attitude to Judaism and Jews was a high priority. He greeted a delegation of Jewish leaders early in his pontificate with the words, "I am Joseph your brother" (Gen 45:4; his middle name was Giuseppe). He removed the odious Good Friday prayer: *pro perfidis Judaeis*, ("for the conversion of the perfidious or unbelieving Jews"). On June 16, 1960, he met with a frail Holocaust survivor from France, Professor Jules Isaac, who had failed to involve Pius XII in reevaluating the teachings of the Church on Judaism and the role that "the teaching of contempt" had played in preparing the soil for the *Shoah*. The role of Pius XII in dealing with Nazism, racism and genocide of the Jews of Europe remains a puzzle—a puzzle that may not be solved unless the Vatican archives are fully opened to scholars, and even then we may not find an answer to the question, could Pius XII have done more to save Europe's Jews? But this we do know: 4,447 Italian Jews were sequestered and saved in convents, schools, seminaries, and other Catholic institutions.[1] Did this come about at the behest of the pope? We don't know for sure. And this we also know: Pius XII was pope from 1939 to 1958. That means he served as pope for thirteen postwar years—a term longer than his wartime pontificate. What did he do to reeducate Catholics in their dealings with Jews? What new teachings did he promulgate regarding Judaism? Did he do anything to uproot the religious roots of anti-Judaism? He removed the translation of the odious term *perfidious*, in the Good Friday Prayer, but so far as I can tell, he did little or nothing.

But if Jules Isaac failed to sway Pope Pius XII, he was eminently successful with Pope John XXIII; his appeal to John XXIII fell on receptive ears. John XXIII appointed a German scholar, Cardinal Augustin Bea, to oversee the production of a document on Jews and Judaism that the Council could adopt that would acknowledge the role of Christian teaching in preparing the soil for the *Shoah* and that would chart a new course for the relations between the two faiths. Sadly, Pope John XXIII died before the second session of the Council, and now it was left to his successor, Paul VI, to carry on the remarkable process that John had started.

The document that emerged from Vatican II did not come about easily or readily. Quite the contrary: it was subjected to sharp debates and disagreements. Conservative clergy did not want to say anything benevolent about the Jews, the historic "enemies" of Jesus and the Church who murdered Jesus. Anti-Semitism was rife in certain clergy circles. Moreover, the prelates from the Middle East and Arab lands were very wary lest the Council articulate anything positive about Jews and Judaism and thereby strengthen the State of Israel in its confrontation with the Arab world. But the bitter impact of the *Shoah* was determinative. Pope Benedict XVI, who had as a young priest attended the Council, reflected many years later on what motivated the Council to approve a document on the Jews. "From the very beginning, our Jewish friends were present and said

1. See Renzo de Felice, *Storia degli ebrei italiani sotto il fascismo* (Turin: Einaudi, 1972), 628–32; trans. Robert L. Miller, *The Jews in Fascist Italy* (New York: Enigma Books, 2001), 466ff. & 751–756; Susan Zuccotti, *Under His Very Window* (New Haven: Yale University Press, 2000), esp. 300–326; Zuccotti, "Pius XII and the Rescue of Jews in Italy: Evidence of a Papal Directive," in Joshua D. Zimmerman, ed., *Jews in Italy under Fascist and Nazi Rule* (Cambridge: Cambridge University Press, 2005), 287–307.

to us Germans, but not only to us, that after the sad happenings of that Nazi century, of that Nazi decade, the Catholic Church ought to speak a message about the Old Testament, and about the Jewish people. They said: Even if it is clear that the Church is not responsible for the *Shoah*, those who committed those crimes were, for the most part, Christians, and so we ought to deepen and renew the Christian conscience, even if we know well that the real believers always resisted against those things. And so it was clear that the relationship with the world of the ancient People of God ought to be an object of reflection."[2]

Even more remarkably, several of the key players who helped bring about the positive statement in section 4 were converts from other religions to Catholicism, including converts from Judaism and Protestantism. Rev. John Oesterreicher played a key role in drafting the text of *Nostra Aetate* on the Jews, as did Rev. Gregory Baum—both former Jews. And the writings of Rev. Karl Thieme and Rev. Dietrich von Hildebrand, both converts from Protestant faiths, helped shape the thinking of the Church on Jewish affairs.[3] And then we must record the role that Rabbi Abraham Joshua Heschel played in swaying the opinion of Pope Paul VI, successor to John XXIII, on the matter of converting Jews to the true faith. When a version of the statement called for "the reunion of the Jewish people with the Church" (i.e., the conversion of Jews to Catholicism), Heschel flew to the Vatican, met with the pope and Cardinal Bea and stated that he would rather "go to Auschwitz than give up my religion." The pope struck the noxious passage, and a revised version was submitted for approval by the Council. The Council approved it overwhelmingly and on October 28, 1965, Pope Paul VI promulgated it. It was the first time in two millennia that a Council had issued an authoritative declaration about Jews and Judaism. Hitherto, popes issued bulls and encyclicals dealing with Jews, but never had an Ecumenical Council undertaken such a task.[4]

Section 4 of *Nostra Aetate*, "On the Relations of the Church to Non-Christian religions," is a short but revolutionary declaration. It acknowledges the Jewish roots of Christianity, noting that Jesus and his disciples were all Jewish. It reaffirms that God's covenant with Israel is still very much valid. It deplores anti-Semitism. It states that all Jews then living

2. Vatican Website, http://www.vatican.va , February 15, 2013.

3. See John Connelly, *From Enemy to Brother* (Cambridge: Harvard University Press, 2012).

4. For the full text, see Appendix I.

or in subsequent generations are not to be held guilty for Jesus's death. It urges that preachers and teachers not give rise to anti-Judaism in their preaching and teaching. It calls for fraternal dialogue between the two faiths. And rather than advocating proselytizing Jews, it cites Paul's views in Rom 9–11, which stress that Christianity is the new shoot grafted on the old (nurturing roots of Judaism) and that God does not renege on His promises or calling; and it looks forward to the eschatological joining of the faiths into one in worshipping the one God (Zeph 3:9). By citing Rom 9–11, the document rejects the usual interpretation of Letter to the Hebrews chapter 8 that seems to portray Judaism as obsolete and passé. To put it differently, Romans trumps Hebrews.

On the other hand, *Nostra Aetate* stated that "the Jewish authorities and those who followed their lead pressed for the death of Christ." Who were those so-called leaders? Surely not the corrupt and venal high priest and Roman lackey, Caiaphas, and his stooges! And it reiterated that the Church is "the new people of God," thereby reaffirming the theology of supersessionism or displacement. And it merely "deplored" anti-Semitism rather than condemning it. It remained for Pope John Paul II to condemn anti-Semitism as "a sin against God and humanity." But as Boston's gravel-voiced Cardinal Richard Cushing, a staunch champion of the document, noted, "The declaration we have is not perfect, but, in my opinion, it is a good start." And Cardinal Walter Kasper, long-time president of the Vatican's Commission for Religious Relations with the Jews, described it as "the beginning of the beginning."

However, Paul VI was somewhat ambivalent about the pronouncements of Vatican II and *Nostra Aetate*. True, he was responsible for emending the odious Good Friday prayer for the conversion of the Jews to read, "The Church prays for the Jewish people that they may continue to grow . . . in faithfulness to God's covenant" and to look forward toward "the fullness of redemption" at the end of time. And he established the Commission for Religious Relations with the Jews, headed for some years by Cardinals Johannes Willebrands, Edward Idris Cassidy, and Walter Kasper, and currently by Cardinal Kurt Koch. At the same time, he delivered a Lenten Mass sermon on Passion Sunday in which he called the day "a grave and sad page because it narrates the conflict, the clash between Jesus and the Hebrew people, a people predestined to await the Messiah but who, just at the right moment, not only did not recognize Him but fought him, abused him, and finally killed him."[5] Old stereotypes and prejudices die slowly, it appears. Then, in 1964, he made a somewhat bizarre visit to Israel, entering via the obscure town of Megiddo; he never met officially with Israeli leaders; he never mentioned the State of Israel once during his brief stay. Was his reluctance to acknowledge the existence of the State a concession to the Arab world in which Christian presence was growing increasingly tenuous? Or was it due to the ancient view of the Church, dating back to Justin Martyr in the second century, that the Jewish people having rejected Jesus lost their Temple and their independent state and would never return home until they accept Jesus as their messiah and savior?

Despite the papal ambivalence, a series of very important documents on the relationship of the Church to the Jewish people ensued, fleshing out and expanding on the views promulgated by *Nostre Aetate*. "Guidelines for Implementing the Councilor Declaration *Nostra Aetate*" was produced in 1974. Then came "Notes on the Correct way to Present Jews and Judaism in Preaching and Catechesis" in 1985. "God's Mercy Endures Forever: Guidelines on the Presentation of Jews and Judaism in Catholic Preaching" followed in 1988. An important statement on the *Shoah* was published in the paper "We Remember: A Reflection on the *Shoah*" in 1998. "The Jewish People and Their Sacred Scriptures" was issued in 2002 and was partly the work of Cardinal Joseph Ratzinger, who was later to be elected Pope Benedict XVI. It was remarkable in that it acknowledged for the first time that the Jewish interpretations of Scripture are possible, and that the "Jewish messianic expectation is not in vain." Further, it expressed the belief in a messiah who "will have the traits of Jesus who has already come and is already present and active among us."[6] All these documents are important because they constitute a vital part of the magisterium—the official body of teachings of the Catholic Church, teachings that will undoubtedly shape Catholic understanding of Jews and Judaism for the foreseeable future.

But if Pope Paul VI was somewhat ambivalent about Jews and Judaism and the State of Israel, his remarkable successor, Pope John Paul II (1978–2005), was definitely not. No other pope in history did as much as John Paul II in fostering a new relationship with the Jewish people based

5. Quoted in John Connelly, *From Enemy to Brother*, 269.

6. Pontifical Biblical Commission, "The Jewish People and Their Scriptures." http://www.vatican.va/roman_curia/congregations/cfaith/pcb_documents/rc_con_cfaith_doc_20020212_popolo-ebraico_en.html/.

on understanding, trust, and respect and, yes, even love. Undoubtedly his Polish background was responsible, because he grew up with Jews, had Jewish friends and soccer buddies, witnessed the tragic destruction of over three million Polish Jews, and felt deeply the tragedy of the *Shoah*, describing it as "an indelible stain on the history of the [twentieth] century."[7] Some years ago I met his closest Jewish friend, Jerzy Kluger, who warmly described the devoted and loving relationship between the two men that continued into John Paul's pontificate. When a young bishop in Krakow, he ordered a Jewish child who had been hidden by a Catholic family during World War II returned to its Jewish family. Baltimore's Cardinal William Keeler, who served for many years as president of the U.S. Conference of Catholic Bishops' Committee on Relations with the Jews, and had attended Vatican II as a young priest, remarked that this was a revolutionary change in the Church's policy. In 1848, when little Edgaro Mortara of Bologna was kidnapped by Church police because his nanny had secretly baptized him, Pope Pius IX refused to return the lad to his parents and raised him as a priest—lost to the Jewish people forever. But this was a different pope and a different century. The pope devoted many hours during his almost twenty-seven-year tenure as pope to rectifying some of the terrible wrongs that were the root causes of anti-Judaism. Early on, he visited Auschwitz and begged forgiveness for the crimes committed by Christians against Jews and other peoples, and he called for a "purification of memory." In 1986, he paid his historic visit to the Rome synagogue, embraced and sat with Chief Rabbi Toaff, and chatted amiably. He stressed that Judaism is intrinsic to Christianity, remarking the he regarded Jews as "our elder brother in faith." In a speech at Mainz, Germany (1980), he stressed that Jews are "the people of God of the Old Testament, never revoked by God, the present-day people of the covenant concluded with Moses." He denounced anti-Semitism as a "sin against God and humanity." But strangely he viewed Nazism as a "neo-pagan phenomenon," playing down the religious roots of that abomination.

In December of 1993, at the pope's prompting, the Vatican recognized the State of Israel and established full diplomatic relations. It was a stunning reversal of the ancient theological position—going back to Justin Martyr and developed by John Chrysostom and Augustine among others—that viewed the loss of the Temple and nation of Judea

7. Commission for Religious Relations with the Jews, "We Remember: A Reflection on the *Shoah*." http://www.vatican.va/roman_curia/pontifical_councils/chrstuni/documents/rc_pc_chrstuni_doc_16031998_shoah_en.html/.

as punishment for the Jewish rejection of Jesus, causing the Jews to be eternal wanderers—stateless people forever—until they accept Jesus as the messiah, protected but kept in an inferior status.[8] I remember well the intimate and amiable kosher reception at the home of Cardinal John O'Connor of New York to mark that historic event. The reader should recall that on January 26, 1904, the president of the World Zionist Organization, Dr. Theodor Herzl, gained an audience with Pope Pius X, urging him to recognize and endorse the Zionist goal to rebuild the ancient homeland. The pope rebuffed Herzl, indicating that "we cannot favor this movement . . . the Hebrew people have not recognized our Lord, therefore we cannot recognize the Hebrew people." He insisted that "we cannot support the Hebrew people in acquisition of the Holy Places." However, the pope added: "And so, if you come to Palestine and settle your people there, we shall have churches and priests ready to baptize all of you."[9]

In 1994, John Paul II hosted a remarkable concert to commemorate the *Shoah* at the Vatican with the Krakow Philharmonic Orchestra under the baton of its Jewish conductor, Gilbert Levine. In 2000, John Paul II made his historic visit to Israel. This time it was an official and public visit including a moving event at Yad Vashem where he asked forgiveness for the crimes against the Jewish people and then offered a deeply emotional, poignant prayer at the Western Wall. He inserted a private prayer in the crevice of the Wall, the receptacle of so many tens of thousands of notes throughout the ages that read:

> God of our fathers, you chose Abraham and his descendants to bring Your name to the nations: We are deeply saddened by the behavior of those who in the course of history have caused these children of Yours to suffer, and asking forgiveness we wish to commit ourselves to genuine brotherhood with the people of the Covenant.[10]

The iconic pictures of that extraordinary event still stir me profoundly to this day.

---

8. See Paula Fredriksen, *Augustine and the Jews: A Christian Defense of Jews and Judaism* (New York: Doubleday, 2008).

9. Raphael Patai, ed., Harry Zohn, trans.,*The Complete Diaries of Theodor Herzl* (5 vols., New York: Herzl Press and Thomas Yoseloff, 1960), 4:1601–5, Interestingly, his successor, Pope Benedict XV, expressed support of the Zionist endeavor.

10. Franklin Sherman, ed., *Bridges: Documents of the Christian-Jewish Dialogue*, vol. 2 (New York: Paulist, 2014), 207.

I can state unequivocally that John Paul II accomplished more in his pontificate of almost twenty-seven years to improve Catholic-Jewish relations than had been achieved in all the preceding nineteen centuries, and that the Jewish people will never forget this remarkably benevolent and compassionate friend.

Benedict XVI, who succeeded John Paul II and served from 2005 to 2013, witnessed the calamity of the Second World War but from a very different perspective than that of John Paul II. He was born in Bavaria, Germany, had been a member of the Hitler Youth, and was drafted into the Wehrmacht as a teenager. Nevertheless, he chose a clergy career after the war, was closely associated with John Paul II, and was known as a distinguished theologian and scholar. He carried on the work of John Paul II. He visited synagogues in Cologne, New York City, and Rome. He deepened his Church's understanding of *Nostra Aetate*. He wrote the important introduction to "The Jewish People and Their Sacred Scriptures in the Christian Bible." At the remarkable meeting that I attended in Washington in 2008, he reaffirmed his commitment to the teachings of *Nostra Aetate* and then met privately with the Jewish delegation to wish them a blessed Pesah. He visited Israel in 2009. He stressed on a number of occasions that the roots of Christianity are found in Judaism, without which one cannot understand Christianity.[11] He insisted that "every effort must be made to fight anti-Semitism wherever it is found."[12] He reiterated that the Sinai covenant is enduring and irrevocable. He actually quoted a passage from the Talmud in one of his talks ("The world stands on three pillars: Torah, worship and deeds of kindness"—Mishnah *Avot* 1:2). That in itself is quite remarkable if we recall that throughout the ages, popes condemned the Talmud as a book of lies and blasphemies and insults against Jesus and Christianity, and in 1240 in Paris and again in the 1550s in Italy, they ordered the burning of the Talmud along with other Hebrew volumes.[13]

---

11. For a powerful and scholarly argument stressing the need to study the Hebraic roots of Christianity, see Marvin R. Wilson, *Exploring Our Hebraic Heritage: A Christian Theology of Roots and Renewal* (Grand Rapids: Eerdmans, 2014).

12. Franklin Sherman, ed., *Bridges: Documents of the Christian-Jewish Dialogue*, vol. 2 (New York: Paulist, 2014), 210, 224–25.

13. Benedict XVI was also capable of some original reinterpretations of anti-Jewish biblical texts. For example, the odious curse in Matthew 27:25: "His blood be upon us and our children," so often cited by Christians in condemning Jews to perpetual imprecation, is interpreted by him to mean that Jesus's blood atones for their sins just as the blood of an animal sacrificed in the Temple was sprinkled on the sinners to atone for their errors.

Benedict XVI also referred to the *Shoah* as a neopagan phenomenon, downplaying the religious roots. He committed some strange blunders in his attempt to woo back into the Catholic fold the members of the heretical St. Pius X Society. He lifted the excommunication of four of their bishops, including that of Bishop Richard Williamson, a vile anti-Semite and Holocaust denier. When he learned of the bishop's sordid record, he actually apologized for his blunder (a remarkable departure from the doctrine of papal infallibility!), cautioning about the need to check out backgrounds on the Internet. He also restored a revised version of the Tridentine Latin Good Friday Prayer, *Pro Conversione Iudaeorum* ("for the conversion of the Jews"), although Cardinal Walter Kasper assured the outraged Jewish community that the prayer was eschatological—that it referred to the end of days, not to historical times. And Benedict raised hackles in the Jewish world when he advanced Pius XII one step closer to sainthood. Still, Benedict's pontificate has been marked by continued rapprochement between the Catholic and Jewish faiths.

Cardinal Jorge Mario Bergoglio of Argentina succeeded Benedict XVI in March of 2013, after Benedict XVI resigned, taking the name of Pope Francis I (for Francis of Assisi, whom he admires so profoundly). He is the first pope from Latin America. His record as a warm friend of the Jewish community of Buenos Aires is well documented. He was involved in interfaith activities, visiting the synagogues on several occasions and actually speaking from their pulpits. The picture of him lighting the Hanukkah menorah in the synagogue is iconic. He cultivated a long and warm friendship with the rector of the Seminario Rabbinico Latinamericano, Rabbi Abraham Skorka, and the two of them produced a volume, *On Heaven and Earth*. He was notable in his denunciation of the tragic murder of eighty-five men and women in the bombing of the Jewish Community Center of Buenos Aires in 1994, apparently the work of Iranian terrorists. Francis wrote recently: "The Church officially recognizes that the People of Israel continues to be the Chosen People."[14] He rejects the deicide charge and reiterates that *Nostra Aetate* and Vatican II are the new, official teachings of the Church. He also urges the opening of the Vatican Archives to examine the war years of Pius XII's pontificate

---

14. Jorge Mario Bergoglio (Pope Francis I) and Abraham Skorka, *On Heaven and Earth: Pope Francis on Faith, Family, and the Church in the Twenty-First Century* (New York: Image, 2013), 188; see also Franklin Sherman, ed., *Bridges: Documents of the Christian-Jewish Dialogue*, vol. 2 (New York: Paulist, 2014), 238–39; Pope Francis I, *Evangelii Gaudium*.

and to search out the truth once and for all. Within hours of his election to the papacy, he sent a note to Rome's chief rabbi, Ricardo Di Segni, inviting him to the inauguration of his papacy and assuring him of his friendship and commitment "to contribute to the progress in relations between the Hebrews and the Catholics which has become well known since Vatican Council II, in a spirit of renewed collaboration to the service of a world that may be more in harmony with the will of the Creator."[15] What a striking difference from the Middle Ages! In those times, a delegation of Roman Jews would greet a newly inaugurated pope, carrying a Torah scroll that they would extend to him, while begging the pope to renew the *Constitutio pro Judaeis* that dates back to Pope Calixtus II (twelfth century) but really derives from Pope Gregory the Great's bull, *Sicut Judaeis* (ca. 600). The pope would bless the Jewish delegation and admonish them that while the Church reveres the Torah, it deplores the fact that the Jews remain blind to the truth of the Gospels. Some of the popes would commit the ultimate indignity of dropping the scroll to the mortification of the Jewish delegation.

More recently, Pope Francis noted that "to be a good Christian it is necessary to understand Jewish history and traditions," and he stressed that "a Christian cannot be an anti-Semite." He wondered what of the promises made to them by God: has it all come to nothing? "With the help of God, and especially since the Second Vatican Council we have rediscovered that the Jewish people are still, for us, the holy root from which Jesus originated." The pope reminded himself and others that "I also questioned God, particularly when my mind turned to the memory of the terrible experiences of the *Shoah*." He reiterated the teaching of Paul that God's fidelity to the covenant established with Israel was never abolished, and that "through the terrible testing during those dark centuries the Jews have clung to their faith in God, for which we can never adequately thank them. By persevering in their faith they recall for all of us Christians the fact that we are always awaiting the Lord's return."[16] And on his May 2014 visit to Israel, in addition to visiting the Western Wall and Yad Vashem, he placed flowers on the grave of Theodor Herzl, in a gesture of apology for Pius X's rebuff of the Zionist movement. Clearly, Francis I is warmly and profoundly committed to working for

15. http://www.ccjr.us/dialogika-resources/documents-and-statements/roman-catholic/francis/1206-f2013march13/.

16. For the text of his Exhortation, see Appendix II.

greater trust and respect between the two faiths in the spirit of that historic document, *Nostra Aetate.*

So it is clear that the Catholic Church has come a long way these past fifty years or so. But it would be naive for us to conclude that the work is over, the task accomplished, and that we can now move on to other areas of exploration and exposition. Let us recall that nineteen centuries of the teaching of contempt preceded Vatican II: you cannot undo nineteen hundred years in a mere fifty, I believe. Remember that teaching, preaching, biblical exposition, homilies, and prayers denigrated Judaism during those long centuries. Good Friday and the Easter season were always dangerous times for Jews; often mobs who had just heard preachers denounce the Jews as perpetrators of deicide, as Christ killers, would pour out of churches and set upon the Jewish quarter for a pogrom or a massacre or an expulsion. If you teach your child that the neighbor down the block had killed your god, you surely cannot expect your child to love or respect that Jewish neighbor. Quite the contrary: contempt was bred in the churches and cathedrals down through the ages.[17] I believe it is a serious error to downplay the religious roots of the Nazi horrors and to blame it all on so-called neopaganism. Of course the Nazi phenomenon was partly neopagan. But what prepared the soil of Germany and other lands in Christian Europe where the *Shoah* occurred? I firmly believe that the teachings of contempt, the charge of deicide, the denigration of Jews, their portrayal as devils and demonic creatures fixed in the minds of Christian Europeans a despicable, contemptible and cursed race that would best be eliminated. And whereas it is true that popes officially protected Jews to keep them as living evidence of the truth of Christianity, as Augustine understood it, papal policies consisted of, in the words of Salo W. Baron, "general sufferance with severe restrictions."[18] Let us remember that Pope Innocent III inaugurated the Jew badge at the Fourth Lateran Council in 1215; that the ghetto that unofficially began in Venice in 1516 reflected papal desires to segregate Jews lest they contaminate Christians; that Pope Paul IV in his odious bull, *Cum nimis absurdum*

---

17. See Mary C. Boys, *Redeeming Our Sacred Story: The Death of Jesus and Relations between Jews and Christians* (New York: Paulist, 2013). Sister Mary analyzes the disastrous influence the deicide charge exerted, and she suggests concrete measures for uprooting this malign teaching.

18. See Salo W. Baron, *A Social and Religious History of the Jews* (18 vols., 2nd ed., New York: Columbia University Press, 1952–83), 4:3–149 for a thorough survey of papal policies.

(1555), called for segregation of Jews and for avoidance of any business or social contacts with them, compelled the men to wear a yellow hat and the women a veil, reduced them to dealing in secondhand goods, prohibited them from engaging Christian nurses, and added further oppressive measures to marginalize them and make life more miserable for them.[19] Jews were depicted as having a veil over their hearts to the truth (2 Cor 3:15), a frequent theme in Christian art and architecture. The Hebrew Bible or "Old Testament" was viewed with disdain as merely a prelude to the New Testament, a position that goes back to Marcion in the second century that had been condemned as heretical but never really disappeared until Vatican II. The Church, through the Inquisition office, periodically seized Hebrew writings for censorship or worse: it condemned them to the flames. And although the Catholic Church officially did not espouse a "racial" notion of salvation, teaching that any race or ethnic group was saved by belief in Jesus and no race is superior to any other, the Spanish Church in the days of the Inquisition did preach the notion of *limpieza de sangre,* "purity of blood," as a mark of a true Christian, and the modern German Catholic Church exhibited some strong racial tendencies in dealing with other faiths—especially Judaism.[20] Clearly, the Nazis learned their lesson well and borrowed many of their despicable ideas and actions from the Catholic and Protestant churches and their leaders. Under the Church the pattern was, the Jews *cannot live as equals* among us, so their rights were severely curtailed. The next stage was, the Jews *cannot live among us,* and the ghettos were instituted. The Nazis took it one step further: the Jews *cannot live . . .*

But other media were invoked in the service of this teaching of contempt. Some years ago, my wife and I visited Madrid for the first time, and we rushed to the Prado Museum to see some of its treasures. I was struck and shocked on visiting the European gallery where I noticed two paintings from the School of Rubens (fourteenth- and fifteenth-century Flemish). One depicted God in heaven above a sacrificial lamb (Jesus— *agnus Dei*). Below was a mob of confused and benighted Jews surrounded by a hodgepodge of torn texts and Hebrew letters, symbolizing the

19. See Solomon Grayzel, *The Church and the Jews in the XIIIth Century,* vol. 1 (New York: Hermon, 1966); vol 2, ed. and arr. Kenneth Stowe (New York: Jewish Theological Seminary of America, 1989); Cecil Roth, *The History of the Jews in Italy* (Philadelphia: Jewish Publication Society, 1946), 294ff.; Attilio Milano, *Storia degli ebrei in Italia* (Turin: Einaudi, 1963), 74ff., 150ff. and passim.

20. Connelly, *From Enemy to Brother,* 36–93.

superseded Old Testament. The other displays a madding crowd scream-
ing to crucify Jesus. One man, who looks like a maniac or a devil, has
a rope around Jesus's neck and is dragging him to the cross. Below are
mobs of Jews—fat, vulgar, fingers festooned with gems and rings, reeking
of opulence. The contrast between Jews and Christians was appalling.

Next we visited Paris and of course went to Notre Dame. I stood
outside the main entrance of the famed cathedral and observed two
contrasting statues: one was a disheveled woman, blinded by her crown
that had slipped from her head, clutching a broken staff; the other was
a resplendent woman, crown proudly perched on her head, clutching a
perfect scepter. I knew the symbolism at once: the former represented
Judaism—blind to the new truth and no longer the receptacle of sovereignty; the other represented the new and true faith—Christianity. These
artistic depictions are found in other cathedrals throughout Europe.[21]
Nor should we forget the anti-Jewish biases and stereotypes found in
literature and theater—in Chaucer, Shakespeare, Marlowe, Dickens, T.
S. Eliot—just to mention a few.[22] The Passion Plays at Oberammergau,
a blatantly anti-Jewish production, attracted hundreds of thousands
through the centuries. And even in music (e.g., Bach's chorales), anti-
Jewish themes are explored and developed. All of this is part of the campaign of *adversus Judaeos*—opposing the former truth of Judaism, now
replaced by the new truth of Christianity. In art, architecture, literature,
theater, theology, preaching, teaching, commentaries, and liturgy, this
was the line followed for nineteen centuries.

Vatican II reversed all that and shifted Catholicism away from all
that had preceded that historic Council. The Bishops' Committee on Relations with the Jews meets twice yearly in the United States with the National Council of Synagogues, and I am certain in other nations as well.

---

21. See Heinz Schreckenberg, *The Jews in Christian Art: An Illustrated History*
(New York: Continuum, 1996).

22. In his *Oliver Twist*, Charles Dickens referred to the villainous Fagin some three
hundred times as "the Jew." Several British Jews wrote him letters of protest causing
him to reconsider his portrayal, and in subsequent editions of the novel he removed
most of those references. Furthermore, in his last completed novel, *Our Mutual
Friend*, he introduced a Jewish character named Judah Riah, who is the perfect model
of a Jewish gentleman—honorable and upstanding. But the damage was done, and
Fagin remains in the minds of millions of Christians the symbol of the ruthless and
bloodthirsty Jew. The truth of this can be seen by the fact that when Menahem Begin
was elected prime minister of Israel, *Time* magazine maliciously informed its readers,
"BEGIN (rhymes with Fagin) WINS."

There are frequent visits to both churches and synagogues, with clergy speaking from the pulpits of both institutions. Joint statements on important issues are publicized periodically. There is no current office in the Vatican that targets Jews for conversion. Rabbis and priests are in constant dialogue, and many warm friendships have resulted. It is not unusual to find a Catholic priest or bishop or cardinal at a rabbi's Passover Seder or Shabbat dinner table. Catholic colleges and universities have established departments and centers for Christian-Jewish relations and chairs for Jewish studies. Even the Orthodox Jewish community, which for many years had shunned interreligious conversation or theological discussions, in great part due to the admonition of Rabbi Joseph B. Soloveitchik, has been drawn in. The Israeli Chief Rabbinate meets regularly with its Vatican counterpart. Chief Ashkenazi Rabbi Jonah Metzger met Christian leaders in Jerusalem (March 10, 2013) and reflected on the persecution of Jews through the ages in the Diaspora but noted that the adoption of *Nostra Aetate*, which repudiated the notion of Jewish guilt for the death of Jesus, had provided for an opportunity for reconciliation between the two faiths. He added, "I want to thank you for your support and help for us to fulfill the right to be citizens in the Holy Land, and may God bless you for coming to visit us." In the same month, when the Orthodox Lincoln Square Synagogue in New York City dedicated its new building on a Sabbath morning, Cardinal Timothy M. Dolan was the guest speaker from the pulpit of that synagogue. I submit that all this would have been impossible had it not been for *Nostra Aetate*. I look back fifty years and I marvel at what we have achieved in this Copernican revolution in Catholic-Jewish affairs. We have come a long way since 1960![23]

Apart from the revolution in Catholic-Jewish affairs, the Protestant world has also been deeply affected. Actually, the Protestants preceded the Catholics in seeking to understand the great tragedy of the *Shoah* and the role Christians and Christian thinking had played. Shortly after World War II, some Protestant theologians and clergy began to question how Christian Europe could have been the scene of the atrocious *Shoah*. Some began to suggest that maybe Christian teachings had prepared the soil

---

23. Some years ago, I met the late Cardinal Carlo Maria Martini of Milan. He told me of his love for the land of Israel, his familiarity with the modern Hebrew language, and that he had purchased a tomb in Israel in which to be buried. He asked if I had studied with Professor Abraham Joshua Heschel. When I replied in the affirmative, he eagerly urged me to tell him all I knew about Dr. Heschel because he admired his writings and teachings. This attitude was surely unheard of prior to Vatican II.

for the *Shoah*. The Seelisberg Declaration (1947) was an early joint but unofficial statement of the newly created International Council of Christians and Jews, consisting of Jews, Protestants, and a few Catholics. The ten points reminded all that one God speaks in the Old and New Testaments; that Jesus was a Jew, as were his first disciples and apostles; that the commandment to love one's neighbor is binding on both Christians and Jews; that in extolling Christianity we should not distort biblical or post-biblical Judaism; that Jews must not be depicted as enemies of Jesus; that the Passion must not be presented in a way that brings odium on all Jews then alive or in following centuries; that the curse that his blood be upon us and our children must be mitigated by the statement that God should forgive them for they know not what they do; that we must not teach that Jews are an accursed race; and that we must avoid suggesting that the first members of the Church had not been Jews. These principles anticipated the landmark statement of *Nostra Aetate* and subsequent documents.[24]

Moreover, individual theologians and clergy such as England's James Parkes, America's Bishop James Pike, Reinhold Niebuhr, Roy and Alice Eckardt; Sweden's Bishop Krister Stendhal; and others engaged in deep soul-searching and called for a reevaluation of Christian teachings on Judaism. Gradually, the various Protestant denominations, including Presbyterians, Lutherans, Methodists, Episcopalians, and others, issued statements to this effect and frankly acknowledged the tawdry role Christian teaching had played in that enormous tragedy. For example, in 1988 the Protestant World Council of Churches gathered in Sweden and issued a document titled "The Church and the Jewish People: Toward a New Understanding."[25] The document enumerated five guiding principles: 1) The covenant of God with the Jewish people remains valid; 2) anti-Semitism and all forms of the teaching of contempt for Judaism are to be rejected; 3) the living tradition is a gift of God; 4) coercive proselytism directed towards Jews is incompatible with Christian faith; 5) Jews and Christians bear a common responsibility as witnesses to God's righteousness and peace in the world. The fact that the document cites *Nostra*

---

24. For the full text of the Seelisberg Declaration and background, see William W. Simpson and Ruth Weyl, *The Story of the International Council of Christians and Jews* (Heppenheim: ICCJ, 1995), appendix II, 117–18.

25. "The Churches and the Jewish People," in *The New Relationship between Christians and Jews: Documentation of Major Statements* (Heppenheim: ICCJ, n.d.), 55–60.

Aetate buttresses my argument that *Nostra Aetate* was the catalyst that propelled a Protestant reevaluation of those teachings.[26]

Sadly, mainline Protestant churches have seen relations with Jews break down and founder over the Israel-Arab conflict. Mainline churches have a deep stake in the Middle East, going back to the early nineteenth century as their missionaries worked in Palestine, Syria, Egypt, Lebanon, and other lands in that region.[27] The leadership of those churches has exhibited increasingly hostile attitudes towards the State of Israel and is perceived by many as being anti-Israel and even anti-Jewish. Consequently, the warm relations of the 1970s and 1980s that dominated relations between the faith groups have chilled noticeably to the point of frozen indifference and even outright hostility.

Paradoxically, as relations with mainline churches have soured, evangelical churches are experiencing a rapprochement towards Jewish leaders and organizations. I say paradoxically because the Jewish community and its religious and secular organizations have most in common with the mainline, liberal churches—especially in the area of social justice, whether in the realm of women's rights, abortion, ordination of women, same-sex marriages, ordination of gays, and other issues of concern. But evangelicals are generally passionate supporters of the State of Israel—in part because they view the return of Jews to the Holy Land as a sine qua non for the second coming of Jesus (the Parousia), but also because they are sympathetic to the plight of a small, beleaguered nation in a sea of hostile Arabs, especially after the *Shoah*; and partly because they identify with a Western-style, democratic state in a region replete with brutal dictatorships. Hence, we are witnessing the growing bonds of affection and respect between the Jewish community and the evangelical churches.

Still, despite all the progress we have witnessed, we must not rest or be satisfied with past accomplishments. We need to move forward and flesh out the promise of *Nostra Aetate*. There are still opponents of its great teachings. The late Cardinal Avery Dulles, referred to it as "a hermeneutic rupture with past Church teachings," and he insisted that

26. An important statement by the Christian Scholars Group (Catholic and Protestant) titled, "A Sacred Obligation," was issued in 2003. See the volume that discusses it in depth, edited by John C. Merkle, *Faith Transformed: Christian Encounters with Jews and Judaism* (Collegeville, MN: Liturgical, 2003).

27. See Michael B. Oren, *Power, Faith and Fantasy* (New York: Norton, 2007), esp. 80–97.

we must continue to target Jews for baptism.[28] The heretical St. Pius X Society rejects the new views codified at Vatican II, remains deeply anti-Semitic, and refuses to be reconciled in the Church of Rome despite serious efforts of Benedict XVI to woo them back into the fold. But Cardinals Kasper and Koch, doubtless speaking in the name of the pope, made it abundantly clear that the society and its followers must subscribe to the newer teachings of the Church as codified in Vatican II or else remain excommunicated. Consequently, religious education and educational materials must reflect these newer teachings about Jews and Judaism. The flaccid and feckless responses of many Catholic and Protestant clergy to the Gibson film *The Passion of the Christ*, a film that revived ancient stereotypes and is at variance with many of the teachings of Vatican II, was stark proof that more work needs to be done.[29] The principles of *Nostra Aetate* have yet to be absorbed by too many seminarians, clergy, and laity in America—not to mention in South America, where 40 percent of the world's Catholics reside. And we need to educate Catholics in Asia and Africa and other parts of the world where the newer teachings have yet to penetrate. We have to uproot once and for all the "teaching of contempt" from Christian teaching and preaching if we are to uproot anti-Judaism from society. In short, there is much work left for us to build on the foundations set by Vatican II. But as Rabbi Tarfon observed, "You are not expected to complete the task; neither are you free to desist from making a start" (Mishnah *Avot* 2:16). This is the challenge to the new generation of preachers, teachers, clergy, theologians, and educators.

This volume contains contributions from a wide range of authors from five countries. There are Catholics and Jews, Protestants and evangelicals, Orthodox and liberal, men and women, theologians and congregational clergy represented here in my effort to give voice to the widest possible spectrum. The first section gives us some historical insights into what Vatican II achieved and how *Nostra Aetate* came about.

28. See Cardinal Avery Dulles, "Covenant and Mission," *America* (October 21, 2002) 8–11 and the rejoinders that follow on 12–16 by Mary Boys, Philip A. Cunningham, and John T. Pawlikowski. Also see Dulles's piece, "The Covenant with Israel," *First Things* (November 2005) 16–21. Cardinal Albert Vanhoye also subscribed to this position. For a full discussion and refutation, cf. John Pawlikowski, "Defining Catholic Identity against the Jews: Pope Benedict XVI and the Question of Mission to the Jewish People," in Alan Berger, ed., *Trialogue and Terror* (Eugene, OR: Cascade Books, 2012), 102–20.

29. See Philip A. Cunningham, ed., *Pondering the Passion* (Lanham, MD: Rowman and Littlefield, 2004).

The second section reflects the impact of the Council on various faith groups. The third section describes its educational and pastoral impact. The fourth section spells out for the reader several unresolved issues that still challenge us. The fifth section contains brief, personal statements and vignettes from a variety of contributors assessing how *Nostra Aetate* impacted their lives, thinking, teaching, and relationships. It is my sincere hope that this volume will inspire clergy and laity, educators and students, professional religion leaders as well as ordinary folks who seek a deeper understanding of the roots of their faith and the relationship between "the elder and younger brother"—Judaism and Christianity. Above all, I hope it will stimulate conversation and dialogue between members of the faith groups.

Once upon a time, not that long ago, Jews and Christians rarely spoke to one another. They ignored each other; they vilified each other; they shouted at each other. But they rarely spoke. My long study of history has taught me that *people who do not speak to one another do unspeakable things to one another.* We dare not return to that ancient state of being. The Second Vatican Council and its great pronouncements, especially *Nostra Aetate*, have ushered in a new era of respect, understanding, honor, and friendship. We must move forward in solidifying its achievements. That means that we Christians and Jews alike must expunge and finally remove any teachings or dogmas that demean or denigrate other faiths or show them in an invidious light. And furthermore, religious imperialism must go: the notion that "I'm in and you are out; that I am saved and you are damned; that it is my way or the highway; that I have a monopoly on truth and I possess the keys to the kingdom" must be discarded if we are to foster respect and trust. Vatican II moved away from the age-old doctrine, *extra ecclesiam nulla salus*—there is no salvation outside the one, true Catholic Church—a position that was never de jure part of the magisterium but was certainly de facto ingrained in Catholic attitudes. But now several of the documents ratified at Vatican II affirm that "other religions often reflect a ray of that Truth which enlightens all men."[30]

30. The Vatican II documents that articulate this position are *Lumen Gentium* (the Dogmatic Constitution of the Church), sec. 16; *Nostra Aetate* sec. 2; *Gaudium et Spes* sec. 22; and *Unitatis Redintegratio* sec. 13. See Christian Rutishauser, "'The Old Unrevoked Covenant' and 'Salvation for All Nations in Christ'—Catholic Doctrines in Contradiction?" in Philip A. Cuningham et al., eds., *Christ Jesus and the Jewish People Today* (Grand Rapids: Eerdmans, 2011), 229–50; Clark Williamson, "What Does It Mean to be Saved?", in *Pondering the Passion*, 119–28; Gilbert S. Rosenthal, "Salvation Jewish Style," in *Trialogue and Terror*, 23–36; Rosenthal, "*Hasidei Umot Ha-Olam*: A

Finally, in all of my interreligious work I have been guided by two biblical verses: "Come now let us reason together"(Isa 1:18), and "Then those who revered the LORD spoke to one another and the LORD took note and listened" (Mal 3:16). May those verses inspire us all.

Remarkable Concept," *Journal of Ecumenical Studies* 48 (2013) 467–90.

PART 1

Retrospective Reflections

1

Fifty Years since the Second Vatican Council

Its Significance for Christian-Jewish Relations

David Rosen

THE SECOND VATICAN ECUMENICAL Council convened by Blessed Pope John XXIII fifty years ago embodied a unique and transformative moment in the history of the Catholic Church; but it heralded an absolute revolution in terms of Catholic-Jewish relations. Among the fruits of the Council was the document known by its first words, *Nostra Aetate,* only promulgated in 1965, and section 4 of this document addresses the teaching of the Church in relation to Judaism and Jews, past and present.

In order to understand the significance of its content, we need to have some historical perspective, which, lamentable, is a very tragic one. A problematic aspect of the success of Christian-Jewish reconciliation in our times is that this tragic past is often forgotten or unknown to younger generations, and thus the significance of the transformation is not fully grasped. Accordingly, I recall now the negative attitude towards Judaism

3

that prevailed in the past only in order to highlight the significance of what *Nostra Aetate* has meant for the Jewish-Christian relationship.

As the community of believers in Jesus of Nazareth expanded into the Gentile world, the connection between the movement that became known as Christianity and its Hebrew origins weakened. There were two major forces at work here. The one was the need to gain greater acceptance in the Roman world. Indeed, especially once Christianity was established as the faith of the Holy Roman Empire, it had every pragmatic interest in minimizing if not in denying its connection to the Jewish people. The second fact, theologically more significant, was the unfortunate competition between Church and Synagogue for the title of the heir to the biblical heritage and its promises. In this process, not only was there the desire to affirm legitimacy and authority, but there was also the need to deny the legitimacy of the other.

Thus, not only did the Church see itself as the new Israel and the true Israel, but there was also the prevalent assumption that the old Israel was a failed Israel rejected by God. This was attributed to the Jewish failure to accept the Christian dispensation and to collective guilt for complicity in the crucifixion. Justin Martyr interpreted the destruction of the Temple in Jerusalem by the Romans and the exile as proof of Divine rejection, and Origen declared that "the blood of Jesus falls on Jews not only then, but on all generations until the end of the world." The fourth-century writings of John Chrysostom, particularly his *Orations against the Jews*, reflect how this concept of "replacement theology" had reached a new level of hostility:

> The synagogue is not only a brothel and a theater, it is also a den of robbers and a lodging for wild beasts . . . But when God forsakes a people, what hope of salvation is left? When God forsakes a place, that place becomes the dwelling of demons . . . They [the Jews] live for their bellies; they gape for things of this world; their condition is no better that that of pigs or goats because of their wanton ways and excessive gluttony . . . Indeed, the synagogue is less deserving of honor than any inn. It is not merely a lodging place for robbers and cheats but also for demons. This is true not only of the synagogue but also of the souls of Jews . . . [T]he martyrs have a special hatred for the Jews since the Jews crucified him for whom they have a special love . . . Was it not God who withdrew them [the priests and prophets of the Temple]? Surely, this is clear to everybody. Why, then did God take them away? Is it not obvious that he hated you and turned

his back on you once and for all? . . . Is it not because God has
abandoned you?[1]

This leitmotif of the Jews being of the devil and in league with the
devil was to be a recurrent theme throughout the following almost two
millennia. But it was the deicide charge that was used most of all to justify
the most terrible actions against Jews. Accordingly, Jews were overwhelmingly viewed as the enemy of God and as a diabolical force of evil. This led
to the horrendous and preposterous defamations and accusations such as
the blood libel originating in Norwich, England, in the twelfth century
and repeated thereafter with regularity. It also led to blaming the Jews
for the Black Death and various other plagues and disasters, providing
"justification" for pillaging and destroying Jewish communities and for
burning synagogues. Such was the case especially during the Crusades,
when the call "kill a Jew and save your soul" rang throughout Europe.

Ironically, the negative theological understanding of the meaning of
Jewish survival often served to mitigate some of these excesses. Christian
theologians who believed that the only purpose of the Jewish people was
to prepare the way for the Christian dispensation, and that Jewry had
accordingly now been replaced by the Church in the Divine plan, needed
to explain why the Jewish people continued to exist at all. Saint Augustine
explained that it was precisely part of the Divine intention that the Jewish
people should survive to wander as testimony to their obduracy, thus
confirming the truth of Christianity. Accordingly, Pope Innocent III (in
the twelfth and thirteenth centuries), for example, explained that while
"inherited guilt is on the whole [Jewish] nation [as] a curse to follow
them everywhere like Cain to live homelessly, nevertheless like Cain they
should never be destroyed, but remain as a testimony until the time of
Jesus' truth and the consequences for those who reject it."[2]

Nevertheless, the Council of Trent not only rejected the deicide
charge but stressed that the responsibility for the death of Jesus is upon
all humanity and especially Christians themselves, since, it declared,
they profess him as Lord and Savior yet choose to violate his teachings. A contemporary scholar on anti-Semitism has written that were

1. Saint John Chrysostom, *Discourses against Judaizing Christians*, trans. Paul W.
Harkins (Washington, DC: Catholic University of America Press, 1979), I.3.1, pp. 10-
11; I.4.1, p. 14; I.4.2, p. 15; VI.1.7, p. 149; VI.3.6, p.157; VI.4.4, p. 160. See also Malcolm
Vivian Hay, *Europe and the Jews* (Boston: Beacon, 1960), 29–31.

2. Solomon Grayzel, *The Church and the Jews in the XIIIth Century*, vol. 1 (New
York: Hermon, 1966), 127.

"this understanding of the crucifixion [to have] been widely preached and taught . . . the history of anti-Semitism might have taken a different course."[3]

There were indeed some more sympathetic voices, such as that of Saint Ignatius of Loyola, who, when accused of being Jewish, retorted that he would be greatly privileged if that were so. "What? To be related to Christ our Lord and to Our Lady the glorious virgin?"[4] This approach, however, was not typical.

Indeed, the attitude that we refer to today as "the teaching of contempt" (a term coined by the Jewish historian Jules Isaac) provided theological justification for Jewish homelessness and marginalization. Accordingly, the idea of the return of the Jewish people to assume sovereignty in its ancestral homeland, which assumed political form in the late nineteenth century as the Zionist movement, was not viewed favorably by the Church, and Pope Pius X told Theodor Herzl so at their meeting in 1904.

As indicated, there were notable Christians whose treatment of and even solidarity with the Jewish people transcended this "teaching of contempt." A great exemplar in this regard was the scholar Johannes Reuchlin, who in 1510 published the first Christian defense of the Talmud, which had been consistently defamed and publicly burnt during the preceding centuries. In more modern times, among the notable Catholics who took brave and public stands against anti-Semitism was the theologian Jacques Maritain, who declared that "Israel is the Jesus among the nations and the Jewish Diaspora within Christian Europe is one long Via Dolorosa."[5]

While there were such harbingers of the change in Christian attitudes towards Jews and Judaism, especially with modern scholarly research and perspectives (facilitated in no small part within the Catholic Church by Pope Pius XII's encyclical *Afflante Spiritu*), the process received its greatest impetus in the wake of the tragedy of the *Shoah*, the Holocaust, during World War II. As devastating as the *Shoah* was for Jewry, its implications and ramifications for Christianity were profound.

---

3. Phyllis Goldstein, *A Convenient Hatred: The History of Anti-Semitism* (Brookline, MA: Facing History and Ourselves, 2012), 127.

4. See Thomas M. Cohen, "Jesuits and New Christians," *Studies in the Spirituality of Jesuits* 42/3 (Autumn 2010) 4, http://ejournals.bc.edu/ojs/index.php/jesuit/article/view/4023/3587/.

5. Jacques Maritain, "The Mystery of Israel," in Maritain, *Ransoming the Time* (New York: Gordian, 1972), 141–79.

As the Christian writer David L. Edwards put it, "Righteous Gentiles, including some bishops did save tens of thousands of Jews, but their efforts were small in comparison with the fact of six million murders, a colossal and cold-blooded crime which would have been impossible without a general indifference to the fate of the victims." And he added, "Not only ignorant peasants or monks but also eminent theologians and spiritual teachers had attacked the Jews as the 'killers of Christ', as a people now abandoned by God, a race deserving not its envied wealth but revenge for plots and acts against innocent Christians. Not only had the Jews of Rome been forced to live in a ghetto until the papacy no longer governed that city, not only had Luther allowed himself to shoot inflammatory words at this easy target, but almost everywhere in Europe, Jews had been made to seem strange, sinister and repulsive."[6]

As mentioned, there were many Christian heroes who stood out as exceptions in these most horrific of times, but one man in particular personifies the transition and transformation in Christian thought. He was the nuncio—the papal ambassador—in Turkey during the period of the *Shoah* and was one of the earliest Western religious personalities to receive information on the Nazi murder machine. This man, Archbishop Angelo Roncalli, helped save thousands of Jews from the clutches of their would-be murderers and was deeply moved by the plight of the Jewish people. Within little more than a decade, he was elected as the new pontiff and took the name John XXIII. Contrary to the widespread perception of him, John XXIII proved to be nothing less than a visionary for his time, convening the Second Vatican Ecumenical Council with a determined resolve that one of the major tasks would be to redress what he saw as the theological misunderstandings, if not perversions, in past Christian thought and teaching in relation to Jews and Judaism, and he gave the task of preparing such a declaration to Cardinal Augustin Bea.

Nostra Aetate—only promulgated after Pope John XXVIII's death—was profoundly influenced by the impact of the *Shoah*, and transformed the Catholic Church's teaching concerning Jews and Judaism. It rejected the portrayal of Jews as collectively guilty for the death of Jesus at the time, let alone in perpetuity, reaffirming the position articulated at the Council of Trent. However, it went much further and positively affirmed the unbroken covenant between God and the Jewish people (quoting from Rom 11:29), and in so doing eliminated in one stroke, as it were,

6. David L. Edwards, *Christianity: The First Two Thousand Years* (Maryknoll, NY: Orbis, 1997), 446–47.

any theological objections to the idea of the return of the Jewish people to its ancestral homeland and to sovereignty within it. Furthermore, *Nostra Aetate* pointedly acknowledges the Church's indebtedness to Judaism, declaring that in the latter "the beginnings of [the Church's] faith and her election are already found." As opposed to the idea of having replaced the Jewish people, Christians are described as "included in the Patriarch's [Abraham's] call."[7]

Moreover, the Christian indebtedness is not presented as a thing of the past, but on the basis of Paul's image of the Church as the wild branch grafted on to the "root" of the people of Israel, *Nostra Aetate* affirms, in the *present* tense, that the Church "cannot forget that she draws sustenance from the root of the good olive tree."[8]

Dr. Eugene Fisher, the former director for Catholic-Jewish relations for the United States Conference of Catholic Bishops (USCCB), has noted that in this regard, *Nostra Aetate* resolves an internal Christian debate concerning Romans 9:4–5, where Paul refers to the Divine election and gifts granted to the Jewish people. The tense of the verb used in the Greek is not clear, and the verb may be translated in the past tense. *Nostra Aetate*, however, uses the present tense and clarifies that the Jewish people "have the adoption as sons, and the glory and the covenant and the law and the worship and the promise." Dr. Fisher points out the enormous significance of this, "for if God's covenant remains valid for the Jews today as much as in Biblical times, then the Jews cannot legitimately be described as 'unfaithful,' 'blind,' or 'legalistic,' in remaining faithful to it! Rather, Jews practicing Judaism must be honored by Christians precisely for their faithfulness, and in this way Christians honor God's faithfulness to His promises."[9]

The late Cardinal Johannes Willebrands, the first president of the Pontifical Commission for Relations with Jewry, gave special emphasis on the sentiments expressed in *Nostra Aetate*, which are virtually repeated in the Council's major constitution on the Church and the modern world, *Lumen Gentium*. *Nostra Aetate* section 4 begins: "As the Church ponders the mystery of salvation for all mankind in Christianity, she is able to affirm the deep spiritual bond between Jews and Christians within God's loving plan for the redemption of the world." In paragraph 4 of the

7. See Appendix I.

8. See Appendix I.

9. Eugene J. Fisher and Leon Klenicki, eds., *In Our Time: The Flowering of Jewish-Catholic Dialogue* (New York: Paulist, 1990), 6.

document, we read: "Nevertheless, God holds the Jews most dear for the sake of the Father; He does not repent of the gifts He makes or the calls He issues—such is the witness of the Apostle." *Lumen Gentium* no. 11, citing the same passages of Paul from Romans 9:4–5 and 11:28–29, states: "In the first place we must recall the people to whom the testament and the promise were given and from whom Christ was born according to the flesh [i.e., the Jews]. On account of their fathers this people remains most dear to God, for God does not repent of the gifts He makes nor of the calls He issues. But the plan of salvation also includes those who acknowledge the Creator."

Dr. Fisher highlights the daring theological nature of this state-ment, in which Christians are called "to see the Church as not alone in the unfolding and proclamation of the Divine mysteries; to view another religion, and one traditionally pilloried by Christians, . . . as the Church's special partner *within* God's redemptive design . . . [using] the sacred terminology normally reserved for the sacraments themselves: 'mysteries of salvation,' 'spiritual bonds,' to describe the relationship between the Church and the Jewish people."[10] In addition, *Nostra Aetate* categorically deplored anti-Semitism and also called for "fraternal dialogue" and bibli-cal studies between Christians and Jews.[11]

As significant as *Nostra Aetate* was and is, it was only part of the *ag-giornamento*, the renewal process of the Church ushered in by the Second Vatican Ecumenical Council. One of the Council's major fruits was the emergence of a dynamic movements designed to revitalize and reinvigo-rate the Catholic faith in contemporary life. One of the most notable of these was and is the Neocatechumenal Way, founded by Kiko Arguello and Carmen Hernandez, that sought to inject the spirit and teachings of the Council into Catholic communities.

Pope Paul VI continued on the path forged by John XXIII, but this transformation ushered in by *Nostra Aetate* moved into an even higher gear with the accession of Blessed John Paul II to the papacy. Undoubt-edly, his own personal history contributed extensively to this—both his childhood friendships with Jews and the experience of the *Shoah* in Poland. While significant documents were issued by the Holy See's Commission for Religious Relations with Jewry during his pontificate, and while he himself wrote many significant statements and homilies

10. Eugene J. Fisher and Leon Klenicki, eds., *In Our Time: The Flowering of Jewish-Catholic Dialogue* (New York: Paulist, 1990), 6.

11. See Appendix 1.

pertaining to Catholic-Jewish reconciliation, only a minority of people read and internalized documents and statements. It was John Paul II's profound understanding of the power of images and their capability through modern media to reach millions, which broadcast to the world the rediscovered brotherhood and love between the Church and the Jewish people. This was evident first and foremost with his visit to the Great Synagogue in Rome in 1986, when he described the Jewish people as "the dearly beloved elder brother of the Church."[12] A further stage in this process of reconciliation was achieved with the establishment of full diplomatic relations between the Holy See and the State of Israel, facilitated by the pope's personal involvement, thereby making it clear to all that the Church had completely repudiated the idea that the Jews were destined to remain wanderers from their ancestral homeland. On the contrary! However, it was probably the papal pilgrimage to the Holy Land in the year 2000 that provided the ultimate testimony of the extent of the transformation in Christian-Jewish relations. The images of the pope standing in tearful solidarity with Jewish suffering at the Yad Vashem Holocaust Memorial and in prayerful respect for Jewish tradition at the Western Wall, placing there the text of the prayer he had composed for a service of repentance in the Vatican, asking for Divine forgiveness for sins perpetrated against Jews down through the ages—all had an enormous impact on the Jewish world and, I suspect, on the Christian world as well.

Little more than a month after Benedict XVI's ascension to the papacy, he received a delegation of the International Jewish Committee for Interreligious Consultations. This roof body embracing the principal Jewish advocacy organizations as well as the major streams of contemporary Judaism, is the official partner of the Holy See's Commission for Religious Relations with Jewry, and I was privileged to preside over it for four years. Notably, Benedict received our delegation almost immediately into his pontificate, before he had even received delegations from representative bodies of other branches of Christianity, let alone other religions. At this meeting, he declared: "In the years following the [Second Vatican Ecumenical] Council, my predecessor Pope Paul VI and in a special way, Pope John Paul II took significant steps towards improving relations with the Jewish People. It is my intention to continue on this path."

Moreover, the first place of divine worship of another religious community that he entered as pope was the synagogue in Cologne, which he

12. http://www.ccjr.us/dialogika-resources/documents-and-statements/roman-catholic/pope-john-paul-ii/305-jp2-86apr13/.

visited in August 2005 during his journey to Germany for World Youth Day. On that occasion, he referred to the above-mentioned meeting, stating, "Today I wish to reaffirm that I intend to continue with great vigor on the path towards improved relations and friendship with the Jewish People, following the decisive lead given by Pope John Paul II."

On both occasions he continued to outline his thoughts on the nature and purpose of this relationship. While acknowledging the tragic past and deploring resurgent anti-Semitism, he asserted that "the 'spiritual patrimony' treasured by Christians and Jews is itself the source of the wisdom and inspiration capable of guiding us towards a future of hope in accordance with the Divine Plan. At the same time, remembrance of the past remains for both communities a moral imperative and a source of purification in our efforts to pray and work for reconciliation, justice, respect and human dignity, and for that peace which is ultimately a gift from the Lord Himself. Of its very nature this importance must include a continued reflection on the profound historical, moral and theological questions posited by the experience of the *Shoah*."[13]

Still in the first year of his pontificate, Pope Benedict continued to meet with an army of Jewish organizations and leaders, including the Chief Rabbis of Israel and the Chief Rabbi of Rome. In receiving the latter, he declared: "The Catholic Church is close and is a friend to you. Yes, we love you and we cannot but love you, because of the Fathers: through them you are very dear and beloved brothers to us."[14]

The pope also expressed his gratitude for the Divine protection of the Jewish people that has guaranteed its survival over the course of history. "The People of Israel have been delivered from the hands of enemies on frequent occasions and in the centuries of anti-Semitism and during the tragic moments of the *Shoah*, the hand of the Almighty sustained and guided them."[15]

Indeed, already in December 2000 in an article titled, "The Heritage of Abraham: The Gift of Christmas," published in *Osservatore Romano*, then-Cardinal Joseph Ratzinger wrote, "Abraham, Father of the People of Israel, Father of Faith, has become the source of blessing, for in him 'all the families of the earth shall call themselves blessed.' The task of the

13. http://www.vatican.va/holy_father/benedict_xvi/speeches/2005/june/documents/hf_ben-xvi_spe_20050609_jewish-committee_en.html/.

14. http://www.vatican.va/holy_father/benedict_xvi/speeches/2006/january/documents/hf_ben-xvi_spe_20060116_rabbino-roma_en.html/.

15. Ibid.

Chosen People is, therefore, to make a gift of their God—the one true God—to every other people. In reality, as Christians we are the inheritors of their faith in the One God. Our gratitude, therefore, must be extended to our Jewish brothers and sisters who, despite the harshness of their own history, have held on to faith in this God right up to the present and who witness to it in the sight of those peoples who, lacking knowledge of the One God, 'dwell in darkness and in the shadow of death (Luke 1:79).'"[16]

Arguably, the most remarkable testimony of Pope Benedict XVI's commitment to continuing to advance the path of his predecessor in Catholic-Jewish reconciliation has been precisely in following the latter's dramatic example, both in visiting the State of Israel and according full respect to the State's highest political and civic as well as religious authorities, and in visiting the Great Synagogue in Rome. For one could have argued that the initiatives of John Paul II were idiosyncratic and personal, born our of his own historical experience and proclivities. In following his predecessor's footsteps, Pope Benedict has actually enshrined these actions, as it were, into the fabric of the papacy, affirming John Paul II's statement that the relationship between the Church and the Jewish people is unique, connected to the very foundation of its faith, unlike the Church's relationship with any other community.

Yet, this stunning transformation in Catholic-Jewish relations has not been internalized universally. This depends to a large extent on the relevant social, cultural, and political content.

The United States of America is arguably the ultimate success story in this regard, for it is here that one finds vibrant and self-confident Jewish and Catholic communities living alongside one another—both minorities, neither dominant—but feeling fully part of and committed to the society at large. Here Jewish-Catholic relations have been able to fully embrace and even lead the path blazed by *Nostra Aetate*, with dozens of institutes of higher learning for Christian-Jewish studies, and with scores of programs involving youth and adults in mutual education and cooperation.

However, in many parts of the world, Jews do not even appear on the Christian radar screen. This is the case in much, if not most, of Latin America; in many parts of Africa and Asia; and even in much of Europe, where significant Jewish communities are no longer to be found. And indeed, even in the United States today, demographic trends are changing

16. http://www.notredamedesion.org/en/dialogue_docs.php?a=2&id=215&categoria=cattolici/.

the makeup of the Catholic Church, and much of a new generation is not the natural beneficiary of the aforementioned changes that have taken place in the U.S. over the last half century.

It is here that the role of educational and formation structures is so important, and where the work of the movements, in particular the Neocatechumenal Way, has become so critical. As one of the most powerful Catholic movements (especially in the Spanish-speaking world but indeed across the globe), its profound commitment to ensuring that the pathway of *Nostra Aetate* becomes a highway for the Church is of inestimable importance. Through its programs in seminaries of Redemptoris Mater, and in particular through its work in Israel in Domus Galilaea, where myriads of the faithful and thousands of the clergy are reimmersed in the Jewish roots of their faith and reconnected to the Jewish people, the message of *Nostra Aetate* is being disseminated on a regular basis. Through this work, a healing process also takes place within the Jewish communities—especially and significantly in Israel—where Jewish people are discovering the true Christian message of love and respect, instead of the tragic image in Jewish minds of Christianity as a hostile and antagonistic force.

This process is not achieved overnight, and indeed in historical terms it has only just begun and will take generations to come to the fullest fruition. Nevertheless, a new era was ushered in by *Nostra Aetate*, not only overcoming the tragic past and paving the way for a rediscovery of brotherhood, but even in opening up the way for us to view each other in a new way theologically, as part and parcel of the Divine blessing for humanity that we are called to be. Today, more and more, Jews and Catholics are coming together to affirm the sacred values we share, while respecting the profound differences that make us each who we are. But our commitment to those shared messages—especially regarding human dignity that flows from each and every person being created in the Divine Image—is the fruit of our historic reconciliation facilitated by *Nostra Aetate*. In the words of Blessed John Paul II, "As the children of Abraham we are called to be a blessing to the world. In order to be so, we must first be a blessing to one another."

2

Abraham Joshua Heschel and the Second Vatican Council
Some Personal Memories

Susannah Heschel

WHEN MY FATHER WAS a child in Warsaw, the pious son of a very distinguished family of Hasidic *rebbes*, he knew no Christians, and he crossed the street rather than walk in front of a church. When he was twenty, in 1927, he entered the University of Berlin, where many of his professors and fellow students were Christian, and he immersed himself in studying the work of German biblical scholars (primarily Protestants). He was displeased with their scholarship on the Bible, and his doctoral dissertation, *Das prophetische Bewusstsein* (*Prophetic Consciousness*) devotes considerable space to exposing and criticizing the assumptions underlying their work. Protestant scholarship on the prophets was biased, he argued, and failed to understand the experience of the prophets, reducing it to epileptic fits or belittling the prophetic message as wrathful. No, he insisted, the prophets had an experience of divine pathos, responding with their own profound sympathy for both God and humanity.

Despite his sharp critique, he maintained cordial relationships with his Christian teachers and colleagues, at least for the first years of his university studies. Within a few years, however, the tone began to change. Christian theologians in Germany, attracted to National Socialism, began to call for the elimination of the Old Testament, as a Jewish book, from the Christian Bible. Jesus was called an Aryan, not a Jew, and Paul was condemned for preaching an alleged "Jewish morality of cattle dealers and pimps," in the words of Reinhold Krause's November 1933 Berlin speech to members of the German Christian movement.

My father's doctorate was delayed once Hitler came to power, and he only received the degree in December of 1935, nearly three years after submitting his dissertation and passing his examinations. By then, he was desperate to find a position outside Germany, but nothing came to fruition until the president of the Hebrew Union College in Cincinnati, Julian Morgenstern, managed to secure five visas for Jewish scholars. My father was one of those rescued, and he arrived in the United States in March of 1940, a penniless refugee.

"Never despair," he used to tell me, and his own courage was extraordinary. He spent the war years terribly lonely in Cincinnati, trying in vain to rescue his mother and three of his sisters, and many friends and colleagues. At the end of the war, he moved to New York, where he became professor at the Jewish Theological Seminary. He married my mother, Sylvia Straus, and quickly the books poured out of him. Within a few years, he published five important books as well as numerous articles, and he became an important figure on the landscape of religious thought in America.

During my childhood, I often heard my parents say that my father was better understood by Christian theologians than by Jews. Indeed, reviewers in Jewish journals were often sharp in their criticisms, whereas Christian scholars praised his work. One of the key moments for my father's career was a glorious review of his book, *Man Is Not Alone*, written by Reinhold Niebuhr for the *New York Herald Tribune*. The review launched a friendship between them, as well as a relationship between my father and most of the faculty members of Union Theological Seminary. Indeed, he was invited to serve as Harry Emerson Fosdick Visiting Professor at Union Seminary during the academic year, 1964–65.

My father's approach to Christians was unique and distinctive among modern Jewish theologians. The modern era opened with Moses Mendelssohn's cordial relationships with Christians and their avoidance of direct discussions of theological differences. Abraham Geiger, the pioneering theologian of the nineteenth century, threw down a gauntlet to Christians (especially Protestants on the quest for the historical figure of Jesus) when he claimed that Jesus was a Jew who said nothing new or original but followed the path of the liberalizing Pharisees. The faith of Jesus was Judaism, Geiger insisted; Christianity was the religion about him, devised by Paul, who polluted Jewish monotheism with pagan ideas to create Christian doctrine. Early twentieth-century Jewish thinkers either were disdainful of Christianity (Hermann Cohen), granted Christianity a role in spreading Jewish ideas that will ultimately lead to redemption (Franz Rosenzweig), or declared Jesus his brother (Martin Buber).

My father's approach was entirely different. Almost never did he mention Jesus or Paul, or engage in exegesis of New Testament texts. He rarely discussed, in public, the history of Christian anti-Semitism, including the role of the churches and the Vatican during the Holocaust. He was never patronizing toward Christian scholars of Jewish texts but had intense discussions of rabbinic ideas with them. What he expected from Christians is precisely what he displayed: respect, affirmation, public support, and never an attempt at conversion, which he considered existential violence. When invited to speak to Christian groups, at colleges or meetings of clergy, he most often spoke about God, prayer, and the nature of human life, making the same points he did to Jewish groups. He sought topics that unite us rather than divide us.

For a Jew from the Hasidic world to have close personal relationships with Christian theologians is remarkable. What did they talk about? The bond was always the Bible and how to understand it. But there were other topics: he discussed rabbinic texts with W. D. Davies, a scholar of Pauline theology; with James Sanders, scholar of the Bible and Dead Sea Scrolls, he would discuss the prophets and related rabbinic passages. Many of those Christian friends joined our family for the Passover Seder or for a Shabbat dinner; indeed, my father invited Martin Luther King Jr. and his family to join us for the Passover Seder in that fateful year of 1968; Dr. King was assassinated just days before Passover. Sometimes his Christian colleagues came to him for advice: a community of nuns asked if he thought they should abandon their traditional habit; Bill Coffin, then the chaplain at Yale University and an active protester against the war in Vietnam, grieved over his divorce.

And they collaborated on efforts to end the war in Vietnam, to understand the meaning of Zionism and the State of Israel, and to conquer poverty. Martin Luther King joined him in speaking out for the release of

Jews from the Soviet Union; Abbott Leo Rudloff, of the Weston Priory in Vermont, was an avid public defender of Israel's security; and my father joined Jesse Jackson in Operation Breadbasket.

In most cases, Christians sought out his friendship, eager to better understand his reading of the Bible and to gain insight into the nature of prayer, but often it was his person, as a religious Jew, that attracted them: theirs was a dialogue of depth-theology, an encounter of a religious person with another, as he describes in his writings. The purpose, he said in his inaugural lecture as the Harry Emerson Fosdick Visiting Professor at Theological Seminary in 1964, was not to discuss what divides Jews and Christians—the divinity of Jesus, for example—but "to help one another; to share insight and learning, to cooperate in academic ventures on the highest scholarly level and, what is even more important, to search in the wilderness for wellsprings of devotion, for treasures of stillness . . . helping one another in the terrible predicament of here and now by the courage to believe that the word of the Lord endures forever as well as in the here and now." Indeed, his lecture was entitled, "No Religion Is an Island."[1]

His encounters with Pope Paul VI, Cardinal Augustin Bea, and other leading Catholics during the Second Vatican Council were meetings of the spirit. Their conversations centered on what Jews and Christians share: the Hebrew Bible, experiences of prayer, belief in God's presence in their lives. While some Jews criticized my father for his ecumenical work, he believed it was a sacred task. When he arrived for a private audience in March of 1971, Pope Paul VI, my father wrote in his diary, "smiled joyously, with a radiant face, shook my hand cordially with both hands . . . telling me that he is reading my books, that my books are very spiritual and very beautiful, and that Catholics should read my books." Toward the end of the meeting, my father writes,

> I told him how grateful we Jews are for the understanding he has shown for the spiritual link of the Jewish people with the Holy City of Jerusalem. All of Jewish history is a pilgrimage to Jerusalem, and the union of the Jewish people and the city of Jerusalem we regard as a sign of divine grace and providence in this age of darkness. The Pope then said: "I will remember your words" and added: "I hope that you and I will meet together in Jerusalem." I then said he may feel assured that the Jews of Israel

1. Abraham Joshua Heschel, "No Religion Is an Island," in *Moral Grandeur and Spiritual Audacity*, ed. Susannah Heschel (New York: Farrar, Straus & Giroux, 1996) 235–50.

will treat the holy places of Christianity with deep reverence. He then said: "God bless you." I said: "God bless you."

My father's involvement with the Vatican had begun during the Second Vatican Council, conceived by Pope John XXIII. He was asked by the American Jewish Committee (AJC) in 1962 to help draft a memorandum that would alter the tone of discussions concerning Catholic-Jewish relations and he wrote:

> With humility and in the spirit of commitment to the prophets of Israel, let us consider the grave problems that confront us all as the children of God. Both Judaism and Christianity share the prophets' belief that God chooses agents through whom His will is made known and His work done throughout history. Both Judaism and Christianity live in the certainty that mankind is in need of ultimate redemption, that God is involved in human history, that in relations between man and man, God is at stake.[2]

My father held meetings with various Vatican representatives, both in New York and in Rome, although he was frequently attacked in bitter terms by some of his Jewish colleagues who felt that theological dialogue with Christians was forbidden to Jews, and that Jews were demeaning themselves by negotiating with the Church over *Nostra Aetate* ("In Our Age," the Vatican's Declaration on the Relation of the Church with Non-Christian Religions). But my father felt that the lives of Jews were at stake in Christian teachings about Judaism. He had lived through too much not to be aware of the power of language. He used to point out that Hitler had come to power not with tanks and machine guns, but with words, and he always emphasized the importance of guarding one's tongue. In his memorandum for the AJC, he wrote:

> It is from the inner life of men and from the articulation of evil thoughts that evil actions take their rise. It is therefore of extreme importance that the sinfulness of thoughts of suspicion and hatred and particularly the sinfulness of any contemptuous utterance, however flippantly it is meant, be made clear to all mankind. This applies in particular to such thoughts and utterances about individuals or groups of other religions, races and nations.

Most significant was the personal dimension of my father's encounters with Christians. He never reproached them; his topic was not to

2. Gary Spruch, *Wide Horizons: Abraham Joshua Heschel, the American Jewish Committee and the Spirit of Nostra Aetate* (New York: AJC, 2008).

speak about the specific anti-Jewish prejudices of Christian theology, or about the failures of the Vatican during the Holocaust. But he didn't need to be explicit: in his sheer being as a religious Jew, without saying a word, Christians who encountered him suddenly confronted their conscience. He used to ask his Christian friends, is it really *ad majorum Dei gloriam*, to the greater glory of God, that there should be no more Jews in the world, that the Sabbath should come to an end, that the Torah should no longer be read in synagogues? Thus, when the Second Vatican Council proposed a draft resolution in 1964 calling for the eventual conversion of the Jews, my father responded, "I would rather go to Auschwitz than give up my faith." The final declaration, *Nostra Aetate*, affirmed the continuing covenant between Jews and God, and clarified that not all Jews are responsible for the crucifixion. Further, it deplored anti-Semitism and did not call for the Jews' conversion, a remarkable turning point that Rabbi Gilbert Rosenthal has called "a Copernican revolution in Catholic thinking about the Jewish religion and people."[3]

The declaration was the result of intellectual changes, to be sure, but also of personal encounters between Catholics and Jews. It was a surprising experience for Christians in those days to discover they could learn something about God from a Jew, that the theology of a Jew could make them better Christians. Many thought that had not happened for two thousand years, since Jesus and Paul. Experiencing the Sabbath in our home, listening as my father prayed, they found themselves brought to a deeper level of their own spiritual lives. Watching as a child, it seemed to me that the nuns who came to our home for a visit were on a pilgrimage, coming home to the Judaism that was the womb of their own faith. This was the first Shabbat dinner or Passover Seder for many of the Christian religious who visited us, though some quickly became regular guests. Some of the nuns in their habits were tentative at first but quickly responded to my father's gentle humor; others, especially Father Felix Morlion from Rome, regaled us with jokes and theological banter. "My friend," my father would say, putting his hand on the arm of his good friend, Reverend William Sloan Coffin, then chaplain at Yale University, "would you like to learn the prayer for bread, the *hamotzi*?" And then he would teach Bill the Hebrew words. Discussions of theology would lead him to tell a story, sometimes from the Midrash, often about one of his Hasidic ancestors, and always illustrating an aspect of his love of Judaism.

3. Gilbert S. Rosenthal, *What Can a Modern Jew Believe?* (Eugene, OR: Wipf & Stock), 210.

What was clear to me was the revelation these devout Christians were experiencing: Judaism, they discovered, was not about legalism or outdated rituals but spiritual vitality. Were those who rejected Christ to be denied salvation, as the church had long claimed? Suddenly they realized that my father too would of course be welcomed into heaven—and please recognize what a profound theological earthquake that represented for so many Christians in that era.

For my father, the personal friendships with Christians were deeply moving. He was able to speak freely about theology and spirituality in a discussion that had not yet taken shape in the Jewish community in America; many American Jews were still insisting, anachronistically, that Judaism has no theology. But imagine: as a child, my father had crossed the street rather than walk in front of a church, and now he found himself consulted by Christians about liturgical reform, social justice, biblical interpretation, and meeting with the pope and Vatican officials to overcome centuries of Christian efforts to convert Jews and blame them for the death of Jesus. For my father, such encounters were momentous. He considered it an upheaval in the history of the West, and a God-given mandate for his work.

For Christians, my father was an inspiration. His work continues to be read widely, and rarely does a week pass when I do not receive a warm letter from someone I've never met, thanking me for my father's writings.

3

Vatican II's *Nostra Aetate*

Its Impact on the Church's Theological
Self-Understanding

John T. Pawlikowski

VATICAN II's *NOSTRA AETATE* was a complicated and contentious document during the conciliar discussions. It was complicated because after
Pope John XXIII decided to add something on the Church and the Jews
to the conciliar agenda after a historic meeting with the French Jewish
historian Jules Isaac, uncertainty developed as to where a statement on
the Church and the Jewish people might be placed. A number of the
advocates of such a statement, mostly biblical scholars and Catholics
connected with resistance movements against the Nazis, favored incor-
poration of such a statement in what eventually became *Lumen Gentium*,
the dogmatic constitution on the Church. For various reasons, however,
this proposal was not accepted. In turn, the conciliar leadership decided
on a separate statement. Eventually, because of the situation faced at
home by the bishops from the Middle East, it was decided that the document should be expanded to include reflections on the Church's relationships with Islam and other non-Christian religions. The heart and soul

of the document, and its most developed section, nonetheless remained chapter 4, which dealt with the Christian-Jewish relationship.

Let me first focus on the first three chapters, which briefly cover Catholicism's basic approach to all non-Christian faiths and introduce the Church to a far more positive outlook on non-Christians than had been generally the case in Christianity for centuries. While these three chapters remain very underdeveloped in comparison to chapter 4 on the relations with the Jews, they did open the door and lay the groundwork for a far more expansive treatment of interreligious relations, including relations with specific traditions such as Islam and Hinduism in follow-up ecclesial documents.

The first three chapters of *Nostra Aetate* fundamentally refocused Catholic attitudes towards non-Christians. While it did not solve some basic questions (such as missionizing people of non-Christian faiths) or reflect in any significant ways on possible theological links with these religious traditions (Islam in particular, where some biblical links exist), it did acknowledge some truth in these religious traditions and affirmed the value of dialogue with their religious leaders. This represented a marked contrast with the long-standing outlook within the Church, which spoke of these religious communities with negative, sometimes even contemptuous, language and basically regarded them as enemies of the Church.

The obvious challenge still remaining for Catholic Christians today is whether we can build on the groundwork laid in *Nostra Aetate*. Despite some lapses, even at the papal level, Catholics and their leaders now speak of other religious traditions in a positive vein and often stand ready to cooperate with them in the social sphere. But any implications of this fundamental perspectival shift to a positive mode for theological understandings, including Christian theological self-understanding, have been largely ignored, except by individual theologians. Ecclesial documents such as *Dominus Iesus,* issued by Cardinal Joseph Ratzinger when he was president of the Congregation for the Doctrine of the Faith, have tended to cast a chill over such efforts. But questions remain about Christian exclusivity in terms of salvation and about the consequent meaning of evangelization in the global, interreligious context in which Christianity finds itself today. It is highly unlikely they will be buried. At some point Catholicism, and Christianity overall, will need to address the issues involved. Hence while the fundamental shift in perspective towards other world religions, introduced in *Nostra Aetate,* may appear rather simple and undeveloped, it nonetheless set the Church on a fundamentally new course that sooner or later will alter some of its traditional theological self-understandings.

Turning now to chapter 4 of *Nostra Aetate,* we need to take very seriously what the Canadian theologian Gregory Baum (who may have written a very early draft of this chapter as a Council expert) said in 1986 at the annual meeting of the Catholic Theological Society of America in Chicago. In a plenary address, Baum termed chapter 4 of *Nostra Aetate* the most radical transformation of the Church's ordinary magisterium to emerge from Vatican II.[1]

So why did Baum make this strong assertion? In order to appreciate its full significance, we must look back at the classical theology of the Church and Judaism. A major part of that classical theological tradition, particularly in the patristic writings, understood the meaning of Christology and ecclesiology as involving the displacement of the Jewish people from any covenantal relationship with God after the Christ event. Jews were now viewed as rejected people who never would have a homeland of their own. This situation was viewed by ecclesiastical writers both as a punishment for having rejected Jesus and putting him to death, and as a warning to Christians of what would happen to those who refused to accept Jesus as their Savior. This came to be known as the "perpetual wandering" theology, and Jews, following the lead of Saint Augustine, became seen as "witness people" in terms of divine punishment. However, Christian theology did not argue for the extermination of the Jews in the same way as subsequent Nazi ideology. It wanted to insure the continuity of the Jewish people because of their "witness value," kept in a miserable state on the margins of society. We see clear evidence of this theology in such places as the papal states.[2]

The classical theology of perpetual wandering on the part of the Jewish people took hold within important sectors of modern biblical scholarship—a situation that persisted well into the twentieth century. Noted exegete Martin Noth, whose book *History of Israel* became standard fare in many theological programs, described Israel as a strictly "religious community," which died a slow, agonizing death in the first

---

1. Gregory Baum, "The Social Context of American Catholic Theology," *Proceedings of the Catholic Theological Society of America* 41 (1986) 87.

2. Nancy Nowakowski Robinson, *Institutional Anti-Judaism: Pope Pius VI and the "Edict Concerning the Jews" in the Context of the Inquisition and the Enlightenment* (Pittsburgh: Xlibris, 2003).

century CE. For Noth, Jewish history reached its culmination in the arrival of Jesus. His words are concise and to the point in this regard:

> Jesus himself . . . no longer formed part of the history of Israel, in him the history of Israel had come, rather, to its real end. What did belong to the history of Israel was the process of his rejection and condemnation by the Jerusalem religious community . . . Hereafter the history of Israel moved quickly to its end.[3]

Nostra Aetate, in chapter 4, put forth three basic affirmations with regard to the Jewish people. The first, and the most fundamental, rejected the traditional deicide charge against the Jews. Jews could not be held collectively responsible for the death of Jesus. While some Jewish leaders may have played a secondary role, blame could not be extended to the entirety of the Jewish community then or now. This assertion totally undercut the basis for the perpetual-wandering and witness-people understanding of Jews and Judaism within Catholicism. Hence the second affirmation in *Nostra Aetate*: Jews remain in a covenantal relationship with God after the Christ event, and hence any Christology or ecclesiology in Christianity cannot base its perspective any longer on a notion of Jesus as the initiator of a totally new covenant with no ties to the ongoing Jewish covenant or proclaim an ecclesiology without positive roots in Judaism.

The final major assertion found in *Nostra Aetate* is meant to fundamentally reorient the church's theological understanding of its relationship with the Jewish people. It declares that Jesus and his disciples were profoundly influenced by parts of Jewish belief and practice at their time. Judaism was a very complex religious reality in this period with many internal disagreements. Jesus appears to stand closest to groups within the Pharisaic movement (as the 1985 *Vatican Notes* on teaching and preaching about Jews and Judaism asserted),[4] though the Jewish scholar Daniel Boyarin recently claimed that Jesus argued against the Pharisees because he saw some of them as threatening the integrity and continuity of Jewish Torah.[5]

3. Martin Noth, *The Laws in the Pentateuch and Other Studies* (Edinburgh: Oliver & Boyd, 1966).

4. For the text of the Vatican *Notes*, cf. Franklin Sherman, ed., *Bridges: Documents of the Christian-Jewish Dialogue*, vol. 1, *The Road to Reconciliation (1945–1985)* (New York: Paulist, 2011), 202–15.

5. Daniel Boyarin, *The Jewish Gospels: The Story of the Jewish Christ*, foreword by Jack Miles (New York: New Press, 2012).

It is unlikely we will ever be able to precisely place Jesus's relationships within the broad and complex Jewish community of his day. But with *Nostra Aetate* we have clearly shifted from an essentially negative view of those relationships to one that is fundamentally positive. The 1985 *Notes*, issued to commemorate the twentieth anniversary of *Nostra Aetate*, confirmed the about-face in Catholicism. Jesus was and always remained a Jew. Jesus is fully a man of his time and his environment—the Jewish-Palestinian one of the first century, the anxieties and hopes of which he shared.[6]

This about-face has been further confirmed by the late cardinal and biblical scholar Carlo Martini, SJ, who wrote in the same vein as the *Notes*:

> Without a sincere feeling for the Jewish world and a direct experience of it one cannot fully understand Christianity. Jesus is fully Jewish, the apostles are Jewish, and one cannot doubt their attachment to the traditions of their forefathers.[7]

The growing awareness of the deep-seated linkage between the first-century Church and the Jewish community of the time has had a major impact on how Christian scholars view both the Hebrew Scriptures, or Old Testament, and the New Testament. While the issue of how to name the first section of the Christian Bible has seen considerable discussion in recent years—with some urging a change to "Hebrew Scriptures," "First Testament," or "Tanach," and others insisting that the traditional term "Old Testament" better reflects the different approach to these writings in the Jewish and Christian communities—no resolution of the disagreement is in sight. Nonetheless, most would admit that a major perspectival change is occurring in contemporary scholarship.

For centuries, the Hebrew Scriptures were generally seen in their better moments as a prelude to the New Testament and in their worse moments as a foil for supposedly superior insights in the New Testament. To a great extent, the selection of liturgical texts from the Hebrew Scriptures was based on this perspective. Interpretation of passages in the Hebrew Scriptures by Jewish scholars was generally ignored within the Church. The belief persisted that correct interpretation of the Hebrew Scriptures was possible only through the lens of the New Testament.

---

6. Franklin Sherman, ed., *Bridges*, 208.

7. Carlo Maria Martini, SJ, "Christianity and Judaism: A Historical and Theological Overview," in James H. Charlesworth, ed., *Jews and Christians: Exploring the Past, the Present, and Future* (New York: Crossroad, 1990), 19.

The "inferiority-superiority" model of the relationship between the two testaments affected Christian theology in many areas, one of the most important being that the "Old Testament" moral vision was inferior to the moral outlook found in the Gospels and Epistles. One still finds such a contrast in the writings of some progressive Catholic ethicists, such as John Coleman, SJ.

Slowly we are witnessing a significant change within biblical scholarship and, to a lesser extent, within the wider Christian theological community. A growing recognition is emerging that the Hebrew Scriptures need to be understood as a positive resource for Christian theology and not merely as a prelude or foil, in part because these writings exercised a profound impact on the teachings of Jesus. There is now an increasing willingness in Christian circles to include the interpretations of the Hebrew Scriptures by Jewish scholars in the construction of contemporary Christian theology and to regard these writings as an indispensable, ongoing resource for the understanding of key Christian theological themes, such as Christology and ecclesiology.

In part because of the enhanced recognition of the role played by the Hebrew Scriptures and some postbiblical Jewish materials from the first century on the mindset of Jesus and first-century Christianity, a growing number of Christian scholars have begun to paint a transformed picture of the initial relations between the Church and the Jewish community and their eventual separation. For most of Christian history, the prevailing view had been that Jesus fully established the Church as a separate institution from Judaism in his own lifetime. But increasingly that traditional understanding is coming under severe scrutiny.

This process of taking a new look at Christian origins and how the Church emerged out of Judaism is now several decades old. One of the first contributors was Robin Scroggs, who taught both at Chicago Theological Seminary and subsequently at Union Theological Seminary in New York. Scroggs emphasized the following points: (1) The movement begun by Jesus and continued after his death in Palestine can best be described as a reform movement within the Judaism of the period. There is little evidence during this period that Christians had a separate identity apart from Jews. (2) The Pauline missionary movement as Paul understood it was a Jewish mission that focused on the Gentiles as the proper object of God's call to his people. (3) Prior to the end of the Jewish war with the Romans in 70 CE, there was no such reality as Christianity. Followers of Jesus did not have a self-understanding of themselves as a religion over against Judaism. A distinct Christian identity only began to emerge after the Jewish-Roman war. (4) The later portions of the New Testament all show some signs of a movement towards separation, but they also generally retain some contact with their original Jewish matrix.[8]

While not every New Testament scholar would subscribe to each and every point made by Scroggs, the consensus is growing that the picture he presents is basically accurate. Such a picture clearly contradicts the classical depictions of Church-Synagogue separation held by most people in both faith communities. It should be noted that the late Cardinal Joseph Bernardin, an episcopal pioneer in promoting constructive Christian-Jewish relations, basically endorsed the Scroggs perspective in his own writings.[9]

The biblical scholar John Meier, in the third volume of his comprehensive study of New Testament understandings of Jesus, argues that from a careful examination of New Testament evidence, Jesus must be seen as presenting himself to the Jewish community of his time as an eschatological prophet and miracle worker in the likeness of Elijah. He was not interested in creating a separatist sect or holy remnant along the lines of the Qumran community. Instead, he envisioned the development of a special religious community within Israel. The idea that this community "within Israel" would slowly undergo a process of separation from Israel as it pursued a mission to the Gentiles in this present world—the long-term result being that this community would become predominantly Gentile itself—finds no place in Jesus's message or practice.[10]

More recently, David Frankfurter adds further to the notion of significant intertwining between Christians and Jews in the period well after Jesus's death. He has insisted that within the various "clusters" of groups that included Jews and Christians, there existed a "mutual influence persisting through late antiquity [and] evidence for a degree of overlap that, all things considered, threatens every construction of an historically distinct 'Christianity' before at least the mid-second century."[11]

---

8. Robin Scroggs, "The Judaizing of the New Testament," *The Chicago Theological Seminary Register* 76/1 (Winter 1986) 36–45.

9. Cf. Cardinal Joseph L. Bernardin, *A Blessing to Each Other: Cardinal Joseph Bernardin and the Jewish-Catholic Dialogue* (Chicago: Liturgy Training Publications, 1996), 78–79.

10. John P. Meier, *A Marginal Jew: Rethinking the Historical Jesus*, vol. 3, *Companions and Competitors* (New York: Doubleday, 2001), 251.

11. David D. Frankfurter, "Beyond 'Jewish Christianity': Continuing Religious

Important Christian and Jewish scholars are now arguing that the actual separation between the Church and the Synagogue, while well advanced by 100 CE, was not completed for several centuries after that. Scholars such as Robert Wilken, Wayne Meeks, Alan Segal, and Anthony Saldarini have uncovered continued ties between certain Jewish and Christian communities, particularly in the East.[12] Evidence of such continuing ties is apparent in the second, third, and (in a few places) even in the fourth and fifth centuries. And the ties were not just on a theoretical level. They also affected popular practice as well. John Chrysostom, for example, launched a harsh critique of Judaism partly out of frustration that Christians in his area were continuing to participate in synagogue services on a regular basis. What sort of role these Christians played in the synagogue services is unknown and likely will remain so unless some new documentation is uncovered. It would be terribly illuminating to have such information.

But short of this, we can say that on the Christian side, at least some believers in Christ did not regard such belief as necessitating a break with Judaism and its ritual practices. And on the Jewish side, this openness to Christians involved some recognition that they authentically belonged to the Jewish community since no evidence exists to suggest that the Christians had to fight their way into the synagogue for such services. One important collection of essays on this topic of the gradual separation of Church and Synagogue has the intriguing title of *The Ways That Never Parted*.

Within the overall "Parting of the Ways" scholarship, one of the most important results has been the significant re-examination of Paul's outlook on Judaism. Traditionally Paul has been viewed both in popular and scholarly circles as, in many ways, Christianity's founder. Pauline theology has played a crucial role in the formulation of christological perspectives, especially in Protestant theology. Pauline theology has

---

Subcultures of the Second and Third Centuries and Their Documents," in Adam H. Becker and Annette Yoshiro Reed, eds., *The Ways That Never Parted: Jews and Christians in Late Antiquity and the Early Middle Ages* (Tübingen: Mohr/Siebeck, 2003) 132. Also cf. Matt Jackson-McCabe, *Jewish Christianity Reconsidered: Rethinking Ancient Groups and Texts* (Minneapolis: Fortress, 2007).

12. Cf. Wayne A. Meeks and Robert Wilken, *Jews and Christians in Antioch in the First Four Centuries of the Common Era* (Missoula, MT: Scholars, 1978); Robert Wilken, *John Chrysostom and the Jews: Rhetoric and Reality in the Late 4th Century* (Berkeley: University of California Press, 1983); and Anthony J. Saldarini, "Jews and Christians in the First Two Centuries: The Changing Paradigm," *Shofar* 10 (1992) 32–42.

also defined the foundation for Christian ethical thought. Paul has been credited with bringing about the decisive break between Christianity and Judaism through his supposed rejection of any Torah obligations for Gentile converts in the first century at the so-called Council of Jerusalem. Paul has often been portrayed as espousing a view in which Christianity clearly holds a position of theological superiority over Judaism.

Much of this perspective on Paul as fundamentally anti-Jewish has been due to the dominance of a master narrative in Christian circles rooted in the book of Acts. This master narrative begins with Stephen's decisive break with Judaism in chapter 7 of Acts. So-called Jewish Christians then began to disappear from this master narrative until chapter 11, when they are totally removed from the storyline following Peter's revelatory vision whereby he becomes convinced to abandon his previous adherence to continued Torah observance. From that point onwards, the master narrative focuses exclusively on Gentiles as the new people of God and moves the epicenter of Christianity from Jerusalem to Rome. Thus in the account of Christian origins that has tended to dominate Christianity's perspective, Judaism is superseded and even annulled, with Paul being viewed as the primary messenger of this teaching. This master narrative from Acts has been especially influential in the liturgy of the Easter season, during which the Church celebrates its fundamental self-identity. Continued ties to Judaism play little or no constructive role in the presentation of this self-identity.

This classical perspective on Paul and Judaism was significantly reinforced in the mid-nineteenth century in the writings of F. C. Baur. In his work, *Paul the Apostle*, written in 1845,[13] Baur argued for the existence of only two factions in the early church. One was the Jewish Christians whose leader was Peter, and the other Gentile Christians, who looked to Paul for spiritual guidance. The Jewish Christians, in Bauer's perspective, stood mired in a narrow legalism that blinded them to the universalistic elements in Jesus's teachings supposedly championed by Paul.

Increasingly this classical perspective on Paul is being pushed aside by insights coming from "the Parting of the Ways" scholarship. Paul is now being portrayed as an integral part of the complicated Jewish-Christian

---

13. F. C. Baur, *Paul the Apostle of Jesus Christ: His Life and Works, His Epistles and Teachings* (Peabody, MA: Hendrickson, 2003). On recent thinking on Paul and Judaism, cf. Reimund Bieringer and Didier Pollefeyt, eds., *Paul and Judaism: Crosscurrents in Pauline Exegesis and the Study of Jewish-Christian Relations* (London: T. & T. Clark, 2012).

scene of his time, rather than as someone who completely repudiated Judaism and its Torah tradition. Shortly before his death, the noted New Testament scholar Raymond Brown said in a public speech in Chicago that he had now become convinced that Paul had a very high regard for Torah, including its ritual dimensions, and that if he had fathered a son, he would likely have had him circumcised. Even Paul's more christological reflections are seen by some scholars now as having roots in the Jewish mystical tradition of the day.

What is beginning to emerge in important sectors of Pauline scholarship is the picture of a Paul still very much a Jew, still quite appreciative of Jewish Torah, with seemingly no objection to its continued practice by Jewish Christians so long as their basic orientation is founded in Christ and his teachings, and still struggling at the end of his ministry to balance his understanding of the newness he experienced in the Christ event with the continuity of the Jewish covenant. This is quite apparent in the famous chapters 9–11 of Romans, which Vatican II used as the cornerstone of its declaration about continuing Jewish covenantal inclusion in chapter 4 of *Nostra Aetate*. A few of the biblical scholars involved in this new Pauline research even go so far as to maintain that Paul regarded Torah observance so highly that he feared that if Gentiles tried to practice it, they would only corrupt its authentic spirit. Such a view admittedly pushes the envelope of scholarly evidence a bit far, but it is presently under discussion in some scholarly circles.

The biblical and theological reflections that have emerged as a result, at least in part, of the fundamental reorientation on the Christian-Jewish question brought about by *Nostra Aetate* carry significant impact for various areas of Christian theology. I would include here Christology, ecclesiology, ethics, mission, and the Christian relationship with other religions.

In terms of Christology, two new imperatives arise. First, the reality of Jesus' deep involvement in a constructive way with segments of the Jewish tradition must be included in any discussion of his divine sonship. While we can certainly continue efforts to present christological understanding in multicultural ways, this should not happen at the expense of highlighting Jesus's Jewish roots, particularly in the interpretation of his message. There is simply no way of properly interpreting Jesus's three years of preaching without setting that teaching in the Jewish context of the period.

Some years ago, the prominent Asian theologian S. Wesley Ariarajah, who worked for many years in the interreligious office of the World Council of Churches, termed the effort to return Jesus to his Jewish context a "futile attempt in terms of creating Christian faith expression in a non-European context." He acknowledged Jesus's positive connections with the Jewish community of his day. But this linkage carries no theological significance today for Ariarajah. For him, relating Christology to the Buddhist tradition represents a far more important challenge.[14]

While I am certainly sympathetic to an effort to relate christological understanding to Buddhism and other Asian religions, we must first try to grasp what Jesus was actually saying. And that cannot be done, as the American Vietnamese Catholic theologian Peter Phan has quite properly argued, apart from investigating its original setting.[15] Doing proper contextual theology today requires doing contextual interpretation of its initial formulation in the first century.

A younger Protestant theologian, R. Kendall Soulen, in contrast to Ariarajah, has got it right. Soulen sees the link to Judaism in Christian self-identity as indispensable and an essential cornerstone. The fundamental link with Judaism is important not only for interpreting Jesus's specific teachings but also for the basic theological understanding of the Christ event. The permanent link to Judaism he regards as a constant check against ever-present gnostic tendencies in christological interpretation. Soulen's unwavering affirmation of this reality is one of his singular contributions to the current christological discussion within the Christian-Jewish dialogue.[16]

The second implication of the post-*Nostra Aetate* vision relative to Christology is the need to insure that in any attempt to state a contemporary Christology, a salvific path for the Jewish people in and through their faithfulness to their continuing covenant is clearly affirmed. This necessity was underscored by Cardinal Walter Kasper during his tenure as president of the Holy See's Commission for Religious Relations with

14. Wesley Ariarajah, "Towards a Fourth Phase in Jewish-Christian Relations: An Asian Perspective," Unpublished Paper. Conference on Christian-Jewish Dialogue, Temple Emmanuel, New York, Cosponsored by the Center for Interreligious Understanding and the Office of Interreligious Affairs of the World Council of Churches, November 2003.

15. Peter Phan, "Jews and Judaism in Asian Theology: Historical and Theological Perspectives," *Gregorianum* 86 (2005) 806–36.

16. R. Kendall Soulen, *The God of Israel and Christian Theology* (Minneapolis: Fortress, 1996).

the Jews.[17] And any number of theologians, such as Paul van Buren, Clark Williamson, Franz Mussner, and the contributors to the volume coming from the joint European-American study group on Christ Jesus and the Jewish people have tried to work out the specifics of Christology along these lines.[18]

With regard to ecclesiology, the implications of the "Parting of the Ways" scholarship are crucial for articulating the understanding of the Church today. Most of us grew up thinking that by the time Jesus died on Calvary, or very shortly thereafter, the church had come into being as a separate institution apart from the Jewish community. But clearly that is historically inaccurate in light of the new research. The church and the Jewish community did part company eventually. And this will remain the situation for the future, even if Meier's contention that Jesus never envisioned a totally new religious community is proven correct. But there is a need in ecclesiological presentations to portray the separation for what it actually was—gradual and complex—and to ask what ties ought to be restored to some extent, even within the separatist model. One possibility is to envision the church and the Jewish community as two distinctive covenantal paths that remain connected in some measure; they are distinctive paths, but not totally distinct.

On the ethical front, the primary learning from the post–*Nostra Aetate* scholarship concerns the foundation of Christian ethics. That foundation has often been presented in a way that roots it in grace rather than law. The so-called law of Christ has been seen as standing in superior contrast to the inferior nature of the Jewish legal tradition. Much of the argumentation for such a perspective has come from interpretations of Pauline literature. Now that the perception of Paul's outlook on Jewish law has been redirected in a positive direction by a growing number of biblical scholars, Christian ethicians will have to do a major readjustment of the Christian approach to ethical thinking.

Finally, post–*Nostra Aetate* scholarship forces us to raise some major questions about how we understand Catholic Christianity's relationship with other world religions. Traditionally we have viewed Catholicism as fully complete as a religion with nothing fundamental to learn from any other religious community, Christian or not. There has been a sense of

17. Walter Cardinal Kasper, "The Good Olive Tree," *America* 185. 7 (17 September 2001) 12–14.

18. John T. Pawlikowski, *Christ in the Light of the Christian-Jewish Dialogue* (Eugene, OR: Wipf & Stock, 2001).

superiority over all other religious perspectives. Catholicism, and Christianity in general, in large measure defined their self-identity over against the Jewish tradition.

Now that the "over against" model has been shown as deeply flawed, there will be a need to rethink this self-definition: first and foremost relative to Judaism but also with respect to other non-Christian religious traditions. This also carries significant implications for evangelization.[19] Cardinal Walter Kasper has argued that there is no necessity for organized evangelization of the Jews because they are in the covenant and have authentic revelation from the Christian theological perspective.[20] But that discussion will need to be expanded to Islam and even beyond.

In sum, *Nostra Aetate* and the scholarship it has generated have the potential for a major reformulation of Christian thought in the key areas outlined above. Obviously such reformulation must be undertaken with care and with a respect for tradition. But it cannot be halted without undermining the process launched at Vatican II in its declaration *Nostra Aetate,* which defined its self-identity.

19. Gavin D'Costa et al., "What Does the Catholic Church Teach about Mission to the Jewish People?" *Theological Studies* 73 (2012) 590–640.

20. Walter Cardinal Kasper, "Christians, Jews and the Thorny Question of Mission," *Origins* 32/28 (19 December 2002) 464.

4

Nostra Aetate: Fifty Years On

Edward Kessler

NOSTRA AETATE, PUBLISHED ON 28th October 1965, towards the end of the Second Vatican Council, helped transform Jewish-Christian relations. Pope John XXIII had already received wide attention a year earlier for publicly greeting Jewish visitors with the words, "I am Joseph your brother." According to Roman Catholic scholar Fr. Edward Flannery, *Nostra Aetate* "terminated in a stroke a millennial teaching of contempt of Jews and Judaism and unequivocally asserted the Church's debt to its Jewish heritage."[1]

It marked the beginnings of a fresh approach to Judaism when the Roman Catholic Church "came in from out of the cold." Although it omitted mention of the Holocaust or the existence of the State of Israel, *Nostra Aetate* was forceful in its condemnation of anti-Semitism. Most important of all, it ushered in a new era, fresh attitudes, a new language of discourse never previously heard in the Catholic Church concerning Jews. The concept of a dialogue now entered the relationship.

---

1. Edward Flannery, "Seminaries, Classrooms, Pulpits, Streets: Where We Have to Go," in Roger Brooks, ed., *Unanswered Questions: Theological Views of Jewish-Catholic Relations* (Notre Dame: University of Notre Dame Press, 1988), 128–29.

THE JEWISH ORIGINS OF CHRISTIANITY

One consequence was a reawakening among Catholics to the Jewish origins of Christianity. They were reminded that Jesus was a faithful Jew, and, as *Nostra Aetate* stated, "that from the Jewish people sprang the apostles," the foundation stones and pillars of the Church, who "draw sustenance from the root of that good olive tree onto which have been grafted the wild olive branches of the Gentiles."[2]

The ramifications were manifold. Christians were taught that Jesus, his family, and his followers were Jewish, and the Jewish background to Christianity was stressed. Christians were taught that Jesus "had very close relations" with the Pharisees. They learnt that the final text of the Gospels was edited long after the events described, which meant that the authors were sometimes concerned with denigrating those Jews who did not follow Jesus, and equally concerned with vindicating the Romans, whose good-will they were seeking. This was courageously admitted by the Vatican's 1985 document on the teaching of Judaism, which stated forthrightly:

> It cannot be ruled out that some references hostile or less than favorable to the Jews have their historical context in conflicts between the nascent Church and the Jewish community. Certain controversies reflect Christian-Jewish relations long after the time of Jesus. To establish this is of capital importance if we wish to bring out the meaning of certain Gospel texts for the Christians of today.[3]

ANTI-SEMITISM AND THE HOLOCAUST

As a result of a soul change, epitomized by *Nostra Aetate*, Christianity shifted from what was, for the most part, an inherent need to condemn Judaism to one of a condemnation of Christian anti-Judaism. This led not

2. There were of course earlier documents than *Nostra Aetate* that emphasized the Jewishness of Jesus such as the 1947 Seelisburg document, which commended Christians to "remember that Jesus was born of a Jewish mother of the seed of David and the people of Israel, and that His everlasting love and forgiveness embraces His own people and the whole world; remember that the first disciples, the apostles and the first martyrs were Jews" (*The Ten Points of Seelisberg: An Address to the Churches*, 1947), http://www.ccjr.us/dialogika-resources/documents-and-statements/ecumenical-christian/567-seelisberg/.

3. *Notes on the Correct Way to Present the Jews and Judaism in Preaching and Catechesis.*

to a separation from all things Jewish but in fact, to a closer relationship with "the elder brother." In the words of German theologian Johannes Metz, "Christian theology after Auschwitz must stress anew the Jewish dimension of Christian beliefs and must overcome the forced blocking-out of the Jewish heritage within Christianity."[4]

Yet, while condemning anti-Semitism, *Nostra Aetate* avoided the topic of the Holocaust, possibly because few leaders of the Christian churches did much to help Jews. Eugenio Pacelli, Pope Pius XII from 1939 to 1958, was (and remains) a controversial figure; some claim that he knew much and did nothing of importance to help Jews whereas others retort that he did what he could and encouraged others to do more.[5] The impression of Vatican policy of the 1930s and '40s, indeed, of the two popes of that time, Pius XI and Pius XII, is hardly a positive one. Yet, it is essential to remember that in Nazi-occupied countries other than Germany, the churches were often targeted themselves, and were thus preoccupied with protecting their own flocks rather than with the fate of Jews.

However, individual Christian leaders did extend their support to Jews, and one of the most honorable examples was Angelo Giuseppe Roncalli, who, as papal nuncio for Turkey and Greece, made available baptismal certificates to thousands of Hungarian Jews in a bid to persuade Germans to leave them unmolested. He later became Pope John XXIII and initiated Vatican II.[6]

In 1987, in the wake of the controversy over the pope's reception of Austrian president Kurt Waldheim, who had been an active Nazi, the Vatican promised to reflect on the Holocaust, and *We Remember: Reflections on the Shoah* was published in 1998. It stresses the evils of anti-Semitism, concluding, "we wish to turn awareness of past sins into a firm resolve to build a new future in which there will be no more anti-Judaism

---

4. Johannes-Baptist Metz, "Facing the Jews: Christian Theology after Auschwitz," in Elisabeth Schüssler Fiorenza and David Tracy, eds., *The Holocaust as Interruption* (Edinburgh: T. & T. Clark, 1984), 27.

5. See, e.g., Pierre Blet, *Pius XII and the Second World War: According to the Archives of the Vatican*, trans. Lawrence J. Johnson (New York: Paulist, 1999); John Cornwell, *Hitler's Pope: The Secret History of Pius XII* (New York: Viking, 1999); Carol Rittner and John K. Roth, eds. and intro., *Pius XII and the Holocaust* (London: Continuum, 2002); José M. Sánchez, *Pius XII and the Holocaust: Understanding the Controversy* (Washington: Catholic University of America Press, 2002).

6. See Peter Hebblethwaite, *Pope John XXIII: Shepherd of the Modern World* (Garden City, NY: Doubleday, 1985).

among Christians or anti-Christian sentiment among Jews but rather a shared mutual respect."[7]

There remains a special European and a special Christian angle to dealing with the *Shoah*. It happened in the midst of a supposedly liberal, democratic, and well-developed civilization. The vast majority of Europeans looked on while their Jewish neighbors were being taken away and murdered. As far as Christianity is concerned, and most Europeans were of course, at least nominally, Christians, the problem is even more serious: some nineteen hundred years after the life of Jesus the Jew, his people were murdered by baptized pagans, who, by their action and inaction, denied their baptism, while most other Christians, from the highest to the lowest, looked aside.

In my view, the Holocaust remains a threat to Christian self-understanding today, as it did at the end of World War II. It is perhaps no coincidence that John Paul II, the Polish pope (whose pontificate witnessed more progress between Catholics and Jews than any other) was the first pope to visit a concentration camp (Auschwitz) and to pray there (1979); was the first pope to visit Yad Vashem in his pilgrimage to Israel (2000); and was the first pope to place words of apology for the Church's anti-Semitism in cracks of the Western Wall.

OVERCOMING SUPERSESSIONISM

One key feature of *Nostra Aetate* was its assertion that "Jews remain most dear to God," who "does not repent of the gifts He makes nor of the calls He issues."[8] In other words, it stated that God's covenant with the Jewish people had never been broken, retained eternal validity; God did not renege on his promises. If Jews were not rejected, then Judaism was not a fossilized faith, as had been taught previously, but a living, authentic religion.

Few biblical concepts have been as troubling to Christian-Jewish relations than the Christian claim to be the successor covenant people, elected by God to replace Israel because of the latter's faithlessness. Known as substitution theory or replacement theology, it argues that

---

7. *We Remember: Reflections on the Shoah*, V, par. 3. For a review of official Roman Catholic statements, see Kessler, "Jewish-Christian Relations in the Global Society: What the Institutional Documents Have and Have Not Been Telling Us," in Kessler et al., eds., *Jews and Christians in Conversation: Crossing Cultures and Generations* (Cambridge: Orchard Academic, 2002), 53–73.

8. See Appendix I.

since the time of Jesus, Jews have been replaced by Christians in God's favor, and that all God's promises to the Jewish people have been inherited by Christianity.

This raises a crucial question in today's relationship: can Christians view Judaism as a valid religion on its own terms (and vice versa)? Directly related to this is the need, from a Christian perspective, for reflection on the survival of the Jewish people and of the vitality of Judaism over nearly two thousand years: this is the "mystery of Israel," upon which Paul reflected in his Epistle to the Romans. For Christians, the question is whether Christianity can differentiate itself from Judaism without asserting itself as either opposed to Judaism or simply the fulfilment of Judaism.

Questions also need to be considered from the Jewish perspective. What was the divine purpose behind the creation of Christianity? What are the implications for Jews that as a result of the Jew Jesus, two billion Christians now read the Jewish Bible? Martin Buber suggested that Jesus was "my elder brother."

Nostra Aetate (and many Christian statements) turn for help to Paul of Tarsus, in whose view both Israel and the Church are elect and participate in the covenant of God. For Paul, it was impossible that the Jewish people as a whole could first have been elected by God and then later displaced. God would not simply elect and then reject. The Church's election derives from that of Israel, but this does not imply that God's covenant with Israel is broken. Rather, it remains unbroken—irrevocably (Rom 11:29). For Paul, the mystery of Israel is that their rejection and their stumbling do not mean that they cease to be accepted by God. Rather, they allow the Gentiles to participate in the peoplehood of Israel. For Paul, God would not simply elect and then reject. As *Nostra Aetate* states:

> Nevertheless, God holds the Jews most dear for the sake of their Fathers; He does not repent of the gifts He makes or of the calls He issues [Rom 11:28–29 referenced here]—such is the witness of the Apostle. In company with the Prophets and the same Apostle, the Church awaits that day, known to God alone, on which all peoples will address the Lord in a single voice and "serve him shoulder to shoulder" (Zeph. 3:9).

Indeed, so strongly does Paul make this point that he offers a severe warning that Gentile Christians should not be haughty or boastful toward unbelieving Jews—much less cultivate evil intent and engage in persecution against them. Christians have remembered the Jews as "enemies" but not as "beloved" of God (Rom 11:28) and have taken to heart Paul's criticisms and used them against the Jews while forgetting Paul's love for the Jews and their traditions (Rom 9:1–5).

Romans 9–11 therefore provided *Nostra Aetate*, and the Church as a whole, a means to reassess attitudes towards Jews and maintain the continuing validity of God's covenant with his Jewish people.

One might argue against Paul by saying that if Jews have not kept faith with God, then God has a perfect right to cast them off. It is interesting that Christians who argue this way have not often drawn the same deduction about Christian faithfulness, which has not been a notable characteristic of the last two millennia. Actually, God seems to have had a remarkable ability to keep faith with both Christians and Jews, when they have not kept faith with him—a point of which Paul is profoundly aware in Romans 9–11. He goes out of his way to deny claims that God has rejected the chosen people, and asserts that their stumbling does not lead to their fall.

The question that needs to be considered by Christian theologians today is, what replaces replacement theology? In their search for a replacement of replacement theology, they may do well to reflect on a speech by John Paul II in 1997:

> This people has been called and led by God, creator of heaven and earth. Their existence is not a mere natural or cultural happening. . . . It is a supernatural one. This people continues in spite of everything to be the people of the covenant, and, despite human infidelity, the Lord is faithful to his covenant.[9]

Some years ago, I heard Cardinal Kasper, former president of the Pontifical Commission for Religious Relations with the Jews, explore the same topic and suggest that the term "unabrogated covenant" should become the starting point for a renewed theology of Judaism. He hoped that conversation about covenant would further a sense of *chevruta*—partnership—between Jews and Christians.[10]

---

9. Quote is from *Documentation Catholique* 94 (1997) 1003.

10. A lecture, titled "The Meaning of Covenant in Judaism, Christianity and Jewish-Christian Relations," held at the Woolf Institute, Cambridge, 6 December 2004. For a transcript of the lecture, see http://www.jcrelations.net/en/?id=2446/.

ISRAEL-PALESTINE

One topic not mentioned in *Nostra Aetate*, but which causes more controversy than any other is the subject of peace and understanding between Israelis and Palestinians, or (perhaps more realistically) conflict and misunderstanding.

Political factors alone do not fully explain why the State of Israel is such a controversial topic. For Jews, of course, the centrality of the land of the Bible, as well as the survival of over a third of world Jewry, is at stake. Christians, for their part, not only disagree as to the place of the people of Israel in Christian theology, but feel particular concern for Christians who live in the nation-state as well as Palestinians. There of course are also many Christians and Jews who are deeply concerned about the "other," making this a complicated picture to understand. Political factors alone do not fully explain why Israel is such a controversial topic. Why do conversations brim with so much emotion and passion?

Although there have been great changes in Christian teaching on Judaism, attitudes toward Israel continue to be difficult. Simply put, it has been easier for the Church to condemn anti-Semitism as a misunderstanding of Christian teaching than to come to terms with the re-establishment of the Jewish State. Once again, it was John Paul II who was not only the first pope to visit a synagogue and to pray there with its congregation (in 1986) but the first to exchange ambassadors with the State of Israel (in 1994), making pilgrimage to the Holy Land in the millennium. His visit and that of Benedict XVI in 2009 helped mark the final repudiation of a "theology of perpetual wandering" for the Jewish community on the part of Christianity—a theology that argued against the very possibility of a restored, sovereign Jewish State, as part of the punishment Jews incurred for rejecting Jesus and supposedly putting him to death.[11]

Of course, some Christians are extremely critical of Israel, such as the authors of *Kairos Palestine*, a document issued by a number of leading Christians from the Holy Land in 2010, which depicts Israel as responsible for a complex conflict. When churches adopt divestment initiatives directed against Israel, a country whose policies they sometimes liken to

11. See John T. Pawlikowski, "The Vatican-Israeli Accords: Their Implications for Catholic Faith and Teaching," in Eugene J. Fisher and Leon Klenicki, eds., *A Challenge Long Delayed: The Diplomatic Exchange between the Holy See and the State of Israel* (New York: Anti-Defamation League, 1996), 10–19.

the former apartheid regime in South Africa, many see these as attempts to delegitimize Israel's very existence, although that may not be the intention. The fact that the churches do not act similarly regarding human rights abuses and state violence in many other places, especially in the wider Middle East, adds to the strain.

There is another complicating factor. For Christians in the Holy Land the relationship with Jews exists within a framework of a larger dialogue with Muslims. Christian Palestinians are concerned at the prospect of the gradual Islamization of the nascent state and of a time when Hamas and other Islamist parties might take over completely. Nablus, a city that once had a sizeable Christian population, now has almost none. The significant reduction in the Christian population elsewhere in the Middle East adds to feelings of insecurity, but there is one contribution Jews and Christians can bring from thousands of miles away: hope.

PAPAL LEADERSHIP

Ever since *Nostra Aetate* and the opening of the citadels of the Vatican to the fresh winds of change, successive popes have surprised commentators by their warm relations with the Jewish people. While John Paul II was renowned for his desire for reconciliation, the German emeritus pope, Benedict XVI was also keen to foster good relations with Jews and Judaism and surprised many with a visit to Auschwitz in 2006 and a pilgrimage to Israel in 2009.

Since March 2013, when Francis I was elected pontiff, we have learned that the Argentinean pope has his own deep commitment to Jewish-Christian relations, nurturing life-long friendships with the Jewish community in Buenos Aires, and coauthoring a book with Argentinian rabbi, Abraham Skorka, that has been translated into Hebrew (*On Heaven and Earth*). He is also expected (at the time of writing this article) to make a pilgrimage to Israel in 2014.

At the forefront of the modern papal conscience is a deep awareness of the intrinsic relationship with the "elder brother." Even the Chief Rabbi of Rome, Riccardo Di Segni, known for his cautious approach to interreligious conversation, has said of the present pope: "This pontiff does not cease to surprise." Rabbi Di Segni was referring to comments expressed publicly by Francis I at an occasion in Rome to mark the seventieth anniversary of the Nazi deportation of Roman Jews. "God never abandoned his covenant with Israel," he said, echoing the words of his predecessors, "and notwithstanding their terrible suffering over the centuries, the Jewish people have kept their faith. For this, we will never be sufficiently grateful to them as a Church, but also as human beings."

While it is difficult for any pope to surpass the efforts of John Paul II to foster reconciliation, Pope Francis has generated a new enthusiasm. For Rabbi David Rosen, Interreligious Director of the American Jewish Committee, "there has never been a Pope with as deep an understanding of Jews as Pope Francis." What lies ahead, Rabbi Rosen suggested, is the educational challenge: there remains a need to deliver programs, to tackle some of the pre-Conciliar attitudes that still prevail in parts of the Catholic world. This pope will continue to surprise. He has called on Jews and Christians "to walk together . . . along a joint path of friendship and trust."

His friendship with Rabbi Skorka is illustrative: I cannot think of any occasion in the history of the Roman Catholic Church when a pope and a rabbi celebrated their friendship by spending four days together in Rome as the two did recently, sharing all meals, including two Jewish festivals and Shabbat. This is an extraordinary friendship and an extraordinary moment in the relationship between the Catholic Church and the Jewish people.

CONCLUSION

Nostra Aetate was a milestone in Christian-Jewish relations and began an immensely difficult but rewarding exercise—namely, to take the "other" as seriously as one demands to be taken oneself. In the words the Vatican's 1975 *Guidelines on Nostra Aetate*, Judaism and Christianity must be understood on their own terms: "Christians must strive to learn by what essential traits the Jews define themselves in the light of their own religious experience."[12]

12. Commission for Religious Relations with the Jews, Guidelines and Suggestions for Implementing the Conciliar Declaration "*Nostra Aetate*" (no. 4) (1974). See also similar Protestant statements such as the World Lutheran Federation's assertion that "Christians also need to learn of the rich and varied history of Judaism since New Testament times, and of the Jewish people as a diverse, living community of faith today. Such an encounter with living and faithful Judaism can be profoundly enriching for Christian self-understanding" (Church Council of the Evangelical Lutheran Church in America, Declaration of ELCA to Jewish Community [1994]), http://www.elca.org/Who-We-Are/Our-Three-Expressions/Churchwide-Organization/Office-of-the-Presiding-Bishop/Ecumenical-and-Inter-Religious-Relations/Inter-Religious-Relations/

The last fifty years have seen a demonstrable shift from a pre–*Nostra Aetate* monologue about Jews to an instructive (and sometimes difficult) dialogue with Jews. A monologue generally fails to understand the reality of the "other," while a dialogue requires a respect for the "other" as it understands itself. The challenge of making the transition from monologue to dialogue remains immense, as the controversy following the 2002 publication of *Reflections on Covenant and Mission* by the National Council of Synagogues and the Bishops' Committee for Ecumenical and Interreligious Affairs, USCCB, demonstrated.[13]

It is clear today that many of the main divisive issues have been either eliminated or taken to the furthest point at which agreement is possible. The efforts of Catholics towards respect of Judaism project attitudes that would have been unthinkable half a century ago. During five decades Jews and Christians have witnessed a massive change and giant strides have been made but we are talking of a dynamic and relentless process. We will never be able to sit back and say, "The work is done. The agenda is completed." However, on many major issues, Jews and Christians find themselves on the same side of the fence, faced with the same challenges, and they are in the unusual position of seeking to tackle them together.

Christian-Jewish-Relations/Declaration-of-ELCA-to-Jewish-Community.aspx.

13. http://www.usccb.org/beliefs-and-teachings/ecumenical-and-interreligious/ jewish/upload/Reflections-on-Covenant-and-Mission.pdf/.

5

"God Holds the Jews Most Dear"
Learning to Respect Jewish Self-Understanding

Philip A. Cunningham

1. INTRODUCTION

As is well known, a new and positive relationship between Catholics and Jews became possible on October 28, 1965, with the promulgation of the Second Vatican Council declaration, *Nostra Aetate*. It is perhaps less well known that intense opposition and parliamentary maneuvering almost scuttled the prospects for such a document.[1]

In this essay, I will focus on one particular cause of difficulty: the pervasive Christian outlook that saw suffering and vulnerability as the

---

1. See Giovanni Miccoli, "Two Sensitive Issues: Religious Freedom and the Jews," in Giuseppe Albergio and Joseph A. Komonchak, eds., *History of Vatican II*, vol. 4, *Church as Communion: Third Period and Intersession, September 1964—September 1965* (Maryknoll, NY: Orbis, 2003), 95–193; John W. O'Malley, *What Happened at Vatican II* (Cambridge: Belknap, 2008), 218–26, 250–52, 275–77; Alberto Melloni, "*Nostra Aetate* and the Discovery of the Sacrament of Otherness," in Philip A. Cunningham et al., eds., *The Catholic Church and the Jewish People: Recent Reflections from Rome* (New York: Fordham University Press, 2007), 129–51.

inevitable fate of Jews until they accepted Christ. An unchallenged part of the air Christians breathed, this stance gave them little reason to think they had much of anything to learn from Jews. Regarding Jews as lost until they accepted Christ fostered a perennial Christian interest in organizing initiatives to bring Jews to baptism. So long as Jews were seen only as prospective and destined converts to Christianity, there was little likelihood of any Jewish and Catholic rapprochement.

This essay explores these themes by discussing certain events before, during, and after the Council. It begins with one of the unsung heroes of this story, a German theologian named Karl Thieme. Baptized a Lutheran, he became Catholic before the Second World War and dedicated his life to combating anti-Semitism among Christians.

2. "THE JEWISH PEOPLE ENJOYS SPECIAL GUIDANCE AND SPECIAL GRACE."

In an intriguing book, John Connelly traces the slow, incremental progress of Catholic pioneers in mid-twentieth-century Europe, who struggled against the attraction that Nazi racism held for many Catholics.[2] Ensnared themselves by the long-lived notion that Jews were destined to suffer and that only baptism into the church could save them, their theological hands were tied, so to speak, as they sought to devise effective religious arguments against anti-Semitism.[3]

As Connelly relates, Karl Thieme experienced a five-year crisis of conscience between 1945 and 1950 after being accused of writing an anti-Semitic book. The allegation was based on Thieme's use of a mistranslation of Rom 11:28 to characterize Jews as "enemies of God." As someone who had labored for years to fight anti-Semitism, Thieme was greatly distressed by this charge from a prominent rabbi.

During his period of soul-searching, Thieme corresponded with several Jewish thinkers, including Martin Buber. His encounter with

2. John Connelly, *From Enemy to Brother: The Revolution in Catholic Teaching on the Jews, 1933–1965* (Cambridge: Harvard University Press, 2012).

3. This is also evident in the draft of a prospective encyclical prepared for Pope Pius XI, *Humani Generis Unitas*. Although it condemned Nazi racism, it asserted that there was an "authentic basis of the social separation of the Jews from the rest of humanity" because their leaders "had called down upon their own heads a Divine malediction" by rejecting Jesus Christ. See Georges Passelecq and Bernard Suchecky, *The Hidden Encyclical of Pius XI* (New York: Harcourt, Brace, 1997), 246–59.

Jewish self-understanding caused him to reevaluate unexamined theological presuppositions. In one notably frank letter, Buber wrote:

> I had been persuaded up to now that you were interested in real understanding with those religious Jews who have understanding for people acting as faithful Christians. But how should such understanding be possible if you identify spiritual life for the Jews with their readiness to be converted? I have my spiritual life in a direct contact between God and myself, and in addition I have my bodily life. I cannot believe that God would allow a Christian to question this fact, and equally I cannot believe that God would allow me to act this way toward a Christian.[4]

Buber's matter-of-fact reference to a direct connection with God called into question the widespread Christian view that this was possible only by explicit faith in Christ. His combining of his "spiritual life" and his "bodily life" also flew in the face of a long-lived Christian distinction (based on a certain reading of 1 Cor 10:18) between "Israel after the flesh" (i.e., living Jews) and the church as the "spiritual Israel." Thieme must also have been taken aback by Buber's suggestion that thinking of Jews only as the likeliest candidates for baptism would be offensive to God.

By 1950, after similar exchanges with other Jews, Thieme spoke of undergoing a personal "conversion." He began saying that Christians must abandon their efforts to baptize Jews, writing to Buber in 1954 that the Jewish people are "God's 'special possession,' and remains sanctified in a way that is hardly accessible to us 'believers from the peoples of the world.'"[5]

Thieme's breakthrough insight was perhaps best expressed in a 1950 article in the *Freiburger Rundbrief*: "a Jewish person not only as an individual person, but also in a certain sense precisely as '*Jew* can be pleasing to God.' Precisely for the Jews according to the entirety of divine revelation certain promises continue to be in force, so that one can assume that even in distance from Christ the Jewish people enjoys special guidance and special grace."[6]

In this period, Thieme was wrestling with key Christian questions about Jewish identity. First, were living Jews the "same people" as the biblical Jewish people? Second, if so, were today's Jews still in covenant with God, and could Christians acknowledge this without relativizing the new

---

4. Buber to Thieme, June 25, 1949. Quoted in Connelly, *From Enemy to Brother*, 201.

5. Ibid., 199.

6. Ibid., 204–5.

covenant of Christ? Third, if Jewish covenantal life endured, what was the relationship between the Jewish people and the Church?[7] Thieme would give affirmative answers to the first two questions, and for the third he spoke of Jews as "elder brothers." He used this phrase with the Parable of the Prodigal Son in mind (Luke 15:11–32). Thieme wrote to Buber that if Jews were the elder son, the one who was always loyal to the father, then it was to them that the father said, "Son, you are always with me, and all that I have is yours" (15:31). This, reasoned Thieme, amounted to the "legitimation of Jewry" until the end of time.[8]

Thieme fully expressed his new perspectives in a series of theses prepared for a 1954 conference of the World Council of Churches in Evanston, Illinois. He urged dialogue with Jews "until the day arrives where 'there shall be *one* fold, and *one* shepherd' (John 10:16), where 'all the peoples . . . may serve him shoulder to shoulder' (Zeph. 3:9)."[9]

Thieme's new perspective was such a change that his longtime co-worker, John Oesterreicher, long argued against it. Oesterreicher, an Austrian Jew who had become a Catholic priest in 1927, had lost his family to the *Shoah*. For many years, he vigorously opposed Nazi anti-Semitism and its corruption of the Christian gospel, but he was also dedicated to the conversion of Jews to Christianity. He gradually changed his mind, in part because of his exchanges with Thieme.

Connelly nicely sums up their relationship: "Their views, the explicitly pro-Jewish (Thieme) and the explicitly anti-racist (Oesterreicher), though in tension, in fact complemented each other."[10] But in the 1950s, Oesterreicher strongly opposed calling Jews "elder brothers" and resisted Thieme's contention that Catholics ought not to proselytize Jews. After 1960 they ceased their decades-long correspondence, but Oesterreicher would remember Thieme's arguments and writings.

---

7. Ibid., 219.

8. Ibid., 202.

9. For the full text of Evanston theses, see http://www.ccjr.us/dialogika-resources/documents-and-statements/roman-catholic/second-vatican-council/naprecursors/1227-evanston1954/.

10. Connelly, *From Enemy to Brother*, 237.

3. "THE CHURCH AWAITS THAT DAY . . . [WHEN] ALL PEOPLES WILL ADDRESS THE LORD IN A SINGLE VOICE."

On June 13, 1960, the French Jewish historian Jules Isaac arrived at the Vatican for a private audience with Pope John XXIII. He presented the pope with a dossier summarizing his research into the history of the Christian "teaching of contempt." Also included was a text from a 1947 conference in Seelisberg, Switzerland, in which Isaac had participated, sponsored by the nascent International Council of Christians and Jews.[11] Titled "An Address to the Churches," it offered ten points "to prevent any animosity towards the Jews which might arise from false, inadequate or mistaken presentations or conceptions of the teaching and preaching of the Christian doctrine."[12] Isaac asked for the upcoming Second Vatican Council to issue a statement on these topics that would condemn anti-Semitism.

John XXIII was sympathetic. As a Vatican nuncio during World War II, the future pope had provided false baptismal certificates and visas to thousands of Jews fleeing the Nazi persecution.[13] Three months after Professor Isaac's visit, he instructed Cardinal Augustin Bea, SJ, president of the Secretariat for Christian Unity, to prepare for the Council's consideration a draft on relations between the Church and the Jewish people. Bea assembled a team of experts to undertake this task, including John Oesterreicher. But the road ahead was not easy. Looking back afterward, Bea is reported to have said, "If I had known all the difficulties before, I do not know whether I would have had the courage to [proceed]."[14]

Four years later, on September 25, 1964, after surmounting various parliamentary maneuvers, Bea was finally able to introduce to the Council Fathers a text titled, "On the Jews and Non-Christian Religions." For various reasons the draft displeased him. His secretariat's previous text had been significantly reduced and altered by the Coordinating

11. O'Malley, *What Happened*, 219.

12. http://www.ccjr.us/dialogika-resources/documents-and-statements/ecumenical-christian/567-seelisberg/

13. George H. Tavard, "*Nostra Aetate*: Forty Years Later," in Michael Attridge, ed., *Jews and Catholics Together: Celebrating the Legacy of "Nostra Aetate"* (Ottawa: Novalis, 2007), 21.

14. Cardinal Walter Kasper, "The Commission for Religious Relations with the Jews: A Crucial Endeavour of the Catholic Church," Address at Boston College, Nov. 6, 2002, §1.

Commission of the Council, apparently to more closely resemble conventional, hostile teaching about Jews.[15] Over the summer this "watered down"[16] draft was leaked in American media and provoked public controversy with the words,

> The union of the Jewish people with the Church is a part of Christian hope. With unshaken faith and deep longing, the Church awaits, in accordance with the teaching of the Apostle Paul, the entry of this people into the fullness of the People of God which Christ has founded.[17]

These words were understood by many to mean that Catholics should actively seek to bring Jews into the Church. On Sept 3, 1964, a prominent American rabbi and scholar, Abraham Joshua Heschel, who had been corresponding with Bea for some time, wrote the cardinal that this phrasing amounted to "spiritual fratricide," and that he was "ready to go to Auschwitz any time, if faced with the alternative of conversion or death."[18] Other Jewish leaders expressed similar sentiments in media reports.

In his presentation to the Council on September 25th, by setting forth counterarguments, Bea implicitly challenged the Coordinating Commission's text for suggesting that all Jews in the time of Jesus bore guilt for the crucifixion. His remarks were clearly intended to spur the Council Fathers to make corrections. Cardinal Joseph Ritter of Saint Louis obliged by saying,

15. Miccoli, "Two Sensitive Issues: Religious Freedom and the Jews," in Giuseppe Albergio and Joseph A. Komonchak, eds., *History of Vatican II*, vol. 4, *Church as Communion: Third Period and Intersession, September 1964—September 1965* (Maryknoll, NY: Orbis, 2003), 149.

16. See a June 13, 1964, letter from New York's Cardinal Francis Spellman to the Vatican Secretary of State and to the Council's Secretary: "any watering down of the text presented during the [Council's] second period would have disastrous consequences" (in Miccoli, "Two Sensitive Issues," 147). This was likely a reaction to a front-page story in the previous day's *New York Times*, with the headline "Vatican Said to Mute Its Text on the Jews," which described that the Coordinating Commission of the Council had "dramatically watered down" the previous draft from Bea's secretariat. See http://www.nytimes.com/1964/06/12/vatican-said-to-mute-its-text-on-the-jews.html?_r=0/.

17. John M. Oesterreicher, *The New Encounter between Christians and Jews* (New York: Philosophical Library, 1986), 186.

18. Beatrice Bruteau, ed., *Merton and Judaism: Recognition, Repentance, and Renewal* (Louisville: Fons Vitae, 2003), 223–24.

> Let the declaration more fully and more explicitly speak of the religious patrimony that so closely, even today, unites the Jewish and Christian peoples. The promises that God . . . made to Abraham still belong to the Jews. The same divine love is extended to Jews and Christians in a special way; because of it a very close unity of love and esteem should thrive between us and them. Therefore, that spirit of love that was found in the original draft should shine out even more in this declaration. Let our debt and relationships to the Jews, which are hesitantly and, as it were, unwillingly acknowledged in this draft, be proclaimed with great joy.[19]

Some speakers took up the controversial addition that spoke of the union of the Jewish people with the Church. They urged that the question of Jewish conversion to Christianity be understood as an eschatological matter; in other words, that it was not the task of Catholics in historical time to try to baptize all Jews. Coadjutor-Archbishop Arthur Elchinger of Strasbourg, for example, stated, "We Christians . . . are not permitted to look upon the Jews as the rejected members of God's people." He concluded that the "declaration should avoid . . . every type of any present calling to conversion of the entire Jewish people . . . We do not yet know, nor can we know, that hour of God, that Paul speaks of in the Epistle to the Romans concerning the definitive union of all the chosen people."

Archbishop Patrick O'Boyle of Washington DC echoed this: "The destiny of the Jewish people depends completely on the dispositions of divine Providence and the grace of God. [If our words lead Jews] to interpret them as a definite and conscious intention to work for their conversion, we will build another high wall that separates us from a holy and fruitful dialogue with the Jewish people . . . Better if we would admit the limitations of our knowledge, and the hidden ways of divine Providence."

After two days of deliberations, it was the task of Bea's team to revise the text accordingly. John Oesterreicher incorporated a phrase from Thieme's 1954 Evanston theses: "the Church awaits the day, known to God alone, when all people will call upon the Lord with a single voice and 'serve him with one accord'(Zeph 3:9)." The Council record explained this specific revision in this way: "The paragraph concerning the church's eschatological hope is changed. Many fathers asked that in the expression

---

19. The texts of all the statements during the so-called Great Debate of September 28–29, 1964 have been translated into English by Patrick T. Brannan, SJ, and may be found at http://www.ccjr.us/dialogika-resources/documents-and-statements/roman -catholic/second-vatican-council/na-debate/.

of this hope, since it concerns the mystery [of Israel], any appearance of proselytism be avoided. Other fathers requested that it somehow be expressed that Christian hope also embraces all peoples. By this present paragraph we wish to satisfy all these desires."[20] The formulation was retained into the final version of *Nostra Aetate* despite the many hurdles the declaration still had to overcome.

About a year later, when the vote on a final text was imminent, the *New York Times* described the new phraseology as "an expression of the long-term 'eschatological' hope of the Church for the eventual unity of all mankind . . . But there is no call to active proselytization and no presentation of conversion as the price of brotherhood" (Oct 4, 1965). Three days before the vote, the self-designated "International Group of Fathers" (the *Coetus Internationalis Patrum*) protested the eschatological perspective. A handful of bishops, including the later excommunicated Archbishop Marcel Lefèbvre, declared it "unworthy of the Council" to have framed "the future conversion of Israel" so as to preclude proselytizing.[21] Nonetheless, when the Council voted on October 14–15, 1965, there were 1,937 votes in favor of the section that included Thieme's eschatological phrase, and only 153 votes against it.[22] Heschel later rejoiced that the declaration was "devoid of any expression of hope for conversion."[23]

Since both friends and foes of *Nostra Aetate* and media reports all shared a common understanding of the words "the Church awaits the day . . . ," it seems clear that the Council Fathers were aware its implications when they overwhelmingly voted their approval. Sadly, Thieme had died of cancer in 1963 and so didn't live to see his contribution enshrined in the conciliar declaration.

Among the many notable features in the story thus far is the importance of personal interactions between Christians and Jews. Constructive exchanges—such as those between Karl Thieme and Martin Buber, John XXIII and Jules Isaac, Augustin Bea and Abraham Heschel—gave Catholics a transformative glimpse into Jewish self-understanding. The

---

20. *Acta Syn.*III.8, 648. My thanks to Thomas Stransky, a member of Bea's team, for this reference.

21. See Oesterreicher, *New Encounter*, 272, 274.

22. Ibid., 275.

23. Reuven Kimelman, "Rabbis Joseph B. Soloveitchik and Abraham Joshua Heschel on Jewish-Christian Relations," *The Edah Journal* 4/2 (2004) 6, citing Abraham J. Heschel, "From Mission to Dialogue," *Conservative Judaism* 21 (Spring 1967) 10.

experience made intolerable the idea that Jews were not in genuine relationship with one, true God.

This newfound respect for Jewish covenantal life found expression in *Nostra Aetate*'s rendering of Rom 9:4–5 in the present tense ("theirs *is* the sonship and the glory and the covenants and the law and the worship and the promises") and its quotation of Rom 11:28–29 ("God holds the Jews most dear for the sake of their Fathers; He does not repent of the gifts He makes or of the calls He issues").

It also led the 1974 Vatican document to implement *Nostra Aetate* to state that "Christians . . . must strive to learn by what essential traits Jews define themselves in the light of their own religious experience."[24] This principle could be negatively expressed as an enduring commandment to future Catholic theologians: "When speaking of Judaism, thou shalt not theologize without respect for Jewish self-understanding."

In the decades of the "reception"[25] of *Nostra Aetate* into the Church community, Catholics came to see Jews more as dialogue partners and less as prospects for conversion. As John Paul II said in 1979, "we recognize with utmost clarity that the path along which we should proceed with the Jewish religious community is one of fraternal dialogue and fruitful collaboration."[26] Though the Council's eschatological perspective effectively "took the wind out of the sails" of conversionary efforts and focused on dialogue with covenantal colleagues in the here and now, Catholics continued to debate the question.

4. "THE CHURCH MUST NOT CONCERN HERSELF WITH THE CONVERSION OF THE JEWS."

The ramifications of the new Catholic respect for Jewish self-understanding have unfolded ever since the Council. John Paul II, for example, repeatedly insisted that God's covenant with the Jewish people was never

---

24. Commission for Religious Relations with the Jews, "Guidelines and Suggestions for Implementing the Conciliar Declaration *Nostra Aetate*, No. 4" (1974), preamble.

25. In Catholic usage, "reception" is the process by which teachings or practices may be assimilated by the people of God.

26. "Address to Representatives of Jewish Organizations," March 12, 1979. See http://www.ccjr.us/dialogika-resources/documents-and-statements/roman-catholic/pope-john-paul-ii/231-jp2-79mar12/.

revoked,[27] and expounded on its significance in writings that today occupy a hefty volume.[28]

An important corollary to this developing tradition was expressed in 2001 when Cardinal Walter Kasper, the new president of the Pontifical Commission for Religious Relations with the Jews, stated at an official Vatican dialogue with worldwide Jewry: "[The Catholic Church] declares that God's grace, which is the grace of Jesus Christ according to our faith, is available to all. Therefore, the Church believes that Judaism, i.e. the faithful response of the Jewish people to God's irrevocable covenant, is salvific for them, because God is faithful to his promises."[29] Considering that for centuries Christians felt Jews were destined to suffer until they accepted Christ, the idea that Jews in divine covenant experience God's saving grace—the grace of Jesus Christ in Christian understanding—bespeaks a remarkable transformation. This includes thinking of covenant as primarily an intimate and living relationship, instead of a lifeless legal contract.

In 2002, after American evangelicals launched new conversionary projects toward Jews, a paper from the dialogue between the U.S. Bishops' Committee on Ecumenical and Interreligious Affairs and the National Council of Synagogues discussed why Catholics did not mount similar efforts. After being vetted by relevant USCCB staffers, "Reflections on Covenant and Mission" (RCM) explained that, "A deepening Catholic appreciation of the eternal covenant between God and the Jewish people, together with a recognition of a divinely-given mission to Jews to witness to God's faithful love, lead to the conclusion that campaigns that target Jews for conversion to Christianity are no longer theologically acceptable in the Catholic Church."[30]

The cochairs of the dialogue saw the text as part of a larger process. Cardinal William Keeler noted that it "echoed the words of Pope John

27. Mainz, Germany (Nov 17, 1980); Sydney, Australia (Nov 26, 1986); Miami, USA (Sept 11, 1987); Vienna, Austria (June 24, 1988); in the Vatican (Sept 26, 1990; Nov 8, 1990; Apr 28, 1999; June 29, 1999); and Mount Sinai, Egypt (Feb 26, 2000). All available at http://www.ccjr.us/dialogika-resources/documents-and-statements/ roman-catholic/pope-john-paul-ii/.

28. Eugene J. Fisher and Leon Klenicki, eds. *The Saint for Shalom: How Pope John Paul II Transformed Catholic-Jewish Relations* (New York: Crossroad, 2011).

29. *"Dominus Iesus,"* 17th meeting of the International Catholic-Jewish Liaison Committee, New York (May 1, 2001). See http://www.ccjr.us/dialogika-resources/ documents-and-statements/roman-catholic/kasper/641-kasper01may1/.

30. http://www.usccb.org/beliefs-and-teachings/ecumenical-and-interreligious/ jewish/upload/Reflections-on-Covenant-and-Mission.pdf/.

Paul II, praying that as Christians and Jews we may be 'a blessing to one another' so that, together, we may be "a blessing to the world.'" Rabbi Gilbert Rosenthal felt that the "joint Catholic-Jewish statement on mission is yet another step in turning a new page in the often stormy relationship between the Jewish people and the Roman Catholic Church."[31]

In a fascinating reprise of questions that engaged Karl Thieme in the 1940s and 1950s, critics of RCM made "neosupersessionist" claims about Judaism, questioning or denying the vitality of ongoing Jewish covenantal life with God.[32] Some resorted to hyperbole[33] and even to apocalyptic rhetoric.[34] Sadly, as had occurred during *Nostra Aetate*'s composition, so now: "Messages were conveyed by indirection or through third parties, so that . . . it became impossible to know how to interpret what was really going on and to whom to address grievances."[35] As a result, confusion abounded.

A parallel debate erupted in 2008 when Pope Benedict XVI composed a new intercession for Jews to be used in the Tridentine Good Friday liturgy. It asked God to "illuminate their hearts so that they may recognize Jesus Christ as savior of all men."[36] Since the new prayer was issued without explanation and published as *pro conversione Iudeaorum*, it seemed that the proselytization of Jews was being encouraged. An

31. http://www.ccjr.us/dialogika-resources/documents-and-statements/interreligious/bceia-ncs/1091-ncs-bceianews2002aug12/.

32. See Cunningham, "Official Ecclesial Documents to Implement Vatican II on Relations with Jews: Study Them, Become Immersed in Them, and Put Them into Practice," *Studies in Christian-Jewish Relations* 4/1 (2009) 1–36, http://ejournals.bc.edu/ojs/index.php/scjr/article/view/1521/1374/.

33. Thus, Cardinal Avery Dulles, e.g., alleged that RCM "seems to say that Christians can evangelize without pronouncing the name of Jesus ["Covenant and Mission," *America* (Oct 21, 2002)], though RCM had stated that the Catholic Church "will always witness to its faith . . . in Jesus Christ to Jews and to all other people." RCM argued that the form evangelization takes with regard to Jews is through dialogue in which Catholics give witness to their faith in Christ. See also Cardinal Kasper: "mission understood as call to conversion from idolatry to the living and true God (1 Thess 1:9) does not apply and cannot be applied to Jews" ["Christians, Jews and the Thorny Question of Mission," *Origins* 32/28 (Dec 19, 2002)].

34. E.g., John Echert feared that "we are moving into one of the signs of the end times, namely apostasy." He opined that "precisely because Jews share an expectation of the coming of the Messiah, they *should* be targeted and the primary efforts of our efforts for converts to Christ" [emphasis added]. Quoted in "On File," *Origins* 32/13 (Sept. 5, 2002), 214.

35. O'Malley, *What Really Happened*, 226.

36. http://www.ccjr.us/dialogika-resources/documents-and-statements/roman-catholic/pope-benedict-xvi/425-b1608feb5/.

article by Cardinal Kasper, printed in *L'Osservatore Romano* at the pope's request, argued that the prayer shared the eschatological perspective of Vatican II: "In this prayer the Church does not take it upon herself to orchestrate the realization of the unfathomable mystery. She cannot do so. Instead, she lays the *when* and the *how* entirely in God's hands. God alone can bring about the Kingdom of God in which the whole of Israel is saved and eschatological peace is bestowed on the world."[37]

Meanwhile in the United States, in the absence of any ecclesiastical effort to bring contrasting perspectives into dialogue with one another, the similar questions that had been raised by RCM continued to simmer. In the summer of 2009, critics of RCM, who now staffed relevant offices of the U.S. Conference of Catholic Bishops, released, "A Note on Ambiguities Contained in 'Reflections on Covenant and Mission.'"[38] This statement's most controversial words struck at the very nature of interreligious dialogue as understood ever since the Second Vatican Council: "Though Christian participation in interreligious dialogue would not normally include an explicit invitation to baptism and entrance into the Church, the Christian dialogue partner is always giving witness to the following of Christ, to which all are implicitly invited."

The prospect that occasionally dialogue *could* be the venue for "an explicit invitation to baptism" immediately alarmed Jewish interlocutors. It will be recalled that this potential had been foreseen forty-five years earlier by Archbishop Patrick O'Boyle during the Second Vatican Council when he warned that words that could be interpreted "as a definite and conscious intention to work for their conversion . . . will build another high wall that separates us from a holy and fruitful dialogue with the Jewish people."[39]

The egregiousness of this ill-advised sentence was soon seen in an unprecedented, unanimous letter of the major American Jewish organizations and religious denominations to the U.S. Conference of Catholic Bishops: "We pose no objection to the position that Christians must bear witness to the truth of their faith and expound on it forthrightly, candidly

---

37. "Striving for Mutual Respect in Modes of Prayer," *L'Osservatore Romano* (April 16, 2008) 8–9, http://www.ccjr.us/dialogika-resources/documents-and-statements/roman-catholic/kasper/651-kasper08apr16/.

38. Original text available at http://www.ccjr.us/dialogika-resources/themes-in-todays-dialogue/conversion/559-usccb-09june18/.

39. http://www.ccjr.us/dialogika-resources/documents-and-statements/roman-catholic/second-vatican-council/na-debate/1020-v21964sept29b/.

and passionately. However, once Jewish-Christian dialogue has been formally characterized as an invitation, whether explicit or implicit, to apostatize, then Jewish participation becomes untenable."[40] Subsequently, leading bishops replied that "Jewish-Catholic dialogue, one of the blessed fruits of the Second Vatican Council, has never been and will never be used by the Catholic Church as a means of proselytism—nor is it intended as a disguised invitation to baptism."[41] They also took the exceptional step of deleting the problematic sentence about implicit and explicit invitations, rendering the "Note on Ambiguities" somewhat inchoate.

The fundamental problem was that most of those who thought of Jews primarily as potential converts rather than as covenantal partners from whom they could learn was their disinterest in Jewish spiritual life. In other words, they violated the post–Vatican II axiom, "When speaking of Judaism, thou shalt not theologize without respect for Jewish self-understanding."

However, Pope Benedict plainly *did* respect Jewish covenantal life. At the Great Synagogue of Rome in January 2010, he pointed to Vatican II as marking "our irrevocable commitment to pursue the path of dialogue, fraternity and friendship." He described Jews as "the people of the Covenant of Moses" and called for a renewed Catholic "respect for the Jewish interpretation of the Old Testament." By citing a rabbinic text, he showed that Christians can learn from the ongoing, post–New Testament Jewish tradition.[42] All these points contradicted those Catholics who had treated Jewish covenantal life after Christ as essentially moribund.

Benedict's commitment to respectful dialogue was also apparent in a 2011 book in which he wrote, "After centuries of antagonism, we now see it as our task to bring these two ways of rereading the biblical texts— the Christian way and the Jewish way—into dialogue with one another, if we are to understand God's will and his word aright."[43] Clearly, the pope desires Jews and Christians to learn from each other about God.

40. "National Jewish Interfaith Leadership Letter on USCCB 'Note on Ambiguities'" (Aug 18, 2009), http://www.ccjr.us/dialogika-resources/themes-in-todays-dialogue/conversion/574-njilo9aug18/.

41. "Statement of Principles on Catholic-Jewish Dialogue" (Oct 2, 2009), §3, http://www.ccjr.us/dialogika-resources/themes-in-todays-dialogue/conversion/583-usccbdialogue09oct2/.

42. http://www.ccjr.us/dialogika-resources/documents-and-statements/roman-catholic/pope-benedict-xvi/660-b1610jan17/.

43. Benedict XVI, *Jesus of Nazareth*, Part Two, *Holy Week: From the Entrance into Jerusalem to the Resurrection* (San Francisco: Ignatius, 2011), 35.

This essay has highlighted the inescapable links among respect for Jewish self-understanding, the desire for trusting interreligious dialogue (in which Christians and Jews each witness to their faith), and the disavowal of long-lived Christian efforts to convert Jews. It is, therefore, inevitable that the same connections that were manifested in the story of Karl Thieme, in the deliberations over *Nostra Aetate* at Vatican II, and during the debates over the following decades, should also be evident in Benedict's thinking. In his 2011 book he also discussed the question of a Christian conversionary "mission" to Jews:

> Here I should like to recall the advice given by Bernard of Clairvaux to his pupil Pope Eugene III on this matter. He reminds the Pope that his duty of care extends not only to Christians, but: "You also have obligations toward unbelievers, whether Jew, Greek, or Gentile" (*De Consideratione* III/i, 2). Then he immediately corrects himself and observes more accurately: "Granted, with regard to the Jews, time excuses you; for them a determined point in time has been fixed, which cannot be anticipated. The full number of the Gentiles must come in first . . . (*De Consideratione* III/i, 3)

Hildegard Brem comments on this passage as follows: "In the light of Romans 11:25, the Church must not concern herself with the conversion of the Jews, since she must wait for the time fixed for this by God, 'until the full number of the Gentiles come in' (Rom 11:25)."

> In the meantime, Israel retains its own mission. Israel is in the hands of God, who will save it "as a whole" at the proper time, when the number of the Gentiles is complete.[44]

The question that Benedict answered negatively here—if Catholics should be organizing to seek Jewish converts—can now be seen as a crucial thread that runs through the past seventy-five years or so. The work of early pioneers, the promulgation of *Nostra Aetate*, and specific writings of Popes John Paul II and Benedict XVI are key benchmarks along the way. It is becoming "settled teaching" that Catholics should not seek to convert Jews, but instead should dialogue with them so that we can learn from one another's experiences of covenanting with God.

---

44. Ibid., 44–45, 47.

As noted earlier, an underlying Christian theological question is, can a people be covenantally related to a saving God even if they do not acknowledge the incarnation of God's Word in Christ?[45]

That the answer to this question is becoming more and more a solid yes in Catholic thought is clear in a 2012 address by the president of the Commission for Religious Relations with Jews, Cardinal Kurt Koch:

> On the one hand, from the Christian confession there can be only one path to salvation. However, on the other hand, it does not necessarily follow that the Jews are excluded from God's salvation because they do not believe in Jesus Christ as the Messiah of Israel and the Son of God. Such a claim would find no support in the . . . understanding of St Paul, who in the Letter to the Romans definitively negates the question he himself has posed, whether God has repudiated his own people: "For the grace and call that God grants are irrevocable" (Rom 11:29).[46]

Clearly, a lot of weight has been placed on Romans 9–11 ever since the Second World War. It raises the question of how best to exegete and actualize Paul's eschatological speculations in our world today. But that is a topic for the future. For now, it is good to recall that it was inconceivable in 1940 that Christians could think positively of Jews as covenanting with a saving God in a non-Christ-centered way. Or as Cardinal Koch has put it: "That the Jews are participants in God's salvation is theologically unquestionable, but how that can be possible without confessing Christ explicitly, is and remains an unfathomable divine mystery."[47]

Yet thanks to *Nostra Aetate* it is today the new norm. On its fiftieth anniversary, let us be grateful to the many laborers along the way for all that has been accomplished and all that yet will be.

---

45. See: Philip A. Cunningham et al., eds., *Christ Jesus and the Jewish People Today: New Explorations of Theological Interrelationships* (Grand Rapids: Eerdmans, 2011).

46. "In the Service of Jewish-Catholic Understanding" (Oct 29, 2012) §6, http://www.ccjr.us/dialogika-resources/documents-and-statements/roman-catholic/kurt-cardinal-koch/1177-koch2012oct29/.

47. Ibid.

6

Toward a New Era of Partnership between Judaism and Christianity

A Covenantal Reflection on *Nostra Aetate* as a (Re)Turning Point

Irving Greenberg

A. WHAT WE HAVE IN COMMON

JUDAISM AND CHRISTIANITY ARE uniquely close. The history of their pre-modern relationship—essentially one of conflict, contempt, and mutual rejection—has totally obscured this deeper truth. The core assertions of both religions are profoundly the same. There is an unseen, eternal and infinite God, Creator and Sustainer of the universe. God so loves existence that the Creator self-limits to enable the universe to operate as a "continuing" system based on dependable natural laws. The infinity of the Divine totally transcends and, in a sense, trivializes this planet and humanity. Nevertheless, the Lord is deeply engaged with—nay, loves—this world and all its inhabitants. God expresses this love in wanting this world to be perfected so that humans will flourish and all the enemies of life will be vanquished. To achieve this goal, the Deity reveals God's self and gives instructions for living the good life.

God so loves humanity that the Lord self-limits again and enters into partnership with humans to achieve *Tikkun Olam* (the repair and perfection of this world). The self-limitation means that the Deity will not act alone to make everything perfect through decisive interventions or divine fiats. Nor will God force humans to do the right thing. Through a loving, covenantal self-binding, God commits to stay with existence and work with humans at their pace and capacity until all is achieved. God is so close and so involved that the Lord is tormented by present human suffering and undergoes unlimited agony in their pain. Nevertheless, God absorbs the infinite pain rather than cutting it short by unilaterally doing humanity's job of perfecting the world. God does offer teaching, sends messengers and messages, and serves as a personal role model to inspire humans to do their work. This unending self-restraint grows out of God's boundless love for humanity—a love that is selfless and patient enough to let humans grow into their task and infinite enough to forgive their sins and misbehaviors along the way.

Humans are called to respond to the divine summons to partnership by committing to God and to the covenant. This entails directing every act of life toward God and God's goal, the triumph of life. Human participation in the work of repair means that humans are empowered in the covenant. Their dignity is honored and developed when they play an important role in their own liberation . As they learn to love God and to love God's creatures, their neighbors, as themselves, they mature and become more responsible. Thus they become worthy of eternal loving life with God even as collectively they move the state of the world forward toward the longed-for final (Messianic) perfection.

All of the above statements are primary teachings in both Judaism and Christianity. This is not to deny that there are fundamental differences between the two faiths. Christianity's emphasis has leaned to spiritualizing much of the above message (even as medieval Judaism does), whereas Judaism's approach has tended to hold the material and spiritual dimensions together (as has much of modern Christianity). What could be a more fundamental contradiction than the Christian faith's assertion that Jesus is part of the Godhead? Judaism insists that this understanding represents a violation of the unity of God and is religiously unacceptable, at least to Jews. But if we recognize that it was the will of God that these two religions not coalesce, if we understand that from the very beginning the Lord wanted the two faiths to work in partnership, alongside each other, to realize the goals of the divine covenants, then these very differences serve to assure the continuing distinctiveness and independence of the two. Therefore, the variations and even the contradictions should not be allowed to obscure the common core and the common cause of the two faiths.

B. THE DYNAMICS OF COVENANT IN JUDAISM

The central idea of covenant is that God enters into covenant because God infinitely respects human freedom and dignity. From the initial outreach to humanity (i.e., the Noahide Covenant) the Lord intends to nurture humans to mature and become fully responsible partners whose commitment to God grows out of relationship and shared vision. Therefore, as humans become more capable, God self-limits again and again. Each time, this cosmic movement is intended to evoke a higher level of human responsibility for the process and outcome of the covenant, while God becomes a closer and more sustaining (but less controlling) partner. This insight (or should I say this, this cosmic movement) made rabbinic Judaism possible. The Rabbis believe that in the first stage of covenant, God acts as a parent who is guiding and raising children. God is more directive, more controlling, more openly interventionist in history, more visibly rewarding and punishing in daily life. Revelation, while it is tailored to the capacity of the people, was, nevertheless, communicated through a transcendental "parental" voice and through direct prophetic channeling.

The rabbis believe that God had self-limited again in their time, as it were, renewing the covenant at a different level. God becomes more hidden, more restrained in intervention in history, less obviously rewarding and punishing in daily life. God now operates more like a lover or husband in a partnership than as dominant parent. (The term *shutaf* [partner] makes its first appearance in rabbinic literature). This self-limitation (called *tzimtzum* in later Jewish Kabbalistic thought) enables God to shift from the transcendent mode to an immanent mode of relationship with people. This means that God can come closer to humans and be encountered in many more places without overwhelming humans or "vaporizing" them on contact. The purpose of this Divine "self-reduction" is to make God more accessible and lovable to humanity while simultaneously evoking a higher level of human activity and responsibility in the partnership. Thus rabbinic Judaism teaches that henceforth, God's revelation will come not through a heavenly voice but from the discovery by human minds of "what does the Lord your God ask of you"–now (Micah 6:6). This is mostly accomplished by studying the past record of Revelation (= Scriptures) and discerning additional layers of meaning that speak to this moment, or by applying the instructions and narratives of the past to the present.

As God ceases to speak transcendentally (i.e., directly from heaven or through prophetic carriers), humans respond to the silence; they reaffirm the covenantal dialogue by constantly speaking to God in prayer and not just in moments of need. Prayer becomes a central focus of religious service. Human leadership activity and policy choices become more decisive in historical outcomes because the Divine no longer intervenes so visibly to completely reverse the balance of power (as was done in the exodus). The Divine is more present everywhere—in the home, in the marital bed, in visiting the sick and feeding the hungry— but humans must turn inward to make this connection. The people of Israel had to become more educated and to intensify Torah study so they could become more active participants in religious life. The process of repentance and self-perfection became more internalized and transformative and, correspondingly, less channeled through external sacrifices and sacramental mechanisms.

The fact that Christianity came into being just when biblical Judaism was coming to an end has been noted for a long time. The negative Christian interpretation was that God had "terminated" Judaism and replaced it with a new covenant, Christianity. Supersessionist theology ignored the fact that the biblical Jewish religion morphed into rabbinic Judaism and continued in a vital, living form. The supersessionist grotesquely caricatured Rabbinic Judaism as dead, soulless, legalistic, and external—or as a vampire religion, i.e., dead but kept alive by Satanic forces or by evil acts—including, literally, by eating the blood of Christians. The negative Jewish interpretation was that Christianity was a false Messianism which utterly failed to bring redemption in the first century. Instead it separated and presented a counterfeit religion to the world. It stole Jewish sources, tropes and hopes, then twisted them into a wrongly spiritualized new covenant, which became the mortal enemy of its own parent and source.

Contemporary positive theologians, after initially restoring the relationship of the two as that of mother and daughter, now are developing a model of two siblings growing out of biblical Judaism and turning into rivals. However, if we look at the first century as the moment of Divine self-limitation to renew the covenant, a different model of the religious developments emerges. The *tzimtzum* was an act of divine love in order to come closer to the human partners. It reflected a conclusion that the Israelites, after fifteen hundred years of covenant living, were capable of stepping up and taking on a more active role in the *brit* (covenant). Thereby, they would move to relate to God more out of love and relationship and less out of response to miracle and visible reward and punishment. But this divine act of love would hardly be confined to the Jewish people. The prophets repeatedly made clear that the covenantal lovingkindness expressed in liberating the Hebrews from Egypt was the foreshadowing of (or, if you will, a down payment on) the universal exodus for all humanity. A divine, cosmic movement to bring Jewry deeper into the *brit,* would naturally be matched by a loving outreach to humanity to bring them into the covenant. This would be important not only because God does not want to be the Deity of only a small segment of God's creatures. Such a step also would assure that the gap between those in the covenant and those not yet initiated, would not grow so large as to repel or intimidate those who are outside.

C. THE DYNAMICS OF COVENANT IN THE BIRTH OF RABBINIC JUDAISM AND OF CHRISTIANITY

In this light, the growth of Christianity side by side with rabbinic Judaism is not (*pace* established Jewish views) an accident or random deviation from the Jewish religion. Nor (*pace* traditional Christian views) was God rejecting Jewry. God was coming closer to the already covenanted people of Israel—even as God was coming closer to all of humanity, the potential members of a covenant with God. Christianity represents a divine outreach to other peoples, meant to incorporate them into a covenantal community, operating side by side with the people of the first election. Christianity is an offering to the Gentiles of the covenant of Israel—a *brit* always intended to be the first stage of the covenant of redemption for all humanity. It was God's will that the two communities partner together or, at least, that they offer their models in tandem and thus reach more people with a richer repertoire of covenantal behaviors.

Consequently, Jews should stop dismissing Paul as a radical who replaced Judaism (= faith in God) with Christianity (= faith in Jesus). Paul understood that God does not repent of God's gifts and that the Jews remain dear to the Lord. At the same time, he unmistakably felt the Divine turn to the Gentiles. He understood that outreach could only come from within Israel. He did not fully grasp that the continuing distinctiveness of the two communities was the ultimate Divine wish, so he assigned to the persistence of the original people of Israel only a temporary standing. Some postmodern, pluralist theologians have found the core of a more permanent pluralism in his teaching. *Nostra Aetate* also drew justification from Paul's words to express respect for Judaism as a living religion.[1]

Given how hard it was for a Jew to rearticulate the covenant to reach beyond Jewry, one can be more understanding of Paul's spiritual struggle. Even if we know the historical tragedy that flowed from the Christian inability to affirm Judaism's ongoing role in the divine economy, we can retroactively see that Christianity could only have been born within Judaism. Only a vital Judaism could have raised a group with such a message of God's love and redemption, infused with messianic consciousness and such deep rootedness in the covenant. Only the predestruction Jewish community was dynamic enough to give birth to the group without its immune system attacking it as a foreign body and causing a still birth, or, alternatively, being swallowed up by the new faith. The two functioning together in parallel was the Divine will. The loving divine pedagogy moved the Jews to the second stage of partnership, while the Gentiles entered their first stage. This initiation phase was marked by more visible miracles and transcendental messages (as was appropriate or even essential to them) to enable them to enter. These were the kind of approaches that originally enabled the Israelites to enter the Sinaitic covenant.

Then Jews, too, can see that the Jesus movement is not merely a spiritually erring, frustrated community of messianic dreamers. It was a group of Jews who responded to a cosmic signal that God was coming closer and was seeking an intensified response from them. The rabbis focused on the anthropopathy of God as *Shekhinah* even beyond the prophetic portrait of a transitive God. They immersed more deeply in the divine identification with the human condition and Israel's fate; they emphasized God's experience of human suffering and human needs. This was the same phenomenon that Christians wrestled with in articulating their concept of the incarnation of God. Jacob Neusner has given

---

1. See Declaration on the Relationship of the Church to Non-Christian Religions (*Nostra Aetate*) in Walter M. Abbott, ed., *The Documents of Vatican II* (New York: America Press, 1966), 668.

a detailed description of how far down this road the rabbis went while insisting that in the end only God is God.[2] Then a Jew may argue: *Felix culpa!* The identification of Jesus as God incarnate—however influenced by Hellenist/Gentile modes of thought and however wrong from a Jewish perspective—became the departure that assured that the two communities would not stay together in one, and that they would continue to argue without resolution. Thus the pluralism of God's outreach was upheld in a world and culture where positive models of multiple monotheistic covenants did not exist.

Implicit in this interpretive model is that Christians were called to offer the Sinaitic covenant to the world while reducing the ethnic content and specific rituals, thereby lowering the barriers to entry. Walking in the footsteps of the Jews but directing their outreach to the Gentiles, they offered this understanding of the meaning and purpose of human life to the newcomers. Also implied in this model is that once the neophytes became integrated into the life of covenant (however long that would take), they, too, would eventually move to a higher degree of human agency in the partnership as their covenant unfolded. In the interim, the two communities, side by side, could teach the Divine revelation in a form tailored for and more transformative for their chosen audience.

The objection may be raised: How could it be that a Divine intention for partnership between the two faiths could have been thwarted in the emergence of two warring entities, strongly denying the legitimacy, or even the right to exist, of the other? The answer lies precisely in the nature of covenant. The *brit* is rooted in God's respect for humans, as they are existentially, and in the Divine commitment to allow them freedom in understanding, interpreting and carrying out the word of God. Out of God's love, revelation itself is shaped to the capacity of humans to hear it. But the multiple levels of intrinsic meaning are themselves filtered by the intellectual frames of understanding as well as by cultural channels and context that govern humans' comprehension. Finite humans never hear the full range of God's infinite word. Exercising their interpretive freedom can lead them to a one-sided or unidimensional exposition of a richly dialectical message. Yet God does not "intervene" to stop the process by *force majeure*. Humans must work it out. Sometimes, as in this

---

2. Admittedly, some of this development is a response to Christianity and its spread. See Jacob Neusner, *The Incarnation of God: The Character of Divinity in Formative Judaism* (Philadelphia: Fortress, 1988).

case, it takes millennia—or the impact of further revelatory events—for the community of faith to capture the original Divine intent.

D. THE TRAGEDY OF OUR HISTORY

The tragedy in the lack of pluralist models to understand God's will is now well understood. The very fact that Christianity was born within Judaism and draws upon its foundational covenant to convey a congruent message led to an understanding that the very existence of Judaism was a problem. Christians developed a replacement theology and sought the death of Judaism by conversion, coercion, or by presenting it as dead (i.e., soulless and not connected to God). The continuing problem of accounting for a living Judaism led to more hateful images. Jews were deicides. They prayed in the synagogue of Satan. They clung to a legalistic, external religion of deeds, utterly lacking the Holy Spirit. They worshipped a wrathful God of strict justice and rejected the incarnate God of love.

The trend to impeach the Jews deepened from century to century. The Church Fathers developed commentaries and a comprehensive interpretation of Jewish religion and history that in sum was a "teaching of contempt." Jews were so vile and their faith so benighted that they were to be isolated from others. When the evil picture was completed, Jews were portrayed as well poisoners and as people who slaughter Christian children and eat their blood in Judaism's central sacred rituals. Their degradation, expulsion, and even deadly violence against them seemed to be only appropriate. The result: abhorrence of Jews was injected deep into European culture, and a nimbus that Jews were inhuman (i.e., not human) was attached to them.

This cumulative policy generated three pustulant sores in the body of the Church. First, within the Gospel of Love, a privileged sanctuary was created that enabled sanctioned hatred to survive in its orbit. Second, the influence of Hebrew Scriptures and prophetic values was diminished. This enabled the easier seduction of Christianity to a one-sidedly spiritual focus to the neglect of social-justice issues and world improvement. Third, the conviction of the absolute authority of Christianity as the exclusive road to salvation, and the worthlessness of Judaism, led to a similar dismissal of other religions. In turn, this worldview validated violent repression of internal dissent in the Church. In later centuries, this pride encouraged Christian complicity in imperialist oppression of peoples living in other cultures and faiths.

Jewry and Judaism also paid a heavy price. There were physical and demographic losses as well as political and material deprivations. But there were significant spiritual deformations as well. Judaism developed teachings of contempt vis-à-vis Christians. The dialectic of the universal and particular, which is a distinctive strength of the religion, was distorted; the balance was pushed towards the ethnocentric and tribal pole. Western Jewry developed a typology of Christianity as idolatry, which encouraged an inner sense of absolute validity that left little or no room for other faiths' legitimacy.

Idolatry is a cruel and devastating categorization. To be fair, the Jews suffered very much before they came to such a harsh judgment. The Judaic polemic justification was that Christians were worshiping a human being. I believe that there was a deeper theological level expressed in this judgement. Idol worship is perceived in the tradition as the culture of death—a culture which spawns violence, degradation, and death dealing to others—whereas Judaism is (and all true religions must be) a culture of life. After all, Jewry did not experience Christianity's work of bringing love and help to millions but only encountered the religion as a constant source of threat, attack, and death. If it is any consolation, the political and legal and military weakness of Jews meant that they could not act out the evils of negative theology (as Christians did). Still the seeds of hostility and abuse in Judaism remained—dormant—but subject to being re-vivified in the modern era when religious Jews regained access to power.

E. *TZIMTZUM*, MODERNITY, *SHOAH*

Under the influence of modernity, there were various attempts to break from the past and to improve attitudes on both sides. But the turning point was the Holocaust. Here a genuine idolatry inflicted mass death without limit or mercy. The *Shoah* is the *reductio ad maleficum* of the traditions of contempt and hatred. Although the Nazis were anti-Christianity and driven by racial anti-Semitism and totalitarian ideology, they utilized (or were affected by) the prior demonization of the Jews. They made them the primary victims of the Final Solution that would bring about their promise of redemption. Moreover, the cooperation or the passivity of the Jews' neighbors in Europe made all the difference in the rates of Nazi- inflicted victimization. In devout Poland and Lithuania, more than 90 percent of the Jews were killed. The Danes and Albanians saved 95 percent of their Jews. Bulgaria saved fifty thousand of its Jewish citizens, but it abandoned the twelve thousand Greek Jews of Thrace under its control to extermination because it felt no connection to them. In response, many good Christians concluded that anti-Semitism was a cancer that would destroy the Gospel of Love, and that hatred of Judaism must be excised, lest Christianity's moral credibility bleed to death.

The level of Christian responsibility was recognized by Pope John XXIII and played a key role in his insistence on developing what became *Nostra Aetate*. (See the exchanges between John XXIII and Jules Isaac.) There is also a deeper theological consideration here. For almost two millennia, the assumption was that the two religions had nothing to learn from each other. Now by dint of Christian conscience and empathy, the Holocaust—an event in Jewish history—became a revelatory event in Christian history. By its light, Christians recognized the need for repentance and to take responsibility for the blood of their brother. Thus *Nostra Aetate*, the first fruit of this profound rethinking, represents a turning point. It is the moment when the momentum of the continuing tradition (which constantly pushed toward alienation from Jews and dismissal of Judaism) was turned back toward the primordial Divine will for a parallel witness and outreach to humanity.

In the aftermath of the *Shoah*, many Christians also grasped the failures and, by implication, the limits of their whole past tradition. Perhaps at the unspoken, deepest level, they sensed the idolatrous outcomes of all systems that claim absolute truth and authority while extending no independent value to others. This insight combined with the influence of modern thinking shaped Vatican II's opening to the world. This included a new willingness to recognize the dignity of other religions and the right to religious freedom. *Nostra Aetate* comes out of the same understanding that led to *Dignitatis Humanae* (the Declaration on Religious Freedom).

Let me add another dimension from the parallel-covenants perspective. God's selfless love wills that humans grow to their full capabilities. The Lord welcomes the growth of human capacity and responds to it. The emergence of modernity represents a major advance in human understanding of the nature of material reality, including the laws of Nature. The new consciousness brought with it increased human power and competence to repair the world. Again this should not be seen as a random development; nor should it be understood merely as an episode in the history of the development of human consciousness. Rather, I would argue that modernity in itself represents a broad, cross-cultural human response to another cosmic divine *tzimtzum*. From a Jewish perspective I add a speculation: If the first-century contraction was intended to call humans to a higher, more equal level of partnership in the covenant, then the recent modern contraction is a summons to humanity to take up comprehensive, cutting-edge responsibility for the covenantal goal of redemption.

Indeed, the culture of modernity has stimulated, and inspired, greater human transformational activity to upgrade the world than any previous civilization. Serious improvements in overcoming long-standing banes of human existence such as poverty and sickness have been made. The life span has been significantly extended for billions of people. Concepts of human dignity and inherent rights and freedom have made major gains. True, there is a serious negative dimension too. Precisely because many secular strains in modernity have filtered out the component of divine initiative, the awareness of covenantal accountability has been weakened or rejected. As a result, many of the processes of *Tikkun Olam* have gone out of control, bringing grave pathologies and threats of destruction in their wake. The Holocaust itself is the ultimate signal of the absolute evil that lurks in human power where all limits have been broken. But the breakdowns are everywhere. Industrialization, the source of affluence and improved living standards, uncontrolled, has generated a tide of pollution, climate warming, and exploitation that threatens the future of the planet. Political movements, driven by ideologies of redemption but losing the sense of limits and of answering to a higher power, turn to totalitarianism and even mass murder in the name of utopia. Individual freedom, spinning beyond covenantal limits, leads to irresponsibility and loss of solidarity. Self-expression as a solipsistic end in itself turns into narcissism, breakdown of community, and neglect of the needy.

Religions must take some of the blame for these pathologies. They often have fought growing human capability in the name of protecting God's sovereignty. This encouraged polarization and revolt against God and covenant as an unjust prior restraint on human creativity and progress. Upholding the status quo for the sake of protecting institutional religion, or even to defend the authority of God, was a betrayal of God's self-abnegation for the sake of improving humanity and its lot. This failure of understanding gave credence to secular and atheistic claims that humans are the true liberators and that they are accountable to no one but themselves. The idolatry of human power has been strengthened further by the moral failures of various religions—be it in pursuing murderous fanaticism in the name of God or upholding reactionary social and political policies in the name of tradition, or in waging war and exercising cruelty between faiths. These behaviors cumulatively leave religions morally weakened and credibility damaged. What the world needs—and Judaism and Christianity can supply—is a reassertion of the Divine-human partnership in which human civilization is empowered but channeled by its connection to God. This would encourage a full-throttle use of human power, covenantally guided, restrained, and directed toward life—not death.

Judaism and Christianity have a unique capacity to recognize the Divine *tzimtzum* and respond to it. They have the history to understand the nature and purpose of Divine self-limitation and to identify the source of the pathologies of modernity in the loss of the sense of partnership and accountability. But they themselves must make the connection. They must articulate the implications in their teachings as well as in their behavior in the world and in their approach to each other. In particular, Christianity would have to shift from its inherited model of being a final and absolute covenant and therefore, self-sufficient. While it continues to reach out to all humans, it would move to understand itself as being a vehicle of Divine outreach to humanity. This includes full recognition of its limitations and full appreciation of the contributions that other faiths and secular movements make to fulfill God's plan and bring the kingdom of God into being. In doing such an act of *tzimtzum*, it would be following its maker in realizing that in making one's self smaller, one is becoming more helpful and more redemptive in the world.

F. RESPONSE TO *TZIMTZUM*: *NOSTRA AETATE* AND HUMAN ASSUMPTION OF RESPONSIBILITY

Implicit in the model of *tzimtzum* is the concept that eventually the Christian faithful would mature into a higher level of responsibility in their covenant. I am not sufficiently a scholar of Christian history to judge whether and when an inner transformation of the covenant roles, comparable to the emergence of rabbinic Judaism in the Jewish religion, has occurred yet. Perhaps the development of the conciliar tradition and the emergence of Protestantism are comparable moments when the dominance of the revealed instruction is restrained and human assumption of greater responsibility for the meaning of the covenant is enacted. I leave it to greater scholars of Christianity to make such a determination about these or other moments in the faith's history.

Vatican II is such a moment—when the human partners take responsibility for a new iteration of the covenant that reshapes the past and the future. Several of its documents include an affirmation of the greater weight and spiritually shaping influence of the people of God and their expanded role in the unfolding covenant. Furthermore, the Council's declarations in *Nostra Aetate*—repudiating the deicide charge, rejecting the classification of Jews as cursed (even the disavowing of anti-Semitism "directed against the Jews and any time and from every source"[3])—override passages and traditions authorized by Sacred Scriptures and/or canonical Church Fathers. This represents, therefore, the living generation of covenantal leadership stepping up and taking additional responsibility in their covenant, even as the rabbis did in theirs. These actions represent not a repudiation of the sacred, revealed sources but a positive response to the Divine self-reduction, asking humans to take the covenant and move its values and policies a step closer to the divinely sought ideal outcomes. This was a movement of *imitatio Dei* in which the Church followed in Jesus's footsteps, "sacrificing" earthly power and claimed authority in order to come closer to the pure Gospel of Love that Christianity is intended to be and wants to be.

There is a deep theological logic in that the influence of modernity combined with the impact of the Holocaust to generate this new Christian approach to Jewry and Judaism. In my view, the most decisive proof of the cosmic movement that evokes modernity—if you will, the most profound signal of a new Divine *tzimtzum*—is the absence of visible, transcendental intervention to stop the Holocaust. What is the Divine message in coming closer, in suffering infinite agony in the ghettoes, concentrations camps, and gas chambers—yet not stopping the destruction by heavenly *force majeure*? It was the inevitable outcome of this millennium's *tzimtzum*, the Divine call for humans to take full responsibility to protect life and uphold the fullness of human dignity and justice, in this world. This is precisely what the evidence of Jewish survival in the *Shoah* points to. Where the neighbors were their brothers' keepers, Jews were saved; where humanity failed to uphold life at whatever cost it took (or where it collaborated with evil) the people of Israel were destroyed.

This same expansion of humans' role is reflected in *Lumen Gentium*'s section on the People of God and in *Gaudium et Spes* (*The Church Today*)

---

3. Abbott, ed., *The Documents of Vatican II*, 667.

and in *Apostolicam Actuositatem* (*Decree on the Apostolate of the Laity*). *Nostra Aetate* is not a singular mutation. It reflects the modernized Christian leaders' recognition of the dignity and value in Judaism and other faiths and their desire that Christianity stop being a vehicle of discrimination and hostility. *Nostra Aetate* should always be read in concert with the other Declarations' thrust to give greater spiritual weight to the humans who make up the membership of the Christian faith community.

As for the *Nostra Aetate* declaration itself, let me confess that as an active participant in the emerging Jewish-Christian dialogue, I initially reacted with some ambivalence. I appreciated its acknowledgment of Christianity's roots in Judaism and foundations in Jewry and that "He [God] does not repent of the gifts He makes" (Rom 11:29). But many of the Catholics that I had met were ahead of *Nostra Aetate* theologically. Many had renounced conversion of the Jews. Some were unequivocally pluralist; it was not. Many had shaken off completely the language of negative interpretation of the Jewish majority not following Christ; it had not. Such phrases as " . . . Jerusalem did not recognize the time of her visitation," " . . . by His cross Christ . . . reconciled Jew and Gentile, making them both one in Himself," and "Although the Church is the new people of God . . . " disappointed me.

Over the years, I came to appreciate the Declaration more and more. First and foremost, there was its repudiation of anti-Semitism. At the time, I thought, That is the least the Church can do; and, why wasn't there a clearer, unmistakable apology? I came to see that this action was the needed fundamental step because anti-Semitism was still the most dangerous enemy of the Jews. (With the recrudescence of anti-Semitism in Europe and its flourishing in the Muslim world, I have come to appreciate *Nostra Aetate*'s wisdom even more.) This Declaration was a step toward protecting the Jew, instead of the past pattern of setting them up for attack and weakening their status. Most important, it removed the incubus of idolatry (i.e., the Church being a source of persecution and death for Jews). Only if this factor was removed could the way be cleared for Christians to think in partnership terms, and for Jews to be receptive to joint action. Only after this turn from hatred could Jews move to a rethinking and to an appreciation of Christianity, which I believe was needed for the dialogue's sake and for Judaism's sake. Only now can the two communities open up to a step that was God's primordial will.

As time went on, I came to realize that the Declaration opened the door so that Christianity could exit its trap of triumphalism and walk toward Jewry with open heart and open arms. *Nostra Aetate* invited further development and perhaps that was its most important impact. A millennial covenant tradition cannot be changed in one fell swoop. The essence of covenant is that God respects human capacity and nature. Maimonides explains that this means that God will not miraculously change human nature but will change people's capacity and behavior through education and persuasion. This means that meaningful, lasting change in a tradition and in human behavior can only be achieved by taking one step at a time. Thus I have watched with growing appreciation the continuing expansion of Christian validation of Judaism. It is striking that even as Pope John Paul II sought to check certain religious shifts stemming from Vatican II, he extended and deepened the Council's affirmation of Judaism. The high point of this process (thus far) is John Paul II's affirmation of Judaism as "the covenant never revoked." Yet one could see that John Paul II struggled to avert declaring unequivocal pluralism. He was concerned that the Church would lose its authority and betray its mandate to be the exclusive community/connection to God. Some of his statements vis-à-vis Judaism were ambiguous. Some policies and papal statements on Judaism made during visits to synagogues helped move forward the issue of Judaism's ongoing and independent validity. Other homilies, a draft of a new catechism, and an encyclical on missionary activity seemed to be retrograde. Pope Benedict—both as pope and earlier as Cardinal Ratzinger—struggled with the last step to pluralism, and strove to hold it back.

Now comes Pope Francis, moving us on to the next step with less inner hesitation or need to be opaque. In his papal exhortation *Evangelii Gaudium* (*The Joy of the Gospel*) he says, "We hold the Jewish people in special regard because their covenant with God has never been revoked for 'The gifts and the call of God are irrevocable' (Romans 11:29)."[4] Thus, as no supreme authority has done before him, he links together two fundamental statements of the Christian turning process in a manner that is bolder and unequivocal.

---

4. Pope Francis, excerpted from the section on Relations with Judaism, endnote 247; in *Evangelii Gaudium* (*The Joy of the Gospel*), from the Vatican website. In endnote 249, he adds, "God continues to work among the people of the Old Covenant and to bring forth treasures of wisdom which flow from their encounter with his word." For this reason, the Church also is enriched when she receives the values of Judaism. While he notes the ongoing contradiction between the two faiths, he speaks of "a rich complementarity," which enables Jews and Christians together "to help one another to mine the riches of God's word." Finally, he notes "a common concern for justice and the development of peoples."

Furthermore, Pope Francis has stressed the Church's call to be on the side of the poor and to help them. I see this as a reflection of a deeper connection to the Hebrew prophets as well as of a religious approach emphasizing the importance of *Tikkun Olam*. This places less emphasis on doctrinal authority and purity as the mission of the Church. Latin America, where he served as bishop, is the first continent where a convocation of significant Jewish institutional leaders and Christian authorities called for joint action for *tikkun olam* as the proper focus for future Jewish-Christian friendship.

This brings me back to the Divine *tzimtzum* and outreach to humanity. What does God want in further renouncing control and soliciting greater human responsibility? As ever the Lord yearns for *Tikkun Olam*. I believe that God longs for the two communities to witness together and to finally partner and take responsibility to repair the world in tandem. I believe that God suffered great agony as his chosen children fought or despised each other—in God's name no less. Now both communities can admit that they did not succeed in accomplishing the repair and perfection of the world. They can confess that they cannot alone achieve this goal, and, therefore, they enter into partnership with each other. Let them affirm that they no longer seek the glory of being the exclusive channel of redemption but only want to act together so that God's will be done. Let them proclaim that they need the help of each other and of all individuals and communities of goodwill if they are to succeed.

Let the partners acknowledge that vast numbers of human beings need help to get the basics of life and dignity. Let them show a model of cooperation and humility in offering religious instruction and guidance to a world caught in a vortex of new power and new responsibilities—a world in which new dangers and grave moral risks lurk in the heart of progress and redemption. Let them affirm that they need the help of science and of many who define themselves as secular to achieve repair and solve the ethical conundrums that present themselves. Let them show a living model that one can overcome thousands of years of enmity and self-centeredness, out of love and faith in God. Let them show that a tradition can be treasured, healed, and carried on at once. This would be a sanctification of the Divine Name in a time when murder and violence "for the sake of God" desecrate the Name every day. When that longed-for day of covenantal partnership comes, then *Nostra Aetate* will be honored as a (re)turning marker on the road to redemption. On that day the two communities will truly fulfill the covenantal promise of being a blessing for all the families of the earth.

PART 2

Nostra Aetate and Other Christian Faith Groups

7

In Our Time

The Legacy of *Nostra Aetate* in Mainline Protestant Churches

Joseph D. Small

Nostra Aetate—Vatican II's "Declaration on the Relation of the Church to Non-Christian Religions," promulgated by Pope Paul VI in 1965—is a consideration of "what men have in common and what draws them to fellowship."[1] It begins with some vague thoughts about religion in general before mentioning Hinduism, Buddhism, and Islam in particular. A few nice words are said about each of the three, concluding with a recognition of "quarrels and hostilities" between Christians and Muslims and a call for mutual understanding and cooperation. If *Nostra Aetate* had ended there, it would soon have been forgotten. If it had dealt with Judaism in as cursory a manner as it did with other world religions, it would have been filed away and ignored.

---

1. All citations of *Nostra Aetate* are from http://www.vatican.va/archive/hist_councils/iivatican_council/documents./

Nostra Aetate is remembered only for its lengthy section on "the bond that spiritually ties the people of the New Covenant to Abraham's stock." Unlike its brief references to Hinduism, Buddhism, Islam, and "other religions," the eight paragraphs on Judaism are deeply theological affirmations of the enduring link between God's chosen peoples. *Nostra Aetate* does not treat the relationship of Christianity to Judaism as simply one instance of "various religions," but as the embodiment of "shared patrimony." The 1965 Declaration of the Second Vatican Council broke new ground in Jewish-Christian relations by stimulating an unprecedented expansion of biblical, historical, and theological scholarship and insight. *Nostra Aetate* proved to be more than a Roman Catholic statement, for it prompted other Christian churches to undertake their own examinations of the relationship between Christianity and Judaism. *Decretum de Judaeis.*

Before analyzing post–Vatican II developments in American Christian denominations, it will be helpful to place *Nostra Aetate* in context. Two years prior to the opening of Vatican II, Pope John XXIII instructed the Secretariat for Promoting Christian Unity to prepare a statement on the Jews. Because the pope understood that this bold initiative would not proceed without difficulty, he requested that initial discussion and drafting be treated *sub secreto*.[2] *Decretum de Judaeis* is the designation of a series of draft documents leading to the text that was proposed to the Council. The five-year-long development of the drafts prompted a groundbreaking advance in the Church's understanding of the relationship between Christians and Jews, as each draft built upon and strengthened its predecessor. Concluding debate in the Council itself strengthened the final draft, resulting in the rich biblical and theological text of *Nostra Aetate* itself.

The road to *Nostra Aetate* was not a smooth one, however. Both within the Catholic Church and beyond it there were objections to the Council making any statement about Jews, as well as objections to some of the more positive elements in the draft documents. Although opposition was overcome, the struggle was intense. The debate has endured throughout subsequent decades, however, as recurring objections cast shadows over attempts by other churches to strengthen and deepen their understanding of the unbreakable bond between Christians and Jews.

Opposition during the Second Vatican Council came from several sources. Some feared that a conciliar statement on the Jews would

2. Alberic Stacpoole, ed., *Vatican II Revisited: By Those Who Were There* (Minneapolis: Winston, 1986), 220.

alienate Arab countries, hostile to the state of Israel, and damage relations with Muslims worldwide. Others contended that certain positive declarations about the Jews would represent too great a departure from previous Church teaching. Some feared that emphasis on the Jews would be interpreted as implicit criticism of the Church's stance during the Nazi era in Europe. Finally, overt hostility to Jews persisted in some Church circles, reinforced by anti-Semitic groups outside the Church.

While the road to *Nostra Aetate* was rocky, the Secretariat for Promoting Christian Unity was committed to the goal. Its steadfastness stimulated new insight and conviction along the way. The original *Decretum de Judaeis* draft, designed for discussion within the Secretariat, focused more on the Church than on the Jews. It stated that "the Church, a new creation in Christ (see Eph. 2:15), can never forget that she is the spiritual continuation of the people with whom, in His mercy and gracious condescension, God made the Old Covenant."[3] Although the draft used strong language to repudiate the charge that the Jewish people are "accursed," and to protest "all wrongs done to Jews," it also used strong language to express confidence that "at the appointed time, the fullness of the children of Abraham according to the flesh will embrace [Christ] who is salvation."

The second draft of *Decretum de Judaeis* is notable for its recognition that Jews and the Church are in "a special relationship." This relationship is not merely formal, for "the Church has a common patrimony with the Synagogue, [and so] this Holy Synod intends in every way to promote and further mutual knowledge and esteem." The draft is also significant for its more forceful repudiation of the view that Jews are accursed: "Although a large part of the Chosen People is still far from Christ, yet it is wrong to call them an accursed people . . . or a deicidal people," the draft declared, going on to state that "the death of Christ is not to be attributed to an entire people then alive, and even less to people today." The seriousness of this statement was made clear as the draft stipulated that, "priests be careful not to say anything, in catechetical instruction or in preaching, that might give rise to hatred or contempt of the Jews in the hearts of their hearers." It concludes with an acknowledgment of the history of hatred and contempt, as the Church "deplore[s] and condemn[s] hatred and persecution of Jews, whether committed of old or in our own times."

---

3. All citations from drafts of *Decretum de Judaeis* are from full texts cited at http://wikipedia.org/w/index.php?oldid=543319296/.

The third and fourth drafts incorporated major themes from the previous two, while also deepening the biblical and theological basis of the "special relationship." The penultimate drafts of *Decretum de Judaeis* incorporated biblical material from both Testaments, vowing that the Church "will never overlook Apostle Paul's words relating to the Jews, to whom belong 'the adoption as sons and the glory, and the covenants and the giving of the law, and the worship, and the promises' (Rom.9:4)."

The substantive development of *Decretum de Judaeis* and the process of revision that led to *Nostra Aetate* were guided throughout by Cardinal Augustin Bea, a Jesuit biblical scholar and president of the Secretariat for Promoting Christian Unity. Cardinal Willebrands later celebrated Bea as "not only the mind behind, but the heart within, the hand upon the text of this Conciliar Declaration."[4] When Bea presented the final draft (at this point a formal *schema*) to the full Council in September 1964, he began by reminding the Council Fathers of the enormous public interest in the issue, and cautioning that many would judge the whole Council on its approval or rejection of the *schema*. He reviewed biblical material at length, responding forcefully to critics of the document's positive valuation of the Jews. He concluded his lengthy presentation with the assertion that the Christian relationship with the Jewish people was an essential component of the Council's task:

> Since the Church is focused at this Council on its own renewal . . . this subject too must be taken up, in order that in this area too the Church may be renewed . . . . The issue is our duty to truth and justice, our duty of gratitude to God, our duty of faithfully imitating the Lord Christ himself and his apostles Peter and Paul as closely as possible.[5]

The public debate (and private discussions) that followed made it clear that the overwhelming majority of the Council was committed to maintaining and strengthening the *schema*. What may have begun as an impulse to address the horrors of the Holocaust had become a full-scale expansion of the Church's teaching on the Jews. A remarkable address by Cardinal Lercaro, one of the Council's moderators, indicated both the conclusion and the future trajectory of what was to become *Nostra*

---

4. Johannes Cardinal Willebrands, "Christians and Jews: A New Vision," in Stacpoole, *Vatican II Revisited*, 221.

5. Giuseppe Alberigo and Joseph A. Komonchak, eds., *History of Vatican II*, vol. 4, *Church as Communion* (Maryknoll, NY: Orbis, 2003), 155.

Aetate. Lercaro went beyond gratitude for Israel's history, insisting that "in the eyes of the Church the people of the covenant have supernatural dignity and value not only in relation to the past and to the very origins of the Church, but also for the present time and in relation to what is essential, lofty, religious, divine, and permanent in the daily life of the Church."[6] Lercaro also asserted "an objective and present link between us and them that is very special in its nature and intensity," and so recommended "acknowledgment of a role which the Jews can still play in the present economy . . . as bearers of a kind of *biblical and paschal testimony*."[7] Not all of the Cardinal Lercaro's theology of Judaism found its way into *Nostra Aetate*, but it was a harbinger of future developments in the wider Christian understanding of Judaism.

In spite of continuing maneuvers by conservative elements, the Council strengthened and then decisively approved the *schema* by a vote of 1,763–250, and *Nostra Aetate* was promulgated by Pope Paul VI on October 28, 1965. A mere glance at the five-year history leading from Pope John XXIII's directive, through the drafts of *Decretum de Judaeis*, to the official Vatican II declaration, is sufficient to demonstrate the Church's sustained attention and careful thought given to the fundamental issue of the relationship between Judaism and Christianity. The influence of *Nostra Aetate—In Our Time*—endures into the present time, for it has prompted a continuing exploration by Christian churches throughout the world into the history and theology of the relationship between Christianity and Judaism, Church and Synagogue, Christians and Jews.

THE FORWARD MOTION OF *NOSTRA AETATE*

As with many other aspects of Vatican II, it soon became clear that the significance of *Nostra Aetate* radiated far beyond the Catholic Church. In particular, five aspects of the Decree prompted other Christian churches and ecumenical councils to give focused attention to their understanding of the relationship between Christianity and Judaism.

First, *Nostra Aetate* forcefully affirmed Christianity's continuing debt to the faith of Israel. The earliest Christian heresy was that of Marcion, a second-century teacher who separated the God revealed in Jesus Christ from the God revealed in creation and the history of Israel,

6. Ibid., 161–62.

7. Ibid., 162.

insisting that the gospel displaced the Old Testament. He excluded the Torah, the Prophets, and the Writings from his list of Scripture, and even limited the Gospel accounts to Luke while "editing" Paul's letters to remove Old Testament references and allusions. Marcion and his views were condemned, and the place of the Old Testament as Christian Scripture was confirmed. Nevertheless, the church's preaching and teaching has often privileged the New Testament over the Old Testament. This tacit supersessionism has been reinforced by simplified distinctions between law and gospel, unwarranted contrasts between faithless Israel and faithful church, parodied portrayals of Pharisees, and tendentious readings of Paul's letters.

Nostra Aetate acknowledges the reality that "the beginnings of [the Church's] faith and her election are found already in the Patriarchs, Moses and the prophets," and that "the Apostles, the Church's main-stay and pillars, as well as most of the early disciples who proclaimed Christ's Gospel to the world, sprang from the Jewish people." But the Decree goes beyond historical acknowledgment to affirm that the contemporary Church "draws sustenance from the root of that well-cultivated olive tree onto which have been grafted the wild shoots, the Gentiles." Christian faith and life continuously springs from Israel's faith and life. The relationship of Christians and Jews is enduring.

This profession leads to a second generative affirmation: God's fidelity to the Jewish people is enduring. Far from being rejected or accursed, the Jews are held "most dear [by God] for the sake of their Fathers; He does not repent of the gifts He makes or of the calls He issues—such is the witness of the Apostle." A corollary to this fundamental declaration is that the Jews are not to be held responsible for the crucifixion of Christ. Although Jerusalem authorities pressed for Christ's death, "what happened in His passion cannot be charged against all the Jews, without distinction, then alive, nor against the Jews of today." *Nostra Aetate* underlines its essential pronouncement by giving forceful instruction on this point to all bishops, priests, and teachers: "All should see to it, then, that in catechetical work or in the preaching of the word of God they do not teach anything that does not conform to the truth of the Gospel and the spirit of Christ."

A third creative element is *Nostra Aetate*'s forceful rejection of the long history and present reality of discrimination, hostility, and persecution of Jews. While rejecting every persecution against any people, "the Church, mindful of the patrimony she shares with the Jews and moved not by political reasons but by the Gospel's spiritual love, decries hatred, persecutions, displays of anti-Semitism, directed against Jews at any time and by anyone." This statement was essential in 1965, when the *Shoah* was a living horror for all of the Council's bishops, but the Declaration's ongoing importance lies in its even more comprehensive rejection of centuries of persecution, and its proleptic denunciation of the virulent anti-Semitism that has reemerged in subsequent decades.

Fourth, while *Nostra Aetate* voices the Christian conviction that "by His cross Christ, Our Peace, reconciled Jews and Gentiles, making both one in Himself," and expresses the Christian hope in "that day, known to God alone, on which all peoples will address the Lord in a single voice," it does not affirm evangelization of Jews. Instead, "since the spiritual patrimony common to Christians and Jews is thus so great, this sacred synod wants to foster and recommend that mutual understanding and respect which is the fruit, above all, of biblical and theological studies as well as of fraternal dialogues."

Finally, all elements of *Nostra Aetate*'s decree on the Jews grow from its introductory affirmation of "the bond that spiritually ties the people of the New Covenant to Abraham's stock." The Decree proclaims that the relationship between the Church and the Jewish people is fundamental, enduring, and contemporary. Judaism is not just one of the other religions, and the relationship between Christians and Jews is not merely one case of interfaith liaison. The Church's connection to both historic Israel and contemporary Judaism is intrinsic to Christian faith.

PROTESTANT RESPONSES

Prior to Vatican II, American Protestant churches gave scant attention to Catholic theology, ethics, and church structures except to criticize them. Two years before the opening of the Council, many Protestants remained suspicious of, if not opposed to, the presidential candidacy of Catholic John F. Kennedy. But Vatican II fulfilled John XXIII's desire for Catholic *aggiornamento*, and Protestant churches took notice. The Council prompted deeper academic and ecclesial biblical inquiry, inspiring Protestant liturgical renewal, ecclesiological understanding, ecumenical openness, and ethical development. The Council's Declaration *Nostra Aetate* moved Protestant churches beyond customary censure of anti-Semitism toward sustained consideration of the relationship between Christians and Jews.

The movement toward deeper understanding coincided with a complicating factor, however. The 1967 Six Day War led to Israel's occupation of Sinai, the Golan Heights, the Gaza Strip, and the West Bank. The establishment of military outposts soon led to a policy of Israeli settlements that was commenced in earnest in 1977, particularly in the West Bank and Gaza. Previous Catholic concern about the reaction of Arab states to positive conciliar statements about the Jews now became Protestant concern about Israeli state policy in the West Bank and Gaza. The Episcopal Church statement on Christian-Jewish relations is typical: "The existence of the State of Israel is a fact of history . . . However, the quest for homeland status by Palestinians—Christian and Muslim—is a part of their search for identity also, and must be addressed together with the need for a just and lasting solution to the conflict in the Middle East."[8]

Nevertheless, *Nostra Aetate* had raised the fundamental issue of the Jewish-Christian link, and Protestant churches understood that they too had to address the issue. A survey of all Protestant inquiry into the matter is beyond the scope of this essay, but attention to several mainline denominational statements will exhibit common approaches to the major themes introduced in *Nostra Aetate*. The United Methodist Church has given repeated attention to Jewish-Christian relations, beginning with "Bridge in Hope" (1972),[9] and continuing through "Building New Bridges in Hope" (1996)[10] to "Strengthening Bridges" (2008).[11] The Evangelical Lutheran Church in America followed "Guidelines for Lutheran-Jewish

8. https://www.bc.edu/dam/files/research_sites/cjl/texts/cjrelations/resources/documents/protestant/Episcopal_Guidelines.htm/.

9. www.notredamedesion.org/en/dialogue_docs.php?a=2&id=693/.

10. http://archives.umc.org/interior.asp?ptid+4&mid+3301/.

11. http://www.umc.org/site/apps/nlnet/content2/.aspx?c=lwL4Kn1LtH&b=495 1419&ct/.

Relations" (1998)[12] with related educational materials for use in synods and congregations. The United Church of Christ adopted "Relationship between the UCC and the Jewish Community" at its Sixteenth General Synod (1987).[13] The Episcopal Church followed its adoption of "Guidelines for Christian-Jewish Relations for Use in The Episcopal Church" (1988)[14] with a survey of the level and extent of Christian-Jewish dialogue and relationships at both parish and diocesan levels. These church documents will be considered together, focusing on the ways they deal with the central affirmations of *Nostra Aetate*. My own church, the Presbyterian Church (U.S.A.), approved an extensive treatment of the issue in 1986—"A Theological Understanding of the Relationship between Christians and Jews."[15] I will treat this document and subsequent developments in the PCUSA more extensively in a separate section of the essay.

Continuing debt to the faith of Israel. All the denominational documents acknowledge Christianity's deep roots in the faith and life of ancient Israel as well as the significance of the continuing relationship of Christianity to Judaism. Explication of the relationship's nature is more nuanced than in *Nostra Aetate*, however. For example, the Episcopal Church "Guidelines" acknowledge that historic Christian interpretations of the relationship often led to "overt acts of condescension, prejudice and even violent acts of persecution" that require "a profound sense of penitence." The "Guidelines" also recognize that "many Christians are convinced that they understand Judaism since they have the Hebrew Scriptures as part of their Bible. This attitude is often reinforced by a lack of knowledge about the history of Jewish life and thought through the 1900 years since Christianity and Judaism parted ways." The United Methodists' second statement, "Building New Bridges of Hope," states more positively that "as Christians, it is important for us to recognize that Judaism went on to develop vital new traditions of its own after the time

12. http://www.notredamedesion.org/en/dialogue_docs.php?a+2&id=62&categoria=altrechiese/.

13. http://www.ucc.org/assets/pdfs/87-jewishrelations.pdf/.

14. The Episcopal Church, *Journal of the General Convention of the Protestant Episcopal Church, 1988* (New York: General Convention), 454–60.

15. Presbyterian Church (U.S.A.). Office of Theology and Worship. *Selected Theological Statements of the Presbyterian Church (U.S.A.) General Assemblies (1956–1998)* (Louisville: Office of Theology and Worship, 1998), 510–23.

of Jesus . . . This evolving tradition has given the Jewish people profound resources for creative life through the centuries."[16]

God's enduring fidelity to the Jews. Most denominational documents also acknowledge the inviolability of God's covenantal relationship with the Jewish people. The United Church of Christ uses blunt language to admit that "the Christian Church has denied for too long the continuing validity of God's covenant with the Jewish people, with all the attendant evils that have followed upon such denial." The UCC also notes that, "the Christian communities of recent times have come more and more to recognize that God's covenant with the Jewish people stands inviolate (Romans 9–11)."[17] The UMC's "Building New Bridges in Hope" addresses the issue of supersession head on, declaring that "while church tradition has taught that Judaism has been superseded by Christianity as the 'new Israel,' we do not believe that earlier covenantal relationships have been invalidated or that God has abandoned Jewish partners in covenant."[18]

Rejection of anti-Semitism. All churches condemn all forms of anti-Semitism, and repudiate the long history of Jewish persecution by the church as well as by the state and society. The most dramatic repudiation of past Christian anti-Jewish rhetoric and action is the Evangelical Lutheran Church in America's 1994 "Declaration to the Jewish Community."[19] The ELCA testified to Martin Luther's importance in its life by stating that "the Lutheran communion of faith is linked by name and heritage to the memory of Martin Luther, teacher and reformer." But while expressing gratitude for Luther, the ELCA went on to declare, "we who bear his name must with pain acknowledge also Luther's anti-Judaic diatribes and violent recommendations in his later writings against the Jews. . . . [W]e reject this violent invective, and yet more do we express our deep and abiding sorrow over its tragic effects on subsequent generations." The ELCA was explicit in its declaration that anti-Semitism is "an affront to the Gospel."

No targeted evangelization of Jews. Every Christian church recognizes its calling to bear witness to the grace of the Lord Jesus Christ. Congregations and individuals may live their evangelical witness minimally, casually, or feebly, but its necessity is seldom denied. The tension between

16. http://archives.umc.org/interior.asp?ptid=4&mid=3301/.

17. http://www.ucc.org/assets/pdfs/87-jewishrelations.pdf/

18. http://archives.umc.org/interior.asp?ptid=4&mid=3301/.

19. http://www.elca.org/en/Faith/Ecumenical-and-Inter-Religious-Relations/.

the Christian evangelical impulse and the now widespread Christian conviction that God's covenant with the Jewish people is inviolate leads to denominational struggles with the issue of evangelism directed to Jews. This struggle is apparent in Protestant church statements about Jewish-Christian relations.

The Evangelical Lutheran Church does not mention evangelism directed at Jews with the exception of an odd mention that "conversion," together with "the security of the state of Israel" and "intermarriage," is a matter that indicates "the depth of Jewish concern for communal survival." "Guidelines for Lutheran-Jewish Relations" understands that Jews regard converts to Christianity who retain their Jewish heritage as having forsaken Judaism, but only advises that Lutherans should be aware of this fact.[20] Although the United Church of Christ statement also omits any mention of the issue of evangelism, the implication of its strong statements—"Christianity is not to be understood as the successor religion to Judaism; God's covenant with the Jewish people has not been abrogated; God has not rejected the Jewish people"[21]—would seem to suggest that evangelism is unwarranted and inappropriate. The fact remains, however, that neither the ELCA nor the UCC addresses the central issue of evangelical witness to Jews.

The Episcopal Church states that it must bear witness to God's self-revelation in Jesus Christ but confesses that the Christian witness toward Jews "has been distorted by coercive proselytism, conscious and unconscious, overt and subtle." "Guidelines for Christian-Jewish Relations" commends dialogue as "mutual witness . . . a sharing of one's faith convictions without the intent of proselytizing."[22] The United Methodist Church seems to have wrestled with the issue most forcefully, evidenced by the deferral of evangelism until its third statement on Jewish-Christian relations. Acknowledging the role of Vatican II in addressing this matter, "Strengthening Bridges" states that "With our Catholic sisters and brothers we believe that God has not abandoned God's covenant with the Jews. . . . Therefore, we reject any and all forms of evangelism which are coercive in their nature, violent in their means, or anti-Semitic in their intent." The UMC concludes by stating that it "neither makes the

20. https://www.bc.edu/dam/files/research_sites/cjl/texts/cjrelations/resources/documents/ protestant/ELCA_Guidelines.htm/.

21. http://www.ucc.org/assets/pdfs/87-jewishrelations.pdf/.

22. https://www.bc.edu/dam/files/research_sites/cjl/texts/cjrelations/resources/documents/protestant/Episcopal_Guidelines.htm/.

Jews a unique focus of our witness-bearing nor excludes Jews from our longing that all persons may of their own volition believe in Jesus Christ our Savior and Lord."[23]

From the beginning, Christianity has been an evangelistic missionary movement. Most mainline Protestant churches appear to have some difficulty in reconciling the evangelistic impulse at the heart of their faith with their belief in the inviolability of God's covenant with the Jewish people. This is a profoundly theological issue that is not dealt with fully by recommending dialogue as an appropriate form of Christian-Jewish connection.

The spiritual bond of Christians and Jews is fundamental. While recognizing Christian indebtedness to the faith of Israel, and acknowledging the enduring vitality of Jewish faith, the four mainline Protestant churches do not probe deeply the spiritual bond that inseparably ties Christians and Jews together. The limited purpose of these official church documents is twofold: first to stress repentance for the deplorable history of anti-Jewish invective, persecution, and violence; and second, to encourage Christian-Jewish dialogue as the primary means of overcoming Christian misconceptions and mutual detachment. These purposes, shared with *Nostra Aetate*, are not inconsequential, but they do not deepen Vatican II's foundational declaration of an enduring, present spiritual relationship.

THEOLOGICAL UNDERSTANDING

The most ambitious American Protestant attempt to address Jewish-Christian relations is the 1986 theological statement of the Presbyterian Church (U.S.A)—"A Theological Understanding of the Relationship between Christians and Jews."[24] Prepared as a pastoral and teaching document to facilitate discussion within the PCUSA and to guide conversation, cooperation, and dialogue between Presbyterians and Jews, it addresses the basic *theological* question, what is the relationship which God intends between Christians and Jews, between Christianity and Judaism? The product of seven years of study and development, "A Theo-

23. http://www.umc.org/what-we-believe/strengthening-bridges/.

24. Presbyterian Church (U.S.A.), "A Theological Understanding of the Relationship between Christians and Jews," https://www.pcusa.org/site_media/media/uploads/_resolutions/christians-jews.pdf/.

logical Understanding of the Relationship between Christians and Jews"
is organized around seven theological affirmations, each of which is followed by a careful explication. Space does not permit a thorough review
of the explications, but a few limited comments following the affirmations themselves will indicate the ways they build upon *Nostra Aetate*.

1. *We affirm that the living God whom Christians worship is the same*
    God who is worshiped and served by Jews. We bear witness that the
    God revealed in Jesus, a Jew, to be the Triune Lord of all, is the same
    one disclosed in the life and worship of Israel.

The Presbyterian statement goes beyond the recognition of common
history and shared concepts to affirm that an enduring bond between
Christians and Jews is established by the faith of both in the one true
God. The community of Jews and those who came to be called Christians
parted ways in the first and second centuries CE, and their subsequent
relationship has often been marked by forms of Christian hostility. Nevertheless, "there are ties which remain between Christians and Jews: the
faith of both in the one God, whose loving and just will is for the redemption of all humankind; and the Jewishness of Jesus whom we confess to
be the Christ of God." These ties are God-given and so must be lived out
by Christians and Jews.

2. *We affirm that the church, elected in Jesus Christ, has been engrafted*
    into the people of God established by the covenant with Abraham,
    Isaac, and Jacob. Therefore, Christians have not replaced Jews.

"A Theological Understanding of the Relationship between Christians and Jews" forcefully rejects supersessionism, stating that "God's
covenants are not broken," and "the church has not 'replaced' the Jewish
people." The statement goes beyond rejection, however, to recognize that
"the church, being made up primarily of those who were once aliens and
strangers to the covenants of promise, has been engrafted into the people
of God." Christianity's relationship to Judaism is not that of replacement
but rather that of the younger sibling.

3. *We affirm that both the church and the Jewish people are elected by*
    God for witness to the world and that the relationship of the church
    to contemporary Jews is based on that gracious and irrevocable
    election of both.

The relationship between Christians and Jews is not established by shared history or contemporary choice. Instead, it is God's initiating election that inaugurates shared witness to the world. True to its Reformed heritage, the PCUSA statement probes the reality of election in the life of both Jews and Christians, declaring that "election does not manifest human achievement but divine grace." Because of the theological centrality of God's electing grace, the statement explicates the common calling of Christians and Jews: "God chose a particular people, Israel, as a sign and foretaste of God's grace toward all people. It is for the sake of God's redemption of the world that Israel was elected. . . . God continues that purpose through Christians and Jews. The church, like the Jewish people, is called to be a light to the nations."

> 4. *We affirm that the reign of God is attested both by the continuing existence of the Jewish people and by the church's proclamation of the gospel of Jesus Christ. Hence, when speaking with Jews about matters of faith, we must always acknowledge that Jews are already in a covenantal relationship with God.*

The Presbyterian statement goes beyond condemnation of insolent, coercive, and violent proselytism to affirm that God's covenant with Jews is inviolable, and that the Jewish people continue to bear witness to God's gracious purposes. Yet Presbyterians also struggle with the relationship between their commission to bear witness to Christ, and their recognition of God's covenantal fidelity to the Jewish people. Like other Protestant churches, the PCUSA declares that dialogue, not targeted evangelism, is the appropriate form of conversation about faith between Christians and Jews, but also makes it clear that "dialogue is not a cover for proselytism. Rather, as trust is established, not only questions and concerns can be shared but faith and commitments as well."

> 5. *We acknowledge in repentance the church's long and deep complicity in the proliferation of anti-Jewish attitudes and actions through its "teaching of contempt" for the Jews. Such teaching we now repudiate, together with the acts and attitudes which it generates.*

Together with other Protestant church statements, "A Theological Understanding" repents of the church's central role in persecution of the Jews. However, the statement goes beyond general contrition to catalogue past and present instances of the "teaching of contempt." Recognizing the depth of mutual hostility in the first century CE, the church admits that "in subsequent centuries, after the occasions for the original hostility had long since passed, the church misused portions of the New Testament as proof texts to justify a heightened animosity toward Jews." Perhaps most important is the testimony that "it is agonizing to discover that the church's 'teaching of contempt' was a major ingredient that made possible the monstrous policy of annihilation of Jews by Nazi Germany." The lengthy explication concludes with the church's "personal" oath, "We pledge, God helping us, never again to participate in, to contribute to, or (insofar as we are able) to allow the persecution or denigration of Jews or the belittling of Judaism."

6. *We affirm the continuity of God's promise of land along with the obligations of that promise to the people of Israel.*

The issue of the land, absent from *Nostra Aetate* and mentioned only as a political issue in other Protestant statements, is recognized as a *theological* matter. The PCUSA statement acknowledges that a faithful explication of the biblical material relating to the covenant with Abraham cannot avoid or dismiss the reality of God's promise of land: "The question with which we must wrestle is how this promise is to be understood in the light of the existence of the modern political state of Israel which has taken its place among the nations of the world." The wrestling match that follows resulted in a draw. The briefest of the seven affirmations is accompanied by the longest of the explications, due in part to extensive negotiation and revision at the 1986 General Assembly that approved "A Theological Understanding of the Relationship between Christians and Jews." Eugene March, a member of the committee that produced the draft document, notes that "what emerged [from the negotiation and revision] was more 'compromised' and less coherent. The theological significance of the modern state of Israel was not addressed and remains a debatable subject for many Presbyterians. A degree of 'spiritualizing' the land and seeing it too much as a metaphor was introduced."[25] Even so, the document goes beyond political analysis to attempt a theological understanding of the contemporary meaning of God's promise of land.

7. *We affirm that Jews and Christians are partners in waiting. Christians see in Christ the redemption not yet fully visible in the world, and Jews*

25. W. Eugene March, "Presbyterians and Jews: A Theological Turning Point," unpublished paper, cited with permission.

await the messianic redemption. Christians and Jews together await the final manifestation of God's promise of the peaceable kingdom.

Christians and Jews are bound in hope as well as in memory and present life. Shared hope has a deep theological significance because "Christian hope is contiguous with Israel's hope and is unintelligible apart from it." Jewish and Christian hope is far more than passive waiting, for partners in hope are "called to the service of God in the world. However that service may differ, the vocation of each may differ, the vocation of each shares at least these elements: a striving to realize the word of the prophets, an attempt to remain sensitive to the dimensions of the holy, an effort to encourage the life of the mind, and a ceaseless activity in the cause of justice and peace."

DEEPENING RELATIONSHIPS

"A Theological Understanding of the Relationship between Christians and Jews" took up the themes of *Nostra Aetate*, developing them in consciously theological directions. In this way, the PCUSA statement was faithful to *Nostra Aetate*'s spirit. Yet that spirit is not adequately honored by any one statement issued by a church. Vatican II declared that "since the spiritual patrimony common to Christians and Jews is thus so great, this sacred synod wants to foster and recommend that mutual understanding and respect which is the fruit, above all, of biblical and theological studies as well as of fraternal dialogues." The Catholic Church has been true to its intention in ways that far exceed the follow through of American Protestant churches. The need for, and difficulty of, sustained ecclesial engagement with the theological understanding of the Jewish-Christian bond is illustrated by the Presbyterian Church (U.S.A.) experience subsequent to the 1986 theological statement.

"A Theological Understanding of the Relationship between Christians and Jews" fostered new contacts between Presbyterian congregations and Jewish synagogues while deepening existing associations. Presbyterian pastors and seminary students were encouraged to become familiar with new biblical scholarship that corrected tendentious Christian readings of both the Old and the New Testaments. Yet the denomination did not continue the theological work begun in the 1986 statement. One consequence of this neglect was a controversy at the 2004 meeting of the General Assembly. A proposal to divest Presbyterian holdings in some companies doing business with the Israeli government, and an ambiguous response to a Philadelphia "messianic Jewish" congregation, caused deep distress in the Jewish community and threatened to rupture Presbyterian-Jewish relations. The controversies led to a General Assembly resolution commissioning a study to reexamine and strengthen the relationship between Christians and Jews, deepening the affirmations of the 1986 statement. As a result of the General Assembly's action, the Presbyterian offices of Theology and Worship, Interfaith Relations, and Evangelism joined with the National Council of Synagogues to hold a series of dialogues and conferences designed in part to produce a second theological statement.[26]

The result of the study was the new statement called "Christians and Jews: People of God," proposed for approval by the 2010 Presbyterian General Assembly.[27] It was intended to supplement, not to replace, "A Theological Understanding of the Relationship between Christians and Jews." The statement was organized in three major sections, "Theological Perspectives," "The Land," and "Evangelism."

The theological section furthered the trajectory set out in 1986, expanding and sharpening the explications of the document's affirmations. It also set directions for further explorations of what it means to affirm that Christians and Jews *now* worship the same God, of the singular reality that Christians and Jews share Scripture, and of inaccurate and offensive characterizations of Jews and Judaism.

The long section on the land evidenced the same struggle that was present in 1986, but also recognized that events of the intervening decades had raised the stakes considerably. The statement acknowledged the reality of God's gift of land while denying that this reality resolves the present political conflict or settles territorial disputes. The value of the statement's lengthy consideration of biblical, historical, theological, religious, and political aspects of the land lies in its careful delineation of issues that must be addressed in deepened dialogue between the church and the Jewish community.

26. The history of the controversy and its aftermath, together with papers from three national conferences, can be found in Joseph D. Small and Gilbert S. Rosenthal, eds., *Let Us Reason Together: Christians and Jews in Conversation* (Louisville: Witherspoon, 2010).

27. Presbyterian Church (U.S.A.) "Christians and Jews: People of God," https://www.pcusa.org/site_media/media/uploads/theologyandworship/pdfs/christianandjewschurchseriesno7.pdf/.

The evangelism section reaffirmed the church's obligation to bear witness to Jesus Christ as Lord and Savior while considerably strengthening the disavowal of pointed strategies that attempt to convert Jews to Christianity. The document asks, "Should Christians assume that Jews are without God, cut off from God's covenant, and so must be converted to Christian faith in order to be restored to communion with God?" It answers that "the New Testament makes it clear to Christians that Jews are not empty vessels, without God, who must be filled with Christianity in order to be restored to divine favor." The section also provides more substance to the practice of dialogue.

Unfortunately, "Christians and Jews: People of God" was not approved by the General Assembly but was sent back for revisions based on further consultation with Middle East Christian churches and with American Presbyterians of Middle Eastern descent. The section on the land was the obvious sticking point, and the result of consultations was a reworked land section. Relatively minor editorial changes were made to the theology and evangelism sections. Introductory paragraphs were added to the document, defining uses of the term "Israel," and emphasizing "The Complicating Factor of Middle East Politics." Perhaps most important, the statement was downgraded to "A Contribution of the Presbyterian Church (U.S.A.) to the Interfaith Conversation."

The story of "Christians and Jews: People of God" illustrates both the ways American Protestant churches can honor the living legacy of *Nostra Aetate* by deepening its theological insights, and the ways that the contemporary politics of Israel and Palestine impede that task. Christian churches and the Jewish community must continue to deepen theological and sociological aspects of the relationship of Christians and Jews. They must also recognize that divisions of conviction and opinion within both communities concerning Israel and Palestine must be part of continuing conversation without dominating it.

The text of "Christians and Jews: People of God" concludes with two prayers from Presbyterian worship books. The first was written shortly after *Nostra Aetate*, and the second shortly after "A Theological Understanding of the Relationship between Christians and Jews." Together, they express the reality that response to the groundbreaking advance of *Nostra Aetate* is found most fully in the life of worshiping communities:

God of Abraham, Isaac, and Jacob,
Father of us all, whose Son Jesus was born a Jew,
was circumcised, and was dedicated in the Temple:
thank you for patriarchs and prophets and righteous rabbis,
Whose teaching we revere, whose law is our law fulfilled in Jesus
Christ.
Never let us forget that we, who are your people,
are by faith children of Abraham,
bound in one family with Jewish brothers and sisters,
who also serve your promise;
through Jesus Christ, our Master and Messiah. Amen.[28]

Almighty God, you are the one true God,
and have called forth people of faith
in every time and place.
Your promises are sure and true.
We bless you for your covenant given to Abraham and Sarah,
that you keep even now with the Jews.
We rejoice that you have brought us into covenant with you
by the coming of your Son, Jesus Christ,
himself a Jew, nurtured in the faith of Israel.
We praise you that you are faithful to covenants made
with us and Jewish brothers and sisters,
that together we may serve your will,
and come at last to your promised peace. Amen.[29]

28. Joint Committee on Worship, *The Worshipbook* (Philadelphia: Westminster, 1970), 201.

29. Presbyterian Church (U.S.A.), *Book of Common Worship* (Louisville: Westminster John Knox, 1993), 815.

8

On Jewish–Orthodox
Christian Relations

Antonios Kireopoulos

THE HISTORY OF JEWISH—ORTHODOX Christian relations has its share of good and bad moments. Whether before or after the schism between the Eastern and Western Churches, Eastern Christians have regarded their Jewish neighbors with the same mix of friendship and enmity as have their Western Christian brothers and sisters. While the Christian East can, of course, take comfort in the fact that it does not have to give account for a role in anything as extreme and horrific as the Holocaust, it nonetheless needs to repent for complicity in shocking and systematic violence in the form of pogroms, for example. At the same time, where Catholic, Protestant, and Anglican Christians can point to instances of genuine embrace of their Jewish neighbors (Archbishop Johannes de Jong of Utrecht, Dietrich Bonhoeffer, Nicholas Winton), likewise Orthodox Christians can point to such instances (Metropolitan Chrysostomos of Zakynthos, Archbishop Stefan of Bulgaria, Mother Maria Skobtsova of Paris). In the 1960s, with the issuance of *Nostra Aetate* at Vatican II, this embrace went beyond isolated instances of heroism and love, and became a recognized theological and social imperative. Indeed, while formally this document was issued for the edification of Roman Catholic Christians, it opened up the opportunity for all Christians generally, including the Orthodox, to embrace Jews with whom we have a "bond that spiritually ties the people of the New Covenant to Abraham's stock."[1]

Recognizing this spiritual bond is what has allowed a growing fraternity among Jews and Orthodox Christians. This is evidenced most readily in the three basic areas of interfaith relations: theological dialogue, collaboration on mutual concerns, and the intentional outreach to be together in public events. But it is not a foregone conclusion, nor should it need to be, that increased contact, even in theological dialogue, has led to altered theological conclusions.

In some ways, many Orthodox would agree with Pope John Paul II's refreshing assertion that Jews are our "elder brothers [and sisters]" in the faith, due to a partially common historical, religious, and scriptural heritage.[2] But it is uncertain that these same Orthodox would share this great pope's relative silence in the context of Jewish-Christian relations on the definitive place of Jesus Christ in the unfolding story of these two communities' common legacy. It would be safe to assume that most Orthodox would, in fact, apply an inclusivist approach to Judaism, as they would to other religions. This is not necessarily wrong to do; and it need not necessarily be interpreted negatively. Still, the suspicions of triumphalism attached to this approach are only magnified when applied to Judaism. Perhaps a next step in the relationship would be to explore ways of asserting what are held to be ultimate theological truths without triumphalistic connotations.[3]

---

1. *Nostra Aetate*, part 4.

2. Comments made in visit to Rome Synagogue, 13 April 1986.

3. In a sort of Orthodox primer on interfaith relations, John Garvey notes both the majority Orthodox inclusivist adherence to the "fulfillment" model and likewise offers a helpful reminder to get past the negative connotations associated with this model in terms of Jewish-Christian relations that might point to a future theme for common theological exploration: "As we approach any encounter with Judaism, we must bear in mind . . . the claim that the Messiah would be divine is not found in the Old Testament. The Messiah, when he came, would lead all humanity to a place of peace and reconciliation. We may say that the Messiah's divinity is a revelation that comes with Jesus' resurrection and ascension, and the sending of the Holy Spirit, and we may have to speak of a second coming in which the fullness of messianic prophecy will be realized at last" (John Garvey, *Seeds of the Word: Orthodox Thinking on Other Religions* [Crestwood, NY: St. Vladimir's Seminary Press, 2005], 117).

Going from a turn outward in genuine embrace to theological exploration of deeply held convictions is an open-ended journey marked by milestones along the way. Seven years after *Nostra Aetate*, in 1972, the first national conference in the United States on Greek Orthodox—Jewish relations took place in New York. The spirit of the day was captured in the statement of Archbishop Iakovos. After recounting some of the twentieth century's sins and sinful attitudes directed by Jews and Christians toward one another, he said, "This colloquium . . . is not inspired or initiated by such considerations. It is thrust upon us by God's mercy and providence, both as a challenge and as a possible response to God's commandment that we love one another, even those we have chosen either not to trust or to condemn."[4] This view that dialogue is an imperative of faith, for both Judaism and Orthodox, would guide formal Jewish–Orthodox Christian relations for years to come.

This was already evident even in the papers that were delivered by both Jewish and Orthodox scholars at that 1972 conference. Published five years after the conference, these papers offered historical, scriptural, liturgical, and ethical overviews from the perspective of both communities, a sort of introduction of each community to the other. To reference just two of these papers, both giving a historical perspective on Jewish–Orthodox relations, the history of the relationship was used to spur the communities to contemporary dialogue. From the Orthodox Christian perspective, Demetrios Constantelos said, "I conclude that the past belongs to the past and cannot be brought back to correct its evils and its faults. But we must look forward because both Greeks and Jews are heirs of eternal values and a heritage which can enrich modern humankind . . . Nothing is more important in modern history than a sincere and thoughtful dialogue."[5] And in offering the Jewish perspective on the history of this relationship, Zvi Ankori stated, "Our two nations are looking now to the future with great expectation but also with a considerable measure of anxiety. Very possibly, in the confusion of present-day politics and in the strange alliances that may arise out of the anguish of our times, Greece and Israel, Greeks and Jews, Greek Orthodoxy and Judaism may find themselves groping for a friendly hand and understanding. Let us make sure that our hands reach each other in a true covenant—a cov-

4. Archbishop Iakovos, as reprinted in *The Greek Orthodox Theological Review* 22 (Spring 1977) 2.

5. Demetrios J. Constantelos, "Greek Orthodox–Jewish Relations in Historical Perspective," *The Greek Orthodox Theological Review* 22 (Spring 1977) 16.

enant dictated by our long joint history, by our common suffering, and by ideals we have shared in the past and always will share in the future."[6]

Anticipating the future of this dialogue, a most insightful assessment of mostly theological issues in need of joint reflection was offered by Seymour Siegel.[7] After citing the "common-ness of roots," he continued to list various topics for mutually enriching theological study: God and the world, the nature of the worshipping community, the role of Tradition, eschatology, mysticism, and ethnicism. This list, certainly expanded through continued contact between the two communities over the years, remains a valuable road map. Similarly anticipating the future of this dialogue, but perhaps even more striking in its identification of areas of needed reflection, is the paper by Jacob Agus. What is most striking about this piece is that he calls for internal Jewish theological reflection, not so much on common themes, but on the New Testament and Christianity in general precisely as Jewish themes. In some ways, the first part of this call anticipates the work of Amy-Jill Levine some thirty years later, namely the reclamation of the New Testament as an integral part of Jewish theological study. The second part of this call is to mirror what has over the last several decades become a primary task of the Christian community in terms of Jewish-Christian relations. Just as Christians have attempted to reunderstand Judaism in the positive theological light of kindred communities first called into covenant by God on Sinai, Agus calls on Jews to develop a theology of Christianity that sees it as an extension of Judaism and thus as another instrument of God meant for humanity's redemption.[8]

In 1976, the international dialogue between the Orthodox and Jewish communities began, with the first of what would become a series of academic conferences cosponsored by the Ecumenical Patriarchate and the International Jewish Committee on Interreligious Consultations. The eighth and most recent of these conferences took place in 2013.

Most of the topics of these conferences have been those that get to the heart of our common traditions and history, and the theological affirmations we can make together as sharers of a common legacy. In this way

6. Zvi Ankori, "Greek Orthodox–Jewish Relations in Historic Perspective—the Jewish View," *The Greek Orthodox Theological Review* 22 (1977) 57.

7. Seymour Siegel, "Judaism and Eastern Orthodoxy: Theological Reflections," *The Greek Orthodox Theological Review* 22 (1977) 63–69.

8. Jacob B. Agus, "Judaism and the New Testament," *The Greek Orthodox Theological Review* 22 (1977) 87.

these conferences followed, if not intentionally then certainly nevertheless, the road map offered by Siegel. For example, Ecumenical Patriarch Bartholomew, in his address at the third conference, in 1993, outlined common spiritual ground and common challenge the two communities could address together.[9]

By the time of the fifth conference, in 2003, Ecumenical Patriarch Bartholomew made two interesting moves. First, he cautioned both communities that narrow self-interest was not helpful to either. After lamenting the abuses that can take place due to interreligious strife and the response of self-protection at the expense of reasonable discourse, he stated, "All people, whether Christians or Jews, are susceptible to the danger of having their judgment clouded by what they perceive as being their own interest."[10] Instead, he suggested rightly that "people who are firmly convinced [of their own faith] and who live the truth of their faith in practice are peaceful and imperturbable and friendly to all."[11]

The Ecumenical Patriarch's second interesting move was to charge each community not to avoid the difficult theological differences between them, but to use those differences as an impulse toward better mutual understanding. He stated, "At the center of the differing viewpoints lies the controversial person of Jesus Christ and the fact of the Cross, which the Apostle Paul, a Jew, described epigrammatically as being 'to the Jews a stumbling block and to the Greeks foolishness' (1 Cor. 1:23) . . . [W}e do not seek to change the faith of our interlocutor on these crucial points or on other points of lesser importance. We are seeking to change the dispositions of our interlocutors toward others and to be led to dialogue in good faith, full of love and mutual respect. Beyond this, it is a matter of free choice for each person, that choice being respected and accepted by all as a possibility."[12]

At the sixth meeting of this dialogue series, in 2007, the participants focused on religious identity, religious freedom, and mutual respect. While offering the promise of fruitful dialogue (religious freedom is a key topic for all communities, particularly as the world sees more and more human

9. Ecumenical Patriarch Bartholomew, "Continuity and Renewal: Jewish-Christian Relations: I," in John Chryssavgis, ed., *In the World, yet Not of the World: Social and Global Initiatives of Ecumenical Patriarch Bartholomew* (New York: Fordham University Press, 2010), 244–46.

10. Ibid., 248.

11. Ibid., 247.

12. Ibid., 249.

rights violations rooted in religious extremism directed against religious minorities) it would seem that there was a missed opportunity to heed the Ecumenical Patriarch's earlier call to take on difficult theological questions. At a meeting held in Jerusalem especially, one could imagine challenging discussions around the theology of the land, the meaning of covenant, the place of Israel in the Church, the emergence of the State of Israel as a theological category for Jews, and other such crucial, and perhaps uncomfortable, topics.[13] Perhaps this was on the mind of Thomas Fitzgerald, who concluded his remarks by saying, "As religious leaders, we have a profound responsibility not simply to share our faith traditions with others in dialogue. This is certainly important. Yet even more than this, we religious leaders also have the opportunity to share in the healing and reconciling actions of the God whom we honor. We also have a responsibility to contribute to the well-being of society and the life of the world. Our discussions are not unrelated to wider concerns for peace and justice, especially in this land but also throughout the world."[14]

Where will this dialogue take the Jewish and Orthodox Christian communities in years to come? What will be the reasons for their continued coming together, and the content of their deliberations? What theological fruit will these dialogues produce within the lives of these respective communities?

It seems certain that one topic to remain at the center of dialogue will be Israel and Palestine. With religious, historical, ethnic, and political ties anchoring members of both communities to the land, neither community is exempt from taking up the theological warrants and interpretations that inform their connection to that land. At the same time, with the moral and spiritual values of love and justice at the core of their

---

13. In some ways, these difficult topics have formed the center of the Christian-Jewish dialogue in the United States. While undergoing fits and starts due to tensions surrounding criticism of the Israeli occupation, and while at the time of this writing at a standstill over such tensions, the Jewish-Christian dialogue has not shied away from difficult theological themes, such as theology of the land and applying categories of liberation theology to the Israeli-Palestinian conflict. Even a separate Jewish-Christian dialogue on pastoral issues, at which challenging themes such as interfaith marriage are on the agenda, has been halted as a result of a disagreement over a Christian church call for a U.S. government investigation into unconditional military aid to Israel. Though ecumenical in nature, these dialogues have limited Orthodox participation.

14. Thomas Fitzgerald, "Faithfulness to a Religious Identity in the Modern World: The Jerusalem Consultation between Judaism and Orthodox Christianity," *The Greek Orthodox Theological Review* 52 (2007) 210–11.

respective faiths, neither community is exempt from calling their members to reconciliation with one another.

This latter imperative—to call their respective members to reconciliation—touches upon a key task for leaders of both communities: to eliminate suspicion and prejudice, and in their place to inculcate respect and affirmation, with regard to one another. For Jews, this might begin by clearly reminding their faithful to refrain from equating Western *and Eastern* Christian critiques of the Israeli occupation and related policies with anti-Semitism, and to remember that such critiques are based to a large extent on solidarity with fellow Christians suffering in the Holy Land. Related concerns to the Orthodox would include the dwindling Christian presence there, community issues pertaining to the Palestinian Christian and broader local Arab population, and legal and other problems faced by the Orthodox Patriarchate of Jerusalem and other Christian leadership.

For the Orthodox, this task might begin by dealing forthrightly with textual sources that partly inform popular piety. In an essay on Jewish–Orthodox Christian relations in the Russian context, Yuriy Tabak has highlighted the negative influence of such sources. As is to be expected, he is careful to note that anti-Semitic attitudes were historically not reflected in official Church policy but rather in "the sermons and speeches of the most illustrious clerics and hierarchs of the Russian Orthodox Church [that in turn reflected] the general population's widely held negative attitudes toward the Jews."[15] But he daringly goes one step further by attributing these negative attitudes to an uncritical adherence to Holy Tradition. "This 'Holy Tradition' embraces the whole historical experience of the Church . . . by its very definition is sacred . . . and . . . dating from the period of the fathers is overtly anti-Semitic."[16] To support his statement, he cites anti-Semitic references to Jews in the writings of the fathers. Indeed, with anti-Semitism being an equal opportunity sin, such references are not limited to Russian luminaries but are to be found in the Greek fathers as well.

Most Orthodox writers would put such references in historical and/ or cultural context or ignore them altogether; they would definitely not see them as normative for Orthodox theology. Still, Tabak is correct to

15. Yuriy Tabak, "Relations between Russian Orthodoxy and Judaism," in John Witte Jr. and Michael Bourdeaux, eds., *Proselytism and Orthodoxy in Russia: The New War for Souls* (Maryknoll, NY: Orbis, 1999), 144.

16. Ibid., 145.

show how such sources influence both clergy and laypeople who, with marginal religious education, may "harbor a degree of underlying suspicion and fear of the Jews, arising from their sketchy knowledge of Holy Tradition."[17] The history of Jews in Russia illustrates the extremes to which such influence may lead.

In truth, these texts are part of the historical record. The writings of the fathers, sermons of hierarchs of past centuries, even brow-raising scriptural references—these cannot be changed. But there is one set of texts that can be changed, and these are liturgical texts, particularly those that are read or sung during Holy Week. To cite the hymns of but one service: "O blood-guilty people, faithless Israel, the murderer Barabbas you set free, but delivered your Savior to the cross"; "Be ashamed, O Jews, at the witness of your dead, raised to life by Him whom you condemned to death in malice and envy"; "O the folly of those who killed the prophets! Now they slay the Messiah!" Perhaps most Orthodox faithful singing such verses shrug them off as poetic license; however, to say that these and other such texts liturgically—and thus theologically—reinforce in the mind of the worshipping community the accusation of Jews as killers of Christ is more likely an understatement.

Some Orthodox might take exception to the notion that liturgical texts can be changed, since they are part of the Holy Tradition of the Church. But in reality, Holy Tradition is *living* Tradition, part of the ongoing life of the community as it journeys through the centuries. This is not a call to political correctness of a twenty-first-century mindset; it is a call to accurately reflect the mind of the Church, which cannot rely on spiritualization of texts written in a different age but instead demands truthfulness in the Church's prayer. Indeed, as Harry Pappas has noted about hymns such as those cited above, "we could revise these hymns without compromising anything of our faith commitment."[18] To make

17. Ibid., 147.

18. Harry Pappas, "Continuity and Discontinuity between Jews and Christians" (unpublished presentation, 1998), 9. Such revisions have already been begun. See, for example, Leonidas Contos, trans., and Spencer T. Kezios, ed., *The Services for Holy Week and Easter: in the Original Greek, with a New English Translation* (San Francisco: Narthex, 1994). In the translator's preface, Contos writes: "The texts contain many references to the Jewish people. For us they have the ring of prejudice. Wherever possible, and permissible within the context, such anti-Semitic elements have been tempered by concern for the worshiper's sensitivity, and the more enlightened attitude that prevails today." Looking at the three verses cited above, the first two have been eliminated (along with many others that have been excised presumably to shorten the

such changes would additionally be an appropriate acknowledgement of the ecumenical importance and influence of *Nostra Aetate*, which states, "True, the Jewish authorities and those who followed their lead pressed for the death of Christ; still, what happened in His passion cannot be charged against all the Jews, without distinction, then alive, nor against the Jews of today. Although the Church is the new people of God, the Jews should not be presented as rejected or accursed by God, as if this followed from the Holy Scriptures. All should see to it, then, that in catechetical work or in the preaching of the word of God they do not teach anything that does not conform to the truth of the Gospel and the spirit of Christ."[19]

Pappas made the observation above during a presentation at a Jewish-Christian clergy retreat in Chicago some fifteen years ago.[20] His overall thesis in this presentation was that there is a continuum of continuity and discontinuity that needs to be appreciated by both Jews and Christians that links both communities and yet recognizes their distinct differences. Both Jews and Christians, and among the latter Orthodox Christians, are beginning to appreciate this reality. For the Orthodox, Pappas succinctly articulates the task at hand: "We need to recover knowledge of the Hebrew Scriptures / Old Testament, in order to understand *how* the new covenant in Christ is both in continuity and discontinuity with the covenant of Sinai. This will lead us to know far better the *real* Jesus of Nazareth, enable us to avoid setting our own modern quasi-Gnostic ideas about him that focus too much on his divinity, and come to understand for our own age the brilliant insight of St. Irenaeus of Lyons, who referred to the Incarnation as the 'scandal of particularity,' which could as well apply to the covenants of both Old and New Testaments."[21]

---

service), and the third reads: "What madness, what Christicide, of those who slew the prophets!" Although this particular work eliminates, and in this example softens, the sharpness of the language without compromising the meaning of the overall service, this and other such works have not yet found their way into common usage.

19. *Nostra Aetate*, part 4.

20. Local Jewish-Christian (and specifically Orthodox Christian) dialogues compose another important area of study that deserves fuller treatment at another time. In fact, such local examples in the U.S. could prove instructive in other contexts, given sensitivities to interfaith, and specifically Jewish-Christian, relations in the U.S. over the last generation or so.

21. Pappas "Continuity and Discontinuity between Jews and Christians" (unpublished presentation, 1998), 8.

Fifty years ago, before the promulgation of *Nostra Aetate*, such statements would have been unthinkable. In the five decades since then, increased contact between Jews and Orthodox Christians has broken down walls and allowed for friendly interactions among dialogue participants. The next step is to ensure that the truths demonstrated through dialogue continue to emerge, not only on these issues, but also on the numerous others that pertain to our relationship, and that these truths become a lived reality for those faithful in the congregations of our respective Jewish and Orthodox Christian communities.

9

Vatican II and *Nostra Aetate* at Fifty
An Evangelical View

Alan F. Johnson

The extensive Vatican II Council's document that sets forth the Roman (Latin) Catholic Church's beliefs and practices for modern times was released in parts at various times from 1963 through 1965 and contains a smaller document entitled, *"Nostra Aetate"* (meaning, "in our time"). Released in 1965, the declaration is a statement of how the Catholic Church understands non-Christian religions. Without denying the Church's clear commitment to proclaim Jesus Christ as the way, the truth, and the life (John 14:6), in whom God reconciled all things to himself (2 Cor 5:18–19), and in whom "men find the fulfillment of their religious life," the Church "rejects nothing of what is true and holy in these religions . . . " Further, the Church affirms that their "manner of life, and conduct, the precepts and doctrines which, although differing in many ways from her own teaching, nevertheless often reflect a ray of that truth which enlightens all men." The Church also encourages its sons "while witnessing to their own faith and way of life, acknowledge, preserve, and encourage the spiritual and moral truths found among non-Christians, also their social life and culture."

More specifically in section 4 of *Nostra Aetate* one finds numerous paragraphs explaining the Church's relationship in particular to the Jewish people and to their religion that is called Judaism. In short the "Church of Christ acknowledges that in God's plan of salvation her election begins in the roots of the patriarchs, Moses, and the prophets. She professes that all Christ's faithful who are men of faith are sons of Abraham (cf. Gal 3:7), are included in the same patriarch's call, and that the salvation of the Church is mystically prefigured in the exodus of God's chosen people from the land of bondage." The Church also remembers that "she received the revelation of the Old Testament by way of that people with whom God in his inexpressible mercy established the ancient covenant. Nor can she forget she draws nourishment from that good olive tree onto which her sons as wild olive branches of the Gentiles have been grafted (cf. Rom. 11:17–24). The Church believes that Christ who is our peace has through his cross reconciled Jews and Gentiles and made them one in himself (cf. Eph. 2:14–16)."[1]

While most of the points made are quite positive and respectful to the Jewish people, the following strikes a slightly sadder historical note in saying, "As holy Scripture testifies, Jerusalem did not recognize God's moment when it came (cf. Lk. 19:42). Jews for the most part did not accept the Gospel; on the contrary, many opposed the spreading of it (cf. Rom. 11:28). Even so, the apostle Paul maintains that the Jews remain very dear to God, for the sake of the patriarchs, since God does not take back the gifts he bestowed or the choice he made (cf. Rom. 11:28–29). Together with the prophets and that same apostle, the Church awaits the day, known to God alone, when all people will call on God with one voice and 'serve him shoulder to shoulder' (Soph. 3:9; cf. Is. 66:23; Ps. 65:4; Rom. 11: 11–32)."[2]

"Since Christians and Jews have such a common spiritual heritage. The Council wishes to encourage and further mutual understanding and appreciation. This can be obtained, especially, by way of biblical and theological enquiry and through friendly discussions."

Finally, the section on the Jews ends with two strong denials and an equally strong affirmation. "It is true that the Church is the new people of God, yet the Jews should not be spoken of as rejected or accursed as if this followed from holy Scripture." Further, "the Church reproves every

1. Austin P. Flannery, ed., *Documents of Vatican II* (Grand Rapids: Eerdmans, 1975), 740.

2. Ibid., 741.

form of persecution against whomsoever it may be directed. Remembering, then, her common heritage with the Jews and moved not by any political considerations, but solely by the religious motivation of Christian charity, she deplores all hatreds, persecutions, displays of anti-Semitism leveled at any time or from any source against the Jews." Last, the strong affirmation follows: "The Church always held and continues to hold that Christ out of infinite love freely underwent suffering and death because of the sins of all men, so that all might attain salvation. It is the duty of the Church, therefore, in her preaching to proclaim the cross of Christ as the sign of God's universal love and the source of all grace."[3]

The Jewish community has hailed this statement as marking a "sea change in Jewish-Christian relations." In this volume you will read various Roman Catholic, Jewish, mainline Protestant responses, assessments, and further reflections on what has happened in the last 50 years since *Nostra Aetate* has been released. The editor has graciously added an "evangelical" voice to the mix for this special anniversary edition. I think it is safe to say that most evangelicals including the scholars among them have never heard of or would they be familiar with the wording and content of *Nostra Aetate*! And while this is changing in the last decade or so, Protestant evangelicals have not had much direct contact with the Roman Catholic Church and its documents, discussions, pronouncements, and activities until recently.[4] Nevertheless, evangelicals have had and continue to have a widespread and longtime interest in and love for the Jewish people. There is an almost parallel but mostly independent development in these communities, their organizations, and institutions that have built various relations with the Jewish people. Of course not all interest in Jews has been welcomed. We will trace some of these welcomed as well as unwelcomed overtures in the following essay.

But just who are the evangelicals, and what have they said and believed about Jews, the Jewish faith, the Holocaust, and the modern nation-state of Israel? Even more importantly how have evangelical Christians behaved in their attitudes and actions toward Jews and the Jewish religious communities?

---

3. In 1978 the Commission for Religious Relations with the Jews (CRRJ) issued "Guidelines on Religious Relations with the Jews (N. 4)" as to how *Nostra Aetate* might be effectively implemented. See http://www.christusrex.org/www1/CDHN/v9.html/.

4. See John H. Armstrong, *Your Church Is Too Small* (Grand Rapids: Zondervan, 2010).

Evangelical is an Old English word that comes from the Greek *euangelion* meaning "good news." Another Old English word also means "good news," i.e., "god-spel," that came to be shortened to "gospel." In the very earliest Greek papyri manuscripts that we have of the first chapter of each of the four books we call the Gospels that record the life, teachings, sufferings, death, and resurrection of Jesus, the title reads "*euangelion* according to Matthew," ". . . to Mark," and so on. The English Bibles translate this as "The Gospel according to Matthew," etc.

In the very early and influential English translation of the Bible by William Tyndale (1534), that was to become the predominant basis (80 percent) of the popular King James translation (1611), Tyndale almost always throughout the New Testament translates *euangelion* as "gospel." The verbal form of the word is quite frequent in his New Testament and is translated, "to preach or proclaim the gospel." This is why so many of the contemporary Christian evangelical organizations, and even Bibles are named, "The Good News" this or that. The "good news" or gospel concerns the joyous new thing that the God of Israel (the One true and Living God, the Creator and Redeemer) has done through Jesus Christ in bringing salvation and forgiveness of sin into the world for all mankind, including Jews and all the Gentile nations of the earth.

Now this does not quite explain the present-day presence of those Christians who may call themselves evangelicals (and those who are evangelicals but prefer not to use this name) in order to distinguish themselves in some way from other Christian traditions or to identify with some party within a larger Christian group or to espouse a theological understanding of Christianity that is defined over against a modernist, accommodating (compromised) view of the Christian faith. But who are the evangelicals that without any criticism support Jews and the State of Israel, along with some who are opposed to the State or at least to some of its policies, and some who are also now engaging in dialogue and discussion especially with the Jewish religious communities in America?

Evangelicals are not a separate religion, Christian denomination, or organization; hence there is no central ecclesial authority for all evangelicals, such as there is in the Roman Catholic Church, the Southern Baptist Convention, the Evangelical Lutheran Church in America, the Episcopal Church or Anglican Communion, the United Methodist Church, the Presbyterian Church U.S.A., the Assemblies of God, or in other identifiable church bodies. The closest organization that represents evangelicals in any overall collaborative way in America is the National

Association of Evangelicals (NAE). Founded in 1942, the NAE currently includes over forty Protestant church denominations and thousands of individual churches in its membership, six affiliate organizations, and a compassion/service arm of the organization, World Relief. There is also a public-policy arm of NAE with offices in Washington DC. The NAE also partners with the World Evangelical Alliance (WEA), a network of evangelical churches in 128 nations that have each formed an evangelical alliance with over 100 international organizations joining together to give a worldwide identity, voice, and platform to more than 420 million evangelical Christians. While the NAE does not have a statement relating to Jews and Christians, the WEA does.

Furthermore, what complicates trying to define who is or what is an evangelical is the kaleidoscopic nature of the broadly varied mosaic of Christian communities, organizations, and institutions that make up the vast subculture of evangelical Christianity. Add to this the fact that evangelicals (with a small *e* can be found in all branches of the Christian Church: in the Roman Catholic Church, in the Orthodox church, in mainline Protestant churches, in independent Bible churches, in parachurch organizations such as World Vision, and in many foreign-mission organizations, as well as in the organization called Jews for Jesus, and in many others. Currently it is not possible to give percentages of where and how many evangelicals there are in American Christianity.

Is there a distinguishing core of belief or practice that can be used to identify who is and who would not fit that name? One prominent evangelical church historian has recently commented to me that an evangelical is "anyone who claims to be an evangelical"![5]

Yet it is still possible to identify some core features of those who call themselves evangelicals.

(1) They all regardless of affiliations would subscribe to what is considered a *historical, classical Christian doctrinal formulation* as can be found in the ancient creeds (Apostles' and Nicene). They may not all use these creeds in their worship services, but minimally they would agree with the substance of Christian faith that these creeds affirm.

(2) Evangelicals all hold to both a *high view of the Bible's divine inspiration as the Word of God* and as the *final authority over faith and life* and

---

5. Mark Noll, historian (University of Notre Dame), who sits on a committee of the NAE that is currently attempting to draft an adequate definition for polling purposes.

to the *priority of the Bible* itself, when properly interpreted, to judge and correct all secondary interpretations and theological reflections (church councils, creeds, traditions, and theologies) however valuable and essential these may be to understand the Bible's teachings.

(3) Evangelicals are committed to the *gospel message of the forgiveness of sins* and *new life* through Jesus Christ's atoning death and resurrection and through whom personal relationship with the One God, the God of Israel, is realized through repentance and faith apart from any previous meritorious works. This free gift of "new life" (new birth) is the divine life of the Holy Spirit of God who pours the love of God into the hearts of individual men and women and who simultaneously unites every redeemed Spirit-born person to every other redeemed person, Jew and Gentile alike, into the *One new universal, eschatological entity, the Israel of God.*

(4) Evangelicals so described are enthusiastic and obedient recipients of the command of Jesus himself to go into all the world and *announce this good news (gospel) to every person, Jew and Gentile* alike, inviting them to freely respond with obedient faith and to enter into the eschatological kingdom of God and to await with good works of love the coming of the Anointed, Righteous One who will redeem the people of God completely along with the whole creation and establish the new heavens and new earth. Since the 1940s, evangelicals have recovered an earlier emphasis on *balancing evangelization with societal social concerns* such as feeding the poor, caring for the prisoners, ministering to AIDS patients, saving the environment, and many other broad humanitarian services.[6]

(5) Some add to these above core identity markers the *transdenominational nature of evangelicalism* that leads many different Christian groups to unite in common causes and projects.

There are many other features of evangelicals that could and should be clarified further including some classic, popular mischaracterizations of evangelicals.[7]

6. See http://www.anevangelicalmanifesto.com/docs/Evangelical_Manifesto.pdf/.

7. Wild, emotional charismatics; prophecy nuts; bigots; uneducated; right wingers; superpatriots; war hawks; separatists; biblical literalists; Bible thumpers; narrowminded; fundamentalists, are a few of the popular labels. The earliest use of the term as applied to persons that is recorded by the *Oxford English Dictionary* is a response of a Dr. Arnold (1876) to a query of who an evangelical is. He replied, "An evangelical is a good Christian with a narrow understanding" (p. 329). This would today fit better the description of one in the fundamentalist subcategory. Many of these are corrected

EVANGELICALS AND JEWS IN HISTORY

It is needed, I believe, but somewhat risky, to try to give a brief under-standing as to who evangelicals are and what kinds of relationships different branches of this type of Christianity have had with the Jewish community in more recent history.

Beyond the sixteenth-century identification of the German Luther-an Church as the "Evangelical Church of Germany," a term that spread throughout Europe and the Scandinavian countries and was used to dis-tinguish Lutherans from Calvinistic Reformed churches, evangelicals in our current sense of the word, begin to be mentioned specifically in con-nection with the eighteenth-century revivalists in England and America. Figures such as John and Charles Wesley, who were Anglicans, spawned a movement that became another Protestant denomination called the Methodists. These evangelicals were mostly low-church Anglicans who denied that any supernatural gifts were imparted by ordination, or that saving grace was imparted by the sacraments or good works. They em-phasized that salvation was by faith alone in the atonement through Christ's death, they emphasized the sole authority of the Bible in matters of faith and life, and they denied that any church had absolute interpretive

---

in two fine pieces. One written by a 2008 committee convened by the NAE (National Association of Evangelicals), entitled, "An Evangelical Manifesto" and the other issued by Wheaton College's ISAE (Institute for the Study of American Evangelicals), both found on website of NAE: www.nae.net). But for the purposes of this essay the follow-ing might be mentioned:

(1) "Contrary to widespread misunderstanding today, we Evangelicals should be defined theologically, and not politically, socially, or culturally. Above all else, it is a commitment and devotion to the person and work of Jesus Christ, his teaching and way of life, and an enduring dedication to his lordship above all other earthly pow-ers, allegiances and loyalties. As such, it should not be limited to tribal or national boundaries, or be confused with, or reduced to political categories such as 'conserva-tive' and 'liberal,' or to psychological categories such as 'reactionary' or 'progressive'" ["Evangelical Manifesto," 8].

(2) "Evangelicalism should be distinguished from two opposite tendencies to which Protestantism has been prone: liberal revisionism and conservative fundamentalism. Called by Jesus to be "in the world, but not of it," Christians, especially in modern society, have been pulled toward two extremes. Those more liberal have tended so to accommodate the world that they reflect the thinking and lifestyles of the day, to the point where they are unfaithful to Christ; whereas those more conservative have tended so to defy the world that they resist it in ways that also become unfaithful to Christ" ("Evangelical Manifesto," 8; see also, for distinctions, Gerald R. McDermott, *Can Evangelicals Learn From World Religions? Jesus, Revelation & Religious Traditions* [Downers Grove, IL: InterVarsity, 2000], 28–39).

authority. An American, Jonathan Edwards, an early President of Princeton University, was also a key evangelical figure in the religious revivals that spread throughout America in the eighteenth century. Evangelicalism was also influenced by the German Pietism of Jacob Spener and the Moravian Brethren, especially, Count Zinzendorf, and his relationship to John Wesley.

It is hard to generalize about this period. Most of the references to Jews and Judaism in these evangelical writers were mentioned in connection with their talking first of all about "ancient" Jews in the Old Testament times of Moses and the prophets and then also in the New Testament. They then extrapolated into their present and applied the text's references to the Jews with whom they generally seemed to have had limited contact, except for personal friendships, but with little knowledge of their religious views and life.[8] Lucinda Martin's recent article reviews attitudes toward Jews in eighteenth-century German Pietism, focusing especially on Halle Pietists and their periodical, *Bau des Reichs Gottes*. She remarks,

> Pietists believed that Jews would convert en masse before the Second Coming of Christ. Those who wanted to hasten Christ's return thus promoted Jewish conversion to Christianity. Pietists sought contact to their Jewish neighbors and urged regents to improve conditions for Jews. In their writings, Pietists maintained that good Christians should behave kindly toward Jews, and they portray Jews as learned and good people—unusually

8. Wesley can be seen at times to mouth anti-Judaic statements when he was preaching from texts that mentioned Jewish unbelief in Jesus, though his behavior toward Jewish people displayed no contempt, hostility, or unfriendliness. He can say things like this: "St. John assigns this very reason for the Jews not understanding the things of God; namely, that in consequence of their preceding sins, and willful rejecting the light, God had now delivered them up to Satan, who had blinded them past recovery" (section 6 of sermon 66: "Signs of the Times," in *The Works of John Wesley*, vol. 6, *Sermons on Several Occasions* [Grand Rapids: Zondervan, n.d.], 309.). Yet this account is also told as to his behavior: "When John Wesley arrived in Savannah in 1736 he found a large group of Jews living there. These Jews had arrived soon after the colony was founded by James Oglethorpe. They had left Spain to escape persecution from the Catholics. When their ship appeared in Savannah many of the colonist didn't want to accept them, but Oglethorpe wanted all the settlers he could get. It was a fortunate decision because Savannah was experiencing a severe Yellow Fever epidemic. One of the Spanish Jews was Dr. Nunez who helped stop the disease. John Wesley taught himself Spanish so he could communicate with the Jews. He and Dr. Nunez became friends and John [was] asked to attend an autopsy conducted by the doctor." (John C. English, "John Wesley and His 'Jewish Parishioners': Jewish-Christian Relationships in Savannah, Georgia, 1736–1737," *Methodist History* 36/4 (July 1998) 220–27.

positive images for the period. At the same time, Pietists made Anti-Judaic assumptions: that Jews "sinned" in not recognizing Jesus as the Messiah and that they could stop persecution against Jews by "repenting."[9]

However, in this period we can see one of the roots of modern evangelical prophetic support for Jews and Israel (Christian Zionism) in the hope that by supporting Jewish evangelism one could hasten the return of Christ. But recent studies have also urged caution in seeing a simple, single root cause for this development.[10]

THE NINETEENTH CENTURY IN BRITAIN AND IN AMERICA

Protestant Christian interest in the land of Israel in prior years, due to travel constraints and the general disdain of actual pilgrimages to Palestine as spiritually useless, saw in biblical terms such as "Zion" and "Jerusalem" references to the soul's journey to the heavenly city, and terms such as the "Jordan River" as having symbolic significance. In the early nineteenth century in Britain there was a growing interest in the actual physical Middle East, and especially for Christians the city of Jerusalem became more than just a spiritual metaphor but gradually fused with the physical city itself. The American scholar, missionary, and archaeologist Edward Robinson, on the basis of his research in Palestine in 1838 and subsequent publications, established the beginnings of the scholarly study of biblical archaeology. Coupled with the growing international tourist industry and the yearning of many to travel to the Holy Land there was also the birth of a fascination with biblical prophecy and the possibilities of a more literal fulfillment of these connected with the land of Palestine itself.[11]

Certain premillennialist writers, such as Alexander Keith, A. J. Bonar, and Robert Murray McCheyne, all of whom held that the archaeological evidence being discovered in Palestine was confirming the truth

---

9. *A Journal of Germanic Studies* 48/3 (2012) 301–16.

10. Donald M. Lewis, *The Origins of Christian Zionism: Lord Shaftesbury and Evangelical Support for a Jewish Homeland* (Cambridge: Cambridge University Press, 2010), 37–38; Additionally, "Ian Murray has observed, belief in the future conversion of the Jews became commonplace among the English Puritans," 28; philo-Semitism vs. anti-Semitism, 34–35ff; see also Spener and Simeon and their "teaching of esteem" vs. "teaching of contempt" (*adversus Judaeos*), 64–65.).

11. Lewis, *The Origins of Christian Zionism*, 136, 137.

of the Christian faith, created a desire to visit the Holy Land and see for themselves what had been discovered. However, there was little that was romantically stimulating, and visits led often to disappointment. Jerusalem then was nothing more than a "disease-infested town, very cramped and decidedly unhealthy—reportedly the worst place in Palestine for ticks, fleas, and biting flies. Its Jewish section, the most disagreeable part of the city, was known for how filthy it was. The rotting carcasses of dogs, cats, and even camels decomposing on the streets were a commonplace, with packs of vicious dogs that foraged on them, always ready to attack anyone who interfered with their scrounging."[12]

By the end of the nineteenth century, there were inhabitants from every European nation living in Jerusalem, and it was the most written-about place in the world.[13] Some estimates have it that there were about twelve thousand total residents. But what about the small Jewish population that some Christians were beginning to describe as the "remnant" that would represent not only Jerusalem's past, but also the Jews' future restoration to the land? Estimates are that a little less than 50 percent were Jews (5,500), with about another 4,190 Jews in other cities in Palestine.[14]

A further development in the evangelical interest in Jerusalem was the influence of the British evangelical, Lord Shaftesbury (Lord Ashley, Earl of Shaftesbury). Lewis finds that "he was 'Victorian' Britain's most prominent social reformer as well as its quintessential evangelical lay leader. However, he also became the leading proponent of Christian Zionism in the nineteenth century and was the first politician of stature to attempt to prepare the way for Jews to establish a homeland in Palestine" as a fulfillment of biblical prophecy.[15]

He was instrumental in urging the British government to establish a consulate in Jerusalem in 1838. There were also political reasons for such a move—such as the French Revolution, Russia's expansion policies, increasing Jewish strictures; and later in the century temporary laws legitimizing the severe persecution of Jews were enacted.[16] Lewis details the development of British evangelical factors and government interests in Palestine and concludes that "in one sense the earliest Zionists were

12. Ibid., 139.
13. Ibid.
14. Ibid., 140.
15. Ibid., 107.
16. Ibid., 323.

Christian Zionists . . . By the 1830s, the expectation that the physical 'Restoration' of the Jews would be fulfilled was widespread in Britain."[17]

The rise of dispensationalism in the later part of the nineteenth century has, along with what we have already briefly traced, set the stage for the unfolding of part of the evangelical and Jews' story in America in the twentieth and twenty-first centuries. Dispensationalism is a variant of evangelical premillennial prophetic biblical interpretation. Essentially it is traced to a British pastor named John Nelson Darby (1800–1882), who, after separating from the Anglican established church, joined the Brethren movement, nondenominational groups that met in private homes for Bible study, spiritual edification, and eucharistic celebration.

These groups were distinguished by a view that divided up the biblical history into seven distinguishable dispensations or economies of God's dealing with humanity under which mankind and God's people lived with different responsibilities. Salvation in any economy was always by grace through faith in the revealed God of Scripture. Here are several of the essential characteristics: the use of an interpretive principle that takes the plain, normal (literal) sense of a biblical text as the true sense. This hermeneutic leads the movement to understand that there is a sharp distinction between God's program for Israel (the historic Jewish community) and the Church. "Thus the church did not begin in the Old Testament, but on the day of Pentecost, and the church is not presently fulfilling promises made to Israel in the Old Testament that have not yet been fulfilled."[18] It seems clear, however, that dispensationalists are against supersessionist or replacement understandings of the relation of Israel to the church. Earlier dispensationalists advocated a "two-peoples-of-God" view, with Israel as the "earthly people", and the church as the "heavenly people" (Darby). Today most dispensationalists have abandoned this heavenly/earthly–separation view, but they still hold to a clear distinction between Israel and the church as earthly (Israel) and spiritual (church).

The dispensational view has also included the belief that before the return of Christ there would be a final return of the Jewish people to their land given to them in the Abrahamic covenant, and that they would as a whole nation convert to belief in Jesus as Savior and enter into the millennium (the one-thousand-year reign of Messiah from Jerusalem) at which time all the promises given to Israel found in the Old

17. Ibid., 114–15.

18. Charles Ryrie, "Dispensation, Dispensationalism," in Walter A. Elwell, ed., *Evangelical Dictionary of Theology* (Grand Rapids: Baker, 1984), 322.

Testament would be consistently and literally fulfilled. The church was viewed as an entirely separate program of God heretofore not revealed (i.e., a mystery), but instigated when the majority of Jews rejected Jesus as their Messiah and king. The church age will end with a "secret rapture" (snatching away) of the church out of the world that will take place before a final great tribulation of seven years on earth that will occur, followed by the second coming of Jesus and the conversion of the Jewish nation to Jesus as Messiah.

THE TWENTIETH CENTURY

Early in the twentieth century several events and evangelical persons figure into the eventual establishment of the nation-state of Israel in Palestine. Five weeks before the Ottoman rule of Jerusalem fell (November 1917), Lord Arthur Balfour, the British Foreign Secretary, wrote a letter to Lord James Rothschild, a leader in the international Zionist movement, indicating that the British government was ready to establish in Palestine a "national home" for the Jewish people, and that they would help them to achieve this providing that "nothing shall be done which may prejudice the civil and religious rights of existing non-Jewish communities in Palestine or the rights or political status enjoyed by Jews in any other country."[19] This Balfour Declaration was influenced by British evangelicals, who were prominent publicists (Shaftesbury, Oliphant, Condor) and by members of the War Cabinet itself that had no less than seven Calvinist evangelicals voting on the Declaration.[20] This turn of events highly encouraged the premillennialist evangelicals that their interpretation of the Bible was on target concerning the return of the Jews to their land in the immediate future.

In the early third of the century a particular American Protestant premillennial evangelical Methodist by the name of William Eugene Blackstone (a.k.a., W. E. Blackstone, or simply W. E. B., 1841–1935), the author of probably the most read premillennialist book of that period, *Jesus Is Coming*, became also a highly celebrated person among the Jewish Zionists. Weber captures well the dynamics then and perhaps also today:

---

19. Timothy P. Weber, *Living in the Shadow of the Second Coming: American Premillennialism 1875–1982* (Grand Rapids: Academie, 1983), 129.

20. Lewis, *The Origins of Christian Zionism*, 333.

At a 1918 Zionist Conference in Philadelphia Blackstone was acclaimed a "Father of Zionism." In the same year, at a Zionist mass meeting in Los Angeles, Blackstone addressed the assembled crowd . . . Despite the call for conversion, Blackstone retained a cherished place in the history of the early Zionist movement . . . Unlike other Protestants, premillennialists believed that God was not finished with the Jews as a national entity. Most evangelicals believed in a vague sort of way that somehow at the end of God's redemptive purposes "all Israel shall be saved" (Romans 11:26); but only premillennialists expected a national restoration in Palestine and a powerful Jewish state under the returned Messiah as part of the saving process. Thus premillennialists were able to stress the evangelization of the Jews while at the same time they supported Jewish nationalistic aspirations.[21]

Among his many pro-Jewish activities, Blackstone also sponsored a number of conferences in behalf of Israel, such as one held in 1915 at Moody Church in Chicago that drew seventeen thousand spectators. Earlier he had established what was perhaps the first interdenominational Jewish mission in America in Chicago in 1887 named, "The Chicago Hebrew Mission."[22] At a Jewish Zionist conference in Philadelphia he was also acclaimed as a " Father of Zionism."[23]

During the first half of the century events have taken place that have changed the dynamics of evangelical relations to the Jewish community. World War II and the horrible realities of the Jewish Holocaust (*Shoah*) have profoundly and permanently affected the world's awareness of anti-Semitism and this people's unjust suffering. I will mention later how this has affected evangelical sensitivities, practices, and statements.

Two other events that have indisputably shaped evangelical and Jewish relations are the United Nations partition of Palestine in 1947 and the subsequent establishment of an independent nation-state of Israel in Palestine the following year (1948). This was received well by most Jews and millennially oriented evangelicals. Nonmillennial evangelicals were not at all certain that this had any prophetic significance, and some even were opposed and called the developments an "unjust restoration."[24] All the while many premillennialists were ecstatic that their interpretations

21. Weber, *Living in the Shadow of the Second Coming*, 140–41.

22. Ibid., 143.

23. Ibid., 140.

24. Dwight Wilson, *Armageddon Now: The Premillenarian Response to Russia and Israel since 1917* (Grand Rapids: Baker, 1977), 169.

of end-time events were proving to be correct especially after the Six Day war that saw the expansion of the borders of the Jewish State (June 1967).

Since the initial founding of the nation-state of Israel, there has developed a more noticeable division within American evangelical premillennialists. There are those who follow historic premillennialism, the oldest form of premillennialism, a form that can be traced back to the second-century patristics of the church such as Papias, Justin Martyr and Irenaeus.[25] Others advocate a more novel and recent form of premillennialism known as dispensational premillennialism, a view that, as was already indicated, goes back only to the nineteenth century and John Nelson Darby. This more recent form of premillennialism gained predominance at the turn of the century and is often found associated with evangelical "fundamentalism."[26]

This fundamentalist wing of those who now call themselves evangelicals (most have dropped calling themselves fundamentalists) emerged in the earlier part of the century in connection with the conservative-modernist controversies, a battle that was engaged with liberal theological factions in the mainline Protestant churches. A paradoxical phenomenon can be found in a number of fundamentalist-evangelicals who had a tangible sincere and genuine love for Jews, but also found themselves voicing occasionally anti-Semitic statements. As historian George Marsden observes, between the two wars, fundamentalists "could be both pro-Zionist and somewhat anti-Semitic, favoring the return of Jews to Israel, which would lead eventually to their conversion; yet in the meantime especially distrusting apostate Jews."[27] While they tried to distance themselves from any form of anti-Semitism, they still believed that anti-Semitism was clearly predicted for the last days.

These controversies also spawned a number of evangelical Bible institutes such as, Moody Bible Institute, Multnomah School of the Bible, the Bible Institute of Los Angeles, the Philadelphia School of the Bible, and many others. "Almost without exception, the institutes taught the new [dispensational] 'premillennialism.'"[28] Almost all these Bible schools offered training in Jewish missions especially if they were located in cities

25. Craig L. Blomberg and Sung Wook Chung, eds., *A Case for Historic Premillennialism: An Alternative to "Left Behind" Eschatology* (Grand Rapids: Baker Academic, 2009), 110–13.

26. Weber, *Living in the Shadow of the Second Coming*, 162.

27. Ibid., 188.

28. Ibid., 34.

heavily populated by Jewish residents. Some serious problems inevitably occurred. However, as historian Weber concludes,

> Even though Christian missionaries tended to turn Jewish con-verts into Gentiles, for the most part they were sincerely and deeply concerned about them. They recognized them as the people of God who, as premillennialists pointed out, would one day in the future receive all of the divine promises made to their fathers. Premillinnialists, therefore, were fierce opponents of anti-Semitism in any form, and they frequently called them-selves the friends of Israel.
>
> Yet there was an ironic ambivalence in the premillennialist attitude toward Jews. On the one hand, Jews were God's chosen people and heirs to the promises; but their rejection of Jesus as Messiah placed them in open rebellion against God and ensured their eventual rendezvous with Antichrist during the great trib-ulation . . . Accordingly, at times premillennialists sounded anti-Semitic. Despite their claims that anti-Semitism was a gross and unexcusable sin against God, some leaders of the movement acted like representatives of American anti-Semitism.[29]

Following the establishment of the State of Israel and the Six Day War, a number of dispensationalists began to wed their interpretations of biblical passages directly with analyses of specific geopolitical events in a manner like putting pieces of a grand puzzle together to fit their perceived plan of the last days events. Hal Lindsey's best selling, *The Late Great Planet Earth* (1970) (and other pieces since) is an example of this approach to world events and the dispensational schematic. Perhaps this is a way of dealing with the chaotic, unsettling events of world history and personal distress in life. For others it may be a means of bringing more people into God's kingdom through Christ. Others may be attracted sim-ply because they believe the Bible teaches it, and they want to be faithful to the Scriptures. There are many varieties of expression of evangelical premillennialism today at the end of the twentieth and during the first quarter of the twenty-first century, and we might mention the Interna-tional Christian Embassy in Jerusalem (ICEJ) and the Christians United for Israel (CUFI) organizations on one end of the spectrum. Institutions

---

29. Ibid., 154; see also Robert Michael, *A Concise History of American Antisemi-tism* (Lanham, MD: Rowan & Littlefield, 2005).

such as Dallas Theological Seminary and Biola University in Los Angeles stand on the other side.[30]

However, evangelicalism is not limited to the millenialists (pre- or post-). There is a considerable evangelical constituency of nonmillennial (or *a*millennial) persuasion that can be found scattered in the Protestant mainline bodies and even in Roman Catholic and Eastern Orthodox churches. These evangelical Christians are generally amillennialists or historical premillennialists or postmillennialists.[31]

This type of evangelical Christian may view with some skepticism any theological significance to the establishment of a Jewish State in Israel especially in light of the perceived issues of Palestinian injustices, displacements, settlements, and land occupation. While not denying the right of the Jewish people to have a legal homeland of their own, many would not see this in terms of either divine right or the fulfillment of biblical prophecies that is signaling the end of days or the soon return of Jesus and the Jews' conversion to Christ. Issues of justice have taken central place, not the fulfillment of biblical land promises. Key New Testament passages and their interpretation, such as Rom 2:25–29; 9–11; and Gal 6:16, are understood differently from the way the premillennialists read them. This leads to important questions as to how the terms *people of God* and *Israel* are to be understood vis-à-vis ethnic Israel and today's Judaism. In contrast dispensational premillennialism is almost always associated with the view that biblical prophecies are being fulfilled today. I will probe this area and its implications to *Nostra Aetate* further in the essay.

---

30. Stephen Spector, *Evangelicals and Israel: The Story of American Christian Zionism* (New York: Oxford University Press, 2009), 165ff. Spector, a Jew and university English professor, uses a journalistic method of sketching a critical yet more positive view of Christian Zionism's American political entwinement than prior studies by Weber and Sizer. "Professor Spector's original interviews with 100 evangelicals, American government officers and Jewish leaders, and Israeli officials, along with other research, reveal the range of other motivations" that Christian Zionists have had for supporting the Israeli State than getting the Jews back to Palestine so they could be converted and the second coming would occur (http://www.jnf.org/about-jnf/in-your-area/speakers/stephen-spector.html/).

31. Timothy P. Weber, "Dispensational and Historic Premillennialism as Popular Millennial Movements," in Blomberg and Chung, eds., *A Case for Historic Premillennialism*, 1–22.

CURRENT EVANGELICAL DISCUSSIONS
WITH THE JEWISH RELIGIOUS COMMUNITY
SINCE VATICAN II

With the above, hardly adequate sketch of evangelicals and their Jewish relations since the eighteenth century, we can now attempt to examine what, if anything, has taken place in America within this diverse segment of the Christian community since Vatican II's *Nostra Aetate* declaration (1965). Any attempt to describe this landscape must face an almost impossible task of looking at a kaleidoscope of multifaceted colors and trying to identify a few that might have greater significance in understanding the whole.

Spawned by *Nostra Aetate* there followed in the next decade numerous joint meetings between Jews and Roman Catholics, Jews and Greek Orthodox, and Jews with mainline Protestant Churches (Episcopal/Anglican, Presbyterian, United Methodist, United Church of Christ, Baptist, Congregationalist, and Lutheran). However, these mainline churches were experiencing continuing declines in membership. It was then that the Jews discovered a large, unknown entity of Christians that simply identified themselves as evangelicals, comprising millions of Americans.

So Jews and evangelicals began a similar attempt to understand and respect each other. Perhaps they had something in common at the start. They were both people that were decentralized in authority structures, largely unknown to each other, and (to the general populace) often stereotyped, misunderstood, and misrepresented in the media. Evangelicals tended also to be located more in the South and Southeast parts of the country, while main Jewish populations lived in the Northeast and the upper Midwest; these distinct locations for the populations allowed fewer actual contacts between them. Although smaller regional or institutional meetings were occurring here and there involving Jews and evangelicals in conversations, the first major denominational meeting was with the Southern Baptists in Louisville, Kentucky, in 1969. Jointly sponsored by the American Jewish Committee (AJC) and the Home Mission Board of the Southern Baptist Convention, the conference was held at the Southern Baptist Theological Seminary.

The first national interdenominational meetings were held in 1975 in New York at the Calvary Church under the joint sponsorship of the AJC (Marc Tannenbaum and A. James Rudin) and the Institute of Holy Land Studies, an evangelical study institute located in Jerusalem on

Mount Zion.[32] There was some uneasiness on both sides as we were not sure of what motives brought our dialogue partners to such a meeting. Most of us left sensing respect and trust toward those we met, while at the same time we realized also and articulated matters of deep difference.

Christianity Today and the AJC (A. James Rudin and Marc Tannenbaum) sponsored the second national meeting at the Trinity Evangelical Divinity School in Deerfield, Illinois, in 1980. Different formats were introduced but with the same wide variety of topics and responses—with both continuing and new participants.

In 1984 a third national gathering of similar composition took place at Gordon College in Massachusetts under the joint sponsorship of A. James Rudin from the AJC, and Professor Marvin R. Wilson, a distinguished evangelical Old Testament scholar from Gordon College and a participant in the two previous national meetings. All three of these proceedings were published and have been widely read and cited.[33]

As a participant in these three discussions, I can testify that they were stimulating, eye-opening, very fruitful, sometimes tense, but friendly and trust building. At no time did I feel inhibited in expressing my own reading of Scripture and my faith commitment. Yet we all learned to do this in a way that respected the other's understandings.

There were local and regional attempts to foster evangelical-Jewish discussions across America in the nineties. For example, Rabbi Yechiel Eckstein, then with the Chicago office of the Anti-Defamation League (ADL), brought evangelicals together with representatives of the Jewish religious community from the greater Chicago area for regular discussions around numerous topics of mutual interest for several years. I myself was one of the members of this helpful interchange. These meetings eventually ceased when Eckstein decided to establish his International Fellowship of Christians and Jews (IFCJ) organization and found greater

32. Evangelical leaders among others included Professor Marvin Wilson (Gordon College) and Dr. Douglas Young, founder and President of the American Institute of Holy Land Studies on Mt. Zion, Jerusalem (now The Jerusalem University College). About twenty-five Jewish representatives and the like number of evangelicals gathered.

33. Marc H. Tanenbaum et al., eds., *Evangelicals and Jews in Conversation on Scripture, Theology, and History* (Grand Rapids: Baker, 1978); Marc H. Tanenbaum et al., eds., *Evangelicals and Jews in an Age of Pluralism* (Grand Rapids: Baker, 1984); A. James Rudin and Marvin R. Wilson, eds., *A Time to Speak: The Evangelical-Jewish Encounter* (Grand Rapids: Eerdmans, 1987). Following these conferences Dr. Wilson published his highly read and respected book, *Our Father Abraham: Jewish Roots of the Christian Faith* (Grand Rapids: Eerdmans, 1989).

enthusiasm and monetary support for his vision with charismatic evangelicals such as Pat Robertson.

National meetings between Jews and evangelicals were again resumed in 2009 in Washington DC, convened under the leadership of evangelicals David Neff, Ron Sider, and Joel Hunter; and from the Jewish side by Rabbi Yehiel Poupko, Ethan Felson, and Rabbi Steven Gutow. These yearly meetings continue. There are between twenty and twenty-five participants from each community drawn from institutions, organizations, churches, and synagogues across America and broadly representative of the different branches of each community. The agenda in some ways has revisited previous discussion topics but new ones as well and with almost a totally new group of persons on both sides from those involved in the earlier conferences. Two discussion documents were presented at the 2013 meeting: one titled "An Evangelical Statement on the Jewish People," and the other, "A Jewish Statement on Evangelical Christianity." These were draft discussion statements and with a number of comments voiced on each will no doubt undergo changes before any final documents are accepted.

Additionally, the national group has discussed a preliminary-guidelines document on how the Palestinian-Israeli discussions can go forward without anti-Semitic or anti-Judaism statements and yet with openness to criticisms of specific Israeli government policies. We have not yet found a way acceptable to both parties to include Messianic Jewish participants in the discussions. However, there is hope that this might be bridged in the future.

EVANGELICAL DOCUMENTARY STATEMENTS ABOUT JEWS AND JUDAISM SINCE VATICAN II

Statements on evangelical relations to Jews and Judaism exist but are not plentiful. This probably can be related to the lack of any centralized authority except where there is an evangelical denominational identity, such as the Assemblies of God, or the Southern Baptist Convention, or the Presbyterian Church of America.

The following references are representative and are not intended to be exhaustive.

Several documents have emerged in evangelical circles, which were generated due to the rise of Jewish evangelicals, who engaged in both the formation of Messianic congregations separate from Gentile churches and in Jewish-led evangelism to non-Messianic Jews.

The Willowbank Declaration on the Christian Gospel and the Jewish People was an earlier and longer piece formulated by an international Consultation on the Gospel and the Jewish People (LCJE) in April 1989 at Willowbank, Bermuda, and sponsored by the World Evangelical Alliance (WEA) and more recently endorsed (2008) by the Lausanne Consultation for Jewish Evangelism (LCJE). These men and women were prominent evangelical leaders and scholars from around the world, from different churches and theological traditions. The main concern as expressed in the introduction to the declaration was explained as the confusion in the Christian communities about whether Jews needed to be evangelized equally along with other Gentile peoples of the world. In a lengthy series of twenty-seven affirmations and denials the document strongly supports Jewish evangelism and denies the two-covenant view that would argue that Jews have their own separate covenant and do not need the gospel for their salvation. Further, it fully supports Messianic Jews and their right to follow Jewish practices and worship styles in their communities even though they may differ from the largely Gentile congregations.

However, there are also strong statements condemning anti-Semitism in any form as "wicked and shameful" and acknowledging that "the church has in the past been much to blame for tolerating and encouraging it and for condoning anti-Jewish actions on the part of individuals and governments." "We pledge ourselves to resist every form of anti-Semitism." The declaration also calls for God's and the Jewish people's forgiveness for Christian complicity in the Jews' past unjust sufferings and exhortations to show genuine love to Jews "in every possible way" because of God's gift through them of the Jewish Messiah and Savior.

There is an important statement parallel to *Nostra Aetate*: "We deny that it is right to single out the Jewish people for putting Jesus to death." "WE AFFIRM THAT Jewish people have an ongoing part in God's plan." The document also contains helpful references to the land controversy: "Concerned about humanity everywhere, we are resolved to uphold the right of Jewish people to a just and peaceful existence everywhere, both in the land of Israel and in their communities throughout the world." Yet it calls for justice in land issues: "WE AFFIRM THAT the Jewish quest for a homeland with secure borders and a just peace has our support. WE DENY THAT any biblical link between the Jewish people and the land of Israel justifies actions that contradict biblical ethics and constitute oppression of people-groups or individuals."

On the other hand, there are statements that will not be that welcomed in the Jewish community: "WE AFFIRM THAT the concern to point Jewish people to faith in Jesus Christ which the Christian church has historically felt and shown was right. WE DENY THAT there is any truth in the widespread notion that evangelizing Jews is needless because they are already in covenant with God through Abraham and Moses and so are already saved despite their rejection of Jesus Christ as Lord and Saviour.

"WE AFFIRM THAT all endeavors to persuade others to become Christians should express love to them by respecting their dignity and integrity at every point, including parents' responsibility in the case of their children. WE DENY THAT coercive or deceptive proselytizing, which violates dignity and integrity on both sides, can ever be justified . . . WE AFFIRM THAT the existence of separate churchly organizations for evangelizing Jews, as for evangelizing any other particular human group, can be justified pragmatically, as an appropriate means of fulfilling the church's mandate to take the Gospel to the whole human race."

The following may be read as anti-Judaism: "WE AFFIRM THAT much of Judaism, in its various forms, throughout contemporary Israel and today's Diaspora, is a development out of, rather than as an authentic embodiment of, the faith, love and hope, that the Hebrew Scriptures teach. WE DENY THAT modern Judaism with its explicit negation of the divine person, work, and Messiah-ship of Jesus Christ contains within itself true knowledge of God's salvation."

As to dialogue and discussions with the Jewish community the document says,

"WE AFFIRM THAT dialogue with other faiths that seeks to transcend stereo-types [*sic*] of them based on ignorance, and to find common ground and to share common concerns, is an expression of Christian love that should be encouraged. WE DENY THAT dialogue that explains the Christian faith without seeking to persuade the dialogue partners of its truth and claims is a sufficient expression of Christian love."[34]

This is an important document that I feel would embody the thinking and beliefs of many of today's Protestant evangelicals about Jewish and evangelical relations and Messianic Judaism. The Declaration is not, however, above some points of criticism especially by those evangelicals

34. http://www.lcje.net/willowbank.html/.

who have had sustained contact with the Jewish religious community in America over a number of years.

Other lengthy evangelical statements that have also the above concerns are found in the Lausanne Committee on World Evangelization publication, "Occasional Paper (LOP) No. 60" titled "Jewish Evangelism. A Call to the Church" (2005).[35] This paper is a response to the statement issued by the Jewish community called, "*Dabru Emet* [*Speak the Truth*]: A Jewish Statement on Christians and Christianity," signed by more than two hundred Jewish scholars and published in *First Things* (November 2000).[36] In the *Dabru Emet* statement that affirms many commonalities of the two communities, it is also stated that from the Jewish viewpoint Christianity and Judaism are two separate religions, each with their own covenants, and that both are valid ways of relating to God.[37] This evangelical and Messianic Jewish document should be read by all Jews as well as evangelicals, because it clearly sets forth why evangelicals cannot accept the two-covenant understanding. Likewise the *Dabru Emet* statement is also must reading to understand the current Jewish consensus.

Another more broad and recent evangelical statement is the one issued by the World Evangelical Alliance (WEA) in March 2008, signed by over fifty evangelical leaders and institutions and titled "The Gospel and the Jewish People: An Evangelical Statement." It affirms in briefer form the main points of the previous evangelical statements.[38]

A few statements from evangelical denominations can be found. The Southern Baptist Convention has issued periodic "Resolutions," beginning in 1873 with a Resolution on Anti-Semitism, which reads: "RESOLVED, that we do gratefully remember this day our unspeakable indebtedness to the seed of Abraham, and devoutly recognize their peculiar claims upon the sympathies and prayer of all gentile Christians, and we hereby record our earnest desire to partake in the glorious work

35. http://www.lausanne.org/en/documents/lops/877-lop-60.html/.

36. http://www.firstthings.com/article/2000/11/dabru-emet-a-jewish-statement-on-christians-and-christianity/.

37. The two-covenant view was originally proposed by the German Jewish philosopher of religion Franz Rosenzweig (1886–1929) in Rosenzweig, *The Star of Redemption* (1922) as cited by Nahum N. Glatzer, *Franz Rosenzweig: His Life and Thought* (2nd rev. ed., New York: Schocken, 1961), 341.

38. See www.worldea.org/.

of hastening the day when the superscription of the cross shall be the confession of all Israel 'Jesus of Nazareth, the king of the Jews.'"[39]

The most recent statement was occasioned by the sixtieth anniversary of the founding of the State of Israel in June 2008: "RESOLVED, That the messengers to the Southern Baptist Convention meeting in Indianapolis, Indiana, 2008, rejoice with Israel in this milestone achievement, and be it further RESOLVED: That we join in prayer for the peace of Jerusalem (Psalm 122:6–7), calling upon world leaders to renounce the growing tide of anti-Semitism; and be it finally RESOLVED: That Southern Baptists express our appreciation and pledge our prayers for Israel, the birthplace of our Lord and a bastion of democracy in the Middle East."[40]

A rather remarkedly balanced premillennial statement from the Assemblies of God denomination is on their website; while affirming the church's belief that in the Jews' return to their land prophecy heralding the last days is being fulfilled, nevertheless the statement calls for denouncing supersessionist or replacement views, anti-Semitism, and extreme Christian Zionist views that posit "an unqualified support for a non-Christian nation to be interpreted by Palestinians as setting aside our basic Christian principles of justice, love for enemies, respect for human life, honesty, and fairness." It is one of those few evangelical statements that takes into consideration the present Israeli and Palestinian conflicts and does so with sensitivity to both sides.[41]

Finally, but not comprehensively, there are two statements that have been drafted but not finalized from the last unofficial meeting of over forty various national and local Jewish and evangelical organizations at their annual session in Washington DC in June 2013.[42]

Evangelical Institutional Changes since Vatican II

In looking at many of the evangelical educational institutions in America, there is sparse evidence that most of the colleges and seminaries have entered into serious discussions with the Jewish religious community.

---

39. http://www.sbc.net/resolutions/search/results.asp?query=Jews/.

40. Southern Baptist Convention, "In Celebration of Israel's 60th Anniversary, Indianapolis, Indiana, 2008," http://www.sbc.net/resolutions/1186/in-celebration-of-israels-60th-anniversary/. Also see nos. 479, 914, 437, 653, 654, 1112, 1116, 1186.

41. See http://ag.org/top/Beliefs/topics/sptlissues_israel.cfm/.

42. The statements have not received any formal ratification.

Wheaton College and Graduate School (Illinois) has had an ongoing group (three or four meetings a year for the last eight years) of five rabbis and five Wheaton faculty members, plus the presidents of the institution during this time. Individual faculty have regularly invited rabbis to lecture in classes dealing with Jewish thought and history and on occasion have sponsored an extended lectureship series by a Jewish scholar that is open to the public.[43] Wheaton has no continuing-educational courses or opportunities for students to regularly access firsthand Jewish scholars or rabbis.

Gordon College (Massachusetts) has under the longtime leadership of Dr. Marvin Wilson sponsored not only National Jewish-Evangelical conferences but local events involving Jews and evangelicals in conversation. Courses are offered in Judaism with Jewish scholars frequently participating.

Calvin Theological Seminary (Michigan) has participated for the last twelve years in a regional dialogue with the Jewish community, sponsored by the West Michigan Academic Consortium. During the last years, the focus of the group has shifted from Christian-Jewish dialogue to Christian, Jewish, and Muslim dialogue, and now (more recently) to interfaith dialogue. Calvin is part of the Christian Reformed Church. The denomination used to have a mission to the Jews in Chicago, New York, and Washington DC. Over a period of time, all these have been discontinued.

Westmont College (California) has visiting rabbis invited to teach.

On the other hand, a promising recent initiative at Nyack College (New York) has created the new Graduate Program in Ancient Judaism & Christian Origins, involving both Jewish and Christian scholars in collaboration. Professor Dr. Steven Notely, a former PhD student under David Flusser at the Hebrew University in Jerusalem, is the director of this new program at Nyack.[44] This may become a model for other evangelical institutions. We are not yet at the point of formal appointments of adjunct Jewish professors at the universities and seminaries.

Fuller Theological Seminary in Pasadena, California, has for the last twelve years led an ongoing rabbi-pastor dialogue involving twenty rabbis and forty Fuller alums, faculty and students, and the seminary president—these meet periodically through the year. The Colorado Springs

43. Rabbi Asher Finkle from Seton Hall University: multiple evening lectures on "A Jewish Perspective on the Gospels."

44. http://www.nyack.edu/content/AJCOExplore/ and http://ajcoconference2013-eorg.eventbrite.com/.

campus also holds cosponsored dialogue events. A Fuller student has been funded by the Henry Luce Foundation to establish a journal called *Evangelical Interfaith Dialogue*. At least one course has been inaugurated to expose students to Jewish faith and practice.

According to reports I have received, there are no direct institutional relations with the Jewish religious community at Dallas Theological Seminary (in Texas), Beeson Divinity School (in Alabama), Southwestern Baptist Theological Seminary (in Texas), Southeastern Baptist Theological Seminary (in North Carolina), Trinity Evangelical Divinity School (in Illinois), Fuller Theological Seminary (in California), Northern Seminary (in Illinois), Biola University and Talbot Theological Seminary (in California), and Whitworth University (in Washington State).

As to evangelical churches, I know of only one that identifies itself as evangelical that regularly invites Jewish rabbis and scholars to speak at services on Sunday mornings. In turn the lead pastor has spoken in most of the major synagogues in the Baltimore area.[45] There may be others, but this would still be a rarity—probably in the synagogues as well.

Numerous evangelical scholars are engaged in collaborative writing projects with Jewish scholars and rabbis on a variety of topics. Those evangelicals whom I have contacted are greatly indebted to and have become good friends with those who are their Jewish publishing partners.[46] It may be a surprise to those not overly familiar with the evangelical community that there is a plethora of new published materials in many areas of history, theology, sociology, the land of Israel, and biblical studies related to the Jewish and evangelical interface that have been coming forth from several of the evangelical publishers.[47] *Christianity Today* magazine has also over the years highlighted evangelical-Jewish relations and issues.

45. New Hope Community Church, Pikesville, MD; Rev. Jason A. Poling, DMin, Senior Pastor.

46. A few examples would be Tremper Longmann III at Westmont College, Lynn Cohick and Daniel Block at Wheaton College, James Edwards at Whitworth College, and Bruce Chilton at Bard College. A number of others could be cited.

47. Eerdmans, for some time, and more recently Brazos Press, in particular, have been publishing numerous books on this subject. At least one Christian organization, World Vision, is beginning to work on a dialogue project with Jewish rabbis.

Current Issues, Tensions, Theologies, and Progress

Here I want to describe some of the issues that have arisen in the discussions between Jews and evangelicals, and also between evangelicals of different viewpoints on Jews and the land and nation of Israel/Palestine. Space only allows the barest of treatment in each category and it should be recognized that the major focus of this book deals with the Jewish interface with the Roman Catholic Church and its Vatican II statement on the Jews (*Nostra Aetate*).

Jesus the Jew and the Church of Jews and Gentiles

In more recent Christian research of the biblical texts of both testaments there has been a trend to locate the materials in their Jewish-worldview context. This is especially significant in the New Testament, where to more correctly understand its main character, Jesus of Nazareth, we are recovering the historical reality of Jesus, his life, teachings, condemnation, and death as a first-century Jew in a Jewish context. This Jewish context is a postbiblical Judaism since no scriptural revelation by a prophet was given for nearly four hundred years, and Judaism continued to develop during that period. Likewise Jesus's Jewish life, teachings, sufferings, and conflicts with certain religious leaders of his day must be understood in the context of this postbiblical Judaism—a Judaism that underwent further significant change after the destruction of Jerusalem and the Temple in 70 CE. Understanding this Jewish context in the best possible way will also shed light on what Messianic faith developed in this context.

Anti-Semitism, Anti-Judaism in the History of the Church

Since Vatican II evangelicals for the most part have become aware and have responded with sadness, regret, repentance, and disbelief to the "history of contempt" for Jews by the church down through the ages (the *Adversus Judaeos* Tradition). This is witnessed to by the statements that are issuing from evangelical denominations, institutions, and individual leaders, who have consistently acknowledged with deep regret and repentance the sad history of the Christian treatment of Jews and Judaism. While contempt and discrimination toward Jews, as well as anti-Semitism, have often been rooted in the surrounding pagan cultures and in governmental actions, Christians have not resisted sufficiently this influence from attaching itself to the practices and language in the churches at large and also in the evangelical communities. For example, we can note this language of contempt even in John Wesley himself (in the eighteenth century). When commenting on John 12:39–40 he says,

> St. John assigns this very reason for the Jews not understanding the things of God; namely, that in consequence of their preceding sins, and willful rejecting the light, God had now delivered them up to Satan, who had blinded them past recovery. Over and over, when they might have seen, they would not; they shut their eyes against the light: And now they cannot see, God having given them up to an indiscernible mind: Therefore they do not believe, because that Isaiah said (that is, because of the reason given in that saying of Isaiah), "He hath blinded their eyes, and hardened their hearts, that they should not see with their eyes, nor understand with their hearts, and be converted, and I should heal them" . . . but his Spirit strives with them no longer, and then Satan hardens them effectually.[48]

Likewise, Jonathan Edwards (in the eighteenth century), commenting on Matthew 12:32, says,

> I shall add no more, but my fervent prayers to God, to bless both the author and his discourse, and that he would pour out his Spirit yet more abundantly, both on America and all the British dominions, and thus he would hasten the glory of the latter days, when the Jews shall be brought in with the fullness of the Gentiles, and that all the kingdoms of the world may become the kingdoms of the Lord and of his Christ, that he may reign forever and ever! Amen and Amen.
>
> They not only went on still in that career of corruption which had been increasing from the time of the Maccabees; but Christ's coming, his doctrine and miracles, the preaching of his followers, and the glorious things that attended the same, were the occasion, through their perverse misimprovement, of an infinite increase of their wickedness. They crucified the Lord of glory, with the utmost malice and cruelty, and persecuted his followers; they pleased not God, and were contrary to all men, they went on to grow worse and worse, till they filled up the

---

48. Cited in Robert Michael, *A Concise History of American Antisemitism* (Lanham, MD: Rowman & Littlefield, 2005), 62–63.

measure of their sin, and out of God's sight, with unspeakably greater tokens of the divine abhorrence and indignation, than in the days of Nebuchadnezzar. The greater part of the whole nation were slain, and the rest were scattered abroad through the earth in the most abject and forlorn circumstances. And in the same spirit of unbelief and malice against Christ and the gospel, and in their miserable dispersed circumstances, do they remain to this day.[49]

In hindsight we can say that to remain silent in the face of these statements is tantamount to voicing approval of them.

TWO MODERN EVENTS THAT HAVE CHANGED CHRISTIAN PERCEPTIONS

The first event was The *Shoah* (Heb. "catastrophic destruction") (1939–45). The effect of the Holocaust, an event that some of us remember in our childhood, is calling forth profound reflection on how such a horrible human evil could have possibly happened in our "enlightened" age—six million Jews murdered and cremated! How could the Jewish people suffer so much pain and loss without the church or the largely Christian nations raising sufficient inquiry, protests, and effective actions against such terrible ethnic killings? As one evangelical Anglican theologian has well said, "We must of course recognize fully that there can be no complacency about the past. It was not merely neo-paganism, but Christian complicity with neo-paganism, that sent millions of Jews to their deaths in our own century. Christian arrogance must be renounced entirely."[50] How this reality has affected traditional evangelical mission to the Jews as a people group will be discussed in a following section on the issue of Jewish evangelism.

In addition to the catastrophe of the Holocaust, the political establishment of the State of Israel in Palestine (in 1948) has impacted Christian views on Judaism. By British mandate and United Nations partition of the land, the Jews were given a portion of the territories roughly in the areas of ancient Israel. The sovereign rule of a Jewish State was their first homeland for over two thousand years.

49. Cited in ibid.

50. N. T. Wright, *The Climax of the Covenant: Christ and the Law in Pauline Theology* (Minneapolis: Fortress, 1992), 253.

War immediately broke out, and territorial lines were redrawn, and many who were in the land suffered displacements—both Jews and other residents of the areas. The nation-state of Israel was recognized by the international community with protest and rejection by certain Arab national entities. Subsequent wars expanded Israel's territories even farther. The conflict over territories has continued to be a thorn in the sides of both the Jews and the Palestinians that live in the land.

This division has spilled over into the two religious communities: the Christian and the Jewish. It has also divided the evangelical community over differing theological views of the religious status of the Jewish State (with its relation to the scenario of the end-times, the return of Christ, and the conversion of the Jewish people), and over continuing political issues of justice for the Palestinians. On the Jewish side as well, debate rages over the issue of security and expanded land appropriation for settlements. The one-state solution and the two-state solution continue to be argued among Palestinians.[51] While the Jews favor for the most part a two-state solution, there has been no significant progress between the political parties.[52] Most mainstream evangelicals go on record as favoring both the security of Israel and justice for the Palestinians. However, in actuality few keep the balance and instead lean in favor of one over the other. Jews are caught in a dilemma: Liberal Protestants are enemies of Israel when it concerns the State of Israel but love Jews as a religious community that does not need to believe in Jesus to be saved. On the other hand, many evangelicals love or support the Israeli State but have an offensive belief that make them enemies to Jews, namely, that Jews need faith in Jesus to be saved.

Evangelicals are also divided over whether the State of Israel should be viewed as having some theological (prophetic) significance, or whether it is another expression of an oppressed people seeking national

51. Fr. Elias Chacour, a Palestinian Christian Israeli, Archbishop of Galilee, favors a one–state solution. See Elias Chacour, with David Hazard, *Blood Brothers* (Grand Rapids: Chosen Books, 2003); Elias Chacour, with Mary E. Jensen, *We Belong to the Land: The Story of a Palestinian Who Lives for Peace and Reconciliation* (Notre Dame, IN: University of Notre Dame Press, 2001).

52. See "Proposed Guideline for Evangelical-Jewish Conversation about the Israel-Palestinian Conflict." See also for both Christian sides of the issue of the land: Salim J. Munayer and Lisa Loden, eds., *The Land Cries Out: Theology of the Land in the Israeli-Palestinian Context* (Eugene, OR: Cascade Books, 2011); and Paul Alexander, ed., *Christ at the Checkpoint: Theology in the Service of Justice and Peace* (Eugene Oregon: Pickwick Publications, 2012).

liberation, which is a large part of the cultural and historical landscape since the beginning of the twentieth century throughout the Western world. If the land is a mere national liberation movement, however well justified, it must be judged by the same moral criteria as other emergent national liberation movements.

Evangelicals who are anti-Jewish Zionists and anti-Christian Zionists appear to base their criticisms of the Jewish State on the assumption that most of the residents and the government itself reside in Israel for theological reasons, and seek to hold them accountable to the biblical commandments of the Torah and the Prophets. What many evangelicals do not recognize is that only a small minority of the residents of Israel see a theological or religious significance to the national entity. As the Jews present at our 2013 meeting in Washington DC stated, "For the overwhelming majority of the Jewish people, Zionism is the national liberation movement of the Jewish people; nothing more and nothing less. Like all national liberation movements, it seeks sovereignty and self-determination in its ancestral homeland."[53]

Finally, I do not think that most evangelicals realize how much the land of Israel and nationhood now form a fundamental marker for Jewish identity along with God, Torah, *Mitzvot*, and peoplehood.[54] Therefore, to criticize the legitimacy of the existence of the State of Israel (not specific policies) is viewed as anti-Semitic by the Jewish people. This presents a challenge to evangelicals who are working with Palestinian Christian churches in particular as to how they can speak critically about the Jewish State's policies and actions using historically or culturally sensitive metaphors—but not with anti-Semitic language. Practicing such sensitivity would include (1) refusing to use a double standard when judging Israel (i.e., applying standards of biblical justice to Israel and equally also to other nation-states, (2) avoiding demonizing Israel (i.e., not seeing the good along with what needs to change), and (3) showing respect to Judaism as it is believed and practiced by Jews today.

---

53. See "Proposed Guideline for Evangelical-Jewish Conversation about the Israel-Palestinian Conflict," unpublished, presented to participants for discussion.

54. See "Jewish Statement on Evangelical Christianity," unpublished.

CHRISTIAN ZIONISM, AND CHRISTIAN ANTIZIONISM

We have traced the beginnings and influence of Christian Zionism in establishing the State of Israel in an earlier section. There we pointed out that not all evangelicals share this "end-of-times" viewpoint. The beginning of the State of Israel and questions about the dispossessions, displacements, camps, the occupation of Palestinian lands by the government of Israel (West Bank), and the continual building of Jewish settlements on Palestinian-occupied land has produced a rift in the evangelical communities—some evangelicals siding with the Palestinians and others with the Israelis. Unfortunately, some extremists on the Christian Zionist side, who have taken the view of Israel (right or wrong) on every issue regardless of the government policy, have created an anti-Christian Zionist reactionary group among some evangelicals who favor Palestinian rights. They accuse the Christian Zionists of not only mistaken interpretation of Scripture but of supporting injustice and oppression of the Palestinians and the Palestinian Christian Churches.[55]

Jews care little about this squabble unless Jews come off badly as a result (i.e., if there is a continuation of the contempt-of-Jews tradition or a demonizing and delegitimizing of the State of Israel that in their minds also invalidates their chosen way of identifying themselves as Jews). The middle of both sides claims that they support the safe continuance of the State and also the just treatment of the Palestinians. However, in practice it seems that most end up favoring one side over the other. Only one group to my knowledge seems to actually maintain a credible balance in practice between the two parties. (This group is the Telos Group, in Washington DC, led by Todd Detherage).[56]

---

55. It is difficult to sort out and brand different organizations as to where they fall on this spectrum. For example, some Christian Zionist organizations are identified with Christians United For Israel (CUFI), Bridges for Peace, the International Christian Embassy in Jerusalem, Institute for Hebraic-Christian Studies, Eagle's Wings, International Fellowship of Christians and Jews; anti-Christian Zionists are best illustrated with Evangelicals for Middle East Understanding (EMEU), and the Sabeel Ecumenical Liberation Theology Center in Jerusalem. For a more sympathetic and yet critical view of Christian Zionism and of these and other organizations involved in this debate among evangelicals, see the Jewish author's treatment in Stephen Spector, *Evangelicals and Israel: The Story of American Christian Zionism* (New York: Oxford University Press, 2009).

56. http://www.telosgroup.org/

JEWISH EVANGELISM, EVANGELICALS, AND *NOSTRA AETATE*

Far more controversial in the Jewish communities is the issue of *evangelicals seeking to evangelize Jews* as a people group. Interestingly, the earlier premillennial evangelicals continued to practice both the support of Israel and missions to the Jews as a people group to win them to the gospel of Jesus (Shaftesbury, Blackstone, et al.). Now, since the *Shoah* (Holocaust) and the founding of the State of Israel, some evangelical organizations and churches, it is claimed, have backed off from evangelizing Jews and instead have heavily supported humanitarian efforts to the Jews with promised or understood agreements not to evangelize Jews in these organizations.[57] However, virtually every major evangelical institution, denomination, and parachurch organization that I have inquired into, including the World Evangelical Alliance (WEA) and the Lausanne Committee have said they continue to support Jewish missions with approaches that pass the integrity, sensitivity, full respect, love, noncoercion, and transparency standards expected of all those who follow Jesus in a post-Holocaust age.[58] While the Jewish community continues to resist any attempts to evangelize Jewish people, some Jews argue that Christian witness to Jews is acceptable.[59]

---

57. See http://www.jewsforjesus.org/publications/newsletter/may-2009/01/.

58. The WEA statement, "The Berlin Declaration on the Uniqueness of Christ and Jewish Evangelism in Europe Today 2008," can be found at http://www.worldevangelicals.org/commissions/list/tc/49.htm/. It can also be found in the book by David Parker, ed., *Jesus, Salvation and the Jewish People: The Uniqueness of Jesus and Jewish Evangelism* (Milton Keynes, UK: Paternoster, 2011).

59. "I cannot, in conscience, oppose missionary activity to the Jews, and I endorse missionary witness to Christians. It is an activity I find ultimately unrewarding, for the activity is designed more to enable the missioner to witness to himself than to bring the unbeliever to believe. Needless to say, where the special psychology of the aggressor is self vindication, the temptation to misrepresent, to connive and insinuate, to deceive and to trick is often too great. But if to missionize is to bear witness, not to one's self but to the truth and it is in the discourse of truth that the missionary confronts the missionized, it is justified," Arthur A. Cohen, *The Myth of the Judeo-Christian Tradition* (New York: Schocken, 1971), 216–17.

MESSIANIC JUDAISM: AN UNBRIDGEABLE
DIFFERENCE BETWEEN JEWS AND EVANGELICALS?

Apparently an even more intractable roadblock, if there could be one, in Jewish and evangelical relations is the emergence, since the Holocaust and the establishment of the State of Israel (both in the 1940s), of what is called Messianic Judaism. Some Jews in every age have always accepted Jesus as the Jewish Messiah and Lord and generally found their way into largely Gentile churches to continue their relationship with and worship of the God of Israel. Today there has arisen a new phenomenon of Jews who find Jesus as their Savior and Lord, and who unite with other Jesus-believing Jews in communities where they desire to keep the law of Moses and Jewish customs that are not incompatible with their faith in Jesus as the Messiah.

That this view is receiving growing and worldwide support among evangelical leaders of many strands is evidenced by several documents that have been released. For example, the World Evangelical Alliance (WEA) issued a document of support in 2008 signed by fifty-seven evangelical leaders worldwide called "The Gospel and the Jewish People: An Evangelical Statement."[60] In it there is a strong commitment to stand against any and all "anti-Semitic words" or "deeds" and any use of "deception or coercion in evangelism." At the same time it affirms the justification of "those with specialized knowledge, history and skills to use these gifts to introduce individuals to the Messiah, and that includes those ministries specifically directed to the Jewish people." Additionally, "we reject the notion that it is deceptive for followers of Jesus Christ who were born Jewish to continue to identify as Jews (Romans 11:1)."[61]

Of course this is not acceptable to the Jewish community that views such an attempted combination of Jewish identity with faith in Jesus as cruel, grotesque, and dishonest. A Jew who accepts Jesus as Messiah is no longer a Jew but has changed his religion, because to be a Jew and practice Judaism is to be identified with a people who do not believe Jesus is Messiah and Lord. This is a difficult barrier to find a way over or around. N. T. Wright claims that the nineteenth-century concept of religions as separate, closed entities has muddied the waters so much as a basic assumption that we cannot see how a follower of Jesus can be at one and

---

60. See www.worldea.org/.

61. See the Assemblies of God Statement "Israel—the Church's Response," http://ag.org/top/Beliefs/topics/sptlissues_israel.cfm/.

the same time a faithful Jew. The Christian church is as much to blame for this dichotomy as the Jewish tradition.[62]

This forces believing Jews into forming separate congregations of Messianic Jews without the benefits of being recognized as part of the larger congregation of Israel. There does not seem to be a way around this impasse at present though there are Messianic Jews who are developing theologies that attempt to create bridges over the chasm.[63]

Historically, J. Denny Weaver comments recently in the *Christian Century*,

> Both Daniel Boyarin in *Border Lines* and John Howard Yoder in *Jewish-Christian Schism Revisited* have argued that for several centuries people who recognized Jesus as the Messiah and those who did not worshiped together in church or synagogue. In other words, disagreements on whether Jesus was the Messiah did not get one expelled from the community as a heretic. A division into mutually exclusive camps came later . . . Yoder identifies a possible end point in the fourth century when the Christians gained political power and could change the social meaning of their group. . . . Boyarin with the code of Theodosius in 438, which defined Christianity as the pure religion and Judaism as false.[64]

Both partners agreed that the "absence of a historical consensus on the finality of the schism indicates that Christians and Jews could even now still be engaged in an in-house debate on whether Jesus is the Messiah." Yoder argues that it was a "tragic" and "unnecessary" separation that did not have to be. Boyarin recognizes the logic and the attractiveness of that position but resists it because accepting it would mean at least a partial rejection of his own distinct tradition.

Others suggest as a way forward that we evangelicals could encourage a movement toward a more positive and appreciative view of rabbinic

---

62. N. T. Wright, *Paul and the Faithfulness of God*, parts 3 and 4 (Minneapolis: Fortress, 2013), 2:1408–34.

63. Mark S. Kinzer, *Postmissionary Messianic Judaism: Redefining Christian Engagement with the Jewish People* (Grand Rapids: Brazos, 2005); Markus Bockmuehl, *Jewish Law in Gentile Churches: Halakhah and the Beginning of Christian Public Ethics* (Grand Rapids: Baker Academic, 2003); Gerald R. McDermott, "Covenant, Mission, and Relating to the Other," in Robert W. Jenson and Eugene B. Korn, eds., *Covenant and Hope: Christian and Jewish Reflections* (Grand Rapids: Eerdmans, 2012), 19–39.

64. J. Denney Weaver, "Jewish and Pacifist," *Christian Century*, Nov. 27, 2013, 34–35.

Judaism not only as a worthy way of life for Jews (and possibly what has preserved them since 70 CE) but as a help also to us Gentile believers in understanding more accurately our Holy Scriptures and their largely Jewish context, and thus at least partially reverse centuries of anti-Judaism in the Christian church.[65]

Finally, reference should be made to what is being called "postmissionary Messianic Judaism" as the latest development in the tradition we have been exploring in this section and the attempts at healing the schism. In 2002 the Union of Messianic Jewish Congregations (UMJC) approved a statement embracing a bilateral ecclesiology that affirms both Jewish solidarity with the larger Jewish community and solidarity with the Gentile believing community that is "joined to Israel through the Messiah"; that affirms corporate and Jewish in nature; that affirms commitment to Yeshua the Messiah; that honors the covenantal responsibilities of Torah and Jewish Religious Tradition; that puts a priority on integration with the wider Jewish world, then to be followed by a vital corporate relationship with the Gentile Christian church; and that bears witness to Yeshua within the people of Israel, and to serve and to represent the "Jewish people within the body of the Messiah."[66]

Besides any evidence, that I am aware of, that this approach is working at all in connection with the wider Jewish community in America, there has been some penetrating critiques by evangelical Roman Catholics. Matthew Levering argues that *Lumen Gentium* supports instead a single ecclesiology and Christ as the "fulfillment" and "reconstituting" of Israel rather than Kinzer's bi-ecclesiology and "continuity" and "expansion" model of the relation of the Church and Israel.[67]

CONTEMPORARY EVANGELICAL THEOLOGIES OF THE NEW COVENANT, THE CHURCH AND THE JEWS

Evangelicals have been busy reexamining their theological understandings of Scripture as it relates to Jews, Judaism, the last days, Israel's election, enduring Jewish covenants including land promises, and what kind

---

65. Kinzer, *Postmissionary Messianic Judaism*, 265ff.

66. Kinzer, *Post-Missionary Messianic Judaism: Redefining Christian Engagement with the Jewish People* (Grand Rapids: Brazos, 2005), 299–302.

67. Mark S. Kinzer and Matthew Levering, "Messianic Gentiles & Messianic Jews," *First Things*, January 2009, 41. See http://www.firstthings.com/article/2009/01/005-messianic-gentiles-messianic-jews/.

of future the Bible does or does not project for corporate Israel. Several of these major models can be identified briefly without critique.

I have earlier mentioned the rise of dispensational premillennialism in the nineteenth century and especially its influence on British attitudes that led to the founding of the State of Israel along with its fostering of goodwill toward Jews in general and the increase of end-times prophetic fervor. This view, though under revision since the 1950s, still maintains a strict distinction between Israel and the church; a rapture theology (e.g., *The Left Behind* series), where the believing Christians are taken out from the earth before the judgments of God fall on an unbelieving world, including on Jews; the coming of Jesus back to a restored and converted Israel in the land of Palestine; and the literal fulfillment of all the promises made to Israel in Moses and the Prophets in an earthly rule of Christ for one thousand years before the new heavens and earth commence.

The institutional strength of this viewpoint continues in schools, seminaries, churches, parachurch organizations, and publishing houses. Certain Jewish organizations have benefited and joined efforts with Christian groups with this theology. These groups nevertheless remain staunchly opposed to the two-covenant viewpoint, and are zealous to show Christian love for and also including bringing the good news to Jews. Many are wholehearted or critical supporters of the State of Israel, and some more progressive types also favor support for the Palestinians where they feel they are being treated unjustly. Most have no contact with the present Jewish religious community.

To be distinguished from these dispensationalist premillennial groups are evangelicals who hold what is called a historic premillennialism viewpoint. Their views reflect the ancient church's eschatology more precisely. In the first place there is a methodological difference that can be expressed this way. The dispensational group reads the New Testament through the lens of the Old Testament, while the historic is just the reverse.[68]

Second, historic premillennial evangelicals do not believe in a secret coming of Christ to "rapture" the church away from the earth before the "great tribulation" and then followed by a later second "visible" coming to earth. There is only one second coming at which time God's promise of the land to Abraham (Gen 13:14–17) will be fulfilled, as Irenaeus says: "If, then, God promised him the inheritance of the land, yet he did

---

68. Blomberg and Chung, eds., *A Case for Historic Premillennialism*, 95.

not receive it during all the time of his sojourn here, it must be, that together with his seed, that is those who fear God and believe in Him, he shall receive it at the resurrection of the just. For his seed is the church, which receives the adoption to God through the Lord."[69] "Irenaeus does not say that the Jews forfeited the promise of the land through disobedience (as some amillennialists would say today), nor does he 'spiritualize' the promise of the land in order to argue that believers receive it in a non-physical way, nor does he try to dissociate the promise of the land from the New Testament church (as many dispensationalists would do). Rather, he insists that the promise of an earthly, material land will be fulfilled on earth."[70]

The more Reformed types of evangelical theologies have taken the view that there will be no earthly reign of Christ to come before the new heavens and earth are established (hence, *a*millennial). Further, there will be no large-scale final conversion of the Jewish people immediately proceeding the coming of Jesus, nor a return to the land of Palestine in the last days. The Jewish markers of land, Temple, Sabbath, circumcision, and food laws are all symbolical foreshadows of the final realities of the new covenant fulfilled in Christ. There are several different branches of this understanding. These distinctions can be seen in the way Paul's statement in Rom 11:26 (" . . . and so all Israel will be saved") is understood: (1) Calvin understood that "all Israel" included in this final salvation all the elect from both the nation of ethnic Israel and also from the Gentiles who would believe throughout history. He referred also to "the Israel of God" in Gal 6:16 as a parallel reference. Often overlooked are Calvin's differences from Luther on the relation of law and gospel. He conceived of a substantial unity between the law and the gospel more than Luther. Therefore, he is inclined to see the relationship between Israel and the church in a more positive light. While it cannot be denied that he occasionally had negative comments about the unfaithful Jews of both Testaments, his exegetical treatment of Rom 9–11 is most instructive and shows "he had a higher view of the Jewish people and Judaism than most of his contemporaries."[71]

---

69. Ibid., 121.

70. Ibid.

71. John Hesselink, "Calvin's Understanding of the Relation of the Church and Israel Based Largely on His Interpretation of Romans 9–11," *Ex Auditu*, 4 (1988) 59–69; see also Anthony A. Hoekema, *The Bible and the Future* (Grand Rapids: Eerdmans, 1979), 140.

(2) Other more Reformed types understand the reference to "all Israel" to mean the turning of all the elect from among the Jews (not including Gentiles) to salvation throughout history. This differs from Calvin's view in restricting the word *Israel* to Jews. However, it agrees with Calvin in that the "salvation" of the Jews refers to the turning in belief to Jesus as Messiah and Lord of individual Jews throughout history and not in some end-time, large-scale, more miraculous sweeping of the whole Jewish people into the church. In other words, in Paul's metaphor of the olive tree it would be the regrafting of broken off Jewish branches, of "hardened" individual Jews, back into their own olive tree through their belief in Jesus as Messiah and Lord in response to the gospel: the same way that believing Gentiles are "saved."[72]

Variations of these views include evangelical theologies of "fulfillment" arguing that Jesus is the eschatological center of history, who eschatologically fulfills and reconfigures Israel around himself. As one interpreter puts it,

> Christ makes all things new not as one more actor on the historical stage. If he came merely to renew or to expand Israel, then he would be another Moses. In fact, Christ possessed the eschatological mission of fulfilling and reconfiguring Israel around himself. The Messiah reveals the participation of all things in the eschatological fulfillment that he accomplishes by his cross and resurrection . . . So is there a place for Torah observance? Yes. Jews who do not believe in Jesus continue to observe the Torah. Christians affirm that such observance is praiseworthy both as worship of the true God and as an anticipation of the messianic fulfillment.[73]

Others such as N. T. Wright see the coming of Jesus as Messiah, who is the faithful fulfillment of Torah, the Righteous One, who represents all Israel in his own flesh, and is the Temple of God on earth, as inaugurating in himself God's new thing in Israel's history in his death as Israel's suffering servant who liberates Israel from its sin and opens that forgiveness to all humankind who will receive it as a free gift from the hand of Israel's God. In his resurrection from the grave, he has become also the firstfruits

---

72. Anthony A. Hoekema, *The Bible and the Future*, 140.

73. Kinzer and Levering, "Messianic Gentiles & Messianic Jews," *First Things*, January 2009, 41; see http://www.firstthings.com/article/2009/01/005-messianic-gentiles-messianic-jews/.

of the new creation, that all who believe in him will one day experience through God's indwelling Spirit of life.

Wright sees Jesus as reconfiguring around himself and the Spirit Israel's "monotheistic doctrine of God" (One God, One Lord), their view of election (not limited to Israel only, but to all the elect from every nation), and Israel's "future" (the divine promises to Israel are being fulfilled now and will be completed not in some awesome, miraculous conversion of the whole Jewish nation, but by the coming of Jesus and the fulfillment of Israel's hope of the resurrection of the Messiah's whole people, and the final fulfillment of the kingdom of God in this world with the new heavens and earth. All this is held along with emphatic denials from these evangelicals that such a view is anti-Semitic or anti-Judaic.[74] This view is in one sense a relief to the Jews (historically), since it undermines any motive to coerce Jews to change their minds now about Jesus in that they are not all going to be swept into the Trinitarian church at the second coming of Jesus—in their view something quite "scandalous."[75] On the other hand, since these evangelicals also reject a two covenant understanding of Jesus' command to "make disciples of all the nations" (Matt 28:19), and since they do believe Paul's gospel to be "to the Jew first" (Rom 1:16), there can be no discrimination against the good news of God's love being proclaimed to all modern Jews. For these evangelicals there is only one covenant and only one people of God in a mysterious bonding together of eschatologically redeemed Jews and Gentiles from all nations and ethnicities, never to be separated, though also never to lose their identities.

---

74. N. T. Wright, *Paul and the Faithfulness of God*, part 2 (Minneapolis: Fortress, 2013), 1:1043–1263; Bruce Chilton, "Romans 9–11 as Scriptural Interpretation and Dialogue with Judaism," *Ex Auditu* 4 (1988) 27–36; Christopher Zoccali, *Whom God Has Called: The Relationship of Church and Israel in Pauline Interpretation, 1920 to the Present* (Eugene, OR: Pickwick Publications, 2010) gives a thoughtful overview of current views including those of evangelicals and others, and a critique of each. He argues himself for a "both-and" approach to the identification of the terms "Israel" and "Jews" in the New Testament literature (i.e., the church is "Israel," and is not "Israel") and with strong denials of any replacement or anti-Judaism overtones.

75. Adam Gregermann, "A Jewish Response to Elizabeth Groppe, Philip A. Cunningham, and Didier Pollefeyt, and Gregor Maria Hoff," in Philip A. Cunningham et al., eds., *Christ Jesus and the Jewish People Today: New Explorations of Theological Interrelationships* (Grand Rapids: Eerdmans, 2011), 224–25.

Conclusion, Whither *Nostra Aetate,* Jews, and Evangelicals?

In this concluding overview of evangelicals, *Nostra Aetate,* and Jews, I would like to briefly sum up without further attempts to argue details where this essay seems to be leading. I want to be as transparent, respectful, and personal as I can. I do not speak for all evangelicals.

1. Evangelicals for the most part do not know of *Nostra Aetate.* However, they have followed their own path to much of what the statement suggests and would be largely in agreement and thankful for this initiative in both the areas of Jewish relations and relations to other religions.[76] Reservations would be mainly as to how ambiguous parts of the statement are being interpreted both within and outside the Catholic Church. Some subsequent papal remarks, some Catholic prelates' reflections, and some Catholic theologians have argued for, what seems to many of us, extrapolations that are contradictory to the intent of the document.[77] On the other hand, if the affirmations in the other documents of Vatican II (eg., *Lumen Gentium* et al.) and the revised *Catechism* (1994) form the interpretive context, then I, as a Protestant evangelical, would feel much more comfortable in seeing multiple ways the statement could be clarified and applied without radically revising the early church's Christology, soteriology (Christ is Lord and the universal Savior of all humanity, including Jews), and ecclesiology (Christ is the head of the one eschatologically redeemed body of Jews and Gentiles). *Nostra Aetate* also raises the important question of the relationship of the covenants to salvation.

76. See Dallas Willard, "Knowledge of Christ and Christian Pluralism," in *Knowing Christ Today: Why We Can Trust Spiritual Knowledge* (New York: HarperCollins, 2009), 168–91. There are many areas of agreement between *Nostra Aetate* and evangelicals, some, however, have taken certain ambiguous parts and extrapolated to raise questions about continued mission to the Jews. Others advocate a "two-covenant" approach that effectively disenfranchises Jews from Jesus's eschatological salvation.

77. Philip A. Cunningham et al., eds., *Christ Jesus and the Jewish People Today: New Explorations of Theological Interrelationships* (Grand Rapids: Eerdmans, 2011), along with Marianne Moyaert and Didier Pollefeyt, eds., *Never Revoked: "Nostra Aetate" as Ongoing Challenge for Jewish-Christian Dialogue* (Leuven: Peeters, 2010), have some Catholic essays by theologians and Cardinals that have advocated views on *Nostra Aetate* that in my estimation have gone too far in taking Paul's statement "with relation to election, they are beloved for the sake of the patriarchs" (Rom 11:28), without understanding this in the full context of Romans 9–11 and the rest of Romans, which have led to views Paul never could likely accept. Space does not allow defending this criticism.

2. The evangelical recovery of *Jesus, the Jew*, and the first-century *Jewish-worldview* context for the beginning of the gospel is continuing to greatly enhance our understanding of the New Testament documents and the nature of the early Messianic communities not only in their initial Jewish-only setting but also in the Jewish-Gentile Messianic communities that also began to worship the God of Israel, who, through the Jewish Messiah, Jesus, was understood to be fulfilling the promises to Abraham and to Moses to save the whole world through his people Israel. Noticeably, when the resurrected Jesus appeared to Paul, the Jew, and spoke to him, he identified himself as a Galilean Jew: "I am Jesus of Nazareth whom you are persecuting" (Acts 22:8).

Moreover, when we deepen our seeing the connection between the faith of and in Jesus with the Jews, we stand today in continual debt to the Jews in the way we read and interpret the Old Testament. Paul could say of his own Jewish people, "The Jews were entrusted with the oracles of God" (Rom 3:2). Many evangelicals do not know that there is a wealth of ancient Jewish interpretative materials on the Old Testament that shed light on many biblical passages drawn from a long tradition of minute study of Scripture.[78] In my own case, I have been able to access this wisdom repeatedly from living rabbis, whom I can call or e-mail. For example, the strong emphasis in Judaism on this world (created good by God), our earthly home, and the almost total lack of any Scripture in the Old Testament on life after death, act as a check on our spiritualizing much of the Old Testament and the New in many areas, such as on the topics of faith and creation, and especially in regard to heaven being somewhere else other than on this earth, and in regard to an afterlife of disembodied souls living in a nonspatial life-setting eternally in this condition. What we are looking at here is a much more positive view of Judaism that could be quite productive between evangelicals and Jews.

78. Bruce Chilton well captures this need: " To meet the challenge of Romans 9–11, however, involves reading the whole of the canon in the light of faith; particularly, it means becoming familiar with the traditions of Israel as that which best articulates God's action in Christ. As Paul demands that we articulate our faith in the terms of reference of Israel, he presses us on to a dialogue with Judaism. Because we share a heritage with Judaism, we are bound to agree and to disagree with our Jewish contemporaries regarding the significance of that heritage . . . Judaism represents an authentic (and relatively straightforward) reading of the Hebrew Scriptures, and the gospel is to be grasped as the intersection between that reading and our experience of Christ," ("Romans 9–11," 34).

3. *Supersession* is for evangelicals and Jews an area where more agreement can be effected though there are still tensions. As indicated in a previous section there is widespread agreement among evangelicals and deep and sincere regret over the way Jews and Judaism have been depicted in either negative or antiquated ways by the church and even by some evangelicals. Tensions arise over just how narrowly *supersession* is defined. I have struggled with this in my relations to Jews. Perhaps for me the suggestions of Orthodox rabbi Eugene Korn are most helpful and have significant possibilities for further exploration. Evangelicals believe that in their relationship to the Jewish Messiah, Jesus, they share equally in the same one Abrahamic covenant with the Jewish people.

The first problem was the exclusive and supersessionist character of traditional Christian theology. Christianity's claim to the same covenantal promises God made to Israel was the very source of intense theological rivalry, the delegitimization of Judaism, and Christian persecution of Jews over the course of Jewish-Christian history. Hard supersessionism (i.e., the notion that the doctrine that the new covenant replaced the Jewish covenant and that after Jesus God rejected the Jews in favor of the church) was the long-standing Christian teaching about Judaism and Jews. The "new Israel" has invalidated the "old Israel," and the new covenant of the spirit rendered the Mosaic covenant limited temporally (i.e., during the time the Jerusalem Temple stood).

The concurrent validity of the Mosaic covenant and the new covenant (i.e., soft supersessionism: the doctrine that the church has been grafted onto the living tree of the Jewish people, but that the new covenant is the ultimate fulfillment of the still-living Jewish covenant), with its implication of concurrent validity for both the Mosaic and the new covenants, was entertained by only a few early Christian thinkers but was ultimately rejected by early normative Christian theology, which was so heavily shaped by Augustine's hard supersessionist understanding of covenantal history. With the advent of the new covenant of the Spirit, the Mosaic covenant became meaningless—even an obstacle to future salvation history. And as Gal 3:28 seems to indicate, there is no room left for the continued distinct existence of the Jewish people or its independent covenantal mission.[79]

---

79. In Robert W. Jenson and Eugene B. Korn, eds., *Covenant and Hope: Christian and Jewish Reflections* (Grand Rapids: Eerdmans, 2012), 162–63. Korn's distinction between "hard" and "soft" supersessionism is attributed to David Novak.

Korn's problem with Gal 3:28 is more easily corrected by clarifying that the distinctions made there by Paul do not erase the identities but simply relativize their significance in a common covenantal community, Jews remain ethnically Jews; Gentiles, ethnically Gentiles; slaves, slaves; freed slaves, freed slaves; and women, women.

Rabbi Korn, however, does go on to point out a more important tension point, the matter of "the doctrines of the trinity and the incarnation." However, as he points out, Jewish legal thought has changed since the sixteenth century, and Jewish experience of the Holocaust has led to Christians' reexamining their complicity in this tragic event, and to the Catholic Church's statement in *Nostra Aetate*, and to the development of consequent soft-supersession theologies of the continued validity of the Jewish covenant. Many of these have argued that since the Jews are not rejected, they have a continuing part in salvation history. Therefore for many Catholics and more liberal Protestants this means no more mission emphasis to the Jewish people to call them to repentance and faith in Jesus as Savior and Lord and as God's only way now of relating to him in saving faith and within the one covenant whether Jew or Gentile. Evangelicals will not be convinced that Korn's solution could in any way fit the New Testament teachings about who Jesus is and what his death and resurrection mean for the salvation of the world. So, in this part of his excellent essay I would find inadequacies with his solution.

4. This leads to the question, then, what is the *Divine purpose* for the continuing existence of the Jewish people and Judaism today? Is there an evangelical answer? I confess that this is a difficult question to answer from a biblical viewpoint. It is not a question that has received much theological reflection in our communities. In England they have an expression for a person who has been let go from their job. He or she is declared "redundant." This is the message that most of the church through history has given to the Jews. Yet, as I have already pointed out, Judaism can be viewed positively as a continuing witness to God's revelation in the *Tanakh* (Jewish Scriptures) that forms the whole context of the events when many first-century Jews believed that the God of Israel had visited his people to redeem them and to call them to repentance through first his prophet John, who baptized those who were repentant and pointed them to his successor, Jesus, the Messiah. Without this continuing Jewish witness, including the Jewish apostles, the Jewish New Testament, and the presence of Jews in the world throughout history, the original gospel could scarcely have survived.

So in one sense the promise made to Abraham long ago that "in his seed all the nations on earth would be blessed" is being fulfilled, howbeit not yet fully consummated. From an evangelical perspective, both Jews within the eschatological Messianic community, as well as Jews outside that fellowship as a religious people continue to witness also to a monotheistic, creator, and redeemer God who has revealed himself to humans through the Abrahamic family to both a secular and a polytheistic world.

But this does not seem to get deep enough and go to the heart or core of the mutually interdependent relationship of the Jewish people with the eschatological Messianic community, called the church. According to Paul's analogy of the olive tree, we (Gentile followers of the Messiah, Jesus) are related as wild, grafted-in branches into the "root" (patriarchs?) (Rom. 11: 17–18). The "branches" that have been "broken off" and "hardened by unbelief" (v. 20) are still part of the people that Paul grieves over and still calls his "brothers and sisters in the flesh," who are in the present part of a people chosen by God, and blessed by God with the "adoption, the glory, the covenants, the giving of the law, the worship, and the promises. To them belong the patriarchs, and from their race, according to the flesh, is the Messiah who is God over all, blessed forever. Amen." (Rom 9:4–5). Further, Paul says hardened Jews can still be grafted back into the olive tree by God's power more easily than the wild-branch grafts (Gentiles).

"Sounding the depths of the mystery which is the church" (*Nostra Aetate*) entices us who follow Jesus to search more deeply this paradoxical, but inseparable mutual bonding, and how this is to be respected and held in tension with our profound differences. Perhaps the distinction that Ratzinger makes between the covenants of promise and covenants of commandments can be helpful?[80]

5. As to the *unrevoked covenant and salvation,* an evangelical viewpoint might look something like this: All the covenants that God has made with humankind, including the Adamic, Noahic, and all those with the Jewish people are unrevoked (or better, not regretted) by God. But as to the solution to the human plight of sin and creation's corruption,

---

80. Pope Benedict XVI (Joseph Cardinal Ratzinger), *Many Religions, One Covenant: Israel, the Church and the World* (San Francisco: Ignatius, 1999), 56; but see also Adam Gregerman, "A Jewish Response," 226–28, who points out the fallacy of arguing that Jews continuing to live as Jews in covenantal life today proves that Jewish covenantal life is good and ought to continue. He points out that the exact opposite was suggested by many Christians through the ages who indicated that the presence of Jews indicated God's continued wrath on this people.

the covenants merely provided the revelatory context of where salvation or deliverance from sin could be accessed and a reconciled relationship to God effected and lived out; covenants did not provide the guarantee of salvation for simply being in the covenant or being a covenant people. When the Messiah came, suffered, died, and rose from death, the revelatory activity of God came to a climax with the new and final covenant he inaugurated. In former days Jews came into right relation with God through Torah, sacrifice, and covenant obedience—but never without the faith of Abraham that brought about their justification by God's free grace (Gen 15:6: "And he believed the Lord and it was counted to him for righteousness").

This new covenant did not abrogate the former covenants with Israel, but it required reframing the nature of the community so that Gentiles of Abraham's faith, before he was circumcised, could become equal members of God's people along with faithful Jews. Some rejected this call for reframing the way the people of God from now on were to be reconstituted. Nevertheless, the benefits of being a Jew were never rescinded for those who followed in the footsteps of believing Abraham.[81]

The most objectionable aspect of this reading is the evangelical insistence that the new covenant inaugurated by Jesus, the Messiah, effects forgiveness of sin and relationship with God only as Jew or Gentile come to God, not through the church, but through faith in Jesus, the Messiah. Recognizably, this is not acceptable today to the Jewish community. Does this mean the end of all discussion and dialogue? Absolutely not. But does this not lead us to put the questions up front, once again: Was Jesus a faithful Jew? Was he a prophet? Was he more than a prophet? I think this discussion can be productive to both communities and can be handled in a Jewish context respectfully and open to strong disagreements, but nevertheless essential to further significant progress.

6. What significance does the *Holocaust and the Land of Israel/Palestine* have in Jewish and evangelical relations? Evangelicals now more than ever before are recovering the hideous truths of the Jewish experiences of suffering through the event of the Holocaust.[82] But who would venture without a prophet to give a reason or proffer a meaning why the Sovereign Lord would allow such an evil before our eyes? Nevertheless, the church

---

81. I am indebted to my colleague Dr. John Walton for this framing of the covenant and salvation question.

82. David Gushee, *Righteous Gentiles of the Holocaust: Genocide and Moral Obligation* (2nd ed.; St. Paul: Paragon House, 2003).

universal has had its eyes opened to the long history of its own adverse attitude toward the Jewish people and is attempting to rectify this blemish on its character, and also to acknowledge the harm done to many.

As we have described earlier in this essay, some evangelicals (Christian Zionists) have interpreted their Scriptures as predicting in the latter days both the return of the Jews to the Holy Land in unbelief and the turning of the whole Jewish people to their Messiah in connection with the return of the Messiah to establish his millennial rule for one thousand years. Still others (perhaps an even larger branch of evangelicals), mostly non-Zionists but even some anti-Christian Zionists, do not believe either of these Christian Zionist doctrines can be supported by more careful biblical exegesis of both Old Testament and New Testament texts. Nevertheless, most of these support the right of Israel to have a secure and safe State as long as it conforms to accepted moral and political expectations applied equally to other nationalisms, especially as these pertain to alleged illegal land occupations. They would also be strongly concerned with the rights of Palestinians not only to form their own State, if they so wish, but also to have redress from Israel of genuine injustices such as provable land seizures.

7. The Christian *evangelization of Jews and Messianic Judaism* both remain lightning rods in the Jewish communities. Targeted Jewish evangelism is thought to be insensitive to the Jewish experience of the Holocaust and to the continuing validity of the Jewish covenants. *Targeting* is an ethically acceptable modern marketing term for approaching prospective customers with knowledge of their culture, personal habits, and historical backgrounds, and then tailoring the market approach to produce the most sales. This description, however, would repulse evangelicals as to what they are doing when they believe Jews need to hear the message of the "good news." The word *targeting* can also be understood in a need or health sense (e.g., If *all* are equally sinners—both Jews and Gentiles—then all need the cleansing and healing [saving] word from God of how he has provided forgiveness now in the death and resurrection of the Jewish Messiah, Jesus). If this same message is proclaimed to both Jew and Gentile equally, taking into consideration what aspects of the message may address needs of the given community, it is difficult for evangelicals to see how this in itself (absent deception or coercion, and done with sincere love) could be objectionable on moral grounds. But the objection of David Novak is that "short of anti-Semitic proposals for

the persecution or even the murder of Jews, nothing is more offensive to Jews than concerted programs by adherents of some other religions that target Jews to convert."[83]

One can understand the anguish of a Jew who has suffered the Holocaust's worst nightmares, persons such as Novak describes, and then who is approached to convert to another religion—one that has been complicit in this ghastly event. If Christianity and Judaism are really two different religions, such a charge has merit. However, if Christianity and Judaism are part and parcel of the same religion, then the obstacle is not conversion to another religion, but an objection toward a prophetic call to repent (to change one's mind) and to believe what God has done through the Messiah of Israel. These issues then can be debated scripturally and argued also with consideration of the traditions of the elders (*Halakhah*), that I have argued evangelicals are not opposed to, without this being labeled a supersessionist or replacement theology or as a covert cover for deception.

Part of our problem, as N. T. Wright correctly identifies, is viewing Christianity and Judaism in terms of the eighteenth-century theory of religions. What Paul was *not* doing in preaching to Jews was advocating a new religion to which they should convert (as he did to pagans), instead his message was thoroughly Jewish:

> Declaring that the God whom the Jews had worshipped all along, the God made known in their scriptures, had done at last what he had promised, and that with that divine action a new world order had come into being. Paul's theology and mission were rooted in and defined by this christologically inaugurated eschatology. . . . The one God had not suddenly changed his mind, his plans or his ultimate purposes. The one God had acted suddenly, shockingly and unexpectedly—just as he said he always would.[84]

Messianic Judaism has no acceptance by the Jewish communities and needs further debate and clarification within the evangelical community.

8. Finally, what may be the *future of evangelicals and Jews* in continued conversation and cooperation? A few suggestions may end this essay

---

83. David Novak, "Covenant and Mission," in Robert W. Jenson and Eugene B. Korn, eds., *Covenant and Hope: Christian and Jewish Reflections* (Grand Rapids: Eerdmans, 2012), 45.

84. N. T. Wright, *Paul and the Faithfulness of God*, parts 3 and 4 (Minneapolis: Fortress, 2013) 2:1410–11.

and perhaps spur both communities to further mutual growth, friendship, and understanding of each other's commonalities and significant differences. Perhaps this can only happen in America and at this time in history. These must be brief.

a. Evangelicals need to give *more direct and intentional efforts in their educational institutions to structure relationships with the surrounding Jewish community* through faculty and administrator discussions with rabbinical leaders, conferences, invitations to visiting rabbis, joint evangelical-Jewish publications, course offerings, and consideration of a visiting or adjunct professor from the Jewish community. Little along these lines seems to be currently the norm. This could be reciprocated by the Jewish educational and synagogue community, as is already occurring.

b. More *teaching in the churches about Judaism* should be encouraged along with exposure to the long history in the churches of the *adversus Judaeous* (contempt for Jews) tradition and its harmful effects toward the Jewish people. Teaching about the Holocaust (*Shoah*) should be a part of church educational programs along with understandings about the nature of anti-Semitism and anti-Judaism and its destructive effects.

c. More evangelical-Jewish local and national discussions should be encouraged. Currently there is only one national regular annual meeting being sponsored in Washington DC This could be duplicated around the country.

d. Publishers (of books, magazines, and journals) in both communities should continue to sponsor conferences and seek out good pieces that help the two communities understand each other better, that develop friendships, and that dispel stereotypical caricatures of Jews and of evangelical Christians. More joint publishing efforts of evangelicals and Jews should be encouraged.

e. Additional endeavors that focus on the common good of the country, state , and local communities are worthy joint projects for Jews and evangelicals.

PART 3

Nostra Aetate and Its Communal and Pastoral Impact

10

Nostra Ætate, Kairos and Mysterium

Murray Watson

"Blessed are you, O Lord our G-d, Sovereign of the universe, you who have granted us life, sustained us, and enabled us to reach this season."

REJOICING AND GRATITUDE: THOSE are the sentiments at the heart of the *Shehecheyanu,* a traditional Jewish prayer praising God, who has enabled the speakers to arrive at a moment of celebration (certain holidays, the purchase of a new home, eating the season's first fresh fruits, seeing a friend after a long absence, etc.). *Wikipedia*—that goldmine of all knowledge (!)—speaks of praying the *Shehecheyanu* "when doing or experiencing something that occurs infrequently, from which one derives pleasure or benefit."[1] We praise and thank God who has made it possible for us to live *until this moment,* an unusual or distinctive time pregnant with joy or meaning or possibility. As we prepare to celebrate the fiftieth anniversary

1. See http://en.wikipedia.org/wiki/Shehecheyanu/.

157

of *Nostra Ætate* [*NA*], and reflect on the many blessings that have flowed from it, and built upon it, it seems to me—as a Christian, at least—that, as both Jews and Christians, the *Shehecheyanu* sums up beautifully the sense of thankfulness, wonder and hope that we feel as we mark that momentous half-century. Indeed, as Rabbi Eric Yoffie so correctly noted back in 2000, "more progress has been made in Catholic-Jewish relations in the last fifty years than was made in the previous two millennia."[2]

Being in my forties, I am very conscious of living at a very blessed and providential time in the history of Jewish-Christian relations. I am myself a beneficiary of those fifty years of hard slogging; of slow, patient relationship building; of missteps and learning; of awkwardness and exploration that has made it possible for us to reach this moment. I was born after Vatican II, and my knowledge of Vatican II comes from printed commentaries, yellowed news articles, and from listening to the stories of a few Canadian bishops who actually took part in the Council. Like many of my generation, I largely take for granted where we are at today in that dialogue—but I also know from my study how hard-fought that progress has been,[3] and how different Jewish-Christian relations are today than they were in October 1962, when Vatican II began. Things are enormously different (and better) today, and we who are living in that new situation could perhaps be justified in praying a prayer very similar to the *Shehecheyanu*. God has indeed brought us to a season of new things, which continue to unfold before our eyes.

Perhaps the phrase in *NA* that has most influenced my own life and ministry has been its radical acknowledgement, in #4, that "the Church . . . cannot forget that she . . . draws sustenance from the root of that good olive tree onto which have been grafted the wild olive branches of the Gentiles."[4] Grammatically, *nutriri* in Latin is an infinitive, but an infinitive *in the present tense*—which is to say that the Church *continues* (still

---

2. Rabbi Eric H. Yoffie, "Good News, Bad News: Extraordinary Achievements and Current Tensions in Catholic-Jewish Relations" (The Joseph Klein Lecture on Judaic Affairs, Assumption College, Worcester, MA, March 23, 2000), http://urj.org/about/union/leadership/yoffie/archive/cj-relations/.

3. See, for example, Father Thomas Stransky's article, "The Genesis of *Nostra Aetate*," *America* (Oct. 24, 2005), http://americamagazine.org/issue/547/article/genesis-nostra-aetate/.

4. "*Quare nequit Ecclesia oblivisci se . . . nutriri radice bonæ olivæ in quam inserti sunt rami oleastri Genti.*" The language here is that of Paul's letter to the Romans (11:13–24, especially v. 18: "remember that it is not you that support the root, but the root that supports you" [*ou su tēn rizan bastazeis alla hē riza se*]).

today) to be nourished and fed by the Jewish faith, in a way that cannot be limited (as it so often was in the past) merely to events of the first century CE. Catholicism officially recognizes that, even today, she "draws sustenance" from the root of the good olive tree which is Judaism—and this phrase has made all the difference for me.

Because of that verb, I have been blessed to be a guest at the Seder table of many Jewish friends and colleagues over the years. Because of that verb, my graduate biblical education included courses (in a Vatican university!) on the classic rabbinic commentaries on the Decalogue and the *Aqedah* [the Binding of Isaac], and on the Jewish background of the New Testament. It meant that, as a Catholic, I had opportunities to live and study in the heart of Jerusalem and to learn from distinguished Jewish scholars—because my Church recognized how essential that "sustenance" is for an accurate and nuanced understanding of Jesus's humanity, and of the New Testament as a whole. Indeed, a 1985 successor document to *NA*[5] urged Catholic students of the Scriptures to "profit discerningly from the traditions of Jewish reading."[6] Concepts like *midrash* and *targum*—once entirely foreign to my vocabulary—have deeply enriched my understanding of the Bible, and have opened up exciting new vistas in thinking about my own Christian faith. In very real ways, I continue to "draw sustenance" on a daily basis from Judaism, Jewish sources, and Jewish scholars, and I realize today how impoverished my faith and study would be without them. I believe that I have grown considerably as a Catholic Christian because of the opportunities I have been offered to interact with Judaism, and Jews, in challenging and life-giving ways, that have enlightened, challenged and stretched me . . . and all of that because Vatican II spoke of the Jewish contribution to Christianity as a reality of the *present* (and not merely of the *past).*

5. Vatican Commission for Religious Relations with the Jews, *Notes on the Correct Way to Present the Jews and Judaism in Preaching and Catechesis in the Roman Catholic Church* (June 24, 1985), http://www.vatican.va/roman_curia/pontifical_councils/chrstuni/relations-jews-docs/rc_pc_chrstuni_doc_19820306_jews-judaism_en.html/.

6. Similarly, the Pontifical Biblical Commission's 2002 document called *The Jewish People and Their Sacred Scriptures in the Christian Bible,* said, "Christians can and ought to admit that the Jewish reading of the Bible is a possible one, in continuity with the Jewish Sacred Scriptures from the Second Temple period . . . Christians can . . . learn much from Jewish exegesis practised for more than two thousand years, and, in fact, they have learned much in the course of history." See http://www.vatican.va/roman_curia/congregations/cfaith/pcb_documents/rc_con_cfaith_doc_20020212_popolo-ebraico_en.html/.

In the Christian tradition, time is traditionally spoken of in terms of two Greek terms: *chronos* and *kairos*. As one commentator helpfully distinguishes them:

> *Chronos* time is the time that we can measure with the help of a watch or a calendar. It is the time that can be divided into seconds and minutes or days and years and centuries. Chronological time is measurable time, divisible into equal parts which are all somewhat alike. But when the Greeks use the word *kairos* they mean another kind of time altogether. The New Testament translations usually render the word *kairos* by "the accepted time" or "when the time was fulfilled." This means that time, besides being this divisible, measurable, even stream on which we are carried along, has another quality which is quite disturbing. It becomes *kairos*, the accepted time, the time for decision.[7]

Other writers explain *kairos* this way:

> Greeks commonly used *chronos* to describe the more quantitative aspects of time, such as chronology or sequence. *Chronos* time is what we might call clock or calendar time: discrete units of time that need to be measured (relatively) precisely . . . The ancients used *kairos* to refer to the more qualitative aspect of time, when something special happened. This term is used much more often—almost twice as frequently—in the Bible. Sometimes translated "season," *kairos* time is when something important happens at just the right time. Paul explains, for example, "when *the fullness of the time* [*kairos*] came, God sent forth His Son, born of a woman, born under the Law" (Gal 4:4 NASB, emphasis added). God wasn't waiting for a precise date on the calendar, but for a period in human history in which the conditions were most appropriate.[8]

> *Kairos* moments are described as occurring in between chronological moments, and they offer special or potent opportunities. In Christian thought, *kairos* time marks an appointed time in the purpose of God. Some churches understand *kairos* time to be in effect when the prayers and songs of human worship

---

7. George W. Forell, *The Protestant Faith* (Englewood Cliffs, NJ: Prentice-Hall, 1960), 49–50.

8. E. Randolph Richards and Brandon J. O'Brien, *Misreading Scripture with Western Eyes: Removing Cultural Blinders to Better Understand the Bible* (Downers Grove, IL: IVP Books, 2012), 142.

intersect with the eternal worship of heavenly angels. *Kairos* time is ripe and rich and fulfilling.[9]

Kairos is, therefore, a privileged type of time, a time of invitation and opportunity, pregnant with possibility, in which our actions can (if we act thoughtfully and well) intersect and cooperate with God's own hopes and dreams for the world. It is THE time, "when the time is right," according to God's Providence.

As we look back at the five decades since *Nostra Ætate,* it is hard not to believe that it has been a *"kairos* time" for both of our communities. It has been a unique moment in the history of both Judaism and Christianity, in which God has made it possible for us to meet each other in a new and unprecedented way, a divinely offered moment of promise and possibility that both communities have (largely) seized, in an attempt to radically transform the nature and tone of our interactions. It has been, in so many ways, a decisive and history-making time, when people on both sides were prepared to listen to each other, to take risks, and to extend hands of friendship, in ways that had hitherto been unthinkable. An entire academic field, interfaith studies, is now a prominent area of study in many major universities, but it simply did not exist two generations ago.

There has also been a veritable explosion of interfaith initiatives, groups, documents and meetings. Here in Canada, the Canadian Conference of Catholic Bishops joined with the Canadian Jewish Congress and the Canadian Council of Churches in 1977 to establish a new tripartite national dialogue, the Canadian Christian-Jewish Consultation (CCJC), which for more than thirty-five years has been bringing together representatives of Canada's Jewish and Christian communities for regular study and discussion.[10] In October of 2000, the Canadian bishops issued a pastoral letter on relations with Judaism titled, "Jubilee: Renewing Our Common Bonds with the Jewish Community,"[11] which spoke of the need for repentance and education on the part of Catholics, and proposed a series of concrete steps that Canadian Catholics and Jews could engage in together to further their relationship. Many Catholic postsecondary

---

9. Melissa Miller, "Keeping Vigil." *Canadian Mennonite* 15/7, Apr 4, 2011, 10, , http://www.canadianmennonite.org/articles/keeping-vigil/.

10. In July 2011, the Canadian Jewish Congress formally disbanded, and a new successor organization, the Centre for Israel and Jewish Affairs (CIJA), came into being. Since that time, CIJA has taken the CJC's position at the national dialogue table, as part of the CCJC.

11. http://www.cccb.ca/site/Files/jewishmessage.pdf/.

institutions and seminaries now incorporate extensive teaching about Judaism in their programs, and Canada's first university-level centre for Catholic-Jewish learning was established in December 2004, at King's University College in London.[12] In 2009, Canada's first yeshiva and rabbinical school was established in Toronto—on the premises of a Catholic university (the University of St. Michael's College)—and Canada's Catholic bishops were among the first to offer their congratulations on the inauguration of this unique new institution,[13] which physically embodies the collaboration between Catholics and Jews that has been such an important part of Canadian society.[14] On a national, provincial, and local level, Jewish-Catholic relations in Canada have never been stronger, more vibrant, or more diverse.

We may tend to take the past fifty years for granted, but we also recognize that they have been significantly *unlike* any other fifty-year period that preceded them in the past two millennia. It has been a *kairos* time, a time specially blessed by God, and, fortunately, the leaders of both our communities have recognized the potential and the invitation, and have led us a long way along this journey of discovery and re-discovery. For many people in their '70s and '80s, the Catholic Church of 2015 seems, in its attitudes toward Jews and Judaism, so different from its 1960s incarnation as to be scarcely recognizable. We have made tremendous, life-giving strides.

And yet, even fifty years on, we are still just *beginning* to delve into some of the important questions that *Nostra Ætate* gave us permission to ask. Some people consider the Catholic Church's claims to possess and authoritatively interpret God's truth as a kind of theological presumptuousness. *Nostra Ætate's* chapter 4, however, includes some language that suggests a perhaps surprising degree of humility regarding God's plans,

---

12. See the Centre's website: http://www.kings.uwo.ca/academics/centres-kings/centre-for-jewish-catholic-muslim-learning/. Since May 2010, the Centre's mandate has expanded to include Islam as well, and so it is now the Centre for Jewish-Catholic-Muslim Learning (CJCML).

13. http://www.cccb.ca/site/eng/commissions-committees-and-aboriginal-council/national-commissions/christian-unity-religious-relations-with-the-jews-and-interfaith-dialogue/documents/3223-yeshiva-congratulations-letter-from-archbishop-bohan.

14. According to Statistics Canada, Jews represent just over 1 percent of the Canadian population (330,000, out of a national population of roughly 31 million Canadians).

and has allowed for a flourishing theological literature that explores the contours of the Jewish-Christian relations. Twice, *NA* speaks of "mystery":

> As this sacred synod delves into the mystery of the Church [*Mysterium Ecclesiæ perscrutans*] . . . and that, "according to the salvific mystery of God [*iuxta salutare Dei mysterium*]," "the beginnings of [the Church's] faith and election are found already among the Patriarchs, Moses and the prophets."[15]

In Christian theological language, *mystery* is a technical term—a truth of such *depth* and *richness* and *complexity* that it can never be entirely plumbed by the human mind. It is not something impenetrable or unknowable, but something which has so many possible layers of meaning that we will never *exhaust* its potential.[16] To say that our exploration of the Church-as-mystery necessarily leads us to reflect deeply on our relationship to Judaism alerts us that there are many, many unanswered questions here for us to grapple fruitfully with; it cannot simply be "ecclesiology-as-catechism". To speak of God's salvific plan for humanity as a mystery that somehow incorporates *both* Judaism and Christianity is a word of caution to all those who might be tempted to oversimplify that relatedness for the purposes of catechesis, preaching or apologetics. Such an over-simplification has often been cast in essentially supersessionist categories. The use of *mystery* language in #4 of the Declaration provides a necessary, valuable opening to new models, new concepts, new language—and that is precisely what we have witnessed over the past fifty years, and continue to witness today.

Similarly, drawing on the language of both Zephaniah and Saint Paul, *NA* "looks forward to a day known to God alone" [*Ecclesia diem Deo soli notum expectat*], when all people will call upon God with a single voice, and serve God shoulder-to-shoulder. How will that happen? There is a sense in which, despite the best of our theologizing, what God intends to do with us, Jews and Christians alike (and *how* God will do that), ultimately remains veiled to our speculation—*is mystery.* We know

15. See Appendix I for all quotations to *NA*.

16. "Serious theological reflection is always hard work, and its outcome fragmentary, tentative, and (often) quite technical in its quest for appropriate imaginative and conceptual accuracy, not because God is complicated, but because we are—and so is the world in which we live. It is not possible without complexity to indicate, or point the way toward, the deep simplicity of the mystery of God." Cf. Nicholas Lash, *Easter in Ordinary: Reflections on Human Experience and the Knowledge of God* (London: SCM, 1988), 291.

that, in God's time and God's way, things that now seem humanly, logically irreconcilable (such as the differing faith-understandings of Jews and Christians) may find a common end-point, in ways that we human beings can neither *foresee* nor *force,* nor perhaps even begin to imagine. Such is the immense mystery of God and God's actions.

I am reminded of the famous story told about the Jewish philosopher Martin Buber, who expressed that hopeful (if radical) vision in a somewhat different way: "What is the difference between Jews and Christians? . . . We all await the Messiah. You Christians believe that He has already come and gone, while we Jews do not. I, therefore, propose that we await him together. And when he appears, we can ask Him, 'So, were you here before?' . . . I hope that at that moment I will be close enough to whisper in his ear, 'For the sake of heaven, don't answer!'"[17]

That such conversations can take place, in friendship and utter frankness, is, to me, a proof that ours is a blessed and special time in human and religious history, a *kairos* moment that God calls us to take seriously and engage in responsibly. We live at a time when new questions are possible and welcome, when we, as Jews and Christians, are in a position to share our respective insights in ways that can enlighten and enrich each other's paths, with respect, humility, and openness. After 1,950 years, we can once again speak to each other as brothers and sisters . . . as joint heirs of a common religious heritage . . . as earnest seekers after the one God and God's will. To live in these days is, indeed, a blessing, a privilege and a divinely conferred responsibility. It is a summons to take the precious heritage of these past fifty years and commit ourselves to actively passing it on to future generations, rooting it even more deeply and broadly in the lives of our respective communities. We are still, in so many ways, at the *beginning* of this journey.

Blessed indeed is the One who has granted us life, sustained us, and enabled us to reach this season—this season of newness and hope, this season of promise and joy. Thanks be to God!

17. As recounted by Elie Wiesel in his *All Rivers Run to the Sea: Memoirs* (New York: Knopf, 1995), 354–55.

11

Liturgical Reform and Renewal in the Roman Catholic Church and Its Impact on Christian-Jewish Relations

Liam M. Tracey

As much of the programme of liturgical renewal in the Roman Catholic Church in the twentieth century is codified and found in Church documents, this paper will begin with a consideration of Church documents. In discussing the impact of a Church document—any document whatever its status or importance, a number of immediate clarifications are required. Not every document from Rome is of equal significance; Church documents require interpretation, and it is important to notice the rank, status, and type of document one is reading. Not every document will have an impact nor is it designed to have one; some answer definite historical moments, others are commemorative or exhortative and others treat matters of discipline. Not every Roman document is directly from the pope; some come from Roman congregations that are part of the Roman curia; others are from the pope but do not have a binding force for Catholics.

In terms of liturgical documents, the charter for liturgical reform and renewal in the mid- to late twentieth century is the first document of the Second Vatican Council, *Sacrosanctum Concilium*.[1] This document initiated a process of renewal and reform in the liturgical celebrations of the Roman Catholic Church that are without parallel in its history. Much of this change is embedded in the actual ritual books themselves (i.e., the books that contain the texts for a liturgy). Each of these books contains an Introduction which outlines not just the structure and order of the service but also provides a theological understanding of the celebration that carries with it an official meaning. As Roman Catholic liturgy is highly ordered the books also contain rubrics which are not just instructions about the texts but also indicate gesture. The books contain a normative description of how official celebrations are seen to unfold, but as recent liturgical scholarship has noted, actual liturgical celebrations in given places may be different or indeed very different. This too, despite disapproval by some official Roman Catholic authorities and more conservative groups within the Church, is also part of the influence and heritage of liturgical reform. Trying to assess the impact of a nonliturgical document like *Nostra Aetate* (*NA*) is more difficult; what change is desirable and possible may need to be clarified and discussed in greater detail.

A global understanding of what liturgy is about and what it celebrates is also required. For the purposes of this article, and it will be developed in the course of this exposition, liturgy is understood as the public (and approved) prayer of the Church. Liturgy has featured heavily in discussions both within and outside the Roman Catholic Church over the course of the last century: in order to understand why, it is necessary

---

1. Helpful to this discussion of the authority and nature of a Church document is the distinction of style and a particular Conciliar style outlined by John O'Malley in his study of Vatican II. See John W. O'Malley, *What Happened at Vatican II* (Cambridge, MA: Belknap, 2008), 305–11. On page 305 he notes, "The style of the documents of Vatican II is what at first glance as well as most profoundly sets it apart from all other councils. During the council bishops, following the orientation from John XXIII, consistently and repeatedly described the council as pastoral in nature, and they sought a style for the documents to conform to it . . . To describe the style simply as 'pastoral,' however, is to miss this important specificity and thereby to miss the profound implications of the genre and vocabulary the council most characteristically used to convey its message. The adoption of the new style, which was really an old style, was the most far-reaching of the many *ressourcements* [return to the original sources] in which the council engaged. At the same time it was a repudiation of other styles and of the model derived in the early Christian centuries from political institutions of the Roman Empire." In some critiques of the Council common in the blogosphere, the word *pastoral* is seen as unimportant or as rendering the Council unimportant and nonbinding.

to briefly outline the history of the liturgical reforms over the course of the last century or so and how they came to the fore in the debates about liturgy at the Second Vatican Council. It is the contention of this article that only with an understanding of the profound liturgical changes (both rubrical and theological) that flow from the Council can one then proceed to exam the impact of a document like *NA* and its importance in the unfinished agenda in terms of liturgical renewal.

THE MODERN LITURGICAL MOVEMENT

This is not the place to retell the story of the Modern Liturgical Movement, but it is important to recall just a number of salient points, before looking at the Constitution on the Sacred Liturgy of the Second Vatican Council and the journey of liturgical reform it marked and how it began a new moment in that task. Key to the liturgical reforms of Vatican II and indeed of all reforms of the Roman Rite throughout history is the desire to return to the classical shape of the Rite itself. This has been called the "pure" or classical shape of the Roman Rite, the liturgy of the city of Rome as formed and celebrated in the city between the fifth and the eight centuries. There have been various attempts to return to this classical shape, at various points during the Middle Ages, again at the Council of Trent (1545–1563), and at the ill-fated Synod of Pistoia held in 1786. In 1832 with the refounding of the monastery of Solesmes by the diocesan priest turned Benedictine, Prosper Gueranger (1805–1875), a new period of liturgical development started. Religious life and indeed the life of the Church was at a low point after the French Revolution. Gueranger's solution was, as he saw it, to restore the purity of the Roman liturgy in its celebration and especially its chant, and the monastery at Solesmes was to serve as a prototype for the rest of the French Church to follow. The French Church had been at the forefront of resistance to the liturgical changes of the Council of Trent and had maintained their own distinctive liturgies, which were mistakenly presented as a return to a Neo-Gallican liturgy, itself a revolt against a Roman liturgy, or the liturgy of Gaul, before Charlemagne (c. 747–814) imposed the classical Roman liturgy on his empire. Gueranger's career was not unlike that of the Dominican Jean-Baptiste Henri-Dominique Lacordaire (1802–1861), in that both were refounding religious orders and in some way working for the future of the French Church as something profoundly related to the See of Peter.

While Gueranger's revival of the Roman Liturgy was very much based on the medieval synthesis of that Rite, it was the influence of the great biblical, patristic and indeed ecumenical movements of the early twentieth century and their return to the sources of the Christian tradition, that gave the impulse to what is today called the Modern Liturgical Movement. The insight of the Apostle Paul and his followers, who saw the Church as the Mystical Body of Christ, was recovered by the school of Tübingen and provided the theological underpinning of the agenda of the movement. This was against a prevailing view of the Church as the *societas perfecta* ("perfect society") and the liturgy as an action of that perfect society—a view upheld in the post-Tridentine period by notable theologians and later canonized saints such as Charles Borromeo (1538–1584), Robert Bellarmine (1542–1621), and others. This view of liturgy carried on right into the nineteenth century; it saw the Church as an institution, and liturgy as an action of that state or institution; a channel of grace to the soul was what was necessary, but it rendered the liturgical celebration lifeless.

In 1903, Pius X issued a *motu proprio* titled *Tra le sollecitudini*, which spoke of the liturgy as a true and indispensable source for the Christian life. This instruction of the pope dealt with sacred music and was considered by many to be a retrograde step. For instance it reaffirmed the primacy of Gregorian chant, which had largely fallen out of favour, and the superiority of Renaissance polyphony, especially that of Giovanni Pierluigi da Palestrina, over other, later polyphonic music. It also excluded women from singing in mixed ensembles with men; discouraged music that smacked of modernity or secular influences; and barred the use of piano, percussion, and other instruments. Yet in its introduction we read:

> We deem it necessary to provide before anything else for the sanctity and dignity of the temple, in which the faithful assemble for no other object than that of acquiring this spirit from its foremost and indispensable font, which is the *active participation* in the most holy mysteries and in the public and solemn prayer of the Church.[2]

This phrase "active participation" was to become the core principle of the liturgical movement and its chief inspiration in its call for liturgical reform. The traditional starting point of the Modern Liturgical Movement

---

2. *Tra le sollecitudini* (italics added), http://www.adoremus.org/MotuProprio.html/.

is seen as a 1909 speech delivered at a Catholic Workers conference in Malines near Brussels, by a chaplain-turned-Benedictine-monk, Lambert Beauduin (1873–1960). He went on to found the monastery now known as Chevetogne Abbey in 1925, widely renowned for its ecumenical endeavours. Beauduin, drawing inspiration from both the *motu proprio* of Pius X (1835–1914) and the social encyclical of 1891, *Rerum novarum* of Leo XIII (1810–1903), profoundly linked the task of liturgical renewal with the social teaching of the Church, a link that is also found in Anglo-Catholicism and would be later largely lost. Beauduin's growing commitment to the liturgy came to flower during 1908–1910. Sometime prior to 1909, Beauduin was said to have burst into the class he was to teach and to have exploded, "I've just realized that the liturgy is the centre of the piety of the church!" In 1909, Beauduin presented his paper on the liturgy at Malines, and in November, the journal *Questions liturgiques* (later *Questions liturgiques et paroissales*) began publication with Beauduin as editor. In June 1910, the first Liturgical Week was held at the monastery of Mont César. The goal of the early liturgical movement was "to restore Christian spirituality [and] the means proposed was the restoration of the parochial High Mass on Sunday, with full participation."

These themes were later developed in the 1947 encyclical letter of Pope Pius XII, *Mediator Dei*. This was the first encyclical to treat the liturgy, indeed it has come to be regarded as the *magna carta* of the liturgical movement. While it allowed for certain adaptations and concessions (e.g., the use of the vernacular in certain rites), it was both cautious and indeed critical of some of the aims of the liturgical movement. Perhaps the most important element of *Mediator Dei,* is its insistence on the theological nature of the liturgy. Indeed Anscar Chupungco has noted that

> The classical definition of the liturgy was formulated by Pope Pius XII in his Encyclical letter *Mediator Dei:* Liturgy is "the public worship which our Redeemer as head of the Church renders to the Father, as well as the worship which the community of the faithful renders to its Founder, and through him to the heavenly Father. In short, it is the worship rendered by the Mystical Body of Christ in the entirety of its head and members" (25).[3]

Nevertheless, the pope's intervention was seen as a ratification of the efforts of liturgical reformers and a continuing approval of their desire to

---

3. Anscar J. Chupungco, *What, Then, is Liturgy? Musings and Memoir* (Collegeville, MN: Liturgical, 2010), 130.

make the liturgy the "true and indispensable source" for Christian life and worship. This would reach its culmination in the Constitution on the Sacred Liturgy of Vatican II. Reform and renewal continued apace after the publication of *Mediator Dei*. A commission for liturgical reform was established in 1948 by the pope and it continued its work until its dissolution in 1960. Amongst its achievements were the shortening of the Eucharistic fast to just one hour prior to receiving Holy Communion; this led of course to the possibility of celebrating the Eucharist in the evening as well as the morning. The restoration of the Easter Vigil in 1951 and the reform of the liturgies of Holy Week in 1955 can also be attributed to the work of this so called Pian Commission. They also produced a Code of Rubrics in 1960 and a new edition of the Breviary (for the celebration of the Liturgy of the Hours) and the Pontifical (the books of celebrations presided over by a bishop) in 1962. It is important to note the work of this Commission, established eighteen years before the first session of the Council took place. As we will see later in this paper, there were already requests from Jewish organizations in the late 1950s to address Jewish texts used in the Roman Catholic liturgy.

THE CONSTITUTION ON THE SACRED LITURGY

On 4 December, 1963, the bishops of the Second Vatican Council approved the first document of the Council, *Sacrosanctum Concilium* (*SC*) by 2,147 votes in favour to 4 votes against. As Keith Pecklers observes:

> This represented a great breakthrough despite last minute-attempts in certain circles of the Roman Curia to sideline the process in favor of a rubricial, centralized, and rigidly immutable Roman liturgy celebrated in Latin. Thus, the Constitution was solemnly approved by Pope Paul VI—the first decree to be promulgated by the Ecumenical Council [. . .] At the heart of that document was a return to the solid foundations inherent within the pure and classical Roman Rite, all of which came to be rediscovered in the work of the liturgical movement and, indeed, the wider movement of *ressourcement* theology, which paved the way for the Council.[4]

---

4. Keith F. Pecklers, *The Genius of the Roman Rite: On the Reception and Implementation of the New Missal* (London: Burns & Oates, 2009), 26.

What we call the Roman Rite today is a hybrid of liturgical developments and elements which have developed over the course of time and in many different geographical areas. Indeed a sound liturgical principle is that no liturgical innovation has ever emerged in Rome. The Roman liturgy borrows, is influenced by, and gathers elements from other parts of the Church. Rome never innovates, my doctoral supervisor constantly reminded me. Critics of liturgical reform have often accused those involved in liturgical renewal of liturgical archaeology, of failing to acknowledge that the liturgy evolves over time and wanting us to return to a mythical golden age of pure Roman liturgy. This is of course a caricature; liturgy must always be celebrated in a given context where it responds to the needs of a particular age, time, and place. Vatican II was profoundly aware of its context, of the incomplete First Vatican Council and the history of other Ecumenical Councils that had preceded it. John F. Kennedy was assassinated twelve days prior to the promulgation of *SC*. The world was living in fear of nuclear war and the sharp rhetoric and fears of the Cold War.[5]

The Council's Preparatory Commission of nearly a 100 members and expert consultants from all parts of the globe prepared a schema that was both theological in its understanding of the liturgical mystery and clear in its call for ritual revision. The schema aimed to be comprehensive and did not shy away from difficult issues like the use of Latin and the possibilities of using vernacular languages. It went through several drafts and changes and was finally presented to the Council Fathers as the Liturgy Constitution. It was the first item on the agenda of the Council and may have been perceived by the Council leaders as being unproblematic. This was not to be the case.[6] Not only were there tensions and disagree-

---

5. Gerald P. Fogarty, "The Council Gets Underway," in Giuseppe Alberigo and Joseph A. Komonchak, eds., *History of Vatican II*, vol. 2, *The Formation of the Council's Identity* (Leuven: Peeters, 1997), 106: "Although the Council made no formal mention of the Cuban Missile Crisis, the threat of nuclear war made real the need for the Council not to limit itself to doctrinal matters. It had to be a voice for peace among all nations."

6. An excellent overview of the schema and the initial conciliar debates on the liturgy can be found in Mathijs Lambertigts, "The Liturgy Debate," in Alberigo and Komonchak, eds., *History of Vatican II*, vol. 2, 107–66. Though Massimo Faggioli has recently noted: "The five-volume *History of Vatican II* edited by Giuseppe Alberigo and Joseph Komonchak provided new information about the key role of the liturgical debate within the council and about the dynamics in the preparatory and conciliar liturgical commissions. Nonetheless, studies on *Sacrosanctum Concilium* published almost concurrently with the *History* focused on an ideological continuity between the early twentieth-century liturgical movement and *Sacrosanctum Concilium*, and

ments over the document, but there were also internal conflicts between members of the Commission and various parts of the Roman Curia, which led to the removal of Annibale Bugnini as secretary of the Preparatory Commission. He had been secretary to the Pian Commission and would later emerge as the chief architect of the Conciliar reforms and much hated, even today, by traditionalist groups. Discussions on the schema took place from 22 October until 13 November, 1962, during the course of fifteen general congregations of the Council. There were 328 oral interventions and 297 written proposals.

SC established both the general principles and the norms that were to guide the reform of the Roman liturgy. Key to this is the already-mentioned classical Roman liturgy, in *SC* 34 suggesting "the rites should be marked by a noble simplicity; they should be short, clear, and unencumbered by useless repetitions; they should be within the people's power of comprehension and as a rule not require much explanation." Noble simplicity is seen as a characteristic of the classical Roman Rite before it came into contact with the more dramatic Gallican Rite and their eventual fusion. Perhaps even more pointed is *SC* 50:

> The rites are to be simplified, due care being taken to preserve their substance which, with the passage of time, came to be duplicated, or were added with little advantage, are now to be discarded; other elements which have suffered injury through accidents of history are now to be restored to their vigour which they held in the days of the holy Fathers, as may be useful and necessary.

The framers of the Liturgy Constitution had been influenced by a greater historical consciousness of the development of the Roman Rite. As heirs

---

thus they overlook the impact of the constitution on Vatican II as such." See Massimo Faggioli, *Vatican II: The Battle for Meaning* (New York: Paulist, 2012), 102. Faggioli's point is not without merit if one reads the first number of the Constitution in which the basic aims of the Council are recalled: "1. This sacred Council has several aims in view: it desires to impart an ever increasing vigor to the Christian life of the faithful; to adapt more suitably to the needs of our own times those institutions which are subject to change; to foster whatever can promote union among all who believe in Christ; to strengthen whatever can help to call the whole of mankind into the household of the Church. The Council therefore sees particularly cogent reasons for undertaking the reform and promotion of the liturgy." The decision to reform the liturgy is closely allied to the purposes of the Council itself. Any reform of the Church must be seen in its liturgy, because as the constitution recalls it is in the liturgy that the Church experiences and shows forth its true identity. Hence, the battle over liturgy in these last years are ultimately ecclesiological in nature. Also see Massimo Faggioli, *True Reform: Liturgy and Ecclesiology in "Sacrosanctum Concilium"* (Collegeville, MN: Liturgical, 2012).

to the biblical, patristic, and ecumenical movements they had a greater knowledge of the history of the Roman Rite than those who reformed the Rite after Trent. Sources long lost for many centuries were now available to them in fine critical editions, as they began the renewal of the Roman liturgy. Thanks to the Modern Liturgical Movement, a recovery had taken place in the Church's understanding of liturgy as something theological and spiritual, profoundly linked to the source of the Christian life and not merely rubrical or canonical. The heart of liturgy is the living, dying, and rising of Christ, the celebration of the paschal mystery. This led to a greater clarity in understanding the relationship between the liturgical celebration and the mystery of Christ and his Church. A fruitful mutual clarification took place on this point, where the liturgy as the celebration of the saving mystery of Christ is seen as a celebration of the gathered people of God, i.e. the Church as the mystical body of Christ. This viewpoint of course places the liturgy and its celebration at the heart of the life and mission of the Church, essential to the Church's self-understanding.

Key to all of this is the central principle of the Modern Liturgical Movement, which is taken up time and time again by *SC*: the full, conscious and active participation of all the people of God in the liturgical celebrations of the Church.

> Mother Church earnestly desires that all the faithful should be led to that *full, conscious,* and *active* participation in liturgical celebrations which is demanded by the very nature of liturgy. (SC 14)

This is the main aim of the liturgical reform and what animated the Modern Liturgical Movement in its many struggles. It is both a right and a duty of all the baptised. *SC* 79 reminds us that intelligent, active, and easy participation by the faithful is the "primary criterion" to be observed in the revision of the rites of the sacramentals.

> In the restoration and promotion of the sacred liturgy, this full and active participation by all the people is the aim to be considered before all else; for it is the primary and indispensable source from which the faithful are to derive their true Christian spirit; and therefore pastors of souls must zealously strive to achieve it, by means of the necessary instruction, in all their pastoral work. (SC 14)

Both then, and even more now, this phrase *actuosa participatio* ("active participation") has caused confusion, debate, and even dissension. From an understanding of active participation that means everyone present must get something to do, to a sense that it is only an interior and spiritual sense of participation. Full and active participation is based on the notion of the common baptismal priesthood of all the faithful, already alluded to in *Mediator Dei* and based on the Pauline notion of the mystical body of Christ. This is not optional or dependent on the whim of a particular bishop or priest; rather it is a right and a duty incumbent on all the baptised. The reform and the renewal of the liturgical books following on from the Council were to enable this participation. Rites were to be simple and accessible; hence the vernacular was encouraged. Communion was to be distributed from the altar and certainly not to be taken from the tabernacle. Even communion under both kinds was thought about, if only on special occasions. Renewed attention was paid to Scripture and its preaching in the homily. The desire of the Council was to recover the unity between the table of the Eucharist and the table of the Word.

> With this phrase [active participation] is connected a series of other adjectives that describe, first, the ideal manner of celebrating the liturgy together (communal, true, authentic, appropriate, with understanding, conscious internal and external, in a vital way, devout, full, complete), second, its necessity and frequency (obligatory and frequent), and third, its result (effective, fruitful). Mere presence at the liturgy would not be "participation" as understood by the liturgical constitution. It is possible that for this reason the number of "those" attending the liturgy dropped after publication of the liturgical constitution, because not everyone wanted anything to do with a participation that meant involvement and a real communal celebration.[7]

While the major themes of the Modern Liturgical Movement were taken up and adopted by the Council, *SC* goes further; it is both an affirmation of a century of struggle and a point of departure for liturgical renewal which has gone since the Council. Like many documents, *SC* is a compromise between progressive and conservative camps. It did not abolish Latin, indeed Latin was established as the language of the *editio typica,* from which all vernacular translations must be made. It did, however, call for a full-scale revision of the Roman liturgical books, and not just the editing or updating of the Tridentine books (an issue that causes problems today, not

---

7. Reiner Kaczynski, "Toward the Reform of the Liturgy," in Giuseppe Alberigo and Joseph A. Komonchak eds., *History of Vatican II*, vol. 3, *The Mature Council* (Leuven: Peeters, 2000), 232.

just of a ritual kind but of a profoundly ecclesiological kind in that the 2007 *motu proprio* of Benedict XVI *Summorum Pontificum,* permits the use of the 1962 books!). *SC* in perhaps its most radical or farseeing section deals with the issue of what today is called enculturation (*SC* 37–40), where it establishes the Roman Rite as the base for future adaptations of the liturgy but does admit in article 40, "in some places and circumstances, however, an even more radical adaptation of the liturgy is needed." It may not be enough to adapt the Roman liturgy: some cultures may require liturgy almost from scratch. This article has never been acted on or more accurately, the Roman authorities have not allowed it to be operative.[8]

Clearly in the Constitution one finds the principle of Episcopal collegiality emerging. The Constitution suggests that in local or national liturgical matters these issues are best dealt with by the local bishop or by the national Episcopal conference (*SC* 41). The resulting tension between diocesan bishops and the Roman Curia would continue right throughout the Council and down to today as an unresolved issue.

POSTCONCILIAR REFORM

In January 1964, Paul VI formed an international *Consilium* to revise existing liturgical books in line with the directives of the Council. These books would then be translated into vernacular languages by regional commissions. Cardinal Giacomo Lercaro of Bologna was named

8. The impact of the liturgy constitution on the Christian-Jewish encounter merits greater attention, as noted by Massimo Faggioli in his *True Reform,* 113: "The importance of *Sacrosanctum Concilium* for the *rapprochement* with the Jews lies in the fact that the liturgical reform of Vatican II made a step forward in comparison to the liturgical reforms of Pius XII, not just in terms of the 'quantity' of reforms enforced, but in terms of intimate connections between the issue of 'change' in the Church (liturgy included) and the unfolding of a deep theological debate on the relations between the Church and the Jews. That is why every step back, or deviation, or second thought about the liturgical reform of Vatican II puts at risk much more than merely the way of performing liturgical ceremonies and has consequences even more dire than restoring of the prayer *pro Iudaeis*." Here Faggioli is referring to the changes brought about in the pontificate of Benedict XVI. For Faggioli, key to the liturgical reform of the Council is a new approach to the Scriptures, where a historical-critical approach to the Scriptures leads to both a change in Christian-Jewish relations and a more abundant reading of Scripture in the liturgy, both in terms of quantity and in terms of a greater emphasis given to the Scriptures in the liturgical celebration. This liturgical and biblical renewal together with a change in the relations with Jews and Judaism are for Faggioli inseparable: one has a deep impact on the other.

President and Fr. Annibale Bugnini as Secretary.[9] There would be constant and ongoing tensions with the Congregation for Divine Worship, which was both personal but also systemic. The CDW was a part of the Roman Curia and its post-Tridentine development, founded to ensure order, uniformity and unity in liturgical practice against the Reformation and its liturgical innovations. Its emphasis was on common language, fixed rubrics, and common norms to be observed by all. The *Consilium* existed to facilitate implementation of the liturgical reforms called for by the Council. The interaction between these reforms at a local, regional, national, and international level would be a constant challenge for both bodies. The issue of language, the vernacular and its historical and cultural variants quickly became and remains a contentious issue.

The *motu proprio Sacram Liturgiam* published by Paul VI in January 1964, to guide the work of the *Consilium*, was seen by many as too restrictive, only partially allowing what the Council had promised and an attempt by the Roman Curia to claw back the power it felt was been delegated to the bishops. A key point of disagreement was the decision not to allow episcopal conferences approve vernacular translations of liturgical texts. Local bishops, especially in mainland Europe, saw this as a lack of trust on the part of the Curia and a blocking of the liturgy constitution. Bugnini saw it as a desire to facilitate a gradual implementation of liturgical reform rather than allowing too much too soon.[10] In 1969, the Vatican issued an instruction on the translation of liturgical texts, *Comme le prevoit*. This pivotal document guided the translation of liturgical texts until it was replaced in 2001 by *Liturgicam Authenticam*. These two documents have very different views and methods on the task of translation. For the 1969 document, translation and the task of inculturation are inextricable linked. The guiding principle for the work of translators was to be that of

9. The history of the *Consilium* is dealt with in Piero Marini, *A Challenging Reform: Realizing the Vision of the Liturgical Renewal*, ed. Mark R. Francis et al. (Collegeville, MN: Liturgical, 2007).

10. Rita Ferrone, *Liturgy: "Sacrosanctum Concilium"* (New York: Paulist, 2007), 55: "Aside from the production of liturgical books in Rome, the reform was proceeding on other fronts as well. Permissions for use of the vernacular and for cultural adaptations of the liturgy were sought and obtained around the world. Commissions were formed to do the work of translation of official texts. For example, even before the end of the council, representatives of eleven English-speaking episcopal conferences has gotten together to plan a 'mixed commission' (i.e., one drawn from multiple conferences) to produce English translations for liturgical use. This body, called the International Commission on English in the Liturgy (ICEL), was founded in 1963."

"dynamic equivalence." It also envisioned new texts written in vernacular languages. It guided the work of the translation of the Roman Missal that eventually came into use in 1973 and the ill-fated Sacramentary of 1998. *Liturgiam Authenticam* on the other hand uses the principle of "formal equivalence," which is a more literal translation of the Latin, and in which every word must be accounted for and the exact sentence structure and punctuation followed. Doctrinal orthodoxy and unity is then presumed to follow this exact translation since it is the principle used in the translation of the third edition of the Roman Missal. But Faggioli is probably right when he sees the forces of reaction already in movement in the 1970s:

> The seventies were the age of the liturgical reform's completion: Paul VI's pontificate is still now much identified—especially by the anti–Vatican II component of Catholicism—with that era of decentralizing, pro-laity and innovative reforms. The election of John Paul II meant not only a new attitude toward Vatican II but also the beginning of a new indulgence toward the tiny minority of Catholic traditionalists who rejected liturgical reform as a device for rejecting Vatican II. The traditionalists grasped better than many advocates of the council's reforms the theological force of *lex orandi, lex credendi* for Vatican II.[11]

NOSTRA AETATE AND ITS IMPACT ON THE LITURGY

Liturgical reform and renewal for many Roman Catholics is the most tangible result of the Second Vatican Council, it certainly is the one that affected them the most, and is a process that, as we have seen, still causes debate, a lack of agreement on its necessity, and indeed a great deal of anguish in parish communities. However no element of Catholic life was left untouched by the Council, and as Rita Ferrone has perceptively noted:

> The Vatican II document, *Nostra Aetate*, on the relationship of the Church to non-Christians, articulated a radically new vision of the Jews and Judaism for Catholics. It is an indisputable fact that in the area of Jewish-Catholic relations, the Council represents a break with the past. The Council determined that the sad history of contempt for Jews and disrespect for Judaism

---

11. Faggioli, *True Reform*, 7: "The law of prayer governs/establishes the law of belief."

which had marred the Church's past would not be carried into its future.[12]

An immediate impact of this new vision was to affect the ongoing task of revising the liturgical books, which we have traced above in this article. Ferrone writes, that "numerous anti-Jewish features of the Church's official prayer were quietly removed. The deletion of material hostile to the Jews took place as part of the call to *aggiornamento*."[13] Drawing on archival material Ferrone convincingly shows that these deletions followed requests from Jewish groups already made in 1959.[14] I have written elsewhere that the impact of *NA* and the documents that follow on from it have had a mixed impact on the Church's liturgy and on its portrayal of Jews and Judaism.[15] What needs greater attention by liturgists is how the whole corpus of the documents of Vatican II should be read in the context of liturgical reform and renewal over the last century: otherwise the next step in that process of interiorisation and change to deep structures of thinking about the liturgy will not happen. Of particular importance here is how to read *NA* alongside the journey of the Modern Liturgical Movement and the liturgy document of Vatican II and the reforms that followed from that event. While texts have been changed, more needs to be done in the area of liturgical formation not just for those preparing for full-time ministry in the Church but of whole parish communities—especially but not exclusively of those involved in liturgical music and the leadership of public prayer. If liturgy is seen principally as made up of approved texts, these other issues will not be addressed or seen as needing attention; yet preaching, formation, and music have powerful impacts on the worshipping community. As more communities have other liturgical services besides the Eucharist (often because of the shortage of ordained ministers), it is imperative that those charged with leading the community in prayer have a correct understanding of Jews and Judaism in harmony with the requirements of the Roman documents. This

12. Rita Ferrone, "Anti-Jewish Elements in the Extraordinary Form," *Worship* 84 (2010) 498.

13. Ibid., 511.

14. Ibid., 510.

15. Liam Tracey, "The Affirmation of Jewish Covenantal Vitality and the Church's Liturgical Life," in Philip A. Cunningham et al., eds., *Christ Jesus and the Jewish People Today: New Explorations of Theological Interrelationships* (Grand Rapids: Eerdmans, 2011), 268–86.

is particularly true for popular devotions and practices, which often run alongside the liturgy of the community.

The theological underpinning of how liturgy is understood in worshipping assemblies is still crucial for any real progress. While direct anti-Jewish texts have been removed from the Roman liturgy, its theological articulation still requires deeper reflection.[16] How as Christians can we profess Jesus Christ as the Saviour of all humanity and at the same time affirm the vitality of the covenantal relationship of the Jewish people with God? As long as liturgy is interpreted in an exclusively christocentric way, which is a legacy of the work of the Modern Liturgical Movement (and it did move interpretation away from rubrical concerns), little progress can be made in seeing the liturgy as the celebration of all of God's marvelous works from the moment of creation to the fulfillment of creation in God's good time. This will entail a more expansive reading of the concept of the paschal mystery, which is central to liturgy constitution. The celebration of the liturgy as a realization of the paschal mystery of Christ has been central to a renewed and much-needed liturgical theology; it has served theological reflection well as a means to understanding the saving nature of the liturgical celebration. But perhaps now is the time to widen our view of this central paradigm, namely, how is the paschal mystery present in the liturgy, a celebration and presence of the whole saving work of God? This entails careful theological reflection on the presence of the Risen Christ and the role of the Spirit in the liturgy and its celebrants—the worshiping community. A part of this necessary reflection is a consideration of how the two testaments relate to each other in the liturgy. How are readings from the Hebrew Bible twinned with readings from the New Testament, and what overarching narrative is presented to the community through these readings. While the liturgical reforms led to a greater use of the Hebrew Bible in the liturgy, how it is used and the selections made from it are still a matter of concern. The issue of typology (how one text is mirrored in another) is a difficult one and permeates the Christian liturgy, but greater attention needs to be paid to this particular way of reading Scripture. Of course a temptation for liturgists is to reduce every aspect of the life of the Church to the liturgy.

---

16. I am not suggesting that there is not work to be done in this field, as the excellent study of the lectionary (the book of readings) by Michael Peppard has shown. See Michael Peppard, "Do We Share a Book? The Sunday Lectionary and Jewish-Christian Relations," *Studies in Christian Jewish Relations* 1 (2005–2006) 89–102, http://ejournals.bc.edu /ojs/ index. php/scjr/article/view/1362/1272/.

Closely allied to this task is the teaching of liturgy and especially what is sometimes called pastoral or practical theology in seminaries and theological centres. Greater attention is needed by those who teach preaching and liturgical leadership to the documents dealing with a changed view on the presentation of Jews and Judaism presented to students. This, too, is a result of the liturgical movement and the reforms of the Council and an increased emphasis on the proclamation and preaching of the Scriptures, and they are now seen as central to the liturgical celebration, not just of the Eucharist, but also of the other sacraments.

Those entrusted with teaching the history of liturgy must be conversant with what is a basic revolution in the Christian understanding of Judaism. Crucial to these profound changes is a more complex understanding of the emergence of Christianity from Second Temple Judaism and how Jesus and his disciples are seen in their historical context. This shines new light on the formation of the Jesus movement, the partings of Judaism(s) and Christianity/ies. Greater attention to the inherent plurality of both faiths in these early formative years reminds us how their identities were fluid and their boundaries porous, including the ways they worshipped and who took part in this prayer.

Christian liturgy must never be used to denigrate or offend Jews, not simply out of politeness or a reluctance to offend, but because this is part of the Church's fidelity to the gospel, an understanding heightened by the Council's document *NA* and the Roman and local documents that flow from it. Benedict XVI's consent to the use of the 1962 liturgical books (the extraordinary form) has allowed a question mark to be posed to this affirmation as Ferrone states:

> The Church cannot afford to treat anti-Jewish bias in the extraordinary form lightly or in a piecemeal fashion, pretending that it does not exist or assuming that it is not a problem. Anti-Jewish liturgical texts are unacceptable today, and will be a continuing source of confusion and embarrassment for the Church if the difficulties they present are not addressed in a straightforward and comprehensive manner.[17]

CONCLUSION

This article has traced the development of liturgical reflection in the Roman Catholic Church in the last century or so. It has striven to show that

17. Ferrone, "Anti-Jewish Elements in the Extraordinary Form," *Worship* 84 (2010) 513.

the liturgical reform associated (and often mistakenly seen as beginning) with the Second Vatican Council is the culmination of the work of the Modern Liturgical Movement: a movement associated with the other great movements of the twentieth century in the area of Scripture, patristics, and a return to the sources of Catholic tradition. The document on the liturgy does not exhaust the aims of those associated with liturgical reform and renewal, nor indeed were all the aims of the Conciliar document put into operation as noted already. It is within this context that a consideration of the impact of *Nostra Aetate* must be studied. The reform of the Roman liturgy was already underway in 1965, and while those charged with the reform of the liturgical books were attentive to the new vision brought about by that document, it is difficult to see a direct impact on their work. In line with the insights of the Bologna School and its interpretation of Vatican II, as represented by Massimo Faggioli, the article has also noted that the liturgy document of the Second Vatican Council is also an event in itself: it had a profound influence on the rest of the Council, and in its turn it is a key document of the Council itself. For Faggioli the move towards a liturgical reform is a move toward reform in the Church and of the Church itself.[18]

A return to the documents of Vatican II and to *NA* on the occasion of the anniversary of its promulgation must invite us all to see its radical nature and prophetic challenge to the Church to change its vision of its relations with Jews and Judaism, especially in its liturgical life and celebration. But that renewed attention must read the document in the light of the whole Conciliar events and that which followed on from that significant moment.[19] Finally, in celebrating this achievement, hopefully new energy and hope will be released to enable us to step forward with faith in what already has been achieved and what still needs to be done.

18. Faggioli, *True Reform*, 119–20.

19. Adam Gregerman, "Jewish Theology and Limits on Reciprocity in Catholic-Jewish Dialogue," *Studies in Christian Jewish Relations* 7 (2012) 1–2: "The Catholic Church, more than any other Christian group or institution, has made a dramatic break with centuries of anti-Judaism. It has persisted in revising its teachings despite enormously complex and fraught theological issues about God, Christ, and salvation . . . As a sign of a subtle evolution in recent Catholic views of Jews, the rejection of the accusation that the Jews eternally bear responsibility for the Crucifixion was an especially notable (and controversial) claim at Vatican II in the 1960s. However, it was only after some time that the brief remarks in *Nostra Aetate* about God's continuing covenant with the Jews, not the rejection of the deicide charge, took center stage." This on-line journal can be accessed at http://ejournals.bc.edu/ojs/index.php/scjr/article/view/2074/.

12

Nostra Aetate
At Fifty There Is Wisdom

Michael Reid Trice

In 2014 the Second Vatican Council reached midlife. In infancy, Vatican II (1962–1965) inspired soul-searching by Catholics around the globe. It invited additional Christian communities to go and do likewise. In the late 1960s and '70s, an infectious confidence for liberation swept through ecumenical and interreligious circles around the world. For its part, the Christian imagination was inspired in the hope for deeper unity unseen since before the dawn of the Reformation. At this same moment, the Church was awakening to its own historical complicity in additional communities of culture and faith, in particular, the Jewish people.

Vatican II took place in a global environment that had been dramatically altered by two world wars. In general terms, the second half of the twentieth century responded to the atrocities of the first fifty years by creating *organizations* (i.e., The United Nations, the Pontifical Council for Promoting Christian Unity) and *documents* (i.e., *The Universal Declaration of Human Rights, Nostra Aetate*) that were the results of serious study and reassessment. These documents were crafted as both treaty and embargo: a *treaty* from the hostilities within the modern human soul that opened our eyes to the utter banality of cruelty and evil; and, an *embargo* on human activity that aimed to deter us from the reenactment of these hostilities in the form of tomorrow's genocide. At the dawn of the twenty-first century, we forget that we live in the shadow of the forces that shaped these institutions and documents. In fact, the world's high ambitions for a *new* age were not unalloyed by a latent fear about our conduct in the age previous. The absence of millions upon millions of voices on the planet testifies to this truth.

◆ ◆ ◆

Vatican II emerged in this spirit of new organizational life and study, which aimed to reach serious and significant consensus on the future of the Church in the world. These efforts drew from deep reservoirs of dedicated theological discovery and ecclesiological reassessment brought from scholars and clergy around the earth. "The Church in the Modern World" (*Gaudium et Spes*), the "Decree on Ecumenism" (*Unitatis Redintegratio*), and "The Relation of the Church to Non-Christian Religions" (*Nostra Aetate*) represent the harvest of three of these efforts. But these are of course more than documents; they represent at their best the hopes for a new age.

As a new age, we can easily misconstrue the transformative power of *Nostra Aetate* because we stand in the historical stream of that continuous starlight and don't always see the shadow of its influence on the world. And yet the shadow cast is significant: *Nostra Aetate* put into play a broad discourse about the relationship between Christians and Jews, directly related to both the viability of a doctrine of conversion *and* the long-standing Christian assertion of Deicide against Jews (i.e., the belief that the Jewish people then as now are universally guilty for Christ's death and thus merit Christian indignation).

The document flows this way: God is both the first movement and the final objective of humanity. Human beings are on a spiritual yearning. Religions provide answers to this spiritual yearning that share a ray of truth with one another. These commonalities mean we should have coffee together; we should talk. More specifically, in the Abrahamic faiths we share a common rootstock via Abraham and his sons. Muslims are urged to place former Christian-Muslim conflicts into historical perspective. Jews and Christians share a covenantal language, with clear admission of filial aptitude insofar as Christianity sprang from the Jewish people. *The*

Jews did not kill God. Christian persecution of Jews yesterday, today, or tomorrow is aberrant to human dignity, is anathema to anyone calling himself a Christian, and is impermissible to God. This is the thrust of *Nostra Aetate.* If you place your ear to the tracks you hear the dissonance between a new world's aspirations and fear from the underbelly of anti-Judaic history. It is a history that ruptured families and lives through pogroms and ultimately the *Shoah.* This is a document with soul. So what was so enduringly transformative about its introduction into the world?

There are direct, transformative consequences of *Nostra Aetate.* In terms of direct consequences, first and foremost the Church's about-face on the absurdity of Deicide was a balm toward trustful Jewish-Christian engagement. As a result, through the 1960s and into the twenty-first century, extensive dialogues appear amidst the emergence of vibrant grass-tips local cooperative efforts. National and international exchanges between Jewish and Christian organizational life likewise reveal the direct consequence of a fifty-year-long deliberate reception of *Nostra Aetate* by Christians around the world. It helped of course that at the time a requisite continued centralization of identity (and today emerging crisis of identity) was also shaping Jewish public life in the West.

In light of *Nostra Aetate,* and Christian and Jewish dialogue and cooperation today, what emerged as a second consequence is a deeper appreciation for how transgenerational abuse and trauma is cumulatively degenerative in history. We learned that narrative lies in some epochs or historical episodes are heinous enough to rupture history itself. A narrative lie can tear at the fabric of meaning-making that ultimately renders life incoherent. Literature is filled with ruptures of this kind, symbolically represented in tearing, gnashing, or violent collapse. So, from Job's torn cloths to systematic theologian Paul Tillich's famous 1948 sermon on the "shaking of the foundations" in a post–World War II world, symbols bear powerful witness to ruptured life.

◆ ◆ ◆

In terms of the degenerative historical aspects of anti-Judaism, the image of Cain's dagger in his brother's flesh is perhaps a most appropriate image for a sibling scandal that ruptures the historical relationship between Christians and Jews. If we had an instrument equivalent to a Geiger counter for measuring the ionizing power of fear in the Jewish community, then it would provide evidence of this rupture today. As a consequence, in European history we understand better the insularity of Jewish culture, even as Jewish life thrived in many quarters. Ruptures are no respecters of religion, making them disproportionately dangerous. That is, historical anti-Judaism as a rupture shook the foundations of Jewish culture, socioeconomic vitality, ethnic identity, and family life, which translate directly into a simple tautology: "The world is a fearful place. I don't feel safe in the world." You never feel safe living on the edge of a rupture.

Nostra Aetate was a courageous if not altogether self-aware effort that shone a klieg light on this historical rupture by following its trace to the origin of a theological (and hence moral) Christian *fault*. On the one hand, historical ruptures (like the transition between the Late Middle Ages and the Early Renaissance) take place as a matter of course from multiple sources. On the other hand, specific historical faults (like the Armenian Genocide) originate in an aberrant ideology that can be traced to a source. In this way, *Nostra Aetate* revealed a historical rupture that was grounded in a theological fault. And so, here was the theological fault, the origin point, which was decisive and deadly: Jews killed God. This core origin point was the heart of a rupture, and *Nostra Aetate* unequivocally repudiated it.

Before we deliver heaps of scorn on Christians, consider the following about Christian identity. Christians live at the axis of their theology and ministry in the world: "I do because I believe," or "I act out of faith." There is a tight binary sequence between profession and performance. In this tightness between theology and ministry, it takes the courage of conviction and fortitude to repudiate both doing and believing by accepting that an action was not merely wrong but hateful due to a duplicitous theological lie, the undergirding rationales of which turned out to be an anathema to the heart of God itself. A bruised religion must sustain this conviction and find a new way. This requires a form of sustained Christian vulnerability that we should never undervalue in the postmodern Christian narrative.

A third direct consequence due to *Nostra Aetate* is located in the response of the Jewish community in the document *Dabru Emet* (*Speak the Truth*). *Dabru Emet* reveals deeper trust that both disentangles Nazism from Christianity and seeks mutual theological discovery alongside a shared call for the healing of the world. Jews and Christians alike would not have been existentially ready for *Dabru Emet* (2000) without the former serious efforts of *Nostra Aetate* (1964–65). But these documents also reveal a lack of consensus, including by the main detractors of *Dabru*

Emet, on the grounds that it underestimates a history of anti-Semitism, precisely by Christians. And here is exactly my point: A document's biggest effect is in building trust and contributing to understanding. Even where the critics are correct, these documents serve their purpose in creating a new foundation for dialogue. In this light, Jews and Christians must assess their own history in a difficult yet necessary conversation that must continue for a very long time.

But Jewish-Christian dialogue must not become so focused on its own particular history that these dialogues are not a service to addressing antireligious bigotry everywhere. From local to international contexts, Jews and Christians must endeavor together in fervently speaking out against ethnoreligious stigmatization and violence, from L.A. to Syria and the Central African Republic. The recruitment of child soldiers and the current unspeakable act of beheading children are two instances where we should be unrelenting in our mutual repudiation. That said, I must say that I am often surprised when, in local contexts, Jews and Christians gather in a lackluster way. When they do meet, local Jewish-Christian dialogue tables focus on navigating around the crisis of Israel-Palestine. But what do we do about the atrocities that beg for Jews and Christians to draw from their own histories and speak mutually against these current events? The lack of protest on behalf of other human beings will surely continue to erode the present credibility of a believable Jewish-Christian voice for peace today.

These past decades have revealed the strengths and weaknesses of relationships between Jews and Christians. Taken altogether, *Nostra Aetate* does clear the ground for deeper engagement between Jews and Christians. Pope Francis's visits to synagogues and the Holy Land, or the unprecedented number of Jewish scholars who are experts in the study of the Christian Scriptures, surely reveal great value for relationships of trust and genuine interest between Jews and Christians, and can speak volumes to our relations in the world.

There are also challenges emerging for *Nostra Aetate*, as a document. I'll identify a few of these below.

First, today we live in a world where communication takes place in the speed and substance of a twitter feed—142 characters instantly communicated. Those living on the planet have never had more exposure to one another in the history of humanity. Surrounded by brevity and abbreviation, Jewish-Christian engagement requires a categorical advance in how we think and work together. Dialogues of discovery are required even as we admit of their lack of usefulness in a popular way. A younger generation blogs with the assumption that our first descriptor is our shared humanity—not whether one is Jewish, Christian, or Wiccan, for that matter. This is, in fact, a welcome advance, except when it becomes the sole descriptor. This phenomenon is not due only to the wiles of youth, as those leaving churches and synagogues are not demographically specific. What do we make of this? There are undiagnosed aspects of pluralism that impact religious identity and belonging, and this too will have to be the work of future dialogues. *Nostra Aetate* begins with the shared human need for spirituality, something that should be highlighted by those in our future who access these documents in relevant ways.

A second, continuous challenge will be how we reimagine the hermeneutic for interpreting *Nostra Aetate*, and guiding documents, that emerged from this earlier generation. Until recently, the modern ecumenical and interreligious movement produced documents that were to be received in the world. This monodirectionality (i.e., top-down approach) represents a Modernist presumption on both the place of authority and its transmission. In the modernist age (of which *Nostra Aetate* is a product) religious leadership convened, emphasized unity of perspective, reached consensus, and distributed the results to the masses (i.e., everyone else). In a postmodern age, "everyone else" (i.e., the masses) convene, emphasize particularity of perspective, explore plural views, and distribute the results continuously and immediately through social media. Relevant, thriving religious leadership today is poly-directional. That is, these leaders gather meaning from everywhere and facilitate particularity to show patterns of emerging possible truths. Knowing this, postmodernist readers of modernist documents are encouraged to deconstruct and reconstruct *Nostra Aetate* in order to deepen relationships between communities of faith. Once again, the challenge will be to reimagine how the truths of this document will be meaningful to an age that requires hearing it.

And this presents the third and final challenge, as well as my closing thoughts. We need documents like *Nostra Aetate* because we still live in a world where anti-Judaism specifically, and ethnoreligious phobias generally, pollute the public square. Hate speech in social media, swastikas on graves, Christmas jingles with anti-Semitic verses, Good Friday services with misinformed references to "the Jews," congressional hearings on the civil loyalties of American Muslims—in varying degrees all these perpetuate a single story of yesterday's misery. We require this document for our future because yesterday's well-rationalized ignorance sometimes reinvents itself in the present, and for that we require reminders, not only of who we were, but also of who we can be and should be and in fact must be, in the world. Ultimately we require *Nostra Aetate* for its authoritative voice, to know what we need to say yes to and also no to. At fifty there is wisdom (Mishnah *Avot* 5:21).

13

Teaching, Learning, and Relationships

Nostra Aetate and Education

Elena Procario-Foley

INTRODUCTION

ON ANY NUMBER OF occasions in recent years I have heard variations on an exchange that proceeds in something of the following fashion: A speaker expresses shock and outrage that young people today do not know terms such as *deicide* or *blood libel*. Someone will concur that Catholic education is in crisis, but someone else just might suggest that perhaps the renewing effects of the Second Vatican Council are the reason for this particular ignorance. Such a person believes that the dialogue and education required by *Nostra Aetate* and the subsequent documents inspired by it have been successful, and therefore Catholics, happily, do not now know these terms. In fact, Eugene Fisher, scholar and pioneer in the Jewish-Catholic dialogue, noted in 1999 that "it is an interesting irony that when I started working in this field a quarter of a century ago I could not give a talk to a Catholic group without defining what I meant by the

189

word, Holocaust. Today, 'Holocaust' is part of the working vocabulary of our culture . . . but the term, 'deicide'. . . now, is the term I must define."[1]

Is there a crisis, or is there unqualified success in the implementation of *Nostra Aetate*? *Nostra Aetate* 4 (hereafter, *NA*) taught "the spiritual patrimony common to Christian and Jews is thus so great, this Sacred Synod want to foster and recommend that mutual understanding and respect which is the fruit, above all, of biblical and theological studies as well as of fraternal dialogues." There is no doubt that the many efforts of Catholics and Jews to reconcile their relationship in the wake of *NA* have yielded many positive results. As this volume attests, there has been no lack of biblical, historical, and theological studies to understand and repair the Jewish-Christian relationship. A culture of healthy dialogue exists at the level of official exchange between religious leaders as well as among scholars. Despite the fact, however, that the 1974 *Guidelines and Suggestions for Implementing the Conciliar Declaration "Nostra Aetate"* taught that "Christians must strive to acquire a better understanding of the religious traditions of Judaism," engaging the study of Judaism in a consistent and systematic way has not always been a priority in some sectors of the Catholic world. Consequently, while it is good that *deicide* is not part of the daily vocabulary for the average Catholic, and while it is good that Catholics have learned a great deal about the Holocaust, it is not good that Catholics generally do not ask questions about the relationship between the pre–Vatican II accusation of deicide and the Holocaust, or about how Judaism is a source for Christian self-understanding. Though it is difficult to remember the shameful Christian history of anti-Judaism, it is as much part of Christian identity as is Christianity's positive inheritance of Jewish origins. Thus labels such as *crisis* or *unqualified success* are simplistic and misleading. Much work has yet to be accomplished but it proceeds on well over fifty years of careful research and patient (and courageous) relationship building.[2] The following will examine briefly

1. Eugene Fisher, "Introduction," in *Catholic-Jewish Relations: Documents from the Holy See* (London: Catholic Truth Society, 1999), 6–7.

2. Though the inspiration for this volume is the fiftieth anniversary of the promulgation of the conciliar document *Nostra Aetate* (*NA*), it would be irresponsible for a brief reflection on education and educational encounters after *NA* not to note a longer history of efforts predating *NA* to redress attitudes of Christian anti-Judaism. Historian John Connelly's magisterial volume *From Enemy to Brother: The Revolution in Catholic Teaching on the Jews 1933–1965* (Cambridge: Harvard University Press, 2012) recounts some of this history in Europe, especially as so-called border crossers or converts to Catholicism worked against racism and ultimately worked to change

a catechetical-curriculum outline to provide one representation of how Catholic education has addressed the teaching inaugurated by *NA*; it may demonstrate that crisis and progress, if not success, sometimes proceed simultaneously. Though there are many established Jewish-Christian education programs,[3] the second part will offer just one recent example of a pilot program at a middle-school level.

CURRICULUM

As is well known, extensive textbook studies have been conducted to reveal how Jews and Judaism have been represented in Catholic educational materials. Research from Sr. Rose Thering's 1961 dissertation for St. Louis University, "The Potential in Religion Textbooks for Developing a Realistic Self-Concept: A Content Analysis," was included in dossiers prepared by the American Jewish Community for consideration at the Vatican during the drafting of *NA*. Eugene Fisher's and Philip A. Cunningham's studies chart a trajectory of slow and painstaking progress to implement the new attitude of respect for Judaism represented in *NA* in educational texts.[4] Their work indicates how far Catholic attitudes have developed as well as honestly confronting the work that remains to be done. Much new work should be done analyzing the current generation

the Church's theology of Judaism. Victoria Barnett, Staff Director of the Committee on Ethics, Religion, and the Holocaust of the United States Holocaust Memorial Museum, has written extensively about the efforts in the United States of the National Conference of Christian and Jews between 1933 and 1948, and I am indebted to her for the reference to Mildred Eakin of Drew University, who was conducting textbook studies from the 1930s through the 1950s; see http://depts.drew.edu/lib/archives/online_exhibits/eakin/biography/EakinGeneralBrochure.pdf/.

3. See for instance the Catholic teacher-training program of the Anti-Defamation League, Bearing Witness: http://www.adl.org/education-outreach/holocaust-education/c/bearing-witness-program.html/; the high-school-teacher exchange program of the American Jewish Committee, in which priests go to teach in Jewish schools and rabbis teach in the Catholic school (C/JEEP): http://www.ajc.org/site/apps/nlnet/content3.aspx?c=7oJILSPwFfJSG&b=8451911&ct=12486485/; or the many college programs offered by the member institutions of the Council of Centers on Jewish-Christian Relations at www.ccjr.us/.

4. See Eugene Fisher, *Faith without Prejudice: Rebuilding Christian Attitudes toward Judaism* (New York: Paulist, 1977); and Philip A. Cunningham, *Education for Shalom: Religion Textbooks and the Enhancement of the Catholic and Jewish Relationship* (Philadelphia: The American Interfaith Institute, 1995).

of textbooks. The following will simply present an overview of one document affecting Catholic education.

By way of an example of how interruptions and resolutions in the consistent development and application of *NA* can arise, we can consider the 2008 publication by the United States Conference of Catholic Bishops (USCCB) of *Doctrinal Elements of a Curriculum Framework for the Development of Catechetical Materials for Young People of High School.*[5] Admittedly neither a course syllabus nor a textbook, the framework nonetheless essentially sets guidelines for the production of both.[6] It is, therefore, a good text to examine when trying to determine whether young Catholics are receiving the sustained education regarding Christianity's authentic relationship to Judaism that *NA* and the documents that followed it require. Developed by the Committee on Evangelization and Catechesis of the USCCB, the document provides a detailed curriculum guide for use in high schools, religious education programs, and youth ministry. The *Framework* provides a series of six core courses to be taken in order, and recommends that the curriculum be completed by the student choosing two electives from five possible choices. The last elective listed, "Option E," is "Ecumenical and Interreligious Issues."

Since two of the sixteen documents issued by the Second Vatican Council concerned exactly ecumenism and other religions, it is troubling that these topics were the very last ones listed in the curriculum framework and then only as a possible elective. Since the postconciliar teaching is clear that "at all levels of Christian instruction and education" teaching "a better understanding of Judaism itself and its relationship to Christianity"[7] is necessary for "understanding and dialogue,"[8] one would

5. Find at http://www.usccb.org/beliefs-and-teachings/how-we-teach/catechesis/upload/high-school-curriculum-framework.pdf/. The curriculum was approved in November 2007 by the full body of the United States Conference of Catholic Bishops, and it was first printed in July 2008.

6. See "Introduction" page 1 at http://www.usccb.org/beliefs-and-teachings/how-we-teach/catechesis/upload/high-school-curriculum-framework.pdf/. The introduction explicitly states that "since this is a framework and not a tool for direct instruction, the doctrines and topics designated are not necessarily defined or completely developed."

7. Vatican Commission for Religious Relations with the Jews, *Guidelines and Suggestions for Implementing the Conciliar Declaration Nostra Aetate (No.4)* (3), 1974, http://www.vatican.va/roman_curia/pontifical_councils/chrstuni/relations-jews-docs/rc_pc_chrstuni_doc_19741201_nostra-aetate_en.html/.

8 Vatican Commission for Religious Relations with the Jews, *Notes on the Correct Way to Present the Jews and Judaism in Preaching and Catechesis in the Roman Catholic*

assume that the *Framework* must have woven teaching about Judaism throughout the curriculum, thus providing a solid foundation of knowledge if a student chose to take the ecumenism-and-interreligious elective (hereafter, Option E).

A word search of the forty-eight pages before Option E yielded only seven explicit uses of the terms "Jews," "Jewish people," or "Judaism."[9] They are essentially all nominal uses. Israel as a reference to "the people" appears to be mentioned but once. On my reading of this document, there are at least five missed opportunities to clarify a promise-fulfillment or "Old Covenant" usage and/or to draw connections between Judaism and Christianity in constructive and positive ways. On this brief, unscientific accounting, the *Framework* does not seem to attend seriously to the instruction begun with *NA* and articulated more explicitly in the three subsequent documents from the Vatican Commission for the Religious Relations with the Jews. The documents urge the necessity of *learning* about Judaism and of forging *relationships* through educational ventures, dialogue, and cooperative social action. The 1985 *Notes* addresses the question of education when in the conclusion it states, "Our two traditions are so related that they cannot ignore each other. Mutual knowledge must be encouraged at every level." The poignant and charged question of building new relationships between Jews and Christians is explicitly addressed in *We Remember* (#5): "We pray that our sorrow for the tragedy which the Jewish people has suffered in our century will lead to a new relationship with the Jewish people."[10]

With the importance of relationships in mind, let us examine the *Framework* a bit more closely through the lens of course Option E. This elective course combines the topics of ecumenism and interreligious dialogue and has six sections.

Church, conclusion, 1985, http://www.vatican.va/roman_curia/pontifical_councils/ chrstuni/relations-jews-docs/rc_pc_chrstuni_doc_19820306_jews-judaism_en.html/.

9. In the very first course, however, "The Revelation of Jesus Christ in Scripture," the "Old" Testament and figures therein are mentioned at IB.1a1; IB.2b; and IVA. Nothing acknowledges the integrity of Tanakh, and there is no note or cross-reference to the 2001 Pontifical Biblical Council document *The Jewish People and Their Sacred Scripture in the Christian Bible* (http://www.vatican.va/roman_curia/congregations/ cfaith/pcb_documents/rc_con_cfaith_doc_20020212_popolo-ebraico_en.html/), which would provide an educator with an important resource for a more richly textured presentation of Scripture in the Christian tradition.

10. Vatican Commission for Religious Relations with the Jews, *We Remember: A Reflection on the* Shoah, 1998: http://www.vatican.va/roman_curia/pontifical_councils/ chrstuni/documents/rc_pc_chrstuni_doc_16031998_shoah_en.html/.

The section on the relationship between Judaism and Catholicism has five subsections. The first two sections enumerate why the relationship is "special" (p. 51; E.III.A.1–2) and "unique and special" (pp. 51–52; E.III.B.1–6). The first of the eight points repeats the famous designation of Pope John Paul II that the Jewish people are the elder brothers in faith. This oft-quoted image could be a strong starting point to encourage reflection about the "intrinsic relationship" (another John Paul characterization) between Jews and Christians. Further, though the section on the Jews ends with a subsection about dialogue (E.III.E.1–3) that notes that an aim of dialogue is mutual respect it does not include interreligious relationships or friendships as a goal. It is unfortunate that the *Framework* misses the opportunity to have young people reflect on relationships since both traditions are pathways into relationship with God and community.

Moreover, the *Framework* repeats the *Catechism* (CCC #840) statement that "the Jewish people are the original Chosen People of God; Christians are the new People of God" (p. 51; III.B.3), as well as stating that "the New Covenant with Jesus Christ is the fulfillment of the promises of the first covenant between God and the Jewish people" (p. 51; III.B.5). These statements can easily lead to the misunderstanding that Christians are better than and closer to God than Jews if they are not well contextualized, thus undermining any possibility of the course leading to interreligious dialogue and to relationships that enliven and deepen the faith of the participants. Referencing the 2001 Pontifical Biblical Council document, *The Jewish People and Their Sacred Scriptures in the Christian Bible* (#21), which warns against a reductionist understanding of *fulfillment*, would help to avoid an unintentional anti-Jewish use of *fulfillment*. Number 21 also includes the remarkable statement, "Jewish messianic expectation is not in vain. It can become for us Christians a powerful stimulant to keep alive the eschatological dimension of our faith. Like them, we too live in expectation." The rich conversations students could have reflecting on these statements would certainly yield insights about divine-human relationships in both traditions and lead students to understand the importance of engaging authentic relationships with their Jewish contemporaries.

It is always easier to critique than to construct, and curriculum development is exceedingly difficult. In fact, some may eschew my observations as just so many minor differences in theological emphasis. My purpose is not to propose a full evaluation[11] of a very complex document that has to balance many criteria but to use the *Framework* as an example of how far Jewish-Catholic relations have developed since *NA* and the effect of this reconciliation on education. On the one hand, the good news is simply that the *Framework* includes a course that incorporates interreligious dialogue. The *Framework* clearly takes Vatican II seriously on this issue by including it in the *Framework*; it also refers to sections of *Lumen Gentium*[12] (especially #16) that specify an understanding of the People of God. On the other hand, those who work in ecumenical and interreligious dialogue can make a case that the *Framework* is too tepid in some parts regarding its engagement of dialogue, much as I have indicated.

The *Framework*, however, most clearly demonstrates changes in Catholic-Jewish relations because of a modification the authors of the document effected themselves after its original publication.

The original text[13] included two surprising and distressing statements concerning Judaism:

1. "The Jewish people have no sacramental economy; they continue to rely on the ritual prescriptions of the first Covenant reinterpreted for post-Temple Judaism" (p. 52; E.III.C.2).

2. "Aims of the dialogue include . . . bring all to Jesus Christ and his Church" (p. 52; E.III.E.3.d).

Those who work in Jewish-Christian relations were shocked to find these statements in the curriculum. The first statement (putting aside all the debates about theologies of sacramentality that it provokes) at minimum strongly implies that Jews do not have a pathway to God or a

11. See for example, Carrie J. Schroeder, "The U.S. Conference of Catholic Bishops' Doctrinal Elements of a Curriculum Framework for the Development of Catechetical Materials for Young People of High School Age: Pedagogical and Theological Perspectives of Religious Studies Teachers in U.S. Catholic Secondary Schools," EdD diss., University of San Francisco, 2013. Doctoral Dissertations.Paper 71, http://repository. usfca.edu/cgi/viewcontent.cgi?article=1060&context=diss/.

12. The Second Vatican Council, *Lumen Gentium: The Dogmatic Constitution of the Church*, 1964, http://www.vatican.va/archive/hist_councils/ii_vatican_council/ documents/vat-ii_const_19641121_lumen-gentium_en.html/.

13. Please note that since its first printing in 2008, changes have been made in the text. It is not clear when the changes were made. I printed a copy from the bishops' website in June 2012. In the course of writing this essay, I discovered that the pdf of the document currently on the website had two changes in the section on Judaism. I have no knowledge of the official reasons for changing the text.

relationship with God. The second statement, in a post-*Shoah* world, is simply unconscionable. Texts like these are stumbling blocks in the process of reconciliation between Catholics and Jews, in fact could preclude dialogue entirely, and have no place in forming young people of faith. Earlier I noted that the *Framework* could be criticized as leaning toward a reductionist view of fulfillment; statements such as these confirm a heavy-handed fulfillment theology not conducive to "foster[ing] mutual understanding and esteem" (*Guidelines* #4) or asking "our Jewish friends . . . to hear us with open hearts" (*We Remember* #1).

The *Framework* was developed by the USCCB Committee on Evangelization and Catechesis and first printed in July 2008. At approximately the same time the *Framework* was being written, the Committee on Doctrine and the Committee on Ecumenical and Interreligious Affairs were working on another document, *A Note on Ambiguities Contained in "Reflections on Covenant and Mission"* issued on June 18, 2009, by the USCCB.[14] The Note (#7) claimed that an invitation to baptism was implicit in every interreligious dialogue. (I have no knowledge of whether the authors of the *Framework* and the "Note" consulted with each other, or if the statements about "bringing all to Christ" in the one and "baptism" in the other were independent of each other as the different documents developed.) On August 18, 2009, a group of five national Jewish interfaith leaders representing different streams of contemporary Judaism and different Jewish organizations sent a letter to the USCCB in response to the "Note" writing that, "once Jewish-Christian dialogue has been formally characterized as an invitation, whether explicit or implicit, to apostatize, then Jewish participation becomes untenable." The USCCB responded on October 2, 2009, with a letter to the five Jewish leaders expressing gratitude that they had sent the letter and explaining that they had removed the sentences concerning baptism from the text. The bishops were "deeply grateful for the testimony of friendship which this honest exchange of correspondence represents in the dialogue."

An exchange at very high levels of official Jewish and Catholic leadership led to a significant alteration in a Catholic text. While the episode concerning the "Note" was not irenic, the fact remains that the Jewish-Catholic dialogue was strong enough to withstand a very significant challenge.

14. Documents and quotations within this paragraph can be accessed at http://www.ccjr.us/dialogika-resources/documents-and-statements/roman-catholic/us-conference-of-catholic-bishops and at http://www.ccjr.us/dialogika-resources/themes-in-todays-dialogue/conversion/574-njil09aug18/.

Did this experience affect the *Framework*? As late as June 2012 the problematic statements listed above were still in the text on the website. At some point, however, the bishops changed their pdf and eliminated the statement about sacramental economy. It is no longer in the document at all as far, as I can discover. The statement about bringing all to Christ (p. 52; E.III.E.3.d) was moved out of the section on Judaism and to the section on Proclamation and Dialogue (p. 53; E.V.A.3).[15] Since sentences in the "Note" that were changed were very similar to those in the *Framework*, one has to wonder if the latter were redacted in light of the fruitful exchange that occurred between the Jewish national interfaith leaders and the bishops.

It is significant that the curriculum was changed, regardless of the process. Eliding the statement about sacramental economy indicates that officials at the USCCB were paying attention to how to write their catechetical theology in light of *NA* and the important dialogue between Jews and Christians that has developed over fifty years. While some would advocate for more adjustments to the document to foster an even stronger unit on building Jewish-Christian understanding, it has to be remembered that the *Framework* is a catechetical document, a genre with limitations. Even given those limitations, the only way to insure religious leadership into the future that can effect constructive change such as that which happened with the controversy over the "Note" is to include in a catechetical framework sustained and substantive teaching about the "intrinsic relationship" between Judaism and Christianity. Experience with good dialogues has proven time and again that participants deepen their understanding of their own religion in authentic ways even as they develop a profound appreciation for their dialogue partner. Therefore, a thoroughgoing exploration of the experience of divine presence and relationship in community should be central to a unit on the relationship between Judaism and Catholicism.

Hanspeter Heinz and David Ellenson encourage forging relationships in interreligious dialogue while probing the truest realities of their respective lived faiths.[16] Their dialogue grapples with problems of

15. I discovered another document from the bishops dated 2012 and titled *Handbook on the Conformity Review Process*. Access it at http://www.usccb.org/about/evangelization-and-catechesis/subcommittee-on-catechism/upload/Conformity-Review-full-text-FINAL-Sept.pdf/. This document demonstrates on pp. 210, 212, 268, and 269 that the Framework was changed.

16. See their dialogue in Michael A. Signer, ed., *Memory and History in Christianity*

the potential extinction of memory (*extinctio memoriae*) posed by the exigencies of modernity and secularization. The details of their exchange are beyond the scope of this essay, but they evince a concern for the maintenance of our religious traditions that guide the future as well as create individuals connected to community—surely a concern for those involved in catechetical education.[17] Heinz concludes, 1. "We need relationships today . . . the [Second Vatican] Council's primary and most important objective was . . . to radically alter relationships: the relationship with God . . . relationship as a means to build community;"[18] 2. "Relationships take time," and "they must rise from the foundations of history;"[19] 3. "Relationships and history are nurtured by memory."[20] Ellenson writes, "God's presence, as well as God's blessing, become manifest only through the reality of relationship."[21] Communities of memory instantiate the presence of the divine for both men. Ellenson proposes that "creating living religious communities that . . . interact with the larger world . . . is essential if . . . everyday life is to be transformed and concentrated into the holy."[22] The curriculum *Framework* might better serve the goals of dialogue and understanding between Catholics and Jews if it included an explicit focus on relationships springing from the idea of the intrinsic relationship between Jews and Christians.

CASE STUDY: THE POSSIBILITIES OF INTERRELIGIOUS EDUCATION AFTER *NOSTRA AETATE*

Rev. Dr. Manfred Deselaers writes, "Stronger than the force which perpetrated Auschwitz must be our commitment to create a civilization of

---

and Judaism (Notre Dame, IN: University of Notre Dame Press, 2001). Hanspeter Heinz, "The Celebration of the Sacraments and the Teaching of the Commandments in the Age of Religious Consumerism, or History and Memory in Christian Communities since the Second Vatican Council," 145–69; David Ellenson, "History, Memory, and Relationship," 170–81.

17. Heinz, "The Celebration of the Sacraments," 148; cf Ellenson, "History, Memory, and Relationship," 170–74.

18. Heinz, "The Celebration of the Sacraments," 164.

19. Ibid.

20. Ibid.

21. Ellenson, 180.

22. Ibid., 176.

love 'after Auschwitz,' at the core of which stands the Jewish-Christian revelation about man as being in the image of G'd."[23]

The breach in relationship between Jews and Christians was so deep and so broad that repairing it will continue to require a wide variety of approaches at the levels of the laity, the scholars, and the leaders. What follows is a reflection on one program that illustrates the possible educational responses available to repair the wounded image of God in the Jewish-Christian relationship.

Engaging students in the study of the Holocaust can foster the study of Judaism—as a living religion compelling in its own integrity, and not as a victim—for Catholic students. For two years I worked with the Museum of Jewish Heritage—A Living Memorial to the Holocaust (located in Battery Park, New York City; hereafter MJH) to pilot an interreligious implementation of the Museum's curriculum: *Coming of Age during the Holocaust, Coming of Age Now.*[24] An explanation of the original intent of the curriculum is necessary before I explain the interreligious pilot.

Parents of children in bar- and bat-mitzvah preparation programs approached MJH asking for assistance in making the preparation curriculum more meaningful. In response to the parents' requests and in collaboration with Yad LaYeled—The Ghetto Fighters' Holocaust and Jewish Resistance Heritage Museum in Israel, MJH developed the *Coming of Age* curriculum. The original three goals of the curriculum were

1. "Students will learn about the major events of the Holocaust."

2. "*Students will learn about Jewish identity, community, and responsibility in a way that is personally engaging and meaningful*" (italics added).

---

23. Manfred Deselaers, "God and Evil: An Anthropological-Philosophical Reflection," in Manfred Deselaers et al., eds., *God and Auschwitz: On Edith Stein, Pope Benedict XVI's Visit, and God in the Twilight of History* (Krakow: UNUM Publishing House, 2008), 45–164.

24. See http://www.mjhnyc.org/l_online.html#.UxoBFfldVyU/ and http://comingofagenow.org/. Since the publishing of the original curriculum in hardcopy with DVD interactive portions, MJH now offers the entire curriculum free of charge on the Internet. I am indebted to Elizabeth Edelstein, Director of Education, the Museum of Jewish Heritage—A Living Memorial to the Holocaust, for introducing me to the *Coming of Age* curriculum and initiating our first joint study of the curriculum, which then inspired us to create the pilot program for interreligious use of the curriculum.

3. "Students will feel that their bar- or bat-mitzvah experience is enriched."[25]

MJH developed a curriculum steeped in the lives of twelve Holocaust survivors and one person who was raised in the Mandate for Palestine who all came to bar mitzvah or bat mitzvah age during the Holocaust. Students are able to probe more deeply their own commitment to their identity, their community, and their responsibilities to the same as they assume adult stature within their religion by encountering survivors who were their age during the Holocaust. The survivors represent a wide range of experience. They are chosen from across different years of the war, different parts of Europe, different levels of economic ability, different levels of religious observance, and so forth.

Each memoir is presented as a discrete unit. In the original hard-copy version, each individual workbook is seventeen pages and customized with a glossary, mapping activity, and timeline activity that is particular to that survivor's experience. The text of each memoir is very deliberately paced, and written for engaged learning. Every several paragraphs readers are presented with a "watch-and-listen" instruction, and students play a chapter from the DVD, or click a link and are presented with the adult survivor describing life as a teenager during the Holocaust, deepening the material that is in the text. The video testimonies are a very brief few minutes, but there are a good number of them for each survivor. In addition, flags for "think and write" and "for your research" also interrupt the text and guide students into active engagement with the survivor's story. The questions help the students to make connections to their contemporary situations and the cumulative effect is that students reflect on what they might do if confronted with challenges to identity and community.

---

25. These goals are listed on page 1 of the "Teacher's Guide" in the original print version. See http://comingofagenow.org/about/ for the goals as they are revised for the online version: "Students will reflect on the challenges survivors faced in maintaining their identities, responsibilities they assumed during difficult circumstances, sacrifices they made for others, and lessons they want to impart to the next generation. By studying the lives of survivors, students will grow in their understanding of the Holocaust and themselves, and develop a deep sense of what it means to come of age today." The curriculum's success in generating serious student reflection on identity, community, and responsibility was one reason that the online version of the curriculum was revised to rephrase goals and reflection questions in a universal way so that the curriculum could be successfully employed by any group of students. For instance, instead of beginning a question with "what in your Jewish tradition or experience," the questions will just ask about "your experience."

It is also important to acknowledge the interpretative horizon of the curriculum. The memoirs are crafted according to the logic that governs the floor plan of the permanent exhibit at MJH. It is a three-part movement. Students get to know the survivor's life before the war and to glimpse an insight into the life of an ordinary young person just like themselves. Life during the war is the second movement, followed by life after the war as the last portion of the lesson. The text also uses historically accurate language, eschewing terms such as "Holocaust," "survivor," or "bystander" so that the students encounter the survivor in personal language and not as some distant phantom of history. Students enter into the life story of the survivor and are challenged to consider the choices they might have made under such horrific threats to one's own existence. A generation that is rapidly passing from us is able to share its experiences in a developmentally appropriate way with young people who are learning to understand the factors in their own lives that create their identity as they strive to identify their responsibilities as young adults to themselves and to their communities.

The *Coming of Age* curriculum is expertly executed around focused goals and is not intended to be an introduction or guide through the political or historical dimensions of the Holocaust. Its personal, narrative approach encourages students to confront themselves and to reflect how they wish to live as adults. The curriculum, consequently, was ideal for use in an interreligious encounter even though its original purpose was much different.

Without the consistent teaching of the Roman Catholic magisterium since NA about the responsibility of Catholics to learn about Jews and Judaism, the educators of MJH and I could never have engaged twelve seventh-grade confirmation students from a Catholic parish with twelve bar- or bat-mitzvah students from a Reform Jewish congregation once a month across a religious-education school year to study the Holocaust and learn from each other in doing so.[26] Do not Catholic students in a confirmation program strive to *"learn about [Catholic] identity, community, and responsibility in a way that is personally engaging and meaningful"*? *Coming of Age* is a curriculum tailor-made (though this was not its original intent) to support an interreligious encounter.

26. This program lasted for two years and took place in New Rochelle, New York. Infrastructure challenges suspended the program, but we hope to reinstitute some form of interreligious engagement with the middle school and/or high school students.

From a certain point of view, one might say that the endeavor was an instant success simply because the clergy and religious educators at both institutions even agreed to try the project! Consider what this meant: students were being released from their standard religion curricula at their respective congregations to study with members of another religion during their final year of preparation for an extraordinarily important religious ritual. Even though it is a standard truth for people who research, teach, and practice in the area of interreligious dialogue that studying with members of a different religious tradition enriches one's understanding of one's own religion, in no way should it be taken for granted that these religious-education programs ceded valuable time from their programs. It is a measure of the rapprochement between Christianity and Judaism that these two local religious communities would allow confirmation and bar- or bat-mitzvah students to study together *precisely as part of their preparation.*

Many, but by no means all, of the students in the program knew each other from public school. They were not accustomed, however, to engaging with each other over questions of faith and religion. Our goals for the interreligious program were easily adopted and revised from *Coming of Age*: to learn about the Holocaust *but in the presence of a religious Other whose tradition had a very different relationship to the Holocaust*; to learn about community, identity, and responsibility for oneself as well as to understand perspectives on these values through the lens of a different religion; to enrich the experience of bar- or bat-mitzvah and confirmation; and to learn more about each other's religious tradition and the inherent connections between the religions. Questions in the text already invited reflection from an intra-Jewish perspective on the original goals; we educators had only to recast the questions to a degree and put Jewish and Christian students in study groups together to begin to pursue the interreligious goals. Students were going to be introduced to each other and their religious traditions in a way far more meaningfully than attending each other's postconfirmation or bar- or bat-mitzvah parties.

We employed the tradition of Jewish text study, *havrutah* (study with a friend a partner), and placed the students in groups of four—two from each congregation. Simply explaining the term *havrutah* was a significant moment of learning for each group of students since to talk about text study begged the question, which texts? for all the students. We seized the opportunity to explore the similarities and differences between the Jewish and Christian sacred texts, which led to an additional and important interreligious question—what might be troublesome about using the title "Old Testament" in a Jewish-Christian encounter? In this new context, students were immediately receptive to learning more about their own and each other's traditions; the context of learning with someone from another tradition put one's own tradition in a new light. We planned from the beginning to supplement the Holocaust curriculum with interreligious activities.

Artifact sharing was one such activity suggested by the museum educators. In our first session and at significant moments throughout the year, such as during the December celebrations of Hanukkah and Christmas or during the spring when approaching Passover and Easter, students were required to bring to class something that reflected for them a special and significant connection to their religious traditions. For this activity students worked in pairs and not in groups of four. Each student had to explain the artifact to the partner; when the pairing activity was over, each member of the pair had to explain to the large group the significance of his or her *partner's* artifact. This is a very successful and enjoyable mode of interreligious sharing for middle-school-age children. The particularity of each religion and its cultural variations takes center stage; students have fun struggling with strange new vocabulary words, ask many questions, and do not want the activity to end. Most important, students let their guards down and they begin to discuss what is important about their faith for them, and they witness the serious convictions of their partner in another religion. Stories from parents, grandparents, and even great grandparents were shared, and students witnessed the importance of community and tradition for identity. They begin to see how the friend whom they knew coming into the program or how a new friend just made in the program takes ownership of his or her religious tradition. That witness leads to concomitant self-reflection. Standing within the thick of their own preparation, the students can enter together into the story of survivors who had to have "underground" bar mitzvahs, or who were baptized in order to survive while their parents wept in the shadows in the back of the church. Together they were able to think about the courage of the Christians (not enough, of course) who hid and rescued Jewish children. Throughout learning the story of the survivor chosen by the *havrutah* group, values at the heart of bar- or bat-mitzvah and confirmation preparation—identity, community, responsibility—were consistently raised for reflection.

Staffing and location also factored into the quality of the interreligious engagement. We alternated sites, rotating back and forth between synagogue and church. Students were exposed to the changes in the religious year just by walking through the various spaces of two fairly large complexes; students noticed their surroundings, the people, the activities, and they would ask questions about what they saw or heard. Spontaneous interreligious learning proved to be quite valuable. A teacher from each congregation's religious-education program was tasked to the program. During the first year, the director of education from MJH and I were at each session coteaching; during the second year, the director came for particular events, and I led the monthly sessions. Students benefited from witnessing the religious-education teachers, volunteers with different levels of experience and training, teaching each other and learning together. It is important, however, when working with volunteer educators to conduct preprogram training to address lacunae in knowledge. The teachers, as with the students, were able to develop a relationship reflecting on their traditions and identities together and they reported being moved by how much they learned.

We arranged for students to attend worship services together. Careful attention must be paid to this dimension of interreligious learning to make it constructive. For instance, inviting the Jewish participants to Catholic mass during the Easter season when the lectionary selections (but for the Psalm) are all drawn from the New Testament is perhaps not the best choice. Attending mass when selections from the shared scripture is used would be a better choice. Parents and families of students should be invited to attend together. The congregations need to be advised in advance that the following week they will host visitors. If conducted correctly, observing worship can be a very rewarding experience for the participants. If God's presence is manifest in relationships, as Heinz and Ellenson explained, then interreligious understanding and friendship can be advanced by sharing with each other one's faith in all of its most intimate particularity—the tradition at prayer. No proselytizing, no doctrinal judgment but the chance to experience God's presence in another's community was the goal.

In addition to visiting the two houses of worship, there were other opportunities for parents to be involved. Halfway through the program we all visited the Museum together. Families were allowed to participate in the fieldtrip and it was a very moving experience to have the previously designated *havrutah* groups move through the museum together with parents and grandparents as part of the group. It was an intergenerational, interreligious learning experience. In the session following the museum visit, the students encountered their survivor memoirs with a new depth of understanding for what the survivors experienced. In the second year of the program, we offered an evening of education for adults with a scholar from each tradition providing an overview of the history of contempt and the efforts of Christians to create a new teaching of respect. Ideally, an interreligious program for parents would run concurrently with the middle-school program.

The comments on the surveys at the conclusion of the program indicated that each group was convinced that the students from the other congregation had learned a great deal about the other religion; there was perceptible pride in their written responses. The students were genuinely happy to know that their religious-other partners now knew about their religion. Jewish participants were surprised to discover that Catholic students would care so deeply about the Holocaust; one Jewish participant reported that he never imagined that the Christian kids would be so sad when they learned about the Holocaust. Most of the participants reported learning a lot more about the Holocaust. In *We Remember: A Reflection on the Shoah,* the Vatican taught that the Holocaust demanded a "moral and religious memory and, particularly among Christians, a very serious reflection on what gave rise to it" (#2). Though the latter task of assessing Christian complicity in the *Shoah* because of the Christian teaching of contempt for Jews and Judaism is intellectually beyond the capacities of seventh-graders, interreligious learning around the Holocaust in the context of confirmation and bar- and bat-mitzvah preparation provided a foundation for these students to develop a "moral and religious memory" in the presence of one another.

The *Coming of Age* Interreligious Pilot Program was successful in part because both congregations' leadership trusted the educators at MJH and me to present sensitively and accurately dimensions of both religious traditions. Acknowledgment of responsibility was involved as well. The Catholic leadership of the parish knew that the teaching of the *NA* era needed to be communicated, that the students in its confirmation program needed to learn more about the Jewish roots of Christianity, and that Catholics need to recognize Christian complicity in the Holocaust.

Unlike a discrete curriculum designed for a single faith community whose goal is to communicate to its members the doctrinal truths of its tradition, the *Coming of Age* program is able to engage students in interreligious dialogue by probing fundamental human concerns: identity, community, responsibility. Its success also is grounding in the relationships that develop while studying the Holocaust together and the genuine learning about the traditions that occurs through those relationships. Religious commitments are strengthened, not weakened, through such learning in dialogue. Though the bishops' curriculum document is explicitly a *doctrinal framework* and as such does incorporate the broad lines of the Vatican II theology expressed in *NA, Unitatis Redintegratio, Dignitatis Humanae,* and *Lumen Gentium* and developed thereafter, nevertheless it would benefit from providing more robust direction for educators about the importance of dialogue as a mode of self-reflection.

CONCLUSION

Fifty years after the publication of *Nostra Aetate,* and seventy years after the liberation of Auschwitz, we can speak of qualified success in educating Catholics about the revolution in Catholic teaching about Judaism. The two examples provided in this essay are just that: they are single illustrations of the fundamental progress that has been made in Jewish-Christian relations, the stress points, and the hope for continued growth in mutual understanding and relationships. It would take many more articles to describe the variety of creative educational efforts at the secondary, college, and congregational levels. Catholic curricula, however, that relegate study of the intrinsic relationship that Jews and Christians share to an elective position do not adequately address the directives provided by *Nostra Aetate* and the documents that have followed it. It is clear, though, that the relationships developed over years of working together toward reconciliation sustain the progress of Jewish-Christian reconciliation when problems arise such as the publication of the USCCB's "Note." Relationships and trust allow the development of new initiatives such as the interreligious version of *Coming of Age.* When Pope Francis I gave an address for business, political, and cultural leaders in Brazil on July 27, 2013, he used the word "dialogue" eleven times in two short paragraphs. His words are guidance for the next fifty years: "dialogue, dialogue, dialogue. It is the only way for individuals, families and societies to grow, the only way for the life of peoples to progress, along with the culture of encounter, a culture in which all have something good to give and all can receive something good in return."[27]

27. See full text at http://www.ccjr.us/dialogika-resources/documents-and-statements/roman-catholic/francis/1251-francis2013july27.

14

The Implications of *Nostra Aetate* for Interreligious Dialogue in Israel[1]

Ronald Kronish

INTRODUCTION

THERE IS NO QUESTION that the document *Nostra Aetate*—promulgated by the Second Vatican Council in October 1965—changed the discourse in the field of Jewish-Christian dialogue in particular, and interreligious dialogue in general in the contemporary period. We have moved from persecution to partnership, from confrontation to cooperation, from diatribe to dialogue.[2]

Not only did *Nostra Aetate* open up a new dialogue between the Catholic Church and the Jewish people, but it initiated a dialogue between the Catholic Church and other religions, including Islam. Indeed,

---

1. Rabbi Dr. Ronald Kronish was assisted in the preparation of this paper by Elana Lubka, a student from Macalester College in St. Paul, Minnesota, who served as a student intern with ICCI in the summer of 2013.

2. As documented and stated in a film produced by the Interreligious Coordinating Council in Israel titled *I Am Joseph Your Brother* (directed by Eli Tal-El and Amy Kronish, 2001, 58 minutes).

it made dialogue between leaders and followers of the major monotheistic religions "kosher" and mainstream. It is now accepted practice for leaders of religious communities at all levels to be in dialogue with each other in many places in the world, and to work together in common cause wherever possible to heal the world. It is fair to say that this is a direct result of the major shift in policy of the Catholic Church, which is expressed in *Nostra Aetate*.

This is also the case in Israel, where I have lived and worked for the past thirty-four years. Interreligious dialogue is part of the landscape here. It is an essential part of our common life. It is vital for our present state of being and for our relations for the future.

In this paper, I will describe the work of interreligious dialogue in Israel in four sections:

1. The political context—how is our dialogue special here due the particular political context, especially the Peace Process and the lack thereof;

2. Our new four-stage model for interreligious dialogue in the service of peace;

3. Our current dialogue and action programs;

4. Our role in the future—why dialogue will be ever more important for a sustainable future for Israel and Palestine.

SECTION I: THE POLITICAL CONTEXT

Engaging in interreligious dialogue in Israel among Jews, Christians, and Muslims is unique, due to the ongoing nature of the conflict and the lack of a political solution, as of this writing. The fact that the so-called Peace Process has dragged on for the past 20 years, since the First Oslo Accord in 1993, without a clear political solution in the offing, has made dialogue more difficult here, especially in recent years.

While we do not engage directly in political work, the political processes—or lack thereof—affect us greatly. The politicians, diplomats and lawyers are responsible for the progress of the Peace Process. They know how to negotiate and reach agreements that lead to peace agreements between governments. They are engaged in peacemaking. When they succeed, peace treaties are crafted and signed by the warring parties.

We, on the other hand—along with other nongovernmental organizations which function in civil society—are engaged in peacebuilding. This is the work of rabbis, imams, priests, educators, social workers and psychologists, who bring people together to enter into dialogical and educational processes aimed at helping people figure out how to live in peace with each other, and motivating people to take concrete actions to do so.

There is, of course, a close connection between peacemaking and peacebuilding processes. When the peacemakers are doing their jobs well by making many peace agreements, as they did in the 1990s with the Oslo Accords (1993 and 1994), the Fundamental Agreement between the State of Israel and the Holy See (Dec. 1993), the peace agreement with Jordan (1994) and the Wye River agreement (1998), then it seemed only natural for people-to-people programs to be considered essential. When political peace progresses well, it is logical and sensible for people to get together to figure out how to live in peace. During the last decade and a half—with no new political agreements—fewer and few people are entering into dialogue with "the other," simply because they don't see the point.

Nevertheless, we have continued to do dialogue programs during the last ten to fifteen years while others have given up. Why?

Through genuine dialogue, these programs keep a flicker of hope alive in an ongoing conflict. They point the way to the future. They remind us that the goal of peace is normalization, not separation. They train the people for the possibilities of peaceful coexistence among people and peoples for the future, even if this is not the reality of the present moment.

Moreover, conflicts can be transformed from a violent phase to an educational/social phase, as in the cases of Northern Ireland, South Africa, and Bosnia, where the bloodshed has ended, and now what needs to be done is to overcome decades of hatred and separation. But even though we are not there yet, we need to begin wherever possible to bring people together to experience and learn about the possibilities and benefits of living together in the same country or same region.

Also, as a result of a comprehensive evaluation process of one of our programs,[3] we discovered that there are ten transformative ways in which participants are affected by such programs:

---

3. *Evaluation Report*, prepared by Rebecca Russo, 2009.

1. Seeing that the conflict has two legitimate sides, and being able to accept people who have different opinions

2. Becoming better listeners

3. Realizing that not everything is solvable

4. Looking at the conflict in a more complex and realistic way

5. Realizing that people are similar in many ways yet still have strong differences

6. Allowing them to grow up and become more confident in their own abilities

7. Influencing them to become more active in society

8. Becoming stronger in their own opinions while simultaneously becoming more tolerant and accepting

9. Having more knowledge about other religions

10. Realizing that "the others" are also human beings.

It is because we have seen so much personal transformation among people that have gone through our dialogue programs that we have been motivated to keep going, even in very difficult periods.

SECTION II: OUR FOUR- STAGE MODEL FOR INTERRELIGIOUS DIALOGUE AND ACTION

Over the past twenty-two years, after much trial and error, we have learned a great deal about the process of dialogue in our particular conflict situation, which has led us to develop the following four- part model:

- Personal interaction: getting to know each other as individual human beings

The first thing we do when we bring groups together to engage in long-term systematic and sensitive dialogue is to focus on personal narratives. Members of the group learn to listen deeply to each other's stories in order to understand and respect the identity and personal narrative of each of its members. In doing so, many stereotypes are broken down and we engage in "de-demonizing" the other (i.e., discovering that the other is not the devil who is out to destroy us).

Palestinians and Israelis who have never met each other before coming to our dialogue groups usually see the other through the prisms of the conflict and the negative media stereotypes which dominate our print and electronic media. In our dialogue groups, we shatter these stereotypes by asking each person to share their identities and life stories with the other.

- Interreligious, Text-Based Learning

The second thing we do in our dialogue process is to open up the sacred texts of each other's religious/cultural traditions and learn from them with good teachers. This helps us to overcome ignorance, break down stereotypes about the other's religion and culture, and build trust between members of the group.

Israeli Jews know almost nothing about Islam or Christianity. And, what they do know is usually negative and was learned in courses in Jewish history in which they learned that Muslims or Christians either oppressed or massacred Jews throughout the centuries. Nor do Muslims or Christians who live in Israel or Palestine know much about Judaism. Much of what they do know is negative, as they learn it mostly from the media and from the "street" and the family.

Participants who have gone through this process in our dialogue groups learn to recognize that there are common humanistic values shared by the three major monotheistic religions, and they can sense a spirit of religious partnership, which motivates them to continue the dialogue and to seek meaningful paths of action together.

- Discussing core issues of the conflict

We believe that in a genuine dialogue process the core issues of the conflict can be discussed in an open, honest, and sensitive fashion, guided by careful and consistent professional facilitation, without creating animosity or acrimony. In fact, we have found that participants in our dialogue groups continue to come back to the table year after year precisely because the discussion is frank and forthright.

When significant levels of trust have been developed beforehand, most people find this phase particularly meaningful and enriching as a way to genuinely get to know the other. It leads to deep mutual under-standing of the other's religious, cultural, and existential reality, even if it also delineates where people fundamentally do not—and often can-not—agree with the other.

- Taking action, separately and together: "Dialogue is not enough!"

As responsible members of society, we must take our learning and create change. We are obligated to work for peace, to influence others, and to cause a ripple effect. As a result, we strive for our groups to experience both dialogue and action. In other words, all of our participants—religious leaders, women, youth, young adults, educators—are asked to take some action—separately or together—as a result of the personal transforma-tional processes that they go through within this intensive experience.

Action can take many forms—personal, social, educational and/ or political, but it is agreed that every person who is moved by the dialogue process is obligated to share their experiences with others in whatever ways possible.

Moreover, each person—through personal and professional net-works and associations—should be committed to acting in such a way as to bring the insights and lessons of their dialogue processes to the atten-tion of people in their own communities.

In this way, each person in each dialogue group is a "multiplier" who can spread the message of the possibilities and benefits of peaceful coexistence, and the method of dialogue and education, to many other people in society.

SECTION III: CURRENT DIALOGUE AND ACTION PROGRAMS[4]

Based on the political context and the four-step model described above, we have been engaged in Dialogue and Action Programs with two major target populations in recent years—religious leaders and youth or young-adult leaders:

Religious Leaders. We have focused on grassroots religious lead-ers who can have an impact in their communities over the last several

---

4. Based on the Interreligious Coordinating Council in Israel (ICCI) 2012 *Annual Report*.

years, and we have held important public symposia in Jerusalem with religious leaders.

- Galilee Religious Leaders' Forum, now in its sixth year, reaches out to about forty religious leaders in the Galilee from Muslim, Christian, Jewish, and Druze faith communities. In collaboration with the Division of Religious Affairs of the Ministry of the Interior, this group, which includes rabbis, Druze and Muslim imams and Christian ministers and reverends, comes together to study each other's religious traditions, to discuss issues of contemporary concern, and to do joint study days called "Days of Tolerance" in Arab and Jewish schools in the Galilee.

- *Kodesh*: Co-chaired by ICCI (Interreligious Coordinating Council in Israel) Director Dr. Ron Kronish and Kadi Iyad Zahalka (Kadi of the Sharia Court of Jerusalem of the State of Israel), *Kodesh*, "Religious Voices for Peace," is a new program, started in 2013, designed for Jewish and Muslim Israeli citizens. The *Kodesh* Dialogue and Action Group consists of fifteen Jews and fifteen Muslims, bringing together men and women of different professions: religious leaders, community leaders, academics, educators, and journalists to study sacred texts, to discuss contemporary issues in Israeli society, and to develop concrete plans-of-action programs to be implemented in Jewish and Arab communities in Israel

- Symposia with the Konrad Adenauer Foundation: In conjunction with the Konrad Adenauer Foundation, ICCI coordinates seminar and study days. In 2012, we held two highly successful symposia:

  - *Iftar Seminar and Dinner*: Religious leaders from across Israel gathered in Jerusalem to break the daily fast during Ramadan and discuss charity and justice in Islam. We also held our fourth annual *Iftar* seminar and dinner in July 2013.

  - *Hanukah Program on Confronting Hellenization and Secularization: Then and Now*: Seventy people from three faiths gathered to discuss issues of modernization and religious traditions in December 2012. Topics of conversation included the question, how do we engage in modernity without losing our religious traditions and identity? This event highlighted the shared challenges religious communities face in the line between embracing innovation and assimilation.

YOUTH/YOUNG ADULT LEADERSHIP PROGRAMS

During the last twelve years, we have been very active in developing dialogue-and-action programs for Palestinian (Muslim and Christian) and Israeli Jewish youth and young adults in the Jerusalem area. We have done this because we have felt that young people are less cynical and more hopeful than their elders, and because they have so much at stake in carving out a better future for their generation.

- Face to Face/Faith to Faith (which is partnership between the Auburn Theological Seminary in New York, ICCI in Jerusalem, and similar organizations in Northern Ireland and South Africa) has been our flagship Dialogue and Action program for Palestinian and Israeli teenagers for the past twelve years. In past years, throughout the yearlong program, the group met twice a month with their two facilitators (one Jewish and one Palestinian) to discuss issues of identity and religion. The program was divided into three parts: meetings to discuss identity issues; a two-week intensive summer camp experience in New York State with peers from South Africa, Northern Ireland, and parts of the USA; and the planning and implementation of action projects. During 2012, the participants were forced to deal with the November fighting in Gaza. Refusing to shy away from these difficult issues, these youth addressed head-on issues of attacks on Palestinian youth in West Jerusalem as well as the late November fighting in Gaza. Going through a war together not only highlighted their concern for one another but brought to light their own confusion towards the war. This was a difficult period for them, both as individuals and as a group, but they pushed forward with projects to mobilize their communities into working toward peace through three final projects.

- Alumni programs—Jewish and Palestinian Young Adults for Peaceful Coexistence—The alumni community is composed of young adult Israelis and Palestinians who have demonstrated commitment toward understanding each other, understanding themselves, and working hard to bring peace programs to their communities.

As more individuals participate in ICCI programs and the alumni network continues to grow, we are confident our program graduates will continue turning their experiences with ICCI into real-world change to bring about peace. Sixteen of our alumni—including Jewish and Palestinian participants—participated in a workshop at the Corrymeela Community in Ballycastle at the end of August 2013, where they met with young adults from Northern Ireland, to learn about their conflict, to reflect on our conflict, and to return to Israel invigorated with new ideas of how to spread the message of the benefits and possibilities of peaceful coexistence in Jewish and Palestinian communities. Testimonials from alumni include such statements as the following: Yehuda, 26: "If I want to know my neighbor, I need to know my neighbor." Tarek, 31: "I have been volunteering with ICCI for five years and know . . . that their goals could change people's lives."

- "Present Memory" Trialogue: In August 2012, ICCI conducted a special ten-day trialogue program for thirty-two young adults, made up of Germans (from the organization *Evangelisches Jugend)*, as well as Jewish and Palestinian Israelis. The program was centered on exploring questions of the past, namely, how we remember the past, how the past is apparent in present societies, and how the past designs current attitudes and perspectives. The entire group visited holy Christian, Jewish, and Islamic sites, through which they explored their own religious and spiritual identities. Through dialogue sessions, participants also had a chance to explore each other's religious identities, as well as how they experienced visiting their own religion's holy sites.

- Kickstart Peace: In 2012, ICCI began a new program with the Abu Ghosh Community Center and the Kiryat Yearim Youth Village to unite Jewish and Arab youth around a shared love: the game of soccer. Through this program, which combines sports training, matches as part of the local Jerusalem Mayor's League, and intercultural and social activities, youth get to know each other through sports as they build social relationships, and develop tolerance and mutual understanding. In the 2012–13 year, the program expanded to two teams, one in the Israeli Arab Village west of Jerusalem known as Abu Gosh, and the other in the northern mixed neighborhood of

Jerusalem known as French Hill. When it was all over, one of the participants in this program said: "We play together like friends, brothers. When we play together, there are no Jews or Arabs anymore, we are all friends" (Hossni, from Abu Ghosh).

SECTION IV: TOWARDS THE FUTURE

As I reflect back to the beginning of this essay, I am mindful that as a result of *Nostra Aetate*, I have been privileged to live in The Era of Dialogue, which this groundbreaking initiative of the Catholic Church brought to the world. The Middle Ages of Christian-Jewish polemics are over. We can now cooperate in so many areas from dialogue to social justice to even peacebuilding! We can now look to the future with confidence and optimism, together, in partnership and for perpetuity.

My father, Rabbi Leon Kronish, of blessed memory, who was a rabbi for fifty-four years, always used to respond to the simple question, how are you? with a typically Jewish/Israeli answer: *Yehiyeh tov*—"things will be good." The future will be better than the past.

He believed deeply in Israel's mission as the fulfillment of messianic redemption. And so do I. I inherited this legacy, this optimism, from him. And therefore I say that despite the current difficulties and obstacles in the political Peace Process—and there are many of them—I believe that the process will work itself out (i.e., there will be a political solution, sooner or later, between Israel and the Palestinians, and all the Arab states).

There will be a two-state solution: Israel and Palestine, side by side. This is the new unfolding reality coming about, albeit much too slowly and painfully. And then what? Will we be prepared for the next steps? What will be needed in the future?

What will be needed is what I like to call "the other peace process"[5]— the educational, religious, and spiritual one—to supplement the political one.

There will be a desperate need for a massive religious, spiritual, educational, and psychological campaign to change the hearts and minds of the people on both sides, a serious and systematic set of programs that will educate the next generations about the existential needs to learn to live together.

5. Ronald Kronish, "The Other Peace Process," *Jerusalem Post*, February 2, 1997.

This will not be quick, nor will it be easy. But it will soon become the new educational imperative of the new era.

We will have no choice but to bring people together in large numbers to engage in dialogue, education, and action in order to learn to live in peace:

- Rabbis, imams, priests, and ministers, as the grassroots community leaders

- Teachers, educators, headmasters, assistant principals, curriculum writers, youth-movement leaders, informal educators, in a wide variety of settings, such as community centers, camps, and seminar centers

- Women from all parts of the Palestinian and Jewish societies—professionals as well as laypersons, educators and activists, housewives and mothers, community leaders and laypersons.

I believe that those of us currently engaged in interreligious dialogue and education in Israel and Palestine will have a major role to play in this people-to-people peace process for a long time to come. And religious leaders and their followers from abroad—Jewish, Christian, and Muslim—will be called upon to help.

This will be a time not to divest of the possibilities of peace but to invest in peacebuilding programs in Israel and Palestine, across borders, for the sake of all of God's children in the region.

15

Reflections on the Impact of *Nostra Aetate* on Israeli Life

Deborah Weissman

THE PUBLICATION OF *NOSTRA Aetate* in 1965 was a watershed event in the history of Catholic-Jewish relations in particular and perhaps even Christian-Jewish relations in general. My colleagues writing other articles for this volume will no doubt stress its unique importance. In this short piece, I will, however, attempt to argue that it has had much less impact on the country in which I live, the State of Israel, both among Jews and among the local Christians. I will argue that its relatively minor impact can be explained through at least three factors: the demographic situation of Jews and non-Jews in Israel, the nature of the local Christian communities, and the ongoing political conflict. I will explore two different approaches to Zionism and how they impact on this topic and conclude by presenting some hopeful signs for the future.

Daniel Rossing (1946–2010) was a true pioneer in the field of Jewish-Christian relations in Israel, who in 2004 founded the JCJCR, the Jerusalem Center for Jewish-Christian Relations. Its work focuses on the local Christian communities within Israel. From 1975 to 1988, Rossing headed the division of Christian communities in the Israeli Ministry of Religious Affairs. It is to his blessed memory that I dedicate this essay.

SOME HISTORICAL BACKGROUND

During the Second Vatican Council, most Israelis were preoccupied with other issues. The State of Israel itself was still very young (in 1962, it was only fifteen years old!). The key challenges were, as always, defense, but also nation building through absorption of mass immigration. Shortly before the Second Vatican Council was the trial of Adolph Eichmann, a source of fascination for the Israeli public, which served to reinforce the feelings of isolation of the Jewish people from the rest of the world and its heritage of persecution at the hands of people self-identified as Christians.

The only major Israeli official to be deeply concerned with the Council and with the work that later emerged as *Nostra Aetate*, was Morris Fisher, the fledgling state's Ambassador to Italy.[1] Few of his colleagues in the Israeli Foreign Ministry even knew or cared much about Christianity. Fisher was involved with the work of the Council but died in 1965, several months before "the Jewish document" finally came out.[2]

Meanwhile, in the Arab world, there was general uneasiness about the projected document. Arab Christians felt threatened, fearing that more openness on the part of the Church vis-à-vis the Jewish people would have negative political ramifications for them in their home countries. Not having directly lived through the *Shoah*, they saw Jews not as victims, but as representatives of an enemy state.

The embrace of *NA*[3] by the official bodies of the American Jewish community served to further distance the Israeli establishment from the document. It was perceived as a subject for Diaspora Jews. American Jews were perceived by the Israelis as *shtadlanim*,[4] going out of their way to celebrate a "victory," which, to the Israelis, was really just a very partial improvement; the reaction of officials in the American Jewish commu-

---

1. For this, and other insights, see the Hebrew edition, published in 2006, of Uri Bialer, *Cross on the Star of David: The Christian World in Israel's Foreign Policy 1948–1967* (Bloomington: Indiana University Press, 2005). See esp. 69–119.

2. This is how what was published as *Nostra Aetate* in October 1965, was previously referred to, in some circles.

3. Abbreviation for *Nostra Aetate*.

4. A medieval Hebrew word for Jewish "lobbyists," who represented their communities before the non-Jewish authorities.

nity reminded some Israelis of the fawning attitudes that allegedly had characterized, in history, the relations between Jews in the Diaspora and some of their non-Jewish rulers. The distance also reflects a deeper tension that existed in Israel-Diaspora relations, primarily in the 1950s and 1960s. As I have written elsewhere,

> I've never understood why in Israel things that are American are in such great demand—like MacDonald's hamburgers—while those that are American Jewish—like non-Orthodox synagogues—are perceived as foreign and *galuti*.[5]

The enthusiastic acceptance of *NA* by Jews in the Diaspora was perceived by Israeli officialdom as *galuti*.

Certainly, the major turning point in Catholic-Jewish relations was in 1993, when, as a response to the Oslo process, the Vatican recognized the State of Israel. The process that led up to this and its ramifications are far beyond the scope of the present paper. We will, however, comment briefly on three papal visits.

PILGRIMAGES

Pope John XXIII died in 1963, to be succeeded by Pope Paul VI, who presided over the rest of Vatican II. In early 1964, Pope Paul went on a pilgrimage to the Holy Land, the first ever. The focus of this pilgrimage was a meeting in Jerusalem with Patriarch Athenagoras I of Constantinople and left little impression on the Israeli public.

In 1999, Rabbi David Rosen (another contributor to this volume) and I were invited to attend a meeting at the Israeli Ministry of Education. I thought that the meeting was about the forthcoming trip to Israel on the part of the then-pope, John Paul II, which had been planned for 2000. It was hoped that hundreds of thousands of Christian Pilgrims would follow him and celebrate the new millennium in the Holy Land. I understood that the Ministry called us in to explore educational ways of preparing Israeli Jewish schoolchildren for this important development.

I came to the meeting well prepared with a list of ideas for educational activities, speakers, films, site visits for class trips, how the units could be

5. Weissman, in Allon Gal and Alfred Gottschalk, eds., *Beyond Survival and Philanthropy: American Jewry and Israel* (Cincinnati: Hebrew Union College Press, 2000), 118. *Galuti* literally means "Exilic" and was a derogatory term in the classical Zionist lexicon.

integrated into various aspects of the school curricula, and so on. To my dismay, the chairman of the meeting began by asking why, in view of the Crusades and the Inquisition, we should welcome all these Christians!

Most of the grandiose plans for masses of tourists never materialized because shortly after the pope's visit, which in itself was a very significant experience, the Second *Intifada* broke out. I have never since been reinvited to the Ministry of Education, although many years have passed and another pope, Benedict XVI, has also come to, and gone from, Jerusalem.

The two papal pilgrimages, in 2000 and 2009, had a great impact on how Israeli Jews relate to Christianity. Pope John Paul II impressed the Israeli public with his charisma. I remember hearing Israeli Jews who said things like, "A religious leader who's compassionate? Wow!" Undoubtedly, the visits to Yad Vashem and the Western Wall were pivotal moments. Nothing in Pope Benedict's visit equaled them.

Were there, from a Jewish perspective, any highlights of Pope Benedict's visit?[6] I think there were: During his visit to Jordan, Pope Benedict, like Moses in Deuteronomy, stood on Mount Nebo and viewed the Promised Land; but unlike Moses, he would then actually enter it on the Israeli side. During his talk there, he recalled the "inseparable bond" between Christians and the Jewish people, who share the Hebrew Scriptures. He expressed the desire to "overcome all obstacles to the reconciliation of Christians and Jews in mutual respect and cooperation." He also acknowledged powerfully the deep connection between Jews, the Torah and the land of Israel. The anti-Israeli criticism leveled at these remarks and the need for the Vatican spokesman in Jordan to soft-pedal them, saying that the pope was speaking only in a religious vein, showed how important a statement he had made.

Second, when the Royal Jordanian jet landed at Ben-Gurion Airport, the plane of a predominantly Muslim country bore the blue-and-white flag of the Jewish State and the yellow flag of the Vatican. Finally, at the welcoming ceremony at the airport, the pope condemned unequivocally anti-Semitism and Holocaust denial. I believe that, as on other occasions, as well, the Pope received poor guidance from his advisors. Few people paid close attention to the speech at the airport; the eyes of the Jewish world were focused on the visit to Yad Vashem, which was, at best, lackluster. One might have expected, given his own personal background

6. Deborah Weissman, "Jewish Perspectives on Pope Benedict XVI's Visit to the Holy Land," in Michael McGarry, CSP, and Deborah Weissman, *Pope Benedict XVI in the Holy Land* (New York: Paulist, 2011), 153–59.

as a German, and given the flap over Holocaust-denying Bishop Richard Williamson, that the pope would have used the opportunity to say something more significant and to do so in a way that would be more cognizant of special Jewish sensitivities.

The difference between the two men is not only one of personal warmth and charisma. Pope Benedict XVI—formerly Cardinal Joseph Ratzinger—was and remains a theology professor; his predecessor, Karol Jozef Wojtyla, before entering the Polish seminary, had been an actor and a playwright and remained the master of the symbolic gesture. But many forget that even he, in the late 1980s, was the target of much Jewish criticism for his welcome to the Vatican of former Nazi Kurt Waldheim. In retrospect, Pope John Paul II seems to have been so admired by Jews, that they are unaware of the more complex and controversial aspects of his papacy. It is also important to bear in mind that the general mood in 2000 regarding the prospects for peace in the region was much more optimistic than in 2009, an Intifada and several wars later.

At the time of the writing of this piece, there is a new pope, Francis, a native of Argentina. He probably has more positive personal and professional ties with the Jewish community of Buenos Aires than any previous pope has ever had with his home community. During a June 2013 meeting with Israel's Deputy Foreign minister Ze'ev Elkin, Pope Francis indicated that he is also interested in visiting Israel. In May 2014 the Pope visited Israel and that may impact significantly on the level of knowledge and interest among Israeli Jews regarding the Catholic Church.

MAJORITY-MINORITY RELATIONS

The relative lack of influence of *NA* in Israel can be explained partly by its anomalous situation of majority-minority relations. Throughout the Diaspora, Jewish communities are small and, often, tiny, minorities within the larger societies. The largest Diaspora community, in the U.S., is, by the most liberal estimates, less than 2 percent of the total population. In the next largest Diaspora community, France, the Jews make up less than 1 percent of the total. Thus, the State of Israel, in which about 75 percent of the population is Jews, is truly anomalous on the world Jewish scene.

Diaspora Jews today generally live as a minority among Christians and post-Christians. In some periods of Jewish history, many Jews lived in predominantly Muslim settings. In Israel, the next largest religious group after Jews is Muslims—about 20 percent—with Christians of all denominations, plus a small community of Druze, making up the rest. Rossing noted:

> [There are] . . . frequently overlooked similarities between the Christian communities in Israel and the Jewish people the world over. Today, these communities collectively constitute only about two percent of the population in the land where Christianity was born. They are perhaps the least understood segment of society, not only by the country's dominant Jewish and Muslim populations, but also—perhaps especially—by the Christian majorities in the West.

With the exception of national churches such as the Armenian and Ethiopian, most of the fourteen ancient communities and roughly forty Protestant groups are now largely Arabic-speaking. As Arab Christians, they are a double minority: Arabs in the midst of the majority Jewish population of Israel, Christians within Israel's dominantly Muslim Arab society. The Eastern Christians cannot escape a sense of second-class status relative to the more numerous and powerful Western Christian world. The smallest communities—such as the Ethiopians, Syrian Catholics, and Anglicans—are at a disadvantage relative to the resources of entrenched communities like the Greek Orthodox, Armenians, and Latins. Finally, those who emphasize their Palestinian identity find themselves in an inferior position vis-à-vis the Israelis.

The above notwithstanding, Israeli Jews frequently perceive the Christian communities as a double majority, affiliated with both the vast Arab world and the vaster Christian world. Likewise, most Muslims in Israel identify the local Christians with the powerful Christian West and almost never see them as an imperiled minority.[7]

Rossing was fond of saying that all three groups in Israel—Jews, Christians and Muslims—share certain qualities of majority existence and certain of minority existence. As we have already seen, the Jews, who are the majority in Israel, are minorities everywhere else. The Christians are majorities in many countries and are the largest single religious group in the world; but in Israel, they are a small minority. (In fact, many Israeli Jews—and some of the world's Christians!—seem to be unaware of the existence of Arab or Palestinian Christians.) The largest religious

---

7. Daniel Rossing, "Microcosm and Multiple Minorities—The Christian Communities in Israel," *Israel Year Book and Almanac* 53 (1999), 28.

minority, Muslims, are a vast majority in the Middle East. Recognition of these shared characteristics could, theoretically, facilitate a fruitful interchange but it rarely does.

In Israel, the Arabs are largely fluent in Hebrew and knowledgeable about the Jewish population to an extent that far overshadows the Jews' knowledge of Arabic language and culture. This may reflect practical considerations, such as the need for employment within the Hebrew-speaking sector. The Jewish majority in Israel are by and large not particularly interested in learning about the various minority groups living in their midst. This is certainly reinforced by the history of Christian-Jewish relations and the attitudes that history has produced.

A well-known Catholic journalist has documented additional sources of frustration on the part of the Catholic community:

> Among Catholics, there's also frustration about negotiations that have lingered since 1993 over the Fundamental Agreement between Israel and the Vatican, which among other things was supposed to regulate the tax and legal status of church properties. While talks over a deal drag on, Israel has unilaterally declared important Christian sites such as Mount Tabor and Capernaum to be national parks, overriding Christian control.[8]

NATURE OF THE LOCAL COMMUNITIES

A second explanation involves the nature of the local religious communities. Byzantine rite Christians—divided between Greek Orthodox and Greek Catholic—account for more than 70 percent of the Christians in the Holy Land. Roman (Latin) Catholics make up about 15 percent and Maronites an additional 8 percent. The rest of the Christians belong to a myriad of Eastern and Protestant churches.

Many people in the Middle East—Jews, Muslims, and Christians—have not gone through what is often called the European Enlightenment.

Many Christians who live in the Middle East, uninfluenced by Western categories and education, live under self-understandings that make it difficult for them to appreciate modern categories. Some of these modern categories include the meaning of democracy (as opposed to

8. John L. Allen, "Politics and Christians in the Holy Land," *National Catholic Reporter*, June 14, 2013, http://ncronline.org/blogs/all-things-catholic/politics-and-christians-holy-land/.

majoritarianism), individual self-understanding versus a more communal or tribal self-understanding, and reliance on reason and argument rather than on authority and tradition.[9]

Although Enlightenment ideas were resisted by the Catholic Church for centuries, the Second Vatican Council represented openness to them. *NA* can be seen as a product of this rapprochement between Catholicism and the Enlightenment, but it is clearly grounded in a Western sensibility. The Eastern Churches, with some important exceptions, have never experienced the Enlightenment firsthand. Many of them continue to hold views that Western Christians might characterize as pre–Vatican II.

With the exception of some of the fundamentalist or dispensationalist Protestants, the Christians least open to interfaith dialogue are the Eastern Orthodox. The reluctance to engage in dialogue, however, is more characteristic of the official hierarchies within these churches than it is of their laity. [10] On an individual basis, members of these churches, particularly those who live or have been educated in the West, do participate in interreligious encounters, often adding an impressive dimension of spiritual depth and rootedness in tradition.[11] There are several reasons for the official reticence. Some observers have traced it back to the legacy of the early Church Fathers.[12] Some have suggested that there is a general suspicion of the outside, including of the Western churches, that goes back to the bloody sacking of Constantinople during the Fourth Crusade (1203–1204.) As an excuse for attacking the greatest Christian city of its day, the Crusaders said that they would restore the Eastern Christian Empire to Rome, crushing the Orthodox Church which the pope (Innocent III) considered a heresy. (For this insight, I am indebted to Professor Father Thomas Stransky, former rector of Tantur. According to Stransky, to this day, the Orthodox suffer from the painful memories of this event.) It should be noted that in 2004, Pope John Paul II apologized to the Ortho-

9. Father Michael McGarry, in a private e-mail on May 30, 2013.

10. One characteristic of Orthodox clergy, at all the interfaith events I have attended with them, is that, when asked to offer a prayer, they seem incapable of offering a truly interreligious prayer. Their insistence in praying always in the name of Christ raises problems for both the Jews and the Muslims taking part in the encounter.

11. One of these was the Very Reverend Dr. Sergei Hackel (1931–2005), a Russian Orthodox leader based in the UK. He was very instrumental in trying to rid his Church of anti-Semitism and encouraging more openness to modernity.

12. It has been suggested that the Eastern Churches have derived more from John Chrysostom, who was notably more anti-Jewish, than from others, such as Saint Augustine.

dox for the atrocities committed eight hundred years before. In the interim, for hundreds of years, the Middle Eastern-based Orthodox Churches lived as a persecuted religious minority under the Ottoman Empire.

POLITICAL CONFLICT

From my own experience teaching at places like Ecce Homo and Tantur, I can give some personal testimony. Friends often ask me about the kinds of questions I get asked. They don't vary so much among the Christian denominations as they do between Christians who come from countries in which there are Jewish communities, and those who come from countries that don't have Jewish communities, so that I may very well be the first Jew they've ever met. People like that might ask me, "Are Jews still offering animal sacrifices?" This is a completely logical question, if the only Jews you know about are the ones in Leviticus.

But, as has been argued in this paper, those aren't the only two possibilities: The Middle Eastern Christians are in a third category—they live in or near the world's largest Jewish community, and feel oppressed or at least discriminated by it. That is indeed a different situation and must be approached differently.

One of the great tragedies of recent history is the Arab-Israeli conflict and, increasingly, the Palestinian-Israeli conflict. Assigning major responsibility for the conflict sometimes depends on when you begin the story—1967? 1948? 1929? 1882? Although increasingly there are religious overtones to the conflict, it has always been primarily a political, territorial conflict between two national movements, Zionism, the national movement for a Jewish homeland, and the Palestinian national movement. In the midst of such a long and bloody conflict, Arab Christians do not want to hear that they were the perpetrators of the Crusades and the Inquisition—which, of course, they were not—nor do they feel any guilt for the Holocaust. Since these historical memories inform the provenance of *NA*, most Arab Christians have felt and many still feel alienated from it. Moreover, accusations of supersessionism and even anti-Semitism have a different meaning with regard to the Christian minority in the Land. Many of the important questions that are at the heart of Christian-Jewish dialogue in the West seem irrelevant in our part of the world.

Today both the Israelis and the Palestinians see themselves as the victims of the conflict. They seem to be competitors in what I call a "suffering sweepstakes." One of the problems with victimhood is that it prevents the victim from assuming responsibility for his or her actions, including the victimization of others. In the Israeli-Palestinian conflict, I believe that both sides are victims and both sides are victimizers. I really think that the least helpful thing people can do—and regrettably, many well-meaning people do this—is to portray the situation in terms of a zero-sum game, in which, if you're pro-Palestinian, you must be anti-Israeli, and vice versa.[13]

TWO DIFFERENT APPROACHES TO ZIONISM

For some Zionists, the essential meaning of creating a Jewish state has been to escape from persecution. In some cases, this was even interpreted to mean "escape from the non-Jews." One of the most important philosophers of the State of Israel, Yeshayahu Leibowitz (1903–1994) defined his Zionism as, "We are fed-up with being ruled by *goyim* (Gentiles)."[14]

But there is another approach that emphasizes Zionism as the re-entry of the Jewish people into history, within the family of nations. Yossi Klein HaLevi is an Israeli-based journalist and author with a deep interest in interreligious dialogue. In a lecture to the Interreligious Coordinating Council in Israel on November 27, 2001, Klein HaLevi indicated that one of the great blessings of Zionism and Jewish sovereignty is the opportunity for Jews to engage as equals in such dialogue.

Both from impressionistic evidence and research findings, it would appear that Israeli Jews have not, for the most part, internalized the sense of confidence and security that living in a sovereign Jewish state ought to provide. A well-known joke says that, "Just because you're paranoid, it doesn't mean that they're not out to get you." Even paranoiacs can have real enemies. Jews today in general and Israelis in particular can be characterized as paranoiacs who have real enemies. The classical rabbinic text *Avot d'Rebbe Natan* says, "Who is the greatest of all heroes? One who turns an enemy into a friend" (23:1). The problem with paranoia is that it prevents the paranoiac from recognizing his or her friends or, at least, potential friends. A leading Jewish activist in interreligious dialogue from

13. For a more in-depth discussion of the conflict, see the document "As Long as You Believe in a Living God, You Must Have Hope," issued by the ICCJ on May 13, 2013, available at www.iccj.org/.

14. Michael Shashar, ed., *About the World and All That's in It: Conversations with Michael Shashar* (in Hebrew) (Jerusalem: Keter, 1988), 28.

Australia has said: "it is hard to feel safe even in a safe environment."[15] Apparently, that applies to Israeli Jews as well.

SOME HOPEFUL SIGNS

In the West, many Jews have felt a need for some kind of Jewish response to *NA* and its subsequent developments. In 2000, an important statement was issued and signed by over 200 Jewish scholars and leaders, mostly North Americans, called *Dabru Emet* (*Speak the Truth*). An organization called the Interreligious Coordinating Council in Israel (ICCI) has promoted the translation of this document and others into Hebrew. It has also sponsored conferences in Israel about *NA*, *Dabru Emet*, and the like.

Nine years later, in 2009, the International Council of Christians and Jews (ICCJ) issued the Berlin Document, "A Time for Re-commitment."[16] This statement was groundbreaking, in that for the first time, in an inter-religious framework, there was a call upon Jews and Jewish communities to undertake a process of soul-searching. One of the core components of the Document is the twelve points or calls of Berlin: four calls to Christians and the Churches, four calls to Jews and Jewish communities, and four calls for joint action that Muslims and others are invited to join. Involved in the formulation of the Berlin Document were four Israeli Jews and one (at the time) Israeli-based Christian. To the extent that the Berlin Document is known among Jews, its status has been controversial, with much criticism for its "washing dirty laundry in public."

Point 5 of the 12 Berlin Points states the following:

> *5. To acknowledge the efforts of many Christian communities in the late 20th century to reform their attitudes toward Jews*

> • By learning about these reforms through more intensive dialogue with Christians.

> • By discussing the implications of changes in Christian churches regarding Jews and their understandings of Judaism.

---

15. William Szekely, president of the Australian Council of Christians and Jews, at a talk titled, "Will the New Pope Tango with the Jews?" delivered at the *Limmud Oz* conference in Sydney, June 9, 2013, p. 20.

16. For the full document, go to www.iccj.org/.

- By teaching Jews of all ages about these changes, both in the context of the history of Jewish-Christian relations and according to the appropriate stage of education for each group.

- By including basic and accurate background information about Christianity in the curricula of Jewish schools, rabbinic seminaries, and adult education programs.

- By studying the New Testament both as Christianity's sacred text and as literature written to a large degree by Jews in an historical-cultural context similar to early Rabbinic literature, thereby offering insight into the development of Judaism in the early centuries of the Common Era.

One of the central Christian figures involved in promoting the reception and study of *NA* in the Holy Land was former Latin Patriarch, Michel Sabbah. He established a committee for dialogue with the Jewish community and, together with Daniel Rossing, organized joint Bible study sessions for Palestinian Christians and Israeli Jews.

The organization that Daniel Rossing started, mentioned earlier (JCJCR,) has done some important educational work for the Israeli public. For example, they organized a program on May 30, 2013, in conjunction with the Jerusalem institute for Israel Studies, a well-respected research facility in Jerusalem. The theme of the evening was the Second Vatican Council. The participants were Ms. Hana Bendcowski, Program Director of the JCJCR; Raymond Cohen, professor emeritus from the Hebrew University's department of international relations, with a specialization in the recent history of the Vatican; Father Dr. David Neuhaus, a Jesuit who is the Assistant to the Latin Patriarch and has responsibility for Hebrew-speaking Catholics in Israel; and Dr. Amnon Ramon, an Israeli-born researcher, considered one of the major experts on the local Christian communities. As he said, the evening was organized because "most of the Israeli public thinks that nothing really happened." Ramon attributed the ignorance and relative apathy to two major factors: the influence of the unfortunate historical relationship between the Church and the Jews, and, what he called, "Israeli provincialism."

I must mention as well the efforts of Neuhaus and his colleague, Father Dr. Jamal Khader, who teach *NA* to students at Bethlehem University and Catholic seminarians in Bet Jalla.[17] One of the paradoxes of

---

17. See their paper, "A Holy Land Context for *Nostra Aetate*," *Studies in Christian-Jewish Relations* 1 (2005–2006) 67–88, http://ejournals.bc.edu/ojs/index.php/scjr/

the Occupation is that often, when interreligious gatherings are organized, Palestinian participants are denied permits to come to Jerusalem.
Occasionally, when a positive event has been planned for weeks, the
permit is denied the day before. It should be noted that the Palestinian
Christians have been an overwhelmingly nonviolent community. Patriarch Sabbah unequivocally condemned the use of terror.[18]

In conclusion, one may say that on a small scale, the situation is
changing for the better. More and more people within the Israeli Jewish
and Christian publics are becoming aware of *NA* and its implications,
and of subsequent developments on the world interreligious scene. However, until the Occupation has ended and the Israeli-Palestinian conflict
has been resolved, it is unlikely that the situation of local Christians will
be changed, in a dramatically different manner.

Among Israeli Jews, there seem to be two opposing trends. On the
one hand, there has been an alarming rise in anti-Christian incidents
within Israel, often identified with the slogan, *"Tag M'hir"* (price tag).
These are usually acts of vandalism and graffiti directed at churches or
other Christian institutions. Sometimes, individual Christians have been
spat upon. While these acts are committed by a tiny, extremist minority within the Jewish community, the Israeli police have recognized the
sufficient seriousness of the phenomenon by setting up, in the spring of
2013, a special unit to deal with it.

At the same time, within the wider Jewish community, there are active efforts to rectify the situation, at least of ignorance, mentioned above.
In addition to the ICCI and the JCJCR, there is now the Galilee Center
for Studies in Jewish-Christian Relations, at The Max Stern Yezreel Valley
College, just outside of Afula. The prestigious Van Leer Institute in Jerusalem has inaugurated a multidisciplinary Seminar for Christian-Jewish
Relations. It is to be hoped that these and similar initiatives will not remain purely on the academic level but will filter down to educational
programs for the wider public. In that way, the impact of *Nostra Aetate*
and subsequent developments within the Church may finally become
known and recognized in Israel.

---

article/view/1360/.

18. Ibid., appendices 1 and 2.

PART 4

Unresolved Issues

16

Nostra Aetate after Fifty Years
Covenant and the Election of Israel

David Berger

THE GENESIS OF *NOSTRA Aetate, no. 4* has generally been analyzed in the narrow context of its place in the history of Jewish-Catholic relations, and its passage has been credited in major part to the efforts of Jewish activists and scholars as well as Catholic thinkers engaged in a wrenching post-Holocaust re-examination of the Church's teachings regarding Jews. The validity and importance of this perspective is beyond question, but the wider environment has, I think, been underappreciated.

It hardly needs to be said that the Jewish component of the Vatican Council's deliberations and documents, whatever its undeniable importance, was not the dominant element in the proceedings. More than a decade and a half ago, I made this point near the beginning of an essay dealing with medieval anti-Semitism, which no doubt escaped the notice of most observers concerned with Vatican II. Here, then, is what I wrote:

> Vatican II was convened in a post-colonial age marked by a new
> regard for self-determination and a new respect for cultural
> diversity—as well as minority rights. Exclusivist claims did not

sit well in this environment, and harsh punishment, even divine punishment, for religious dissent surely did not. A telling
expression of the inner struggle triggered by the clash of this
liberal, humanistic sensibility with a narrower, more forbidding
tradition was formulated by a playwright hostile to Catholicism
whose bitter work, *Sister Mary Ignatius Explains It All To You*,
nonetheless has its very funny moments. Sister Mary, an old-
fashioned nun teaching in the aftermath of Vatican II, defines
"limbo" for her classroom/audience. If I remember correctly,
she displays a picture of a baby trapped behind the bars of a crib
and declares, "Limbo is where unbaptized children went before
the Ecumenical Council."

The historical and theological precision of this statement
may leave something to be desired, but it brilliantly captures
a central feature of the ideological atmosphere of the Council,
which had nothing to do with Jews and next to nothing to do
with the Holocaust. It was this spirit that animated the adoption of a more positive attitude toward Islam and the religions
of the East, the assertion that salvation is possible outside the
Church—and *Nostra Aetate, no. 4*. One who locates the fundamental impetus of the historic declaration on the Jews in the
specifics of the Jewish-Catholic relationship loses sight of the
larger process and misses the key point.[1]

On reflection, the assertion that this larger reassessment had "next
to nothing to do with the Holocaust" was too strong, perhaps much too
strong, since even the broader transformation in the Church and beyond
may well have been influenced by the Holocaust, but the basic point, I
think, remains valid. We are dealing with a watershed in the history of
the Church that far transcends the Jewish question, and the reassessment
of that question is a part of that larger phenomenon rather than an essentially independent development.

The clearly revolutionary element in *Nostra Aetate, no. 4* is its unequivocal denial that contemporary Jews bear any responsibility for the
crucifixion. The point is then reinforced by a concomitant denunciation of
anti-Semitism. Because some Catholics are uneasy with the assertion that
these teachings—even the first one—are new, they can be insufficiently

1. David Berger, "From Crusades to Blood Libels to Expulsions: Some New Approaches to Medieval Antisemitism," The Second Victor J. Selmanowitz Memorial
Lecture, Touro College Graduate School of Jewish Studies (New York, 1997), 5–6. Reprinted in David Berger, *Persecution, Polemic, and Dialogue: Essays in Jewish-Christian
Relations* (Boston: University Studies Press, 2010), 15–39, at 19–20.

sensitive to their profound significance. Instead, they are inclined to stress what they see as even more far-reaching implications. Thus, they maintain that the document's allusion to the irrevocability of God's gifts to the Jewish people affirmed in Rom 11:28–29 was meant to effect a historic reevaluation of the status of the original covenant—Abrahamic and even Mosaic. In its strongest form, this understanding of *Nostra Aetate* sees an implication that the covenant at Sinai remains in full force, so that Jews who fulfill it are fulfilling the will of God. This means *inter alia* that such Jews can be saved through their commitment to that covenant, and that mission to the Jews runs counter to the divine will.

The very fact that such conclusions have been drawn from *Nostra Aetate* is itself a historic development that becomes a key element of the document's legacy. Nonetheless, the real meaning of the allusion in question is, I think, less dramatic, and the range of understandings that the passage can and to a large degree has generated illustrates its ambiguities as well as its potential for a variety of applications. While most Jews take maximum satisfaction from the most expansive understanding, the available options present a richer tapestry and evoke the ruminations that follow.

Romans 11 has elicited a wide spectrum of interpretations since the patristic period,[2] so that both the intrinsic options afforded by the text and the history of its exegesis mean that the mere citation of a key verse does not tell us the intent of the authors who cited it. The adoption of *Nostra Aetate, no. 4* was not an entirely smooth process, and even if we are to assume that all those involved in drafting the text understood it in precisely the same way, it is evident that the representatives who ultimately voted for it did not have a uniform understanding of its provisions. It is therefore an exercise in futility to determine *the* import of *Nostra Aetate*'s citation of the affirmation in Romans that God does not repent of the gifts He makes.[3]

The narrowest understanding of the passage in Romans is that physical or carnal Israel will not cease to exist despite its reprobate nature and

2. For an exhaustive survey and analysis, see Jeremy Cohen, "'The Mystery of Israel's Salvation': Romans 11:25–26 in Patristic and Medieval Exegesis," *Harvard Theological Review* 98 (2005) 247–81.

3. Philip A. Cunningham has pointed to evidence that *Nostra Aetate*'s final version reflects a decision by its authors to postpone the collective conversion of Jews to the *eschaton*. See Cunningham, "Response to Bolton's 'Contesting the Covenants,'" *Journal of Ecumenical Studies* 4 (2010) 399–400. Even if this was indeed the intention of the authors, the salvific force of the Jewish covenant does not necessarily follow.

is assured that at the end of days a remnant will be present to embrace the Christian message in its fullness. In this conception, preeschatological Israel has no spiritual value and no longer enjoys a covenantal relationship with God in more than the most minimal sense. All we find in that passage is an affirmation that this relationship guarantees physical survival until the time when Israel will recognize the truth.

Since most Christians through the centuries adopted a reading of Romans more or less identical with this one, and nothing in the text forces one to a more generous understanding, the revisionist interpretations that have emerged since *Nostra Aetate* reflect a striking desire to construct a more positive assessment of Judaism. Thus, the passage in Romans comes to mean that there remains a meaningful spiritual relationship between God and the Jewish people. Once such an affirmation is made, the persistence of an original covenant with vital religious content becomes distinctly possible, perhaps even probable.

If that covenant is the one with Abraham, a narrow reading can fit fairly smoothly into the standard contours of classical Christianity. God maintains this covenant with the original Israel, which remains in some sense his chosen people, but the old law has little if any relevance to that status. Ideally, Jews should embrace Christianity even in historical time, and there is no theological reason why Christians should refrain from urging them to do so. Even if such efforts are undesirable for pragmatic or ethical reasons, there is certainly no reason to refrain from praying for the conversion of the Jews even before the fullness of time.

As I noted earlier, some ecumenically minded Christians are dissatisfied with this step, rightly seeing it as supersessionist, and not so rightly (in my view) taking it for granted that any form of supersessionism is religiously and morally objectionable.[4] Consequently, some ascribe a stronger meaning to the persistence of the Abrahamic covenant, while others take the dramatic step of affirming the continuing validity of the Mosaic covenant as well. This approach sits uneasily with key elements of historic Christian theology, and it is no accident that Cardinal Kurt Koch, in an interview on Israel Independence Day in 2013, manifested evident discomfort as he wrestled with the implications of this position.[5]

4. For a defense of the ethical legitimacy of supersessionism that does not denigrate Jews or Judaism, see Berger, "On *Dominus Iesus* and the Jews," *America* 185/7 (September 17, 2001) 7–12, reprinted in Berger, *Persecution, Polemic, and Dialogue*, 378–84, at 380–82.

5. "Jewish-Catholic Dialogue 65 Years after the Founding of the State of Israel,"

Question: The Apostle Paul says in the Letter to the Romans that God remains true to his covenant. Yet in the history of theology the idea that the Jews were disinherited was predominant for a long time. How did that happen?

Cardinal Koch: This has to do with the separation of Church and Synagogue. As historical research has shown, the process of estrangement took place less rapidly than was long thought to be the case. But the process had increasingly radical consequences in the aftermath. The notion became prevalent that the Church had taken the place of Judaism. Nor was Saint Paul's Letter to the Romans, which very subtly reflects on the mystery of the interpenetration of the New and the Old Covenant, able to prevent this. How we are to think about the eternal validity of the Old Covenant and at the same time about the newness of the New Covenant in Jesus Christ remains even today a major theological challenge.

Question: But what does that mean? Are there two separate ways of salvation, then, for Jews and Christians? Abraham and Moses for the one group, Jesus Christ for the other? Then the Jews would be an exception to the Church's commission to evangelize.

Cardinal Koch: For Christians there is naturally only one way of salvation, which God revealed to us in Jesus Christ. On the other hand we Christians, in dealing with the Jews, do not have to bear witness to a way of salvation that is completely foreign to them, as is the case with other religions. For the New Testament is built entirely on the Old Testament. For this reason the Catholic Church has no organized mission to the Jews, as is the case for instance in certain Evangelical circles. On the other hand, we Christians witness to the Jews also concerning the hope that faith in Christ gives us.

Catholics who adhere to the older position on the salvation of Jews and their suitability as objects of mission will find here a single argument for altering that position: "The New Testament is built entirely on the Old Testament." And they will respond, "Of course this is true (although 'entirely' is an overstatement). But how does it yield your conclusion?

The Catholic World Report, May 15, 2013, http://www.catholicworldreport.com/Item/2259/jewishcatholic_dialogue_65_years_after_the_founding_of_the_state_of_israel.aspx#.UnF3j1_D_cs/.

The New Testament is built on the Old, but it perfects it, transcends it, and provides insight into its deeper, nonliteral meaning. Why should Jews be left to their rejection of these truths, and how does it follow that they are saved?"

Once the persistence of the Mosaic covenant has been affirmed by some Catholics, many Jews engaged in interfaith dialogue (as we shall see presently) have come to regard such an affirmation as a test of a genuinely pro-Jewish stance. Precisely because I recognize the great hurdles that a Christian must overcome to make this affirmation, I do not consider this expectation appropriate, and I even harbor some doubts about its pragmatic usefulness.

Let us turn, then, to a more detailed look at some of the Catholic discussions that have swirled around the question of covenant and mission since *Nostra Aetate*.[6] As early as the 1970s, some Catholic authors proposed a double-covenant theory.[7] When the official declaration *Dominus Iesus* was issued in 2000, Cardinal Walter Kasper responded to Jewish concerns a year later in an article containing the following affirmation:

> The only thing I wish to say is that the document *Dominus Ie-sus* does not state that everybody needs to become a Catholic in order to be saved by God. On the contrary, it declares that God's grace, which is the grace of Jesus Christ according to our faith, is available to all. Therefore, the Church believes that Judaism, i.e. the faithful response of the Jewish people to God's irrevocable covenant, is salvific for them, because God is faithful to his promises. [8]

6. The most thorough survey and analysis of these discussions is that of David J. Bolton, "Catholic-Jewish Dialogue: Contesting the Covenants," *Journal of Ecumenical Studies* 45 (2010) 37–60.

7. Bolton points to Monika Hellwig, "Christian Theology and the Covenant of Israel," *Journal of Ecumenical Studies* 7 (1970) 37–51; Rosemary Radford Ruether, "An Invitation to Jewish-Christian Dialogue: In What Sense Can We Say that Jesus Was 'The Christ'?" *The Ecumenist* 10/2 (1972) 17–24; Ruether, *Faith and Fratricide: The Theological Roots of Anti-Semitism* (New York: Seabury, 1974); and Michael B. Mc-Garry, *Christology after Auschwitz* (New York: Paulist, 1977).

8. Walter Cardinal Kasper, "The Good Olive Tree," *America* 185/7 (September 17, 2001) 12–14. It is noteworthy that this statement does not grant Jews the full special status that dual-covenant theologies normally do. Salvation is available to all in principle; for Jews it is achieved through the old covenant. See note 3 above for my own reaction to *Dominus Iesus*. For an analysis of the views of the author of *Dominus Iesus* regarding our issue, see Richard J. Sklba, "Covenant Renewed: Josef Ratzinger, Theologian and Pastor," in Robert W. Jenson and Eugene B. Korn, eds., *Covenant and Hope: Christian and Jewish Reflections* (Grand Rapids: Eerdmans, 2012), 58–79.

The following year, the issue of the eternity of the Jewish covenant came to the fore in two documents by Catholic scholars: "Reflections on Covenant and Mission" (2002) and "A Sacred Obligation" (2003). Both of these asserted that Jews are in "a saving covenant with God," and the second added that recognition of this reality requires Christians to find "new ways of understanding the universal significance of Christ."[9]

Within a few months of the appearance of "Reflections," Cardinal Avery Dulles published a critical response in the Catholic journal *America*, to which three distinguished theologians who participated in its formulation replied.[10] The reply contains an assertion that illustrates the boldness that can characterize the argument for the abiding efficaciousness of the Jewish covenant. I do not believe that every Catholic who affirms such efficaciousness regards the assertion that we shall encounter as indispensable to the argument, but the willingness of the authors to mobilize it helps underscore the reasons for resistance among many traditional Catholics.

What then does the reply assert?

In arguing for the permanence and salvific nature of the Mosaic covenant, the authors say in so many words that Heb 8:13 and 10:9 contradict this position, but the Church has gone beyond those verses and has the authority to say that the author of Hebrews was mistaken. Similarly, they assert that Paul himself, in the very chapter of Romans that serves as the basis for the most liberal position on covenant, mistakenly thought that Israel now consisted of dead branches detached "from God's unfolding plans" but believed this condition to be temporary and soon to be corrected. However, we now know that he too was mistaken. Today's Church speaks of "the permanence of Israel" as "accompanied by a continuous spiritual fecundity." "The magisterium can explicitly contradict an idea of an individual New Testament author."

The authors go on to quote the Pontifical Biblical Commission to defend the legitimacy of these assertions. The Commission declared that

9. For a summary and analysis of these statements, see Mary C. Boys, "The Covenant in Contemporary Ecclesial Documents," in Eugene B. Korn and John T. Pawlikowski, OSM, eds., *Two Faiths, One Covenant? Jewish and Christian Identity in the Presence of the Other* (Lanham, MD: Rowman & Littlefield, 2005), 81–110, at 100–103.

10. Avery Cardinal Dulles, "Covenant and Mission," *America* 187/12 (October 21, 2002) 8–11; Mary C. Boys, Philip A. Cunningham, and John T. Pawlikowski, "Theology's 'Sacred Obligation': A Reply to Cardinal Dulles," *America* 187/12 (October 21, 2002) 12–16, http://www.bc.edu/dam/files/research_sites/cjl/texts/cjrelations/resources/articles/BoysCunnPaw.htm/.

"interpretation of Scripture involves a work of sifting and setting aside; it stands in continuity with earlier exegetical traditions, many elements of which it preserves and makes its own; but in other matters it will go its own way, seeking to make further progress" (*The Interpretation of the Bible in the Church*, 1993). When they apply this, they make a critical, unacknowledged modification: "We argue that official Catholic teaching today has, in the 1993 PBC formulation, 'gone its own way' and 'set aside' the opinion of the author of Hebrews about Israel's covenant." The PBC spoke of setting aside exegetical traditions. The authors speak of setting aside the views of Paul and the author of Hebrews. I am hardly in a position to assert that the magisterium cannot do what they say, but their prooftext is unpersuasive and the position itself is surely not upheld universally within the Church.

Several years later, Cardinal Dulles devoted a longer article to the questions raised by the recent re-evaluation of the Jewish covenant, acknowledging the challenges they present, citing a multiplicity of positions, and attempting to develop a viable approach. He noted with approval the oft-quoted remark by Pope John Paul II in a 1980 speech in Mainz, where he spoke of dialogue "between the people of God of the Old Covenant, never revoked by God, and that of the New Covenant." However, the Cardinal vigorously rejected the position that the Old Covenant provides Jews a road to salvation separate from the one affirmed in the New.

In a passage that has particular relevance to the questions that I shall soon raise about the content of the Mosaic covenant, Dulles cited an unanswered letter by Michael Wyschogrod to the late Cardinal Lustiger of Paris, a Jewish convert to Christianity, that asks how the Cardinal can assert that he has not run away from Jewish tradition, given his abandonment of Jewish observance. Dulles went on to say, "If Lustiger had responded he might have pointed out that according to the teaching of Paul, which is normative for Christians, circumcision and the Mosaic law have lost their salvific value, at least for Christians, and in that sense been 'superseded.'" The qualifying phrase "at least for Christians" does not sit well with Dulles's later denial of a separate salvific road for Jews , or with his earlier assertion that the ceremonial law survives only "in a super-eminent way in Christ and the Church," and it gives particularly revealing expression, however briefly, to the deep tensions that beset this discussion.[11]

11. Avery Cardinal Dulles, "The Covenant with Israel," *First Things* 157 (November, 2005) 16–21, http://www.firstthings.com/article/2005/11/the-covenant-with-israel/.

In 2009, the United States Conference of Catholic Bishops formally expressed reservations about "Reflections," going so far as to say that although Jewish-Christian dialogue "would not normally include an explicit invitation to baptism . . . the Christian dialogue partner is always giving witness to the following of Christ to which all are implicitly invited." Jewish organizations regarded the affirmation that interfaith dialogue contains an implicit conversionary objective as profoundly objectionable, and I was involved in formulating two reactions. The first was a letter that I wrote on behalf of the Rabbinical Council of America and the Union of Orthodox Jewish Congregations of America, which concentrated on the redefinition of *dialogue*.[12] The other was a jointly written letter from five Jewish organizations. Most of the authors wanted to add an additional point criticizing the new statement for implying that the Mosaic covenant is not in effect. In light of my long-standing reservations about telling Christians what to believe about their own religion, I objected and helped formulate a compromise that produced the following text:

> The second source of concern has to do with the continuing validity of the Mosaic covenant. There is a range of views within the Jewish community about the appropriate Jewish reaction to a Christian denial of the validity of this covenant. But we all recognize that affirming its validity is more likely to result in more positive attitudes toward Jews, and we were consequently encouraged by a series of what appeared to be weighty statements by Church officials over the years that endorsed this affirmation. The new statement has therefore engendered uncertainty as to the position espoused by the Church and its spokespersons as well as an understandable measure of disappointment.

He does offer a concession, which has little impact on our concerns, that "the observance of some of these [ritual] prescriptions by Jews who have become Christians could be permissible or even praiseworthy as a way of recalling the rootedness of Christianity in the Old Covenant."

For an uncompromising polemic against any affirmation of an eternal Mosaic covenant, see Robert A. Sungenis, "The Old Covenant: Revoked or Not Revoked?; Jews and Christians: A Journey of Faith," http://archive.is/GRh44/. This piece is written from an extremely conservative perspective but contains a wide-ranging survey of opinions with references to expressions of the most liberal position. For a more balanced essay rejecting what the authors call "extreme supersessionism" but also arguing vigorously against what they call the dual-covenant position that grants Jews salvation through their covenant, see Michael Forrest and David Palm, "All in the Family—Christians, Jews, and God," http://www.cuf.org/2009/07/all-in-the-family-christians-jews-and-god-2/.

12. See http://www.rabbis.org/news/article.cfm?id=105461/.

To our great satisfaction, the bishops agreed to eliminate the offending passage, but what is worth noting for our purposes is that prominent Jews involved in interfaith dialogue have developed so strong an expectation that Christians will affirm the validity of the Mosaic covenant that they see any deviation from this position as profoundly objectionable and deserving of frontal criticism.

At this point, I am no longer certain that it is even in the Jewish interest to have Christians emphasize the Mosaic rather than the Abrahamic covenant. In addition to the points raised by Cardinal Koch's interviewer, a Christian affirmation that the Mosaic covenant remains in effect leads to some intriguing and potentially disturbing questions, at least from the perspective of a Jew for whom all the commandments in that covenant are fundamental to its essence.

If the covenant remains, does that mean that its actual content remains binding on Jews? Would Christians be impelled to regard Jews who do not observe the law of the Hebrew Bible in its fullness as sinners? Since some Christian texts see observance of the Old Law as a near impossibility, does that mean that Jews are for the most part denied salvation because of the failure to observe the Mosaic covenant properly? What of non-Orthodox Jews, especially Reform Jews, who even in principle observe the Old Law selectively, rejecting major elements? For that matter, Orthodox Jews observe the Old Law through the prism of the Talmud, whose validity Christians do not recognize. Can one be saved by a covenant to which one does not adhere? Should Christians at least engage in missionary efforts directed at nonreligious Jews, who do not observe the Old Law at all except to the degree that their moral instincts lead them to behave in ways that happen to accord with some of its provisions? (This last possibility bears an affinity to the position taken by some Reform Jews in the last few decades that Jews should proselytize unchurched Gentiles.)

A *reductio ad absurdum* of this line of questioning would lead to the rejection of individual Jews who wish to convert to Christianity; they are, after all, bound by the Mosaic covenant. Since no Christian takes this position, it follows that the doctrine that the Mosaic covenant remains in effect in its original form applies only to Jews who do not embrace Christianity.

This limitation explains why Jewish converts may be welcomed (thus dealing with the *reductio ad absurdum*), but it does not address the other questions. The deepest irony that could emerge from this discourse is that Christians, whose tradition regards the so-called legalism associated with the Pharisees of the Gospels with disdain (despite the massive and complex structure of canon law), would be placed in the acutely uncomfortable position of seeing the observance of the laws that mark the Mosaic covenant as a requirement for the salvation of unconverted Jews.

These considerations, then, appear to lead to unacceptable, almost inconceivable, consequences from a Christian perspective. If this is the case, what do Christians mean when they say that the Mosaic covenant remains in effect and that Jews can attain salvation through that covenant? Though they presumably do not restrict this salvation to fully observant Jews, it is difficult to imagine that even the most liberal ecumenicists would affirm that the Mosaic covenant is a vehicle of salvation for any decent human being born of Jewish parents.

Consequently, it appears that their position, while not articulated in quite these terms, consists roughly of the following elements:

God's election of the Jews has not been annulled. That election was manifested in the covenant at Sinai, which remains effective and salvific. Those Jews who continue to adhere to it have been granted a great deal of latitude in determining their obligations under that covenant. That latitude is limited, however, by two broad considerations. First, the moral dimension of the Old Covenant, which has not been superseded by the new one, continues to be obligatory. Second, Jewish modes of relationship to the Old Covenant must be governed by a genuine sense that its core values remain binding; thus, the practices in which committed Jews engage to express that relationship must amount in their minds to continued adherence to its key message. With sufficient effort, one might even argue that many secular Jews meet this criterion on the grounds that a sense of identification with the Jewish people or community qualifies as adherence to the Mosaic covenant. In sum, as long as Jews believe that in some crucial sense they remain loyal to the Sinaitic covenant—even in the absence of a belief that anything noteworthy actually happened at Sinai—that covenant grants them salvation.

The granting of salvation through the Mosaic covenant to people who do not observe much or any of the "ceremonial" law in the Pentateuch is facilitated by the historic Christian devaluation of Jewish ritual, which occasionally even took the form of denial that certain laws were ever intended to be fulfilled literally. Moreover, the acceptability of pentateuchal criticism in the contemporary Catholic Church complicates the question of the very meaning and content of the Mosaic or Sinaitic covenant in intriguing fashion that we cannot pursue here and may further facilitate the conviction that some of its injunctions were never binding.[13] What emerges from this speculative analysis is that the sharp, counterfactual irony where Christians insist on the salvific indispensability of Jewish ritual observance for unconverted Jews is replaced by a mild but real irony: Catholics friendly to Jews, who take the greatest pains to express respect for classical Judaism in its own terms, essentially resort to Christianity's historical devaluation of Jewish law so that they can regard Jews who devalue that law as beneficiaries of the Old Covenant's salvific power. This devaluation—along with its generous consequences—is of course perfectly legitimate from a Christian perspective and cannot justly elicit criticism even from the most traditional Jew.

This chain of reasoning may be entirely misguided, but it makes me uneasy about the potential course of a process in which Christians rigorously confront the consequences of an eternal Mosaic covenant. The great advantage for Jews of a Christian affirmation that the Mosaic covenant remains in effect is that it provides a powerful argument against proselytizing directed at them, and nothing that I will say fully negates this advantage. Nonetheless, among Christians sympathetic to Jews, affirming the persistence of an Abrahamic covenant can yield almost the same benefits and is not beset by the majority of the questions that I have raised. (Christians not particularly sympathetic to Jews will in any event not accept the eternity of the Mosaic covenant.) The Catholic Church has abandoned proselytizing efforts directed at Jews even though the continuing validity and independent salvific power of the Mosaic covenant is by no means generally accepted doctrine.[14]

13. At a small Jewish-Catholic conference on the understanding of the Bible held in Lucerne in 1984, the head of the Pontifical Biblical Institute in Rome discussed Catholic approaches to biblical scholarship. He summarized what he saw as the contemporary approach by saying that every book of the Bible has two authors: God and the human author. I asked whether he thought that the following formulation would do justice to this position: "Every biblical book has two authors: God and the human author, but God does not read the final page proofs." After brief consideration, he answered in the affirmative. This approach can of course provide support—and is probably even a sine qua non—for the position that the magisterium can reject the view of a New Testament author. (The book that emerged from that conference is, Clemens Thoma and Michael Wyschogrod, eds., *Understanding Scripture: Explorations of Jewish and Christian Traditions of Interpretation* [New York: Paulist, 1987].)

14. For an argument against proselytizing Jews that does not flow from theological considerations, see Berger, "Reflections on Conversion and Proselytizing in Judaism and Christianity," *Studies in Jewish-Christian Relations* 3 (2008) R1-R8, http://

Moreover, it is the divine blessing to Abraham, which undergirds much of the empathy with Jews affirmed by many evangelical Christians, and their support for the Jewish right to the land of Israel (currently far more important to most Jews than abstract discussions of salvation through the Old Law) that requires no recourse to the Mosaic covenant. The prophetic passages that these Christians often cite foretelling a restoration of the Jewish people to its land can stand on their own or be understood as a function of the promises to the patriarchs. (As medieval Jews argued in debates about the True Israel, it is difficult to spiritualize those promises and refer them to the Church since they speak about return from exile, and it was the carnal Israel, not the purported spiritual one, that was dispersed.)

And so we need to note an additional consequence of *Nostra Aetate*, namely, its elimination of the key theological argument justifying nonrecognition of Israel. This follows inexorably from the rejection of the view that postcrucifixion Jews bear responsibility for the killing of Jesus. Nonetheless, the Vatican did not translate this implication into practice for many years. The refusal to establish diplomatic relations with Israel was a sore point in Jewish-Catholic interaction, and it is difficult to take seriously the forced theoretical rationales such as the absence of settled borders or a formal peace that were proffered for this refusal. At this point, however, there is no value in rehearsing the problematic character of the Vatican's delay in exchanging ambassadors with Israel; what matters is that the situation has been rectified, and that this was ultimately made possible by *Nostra Aetate*.

In the decades following Vatican II, the central Church and various national conferences of bishops issued a series of documents that flesh out the general prescriptions of *Nostra Aetate, no. 4*. While most Jews have responded to these initiatives with appreciation and enthusiasm, a minority have reacted in a grudging, even churlish fashion. They have complained that *Nostra Aetate* itself did not specifically use the term "deicide" in its denial of Jewish guilt, and that it "deplored" rather than "condemned" anti-Semitism (though the latter "defect" has been rectified by later pronouncements); they have objected to the fact that the 1998 document on the *Shoah* did not hold the Church *qua* Church responsible for

ejournals.bc.edu/ojs/index.php/scjr/article/view/1502/1355/. The piece also appeared in Joseph D. Small and Gilbert S. Rosenthal, eds., *Let us Reason Together: Christians and Jews in Conversation* (Louisville: Witherspoon, 2010), 131–40, and was reprinted in Berger, *Persecution, Polemic, and Dialogue*, 367–77, at 376–77.

anti-Semitism and its most terrible manifestation; they have demanded that the Church explicitly recognize the moral deficiencies of Pius XII's behavior during the Nazi era; they have insisted that even what I regard as benign supersessionism be rejected as an offense against interfaith morality. Some Jews indignantly denounce the historic Church for its teaching of contempt and then dismiss the revocation of that teaching as an overdue triviality. Such responses strike me as inherently unjustified and/or pragmatically unwise.

At the same time, celebratory reactions to these post–Vatican II documents need to be tempered by the recognition that the impact of such statements is often limited, and not only with respect to reception by the laity. Declarations by Church representatives charged to deal with Jews can reflect a perspective different from that of other Church authorities. There can be profound differences, for example, between declarations regarding Israel issued by the Catholic-Jewish Liaison Committee and the equivalent committee of Catholics and Muslims. Even when a statement is issued by a national Catholic body, there is no guarantee that it will be honored when tested in a context involving authorities who do not regularly work with Jews. Thus, the document on *Criteria for Evaluation of Dramatizations of the Passion* issued by the National Conference of Catholic Bishops in the United States was utterly ignored by the Conference's own Office of Film and Broadcasting in its review of Mel Gibson's controversial film.[15]

Let me close with a brief remark about the implications of the deep changes in the official Catholic views of Jews and Judaism for Jewish self-reflection. I am implacably opposed to modifications of what I regard as core Jewish evaluations of Christianity in the service of ecumenical reciprocity. At the same time, Jews have confronted troubling issues relating to their view of Christianity and their general attitude to non-Jews over a period of many centuries when *Nostra Aetate* was not even a glimmer in the eye of the Church. This inner confrontation was stimulated by theological, ethical, economic, and legal factors that were not always connected to Christian attitudes toward Jews; and when they were, the reaction could sometimes move in an unexpected direction.[16] Precisely

15. I commented on this point in "Jews, Christians, and 'The Passion'," *Commentary* 117/5 (May 2004) 23–31 (reprinted in David Berger, *Persecution, Polemic, and Dialogue*, 399–416, at 413), as well as in the exchange in *Commentary* 118/2 (2004) 10.

16. See *inter multa alia* Jacob Katz's classic work, *Exclusiveness and Tolerance* (London: Oxford University Press, 1961), and my discussion: Berger, "Jacob Katz on Jews

because Christianity is simultaneously similar to Judaism and profoundly different from it, limning its contours from the perspective of Jewish law and thought is a daunting challenge, and I have struggled with it for years in a variety of forums.[17] Like the Christian effort to define a proper relationship with Judaism, this task, in the famous words of the Mishnah, is not for us to complete, but we are not free to desist from it.

and Christians in the Middle Ages," in Jay M. Harris, ed., *The Pride of Jacob: Essays on Jacob Katz and his Work* (Cambridge: Harvard University Press, 2002), 41–63, reprinted in Berger, *Persecution, Polemic, and Dialogue*, 51–74. See too my observations in Berger, "Christians, Gentiles, and the Talmud: A Fourteenth-Century Jewish Response to the Attack on Rabbinic Judaism," in Bernard Lewis and Friedrich Niewöhner, eds., *Religionsgespräche im Mittelalter* (Wiesbaden: Harrassowitz, 1992), 115–30, reprinted in Berger, *Persecution, Polemic, and Dialogue*, 158–76, at 176.

17. My most extensive and personal expression of this struggle is an essay titled "Jews, Gentiles, and the Modern Egalitarian Ethos: Some Tentative Thoughts," in Marc D. Stern, ed., *Formulating Responses in an Egalitarian Age* (Lanham, MD: Rowman & Littlefield, 2005), 83–108.

17

Nostra Aetate's Processing of Gospel Texts

Five Substantive Reactions by *Lay* Jews

Michael J. Cook

A RELENTLESS POUNDING ON a dormitory door awakens a Jewish coed at Miami University (Oxford, Ohio). It is 3:00 a.m. in the fall of 1965. At the door is a casual acquaintance from across the hall. "TV just announced that the pope has freed *you* from killing Jesus," she said. "Thought you'd want to know as soon as possible!"

Whether or not that 1965 coed indeed would "want to know" this, countless Jews were assuredly, at that time, enthused over Vatican II: not only for its dismissal of the Jews' perpetual collective blame for Jesus's death but also for the many other gains now possibly to ensue in Jewish-Catholic relations. Accordingly, with the approach of each ten-year anniversary, I have recalibrated my teaching and speaking to emphasize the historic implications of this "turnaround." Yet with the passage of time *lay* Jewish interest in celebrating Vatican II may be on the wane—except, potentially, for an intriguing change of direction from a radically unexpected quarter!

For besides the Vatican "turnaround," a *second* "turnaround," of an entirely different nature, has materialized and is accelerating within the Jewish arena: an unprecedented burgeoning not only of Jewish scholarship on the New Testament but also an outright reversal by *lay* Jews, non-specialists, now favoring such study themselves. Formidable but also symbolic here has been production of *The Jewish Annotated New Testament*,[1] billed as scholarship "clear" and "accessible"[2]—reflecting the editors' intent to earmark also nonspecialist readers, lay Jews among them. And the fifty or so contributors by no means represent the totality of Jewish scholars in the field, not to mention the plethora of their other writings published elsewhere.

Understandably, the rise of even lay Jews' interest, particularly in Gospel study, has redirected some Jews to focus also on how key Gospel texts were appropriated and processed first by *Nostra Aetate*[3] itself, and thereafter by its two implementing documents: the *Guidelines*[4] and *Notes*.[5] This unexpected opportunity poses the question of whether Catholics themselves are comfortable encouraging a convergence of these two developments—i.e., interaction between the Catholic turnaround from 1965 and now the lay Jewish turnaround of more recent vintage. Here lies a key to restimulating lay Jews' interest in ten-year-anniversary celebrations: elevating dialogue along a new avenue that Jews would find inviting.

1. Amy-Jill Levine and Marc Zvi Brettler, eds., *The Jewish Annotated New Testament* (New York: Oxford University Press, 2011).

2. On its back cover.

3. *Declaration on the Relation of the Church to Non-Christian Religions "Nostra Aetate,"* Oct 28, 1965: n. 4.

4. *Guidelines and Suggestions for Implementing the Conciliar Declaration "Nostra Aetate"* (n. 4), Oct 22, 1974, http://www.vatican.va/roman_curia/pontifical_councils/chrstuni/relations-jews-docs/rc_pc_chrstuni_doc_19741201_nostra-aetate_en.html/.

5. *Notes on the Correct Way to Present the Jews and Judaism in Preaching and Catechesis of the Roman Catholic Church,* Jun 24, 1985, http://www.vatican.va/roman_curia/pontifical_councils/chrstuni/relations-jews-docs/rc_pc_chrstuni_doc_19820306_jews-judaism_en.html/.

THE SECOND TURNAROUND: BACKGROUND

Jews' paradigmatic approach to coping with problematic issues—especially involving Jews' place in society—has been to amass rather than to shun knowledge. One glaring exception has been securing familiarity with, let alone competence in, the New Testament, where instead Jewish avoidance strategies have been the rule. This almost two-millennial mindset, initially advised by rabbinic Sages of old,[6] has not proven sage advice. Indeed, often Jews' incapacity to address New Testament matters has only guaranteed that their problems vis-à-vis Christianity could congeal, intensify, and fester, destabilizing Jews' well-being on communal as well as individual bases.

Has the recent reversal of this lingering ghettoization of the Jewish mind itself been a function of Vatican II's new openness? While such a case could be made, more determinative have been factors *internal* to the Jewish communal experience (as I chronicle elsewhere[7]).

Beyond discovering Gospel study to be intellectually stimulating, some lay Jews have experienced it also as cathartic, given their abiding pain and resentment over New Testament castigations of Jews as murderous as well as spiritually blind. Both factors, then—the cerebral and the cathartic—have incentivized even lay Jews to detect the possible "Gospel dynamics"[8] that spawned the New Testament's frequently anti-Jewish tenor. Thereafter, Jews have sought to explain the operation of these dynamics to their children, non-Jewish family members, friends Jewish and Christian, and a broader Christian society. Facilitating this exposure have been adult-education courses taught by rabbis, who now are themselves trained in New Testament,[9] synagogue Scholar-in-Residence programs by specialists in Gospel issues, national and regional study conclaves featuring New Testament topics, increasing attention even in Jewish re-

6. E.g., Tosefta Shabbat 13:5; cf. Tosefta Yadayim 2:13.

7. Ch. 23 in Michael J. Cook, *Modern Jews Engage the New Testament: Enhancing Jewish Well-Being in a Christian Environment* (3rd ed.; Woodstock, VT: Jewish Lights, 2012): changing attitudes by national Jewish organizations, sociological trends (assimilation, intermarriage, blended families, declining birthrate), defensiveness (against millennialism, creationism, missionizing), cultural challenges (Gibson's *Passion of the Christ*), etc.

8. Ibid, 351–54 (Gospel Dynamics Index).

9. Hebrew Union College (Cincinnati) is the first (possibly still only) Jewish seminary in history to *require* technical New Testament facility for ordination, with now over one thousand graduates so trained.

ligious schools to Jesus-related problems,[10] and study of recommended scholarship (or gravitation to such works) on one's own—all enhancing Jews' sense of well-being in a Christian environment.

THE QUESTION OF TRESPASS

Does such Jewish examination of sacred Christian Scripture constitute *trespass*? Over the centuries, Gospel denigrations of Jews have constituted possibly *the* prime external determinant of all of Jewish history. Jews today might have less inducement to explore New Testament terrain if these writings had not irreversibly dislodged Jewish life from courses that Jews would have wished to set for themselves. Moreover, the younger religion, Christianity, co-opted the Scriptures of its elder, Judaism, and interpreted them to the elder's disparagement and detriment. Is it not fair, even necessary, that the newer writings (many later canonized) stand open to Jewish scrutiny?

The *Guidelines* ask Catholics to understand "the manner in which Jews identify themselves" and "by what essential traits the Jews define themselves in the light of their own religious experience"[11] (iterated by the *Notes*[12]). Regarding this clarion call for Catholics, Jews resonate with Chicago's late Joseph Cardinal Bernardin, who urged that "the history of anti-Semitism and of anti-Judaic theology be restored [not eliminated but *restored*] to . . . Catholic teaching materials . . . to tell the full story of the Church's treatment of Jews over the centuries, ending with a rejection of the shadow side of that history and theology at the Second Vatican Council."[13] The more this challenge is known and taken to heart, the more readily Catholics themselves may discern the need for Jews to study Gospel texts as part of the process of conveying how Jews "identify" and "define themselves," and even to apply this study in assessing the threefold *Nostra Aetate* composite.

10. Roxanne (Schneider) Shapiro, "Teaching Jewish Children about Jesus: Is the Advice of Our Sages Still Sage Advice?" Thesis, Hebrew Union College, 2013.

11. Introduction and Preamble, respectively.

12. *Notes*, I ("Religious Teaching and Judaism"), section 4.

13. Joseph Cardinal Bernardin, "Antisemitism: The Historical Legacy and the Continuing Challenge for Christians," a lecture published in a pamphlet for the Hebrew University by the Center for Christian-Jewish Understanding (Fairfield, CT: Sacred Heart University, 1995) 16, 18; cf. Michael Cook, *Jewish Views of Jesus* (The Joseph Cardinal Bernardin Jerusalem Lecture 2007; Chicago: Spertus, 2007).

CLASHING APPROACHES: DOCTRINAL VS. HISTORICAL-CRITICAL

At the close of January 1988, three Jews (nonspecialists) independently sent me press clippings summarizing a memorable program just held in Manhattan. One headline proclaimed: "Ratzinger—Modern Biblical Scholarship Dilutes Church Teaching."[14] According to this particular clipping, Joseph Cardinal Ratzinger, then prefect of the Vatican's Congregation for the Doctrine of the Faith (later Pope Benedict XVI), amiably "chided modern exegetes ... for inserting their presuppositions into their study of the scriptures," adding that "some modern exegesis has 'ceased being theology.'" While endorsing use of the "historical-critical method" of Bible study, he found "the technique . . . subject to perversion by the views of those who use it." During a news conference, he distinguished between "what scholars can discuss and what can be taught in the name of the church."[15] Basing themselves solely on the press reportage (accurate and sufficient or not), each of my three contacts asked me to clarify how this distinction—between what can be *discussed* vs. what may be *taught*—could be viable.

They also shared their abrupt, enthusiastic transformation upon reading cited-responses by Fr. Raymond E. Brown, Auburn Distinguished Professor of Biblical Studies at New York's Union Theological Seminary, and recipient of twenty-four honorary degrees from Protestant as well as Catholic institutions. Both in his own lecture[16] and follow-up conversation (featuring about twenty others), Brown congenially countered that "'moderate biblical criticism' served the church well," even "bolstering the proclamation of the gospel and unifying Protestant, Catholic and Orthodox views." *The New York Times'* Peter Steinfels highlighted Brown's insistence that his type of scholarship represented a search for a new way

---

14. Charles Austin, *Religious News Service Daily Reports,* Jan 29, 1988, 1–2.

15. The 1988 Erasmus Lecture (St. Peter's Lutheran Church), "Biblical Interpretation in Conflict: The Question of the Basic Principles and Path of Exegesis Today," in Pope Benedict XVI (Joseph Cardinal Ratzinger), *God's Word: Scripture, Tradition, Office,* P. Hünermann and T. Söding, eds.; H. Taylor, trans. (San Francisco: Ignatius, 2008), 91–126.

16. Raymond E. Brown, "The Contribution of Historical Biblical Criticism to Ecumenical Church Discussion," delivered at the same conference featuring Ratzinger's Erasmus lecture, in Richard John Neuhaus, ed., *Biblical Interpretation in Crisis: The Ratzinger Conference on Bible and Church* (Grand Rapids: Eerdmans, 1989), 24–49.

of using the Bible that would be "authoritative and church-building,"[17] and that Vatican II actually *supported* the "higher criticism" that characterized and vindicated Brown's approach.[18]

Noteworthy here is unawareness by these three lay Jews (and countless others) of the *innumerable Catholic theologians themselves well-schooled and published in historical-critical matters*. Those Jews knowing this are thus puzzled why, during *Nostra Aetate* discourse, such experts often shift into a doctrinal mode that at times appears to banish, or at least "vanish," the historical-critical approach altogether in favor of the theological: "two-covenants," "chosenness," "liturgy," "supersessionism," "eschatology," "typology," and "mission." Most Jews, meanwhile, instead self-identify by other articulated categories: "peoplehood," "civilization," "culture," "ethics," "festival observance," and above all *"history."* I have employed the foregoing Ratzinger/Brown vignette to dramatize that Catholic understanding of how lay Jews self-identify may remain elusive unless we rebalance dialogue on *Nostra Aetate* matters by welcoming historical-critical dimensions on a par with those doctrinal.

FIVE FREQUENTLY RECURRING ILLUSTRATIONS

In advancing now five typical Jewish lay reactions to *Nostra Aetate's* processing of Gospel texts, I myself will be fleshing out the core of these reactions for fuller clarity. Yet at least two notable problems warrant mention here, at least in passing: (1) Never have *I* heard any of these common Jewish reactions broached, let alone addressed, at a *Nostra Aetate* conference. Has my experience been idiosyncratic or the norm? (2) What of still additional follow-up Catholic writings, ancillary to the threefold *Nostra Aetate* complex, that *clarify*, even *amend*, sections of the original documents but of which most Jews are unaware—or, even if aware, would likely deem to lack the gravitas of an official Church imprimatur?

---

17. Peter Steinfels, "Cardinal Is Seen as Kind, if Firm, Monitor of Faith," *New York Times*, Mon, Feb. 1, 1988, http://www.nytimes.com/1988/02/01/us/cardinal-is-seen-as-kind-if-firm-monitor-of-faith.html/.

18 For full treatment of the program: Pablo T. Gadenz, "Overcoming the Hiatus between Exegesis and Theology: Guidance and Examples from Pope Benedict XVI," in Scott M. Carl, *"Verbum Domini" and the Complementarity of Exegesis and Faith* (Catholic Theological Formation Series; Grand Rapids: Eerdmans, 2014), 41–62.

LAY JEWS' REACTION TO "THE HYBRID RIDDLE"

Unquestionably, here is *the* most frequently posed challenge by lay Jews: If it was indispensable for humanity's redemption that Jesus die, with Jews allegedly a vital cog in effecting that *benefit*, then why were Jews *blamed*, indeed condemned, for Jesus's death? I myself have coined this "the Hybrid Riddle"[19] because it simultaneously affirms two mutually exclusive propositions: "benefit" yet also condemnatory "blame." The pertinence here is that lay Jews spot "the Hybrid Riddle" glaringly ensconced, yet left entirely unresolved, directly within the *Nostra Aetate* paragraph itself!

> *BLAME:* " . . . the Jewish authorities and those who followed their lead pressed for the death of Christ; still, what happened in His passion cannot be charged against all the Jews, without distinction, then alive, nor against the Jews of today . . ."

> *BENEFIT:* "Besides, as the Church has always held and holds now, Christ underwent His passion and death freely, because of the sins of men and out of infinite love, in order that all may reach salvation."

Here especially the word, "besides," signals a hybrid.

Teasing out a seeming parallel from the Judas story, Mark 14:21 (& parallels) has Jesus declare: "the Son of man goes as it is written of him *[BENEFIT]*, but woe to that man by whom [he] . . . is betrayed! It would have been better for that man if he not been born *[BLAME]*." That is, Jesus had to die, but woe to heinous Judas who need not have opted to betray him. If "Judas" by intention intimates "Jew,"[20] then all the more so does Jesus have to die as divinely ordained, but woe to those heinous *Jews* who need not have opted to condemn him.

Given the countless deaths related to this hybrid conundrum, today's lay Jews will be impatient hearing proposals of some theological "mystery" such as the one that posits *by the same people through whom Christ died was the world redeemed*. Nor will Jews welcome explanations that God's plan required human agency, with the Jews that chosen instrumentality. Instead, Jews look for a historical-critical alternative reframing

---

19. Cook, *Modern Jews Engage the New Testament*, 128–29.

20. Note the assonance of "Judas" and "Jew," almost identically spelled in Greek (*Ioudas* [Judas], *Ioudaios* [Jew]) and also Hebrew (*Yehuda, Yehudi*)—suggesting intentional equation: Judas echoed the Jews whom Mark blamed for Jesus's death—hence Judas the Jew *and* Judas *as* the *Jews* betrayed Jesus.

of the matter. I myself, e.g., assign "benefit" vs. "blame" sequentially to respective time frames:

- **BENEFIT** could have originated when Christians, possibly beginning as early as the 30s, came to understand "Christ's" death as *beneficial* since believers' vicarious participation in his death and resurrection cleansed them from evil innate in this life, enabling their salvific rebirth unto life eternal.

- **BLAME** would be the card played only later, especially during the 60s,[21] when Nero scapegoated Christians for the Roman capital's disastrous fire (64),[22] which was followed by the Jews' own homeland revolt against Rome (66–73). How fearful Christians must then have become that the founder to whom they traced themselves had been crucified, a *Roman* punishment often for insurrectionists, and that the "Christian" movement was known to have stemmed from a land now engulfed in fanatical rebellion against Rome by Jewish insurgents with whom Christian-Jews could still readily be *confused*.[23] Lest the stigma of their crucified Lord adhere likewise to his later followers, here was reason enough to invent Pilate's supposed endeavor to release Jesus. By thus shifting blame for Jesus's death from Rome instead to Rome's *enemy*—namely, Jews rejecting Jesus—a Jew put to death by Rome could "become" a Christian put to death by Jews.

LAY JEWS' REACTION TO THE ABSENCE OF "ROME"

Thrice the *Nostra Aetate* documents "free" Jews from collective, perpetual blame for Jesus's death.[24] Shock ensues when lay Jews, upon first genuinely reading these texts, discover that still *solely Jews* are left culpable, only

21. That Paul himself uncharacteristically leveled *blame* already in ca. 48–50 (1 Thess 2:14ff.) is debated as instead by a post-70 hand. (Paul saw Jesus's death as beneficial, not cause for blame.) Inclining toward authenticity: Didier Pollefeyt and David Bolton, "Paul, Deicide, and the Wrath of God," in Thomas G. Casey and Justin Taylor, eds., *Paul's Jewish Matrix* (Rome: Gregorian & Biblical Press, 2011), 229–57.

22. Tacitus, *Annals* xv.44.

23. Christians shared Jewish Scripture, facets of Jewish belief, liturgy, festival practice, in some cases family ties.

24. *Nostra Aetate* 4; *Guidelines*, III Teaching and Education; *Notes*, IV The Jews in the New Testament, 2.

now just fewer of them! Absent here is recourse to the unequivocal position of countless Catholic scholars that *Rome* and *Pilate* were largely if not primarily determinative in Jesus's death.

Irrespective of such admission in ancillary Catholic documents (the problem referenced above),[25] Jews are noncomprehending as to why the *Guidelines* and *Notes*—respectively nine and twenty years later than *Nostra Aetate* itself—still do nothing more than repeat verbatim the original wording with no retouching nuance (thus seeming to affirm the sufficiency of the *Nostra Aetate* formulation). After all,

- Josephus details the subordination of each high priest (e.g., Caiaphas) to his corresponding Roman governor (here Pilate), with the latter empowered to peremptorily dismiss the former.

- The longest joint tenure, that of Caiaphas with Pilate, implies consonance of Caiaphas's actions with Pilate's directives. [26]

- Josephus states that high priests could legally convene Sanhedrins only at a Roman governor's behest.[27]

- Even the historicity of Jesus's Sanhedrin trial must be questioned.[28]

- Sources other than the Gospels portray Pilate's rule as so cruel and counterproductive that Rome had to remove him from office.[29]

25. Eugene J. Fisher and Leon Klenicki, eds., *In Our Time: The Flowering of Jewish-Catholic Dialogue* (New York: Paulist, 1990), 15–16; also *Within Context: Guidelines for the Catechetical Presentation of Jews and Judaism in the New Testament*, Sec. for Catholic Jewish Relations, NCCB; Adult Educ. Dep't, USCC; Interfaith Affairs Dep't, ADL (1986), 67–69. See http://archive.adl.org/nr/exeres/a9659c0f-2958-4e48-8418-530a140f02d4,db7611a2-02cd-43af-8147-649e26813571,frameless.html/.

26. *Antiquities* XX.x.1 (¶¶224–230); cf. *Antiquities* XVIII.ii.1–2 (¶¶26–35).

27. *Antiquities* XX.ix.1 (¶¶197–203).

28. Cook, "Is Jesus' Nighttime Sanhedrin Trial an Aggrandizement of Friday Morning's 'Consultation'?," in *The Bible and Interpretation*, http://www.bibleinterp.com/opeds/2013/coo378023.shtml/. For different skepticism, see *Criteria for the Evaluation of Dramatizations of the Passion* (Bishops' Committee for Ecumenical and Interreligious Affairs, NCCB, 1988), section C, https://www.bc.edu/dam/files/research_sites/cjl/texts/cjrelations/resources/documents/catholic/Passion_Plays.htm/.

29. *War* II.ix.2–4 (¶¶169–77) // *Antiquities* XVIII.iii.1–3 (¶¶55–64); iv.1–2 (¶¶85–89); cf. Luke 13:1; Philo, *Embassy to Gaius*, 299–305.

- Finally, the Gospels may depict Jesus as condemned for "blasphemy," a Jewish crime of no concern to Rome, precisely to displace "sedition" ("King of the Jews"), a severe crime to Rome.

That Rome or Pilate goes unmentioned anywhere, especially in the *Guidelines* and *Notes*, suggests to Jews a reticence by the Church that is disconcertingly inconsistent with what Jews assumed was the Church's intention: to render a more realistic and balanced understanding of what underlay the Passion account.

LAY JEWS' REACTION TO MATTHEW'S "BLOOD CURSE" AS NECESSARILY MEANING *IN PERPETUITY*

Although none of the three major documents cites Matt 27:25 ("His blood be on us and on our children"), this key verse spawned belief that Jews are collectively and permanently culpable for Jesus's death. Understandable is some lay Jews' query: why not read this text as limited to only two generations: with the "on us" referring to the Jews' past generation (namely, Jesus's own day); and with the "on our children" referring to the Jews' present generation (Matthew's own)—correlative to Brown's question: "how far does [must?] the 'us and our children' extend?"[30]

Fleshing out the matter: Matthew was customarily so preoccupied with problems of his *own* community (ca. 85 CE) that, arguably, he could indeed have intended 27:25 to *end with* his own day (rather than to extend into perpetuity). Nor need usage of "on our children" elsewhere (if anywhere) in Scripture determine our view of what Matthew intended *here*.

By analogy, only once does Matthew employ the term "the Jews" (aside from "king of the Jews"[31]), here to counter a rumor that the emptiness of Jesus' tomb was due to his disciples' theft of his body—a tale spread in Matthew's own community "among the Jews *to this day*" (28:15b; italics added). Matthew's singular, and lengthy, vitriol against Pharisees likewise seems directed to those of Matthew's own day and community (ch. 23). So also his formulation of the "Great Commission" (28:19a) which reverses, *for Matthew's own time,* Jesus's presumably original orientation (10:5–6; 15:24).[32] By the same token, then, would not Matthew feel the need to

30. Raymond Brown, *The Death of the Messiah*, vol. 1 (New York: Doubleday, 1994), 839.

31. Which Matthew preserves from Mark, not originates.

32. Matthew reverses the Christian mission from exclusively the lost sheep

account for the *recent* catastrophic destruction of Jerusalem's Temple (70 CE)—all the more so if, as most scholars consider, he wrote from nearby Antioch? By means of 27:25, Matthew could process the *Temple's fall* as recompense for the Jews' own criminality (cf. likewise 23:38, and the opening of ch. 24). This realization by us would also explain why no other canonical Gospel includes a parallel to Matt 27:25—namely, that it reflected specifically Matthew's own day and community.

LAY JEWS' REACTION TO THE ADMISSION: "REFLECT CHRISTIAN-JEWISH-RELATIONS LONG AFTER THE TIME OF JESUS"

Unusual in employing a historical-critical approach, the *Notes* aver: "Certain [Gospel] controversies reflect Christian-Jewish-relations long after the time of Jesus,"[33] explained to mean "actually hav[ing] their historical context . . . in the last decades of the first century."[34] Yet Jewish readers discover no limitation here, so that this (correct) historical-critical admission seemingly allows for untrammeled application elsewhere: i.e., how many additional instances of Gospel references to Jesus, found now in the *Nostra Aetate* complex (even aside from controversies), should be examined as likewise *alterations* due to a post-70 context? Jews may be comfortable with this open-ended implication but confused as to the extent of what the Church here foresaw—or did not foresee—by it.

LAY JEWS' REACTION TO THE SHADOW SIDE OF "TYPOLOGY"

The *Notes* read: "typological interpretation consists in reading the Old Testament as preparation and, in certain aspects, outline and foreshadowing of the New."[35] Examples cited here include the exodus, passing

---

of Israel (10:5–6; 15:24) to include also, or exclusively, "Gentiles" (based on how *ethnē* in 28:19 is understood). See Cook, "'Mind the Gap': Bridging One Dozen Lacunae in Jewish-Catholic Dialogue," Second Annual John Paul II Lecture in Christian-Jewish Relations (Boston College., 2013), http://huc.edu/academics/learn/mind-gap-bridging-one-dozen-lacunae-jewish-catholic-dialogue/.

33. *Notes* IV.A; cf. IV D.

34. *Within Context*, 61.

35 *Notes* II: Relations between the Old and New Testament, 5 and *passim*. Cf. *Dogmatic Constitution on Divine Revelation "Dei Verbum"* (Nov. 18, 1965), n. 16, cited in

through the Red Sea, the rock in the wilderness, and so forth.[36] Even while the *Notes* were being fashioned, however, some Catholic biblicists objected to the any inclusion of typology—that this would appear regressive and inconsistent with the very flavor of *Nostra Aetate*, especially because it could be inferred as supersessionism. (Instructively, however, the *Notes* do recognize that such readings may constitute a problem in Jewish-Catholic relations, and should not preclude the viability of alternative interpretive options.[37])

When lay Jews, unschooled in typology, first hear about it, some typically propose an obvious alternative: that what appears to be typological *prediction* foreshadowing details of Gospel episodes could instead be *conformance* by Gospel tradition to match antecedent Jewish Scripture. Might not Jesus seem to fulfill Isaiah's Suffering Servant because Jesus's image was belatedly *correlated* to Isa 53? Did Jesus genuinely quote Ps 22:1 ("My God, . . . why hast thou forsaken me?"), and then was that Psalm's other imagery (casting lots for garments, derision by passersby wagging their heads, etc.) *imported* into what Mark and Matthew convey—this embellishment to *match* their scenes of Jesus on the cross to the reminder of Ps 22? Is what is understood as Moses's five books of the Torah on Mount Sinai to be seriously construed as an actual foreshadowing of Jesus's Sermon on the *Mount* in five divisions (Matt 5–7)? Is Ahithophel's suicide-by-hanging, after betraying David (2 Sam 17:23), actually a predictive "type" of *Judas's* suicide-by-hanging, after betraying Jesus (Matt 27:5)? Or would each of these themes (and countless others like them) far more likely reflect the Gospels' *conformance* of details to earlier Jewish Biblical narratives?

This becomes most impactful when we view the seeming correlation of *Jeremiah's* Passion with that of Jesus. Jeremiah himself was a righteous Jew speaking for God, defying the religious establishment, arousing enmity from Jewish priests, demanding they amend their ways, and threatening the Temple's destruction (a "den of robbers" [7:11]). Threatened by priests with death, Jeremiah warned they could bring innocent blood upon themselves. A vacillating civil authority (reluctant to heed priests' demands) pronounced him innocent. Later, the Temple was destroyed as the just man warned! Graphically:

Guidelines, III—Teaching and Education.

36. *Notes* II: Relations between the Old and New Testament.

37. See further analysis in Eugene J. Fisher and Leon Klenicki, eds., *In Our Time: The Flowering of Jewish-Catholic Dialogue* (New York: Paulist, 1990), 13–14.

JEREMIAH's Passion		JESUS' Passion
"Has the house . . . become a den of robbers?" (7:11)	→	"Is it not written [Jer 7:11], 'My house . . . you have made ... a den of robbers'?" (Mark 11:17 & parallels)
I will "do to th[is] house [temple #1] . . . as I did to Shiloh [1 Sam 4–6]!" (7:14)	→	"We heard him say, 'I will destroy this temple [#2] . . .'" (Mark 14:58 & paralells; cf. John 2:19)
"All the people laid hold of him, saying: 'You shall die'" (26:8)	→	"All the people" demanded his death (Matt 27:25)
An inquiry convened for Jeremiah (26:10)	→	A Sanhedrin convened for Jesus (Mark 14:53 & parallels)
Priests (and others) said Jeremiah "deserves . . . death" for words "you have heard" (11)	→	The Sanhedrin decided that Jesus "deserves death" (Mt 26:66 [cf. Mark 14:64]) for words that "you have heard" (Mark 14:64; cf. Matt 26:65)
"you will bring innocent blood upon yourselves" (26:15)	→	"His blood be on us and on our children!" (Matt 27:25)
His captors took him for execution to the vacillating King Zedekiah, who replied: "He is in your hands . . ." (38:5)	→	His captors took him for execution to the vacillating prefect Pilate, who replied: "See to it yourselves" (Matt 27:24)
Wanting a private conversation, "Zedekiah sent for Jeremiah" (38:14)	→	Wanting a private conversation, "Pilate . . . called Jesus" to him (John 18:33)
Zedekiah was "afraid" (38:19)	→	Pilate was "the more afraid" (John 19:8)

Some lay Jews have volunteered the analogy of shooting arrows first, then painting a bull's-eye around each. Were Jesus's Passion to any degree modeled on Jeremiah's, this could mean that a literary device (nonhistory) became misapplied as a pretext for murdering countless Jews (not to mention for loss of their yet unborn offspring). Thus the unease even by some Catholic biblicists that "typology could signal supersessionism," does not match the potentially more ominous "shadow side" of the problem overlooked by the *Notes*.

SUMMARY

Since countless Catholic theologians are themselves extraordinarily adroit in dialoguing on the *historical* layering of Gospel texts, could not such historical-critical discussion, so preferred by Jews, be more fully incorporated into at least some Jewish-Catholic symposia—with printed lecture titles reflecting *historical* matters additional to *doctrinal*—so that the two "turnarounds" will interact more than diverge? Of course, what many Jews would most desire is, someday, a *fourth* major document following up the first three (now after a thirty-year hiatus: 1985–2015) and addressing these pointed Jewish reactions.

Jews studying the *Nostra Aetate* complex assuredly respect these documents as earmarked for Catholic constituents—not *for* Jews but for Catholics *about* Jews. And Jews can remind themselves of the overarching importance of the Second Vatican Council in the grand sweep of world history, and of its continued implementation in ever wider circles today. Yet since escalating interest in Gospel study by lay Jews seems here to stay, then progress on what the *Guidelines* term the "still long road ahead"[38] depends on maximizing the number of potentially eager traveling partners.

---

38. This is the opening of the concluding paragraph.

18

In Our Time: *Nostra Aetate* after Fifty Years

Retrospect and Prospects

Eugene J. Fisher

THE DECLARATION *NOSTRA AETATE* was one of the first of the statements of the Second Vatican Council to be taken up for consideration, and one of the last to be promulgated. When it was issued on October 28, 1965, I was a senior in a seminary, the debates of the Council having coincided with our college years.[1] Those were heady years. We used to say that we entered the seminary in the sixteenth century, with the Council of Trent, and graduated on the verge of the twenty-first. Little did I know that I would spend much of my professional life working out the implications and implementing one section, number 4, of this shortest of the Conciliar documents.

Pursuing a love of the Hebrew Scriptures after I left the seminary, I engaged in doctoral work at the Institute of Hebrew Studies at New

1. See Eugene J. Fisher, "A Life in Dialogue," in William Richardson, ed., *Wandering between Two Worlds: The Sacred Heart Seminary Class of 1965* (Royal Oak, MI: Van Antwerp & Beale, 2009), 207–54.

York University, most often being the lone Christian in classes of Jews studying Judaism and Jewish history with Jewish professors. Having grown up in a virtually hermetically sealed Catholic environment, I experienced something of a culture shock relearning Christian history and to a real extent Christian theology from the perspective of its significant other and perpetual minority, the Jewish people. From Jews, I came to understand the teaching of contempt against Judaism, a term coined by French Jewish historian Jules Isaac,[2] whose meeting with Pope John XXIII influenced him to direct Cardinal Augustin Bea to put a renewed look at traditional Catholic teaching on Jews and Judaism on the agenda of the Second Vatican Council. Bea was a Scripture scholar, and with the help of a small group of experts, among them survivors of the Holocaust such as Msgr. John Oesterreicher,[3] he directed the drafters of the document which was to become *Nostra Aetate* (*In Our Time*) to go back to the New Testament to begin to refashion Catholic theology on Judaism from the basis of the newer understandings of Scripture brought about by contemporary biblical scholarship. *Nostra Aetate* is thus unusual in documents of the Council in not referring to the Fathers of the Church or to previous documents of Ecumenical Councils, since none of these directly took up the core issues of the teaching of contempt, such as the canard that the Jews were as a people collectively guilty for the death of Jesus, but simply presumed them. The revolution in Catholic thought begun by the resulting document has been considered by many, among them subsequent popes such as John Paul II and Benedict XVI, as one of the most significant advances made by the Council,[4] Even more, from my Jewish professors and friends at NYU I came to understand something of the beauty and depth of Judaism, both biblical and rabbinic, as Jews

2. Jules Isaac, *Has Anti-Semitism Roots in Christianity?* (New York: National Conference of Christians and Jews, 1961); Isaac, *The Teaching of Contempt: Christian Roots of Anti-Semitism* (New York: Holt, Rinehart & Winston, 1964); and Isaac, *Jesus and Israel* (New York: Holt, Rinehart & Winston, 1971).

3. See Augustin Cardinal Bea, *The Church and the Jewish People: A Commentary on the Second Vatican Council's Declaration on the Relation of the Church to Non-Christian Religions* (London: Chapman, 1966); and John Connelly, *From Enemy to Brother: The Revolution in Catholic Teaching on the Jews 1933–1965* (Cambridge: Harvard University Press, 2012).

4. See Eugene J. Fisher, ed., *Memoria Futuri, Catholic-Jewish Dialogue Yesterday, Today, and Tomorrow: Selected Texts and Addresses of Cardinal William H. Keeler* (New York: Paulist, 2012); and, Eugene J. Fisher and Leon Klenicki, eds, *The Saint for Shalom: The Complete Texts and Addresses of Pope John Paul II on Jews and Judaism, 1979–2005* (New York: Crossroad, 2011).

themselves understand and interpret their own traditions. I also came to understand that the negative attitudes toward Jews of the teaching of contempt over the centuries had also led to negative attitudes among Christians of God's revelation to the Jews in the Hebrew Scriptures, so that reappreciating Jews and Judaism entails a renewal of understanding of the Hebrew Scriptures, and vice versa.[5] It is not coincidental that so many of the key documents of the Church since the Council on Catholic-Jewish relations involve a renewed appreciation of the Hebrew Scriptures, understood on their own grounds and not just through the lens of the New Testament.[6]

I served from 1977 to 2007 as the staff person for Catholic-Jewish relations for the U.S. Conference of Catholic Bishops, as well as a Consultor to the Holy See's Commission for Religious Relations with the Jews and as a member of the Catholic side of the International Catholic-Jewish Liaison Committee. Therefore, I have taken part in many of the controversies that have troubled relations between the Catholic Church and the Jewish people, their resolutions, and the significant advances in understanding that have taken place since the issuance of *Nostra Aetate* a half century ago. Here, I will limit myself to reflecting on a few that I believe hold meaning for us today, and that provide a glimpse of new challenges and possibilities for the future.

Nostra Aetate was warmly received by Jews and Catholics involved in the dialogue when it was promulgated, but some key areas of omission and need for clarification were noted. While anti-Semitism was "deplored", for example, it was not "condemned." Neither the Holocaust (*Shoah*) nor the rebirth of a Jewish State in the Land promised to the Jews by God, as attested in the Hebrew Scriptures, was mentioned. And it remained a

---

5. I also came to understand, and to understand why, many Jewish scholars themselves have negative attitudes toward Christianity that do not always reflect objective history or Christian theology, properly understood. My first article in Christian-Jewish studies, based upon a paper I submitted for a class at NYU, was a study of these. An expanded and updated version of that original 1973 article, originally published in the scholarly journal *Judaism* is "Typical Jewish Misunderstandings of Christ, Christianity and Jewish-Christian Relations over the Centuries," in Zev Garber, ed., *The Jewish Jesus: Revelation, Reflection, Reclamation* (West Lafayette, IN: Purdue University Press, 2011), 228–48.

6. See, for just one example, the 2001 statement of the Pontifical Biblical Commission, approved by then-Cardinal Joseph Ratzinger as head of the Congregation for the Doctrine of the Faith, *The Jews and Their Sacred Scriptures in the Christian Bible*, http://www.vatican.va/roman_curia/congregations/cfaith/pcb_documents/rc_con_cfaith_doc_20020212_popolo-ebraico_en.html/.

bit unclear whether the Church's aim remained that of converting Jews to Christianity or working with Jews for the betterment of humanity.

The first two of these lingering questions were responded to by the *Guidelines and Suggestions for Implementing the Conciliar Declaration, "Nostra Aetate,"* no. 4, issued by the Holy See's Commission for Religious Relations with the Jews on December 1, 1974.[7] In its Preamble the 1974 statement noted the "historical setting" of *Nostra Aetate* as "the memory of the persecution and massacre of the Jews which took place in Europe" during World War II. The *Guidelines* also "restate" *Nostra Aetate* that "the spiritual bonds and historical links binding the Church to Judaism condemn, as opposed to the very spirit of Christianity, all forms of anti-Semitism and discrimination" (against Jews). The *Guidelines* went on to draw out significant implications for Catholic understandings of the Church's liturgy and working together with Jews in "great causes such as the struggle for peace and justice." The *Guidelines* provided important ground rules for the dialogue between Jews and Catholics, and for re-thinking and revising Catholic teaching materials on Jews and Judaism. My doctoral dissertation for New York University and my first book in the field, *Faith without Prejudice*, applied these guidelines to textbooks used in the United States, and explained how they were to be understood and used to interpret the New Testament and Judaism.[8]

One area of tension has been and remains the Holocaust, perpetrated by baptized Christians imbued with the ancient teaching of contempt against Jews and Judaism. Pope Benedict XVI, in his parting statement to the clergy of Rome, acknowledged that this remains a challenge for all Catholics: "Even if it is clear that the Catholic Church is not responsible for the *Shoah*, it was Christians for the most part who committed those crimes; we need to deepen and renew Christian awareness of this."[9] A major controversy between Catholics and Jews erupted in the 1980's over the setting up of a convent of cloistered nuns in a property adjacent to the death camp of Auschwitz-Birkenau. The nuns sought to dedicate their

---

7. http://www.vatican.va/roman_curia/pontifical_councils/chrstuni/relations-jews-docs/rc_pc_chrstuni_doc_19741201_nostra-aetate_en.html/.

8. Cf. Eugene J. Fisher, *Faith without Prejudice: Rebuilding Christian Attitudes toward Judaism* (New York: Paulist, 1977; 2nd ed., New York: Crossroad, 1993).

9. Pope Benedict XVI, Meeting with the Parish Priests and Clergy of Rome, Paul VI Audience Hall, February 14, 2013, http://www.vatican.va/holy_father/benedict_xvi/speeches/2013/february/documents/hf_ben-xvi_spe_20130214_clero-roma_en.html/.

lives to praying there for all the victims of the camp, Polish Catholics as well as Jews. Many Jews, understandably, saw this as an appropriation of the Holocaust, making it an event of Catholic rather than Jewish history.[10]

Ultimately, the Auschwitz-convent controversy was resolved by the personal intervention of Pope John Paul II, who asked the nuns to move to a new location further away from the camp, albeit still nearby. Ongoing tensions, however, remain, and are likely to crop up as well in the future. One such is the issue of how to remember the role of Pope Pius XII during the war. There is already an extensive body of literature on this issue. Many scholars stress the fact that Pius authorized the hiding of Jews in the convents and monasteries of Rome and throughout Italy, a record of saving Jewish lives virtually unmatched in Europe. Others believe that the Church could have done more and that Pius could have made more direct public statements condemning the Nazi roundup and deportation of Jews to the death camps, thus motivating more Christians throughout Europe to save Jews. This is a controversy likely to continue. One point that I would make, and have many times over the years, is that the archives of the Holy See for the period of 1939 to 1946 should be released for scholarly study and analysis as soon as possible. There is no reason to wait until all of the records of Pius's entire pontificate are catalogued, when those for the key years in question could be released virtually immediately. Only after release of these documents should any further moves toward making Pius a saint be considered. A large selection of these documents has already been released, of course. Study of these by Jewish and Catholic scholars has shown that the criteria for selection were objective and thus that it is unlikely that major revisions of the historical record will result from the release of the full materials. But withholding release of the documents has, like the cross at the Auschwitz convent, become symbolic of the Church's unwillingness to fully engage its past, and thus to seek reconciliation with the Jewish people in the present, and to work with Jews for a better future for all.

Another serious misunderstanding between Catholics and Jews took place when Pope John Paul II canonized a Jewish convert, Edith Stein. John Paul had studied her works in his academic career and believed

10. On the Auschwitz Convent, see Carol Rittner and John K. Roth, eds., *Memory Offended: The Auschwitz Convent Controversy* (New York: Praeger, 1991), which includes a selection of "key documents." Also, Alan L. Berger et al., eds., *The Continuing Agony: From the Carmelite Convent to the Crosses of Auschwitz* (Lanham, MD: University Press of America, 2004), which has articles and statements by Polish authorities.

strongly in her cause. Again, the core of the issue was Jewish concern that the Church was appropriating the *Shoah* as its own tragedy, not as the tragedy of the Jews who were its victims. Stein was killed as a Jew, taken to Auschwitz as part of the roundup of Jewish converts to Catholicism by the Nazis in the Netherlands in reprisal for the public condemnation of the deportations of Jews by the Dutch Catholic bishops. Pope John Paul II was very clear that Stein died first as a Jew, no more or less than the other six million victims of Nazi genocide, and only secondarily as a Catholic, a martyr to the Catholic faith because she was taken up as a result of the public witness of the Dutch bishops against the Holocaust.[11] Having a Jewish victim of the Holocaust declared a saint and placed on the Catholic liturgical calendar has meant that at least one day in the year the Catholic Church will officially remember the *Shoah* and be forced anew to discuss its implications for Catholic history and teaching.

In the summer of 1987, just six weeks before Pope John Paul II was to meet with representatives of the world and American Jewish communities for the first time in the New World, in Miami, it came out that the pope had met with Kurt Waldheim, the Catholic leader of Austria and a man whose past as a Nazi sympathizer who had played an indirect role in the *Shoah* was coming out. The Jewish community of course was outraged and questioned whether they could in fact meet with the pope under such circumstances. A hasty meeting was called in Rome with representatives of the Jewish people and the Holy See, in which I was privileged to take part. The outcome, after very serious and difficult discussion, was a promise on the part of the Holy See to take up in a major way the issue of the *Shoah* and Christian responsibility. The meeting in Miami took place and was, by all accounts, very successful. The process of development of the promised document took several years, beginning with consultations with representatives of the Catholic and Jewish communities of Europe. The final product, which was delayed and changed, not for the better, by the Vatican Secretariat of State, after being approved

---

11. Cf. Eugene J. Fisher, "A Painful Legacy: A Response to Daniel Polish," in Harry James Cargas, ed., *The Unnecessary Problem of Edith Stein* (Lanham, MD: University Press of America, 1994), 17–21; Eugene J. Fisher, "Edith Stein and Catholic-Jewish Relations," in Waltraud Herbstrith, OCD, ed., *Never Forget: Christian and Jewish Perspectives on Edith Stein* (Washington DC: ICS Publications, 1998), 165–70; Eugene J. Fisher, "Introduction" to Susanne Batsdorff, ed., *Aunt Edith: The Jewish Heritage of a Catholic Saint* (Springfield, IL: Templegate, 1998), 9–18; and Eugene J. Fisher, "Edith Stein: Tochter des judischen Volkes, reich an Weisheit und Tapferkeit," in *Dialog: Koordinierungsausschuss fur christliche-judische Zusammenarbeit* 90 (2010) 9–17.

in very good form by the Congregation for the Doctrine of the Faith, then headed by Cardinal Joseph Ratzinger, the future Pope Benedict XVI, was finally issued in 1998 under the title *We Remember: A Catholic Reflection on the Shoah.*

On the day it was issued, I was on an airplane flying from Israel to Rome, on a joint trip of U.S. bishops and rabbis, led by Cardinal William H. Keeler, the Episcopal Moderator for Catholic-Jewish Relations of the U.S. Conference of Catholic Bishops, and Rabbis Mordecai Waxman of the National Council of Synagogues and James Rudin of the American Jewish Committee. We were met at the airport by Cardinal Edward Idris Cassidy of the Holy See's Commission for Religious Relations with the Jews, and with copies of the just-released text. The next morning the rabbis, supported by Cardinal Keeler and the American bishops, succinctly stated their concerns with the text as published. Somewhat to our collective surprise, Cardinal Cassidy acknowledged the weaknesses of the text and agreed with our concerns. That May, in an address to the American Jewish Committee, speaking as the signatory of the document, he interpreted it, responding to and resolving the concerns in his official capacity. I have described in detail the process leading up to the text, its ambiguities, and resolution.[12] Subsequently, the U.S. Conference of Catholic Bishops authorized publication of a text implementing the Vatican statement for the Church in the United States, on how the *Shoah* and Christian responsibility are to be understood and taught in Catholic education. It was based upon *We Remember* as officially interpreted by Cardinal Cassidy in the name of the Holy See.[13]

The question of the Holy See's understanding of the State of Israel was resolved with the exchange of ambassadors and has been strongly affirmed by the prayerful visits to Israel of Popes John Paul II and Benedict XVI. The Holy See's approach affirms fully the validity of Israel as a Jewish state while also favoring statehood for the Palestinians by means

---

12. Eugene J. Fisher, "Interpreting *We Remember: A Reflection on the* Shoah: The History and Development of a Document of the Holy See," in Margaret Monahan Hogan and James M. Lies, eds., *History (1933–1948): What We Choose to Remember* (Portland, OR: Garaventa Center for Catholic Intellectual Life and American Culture, University of Portland, 2011), 61–84.

13. Bishops' Committee for Ecumenical and Interreligious Affairs, U.S. Conference of Catholic Bishops. *Catholic Teaching on the Shoah: Implementing the Holy See's "We Remember"* (Washington DC: United States Catholic Conference, 2001), http://www.usccb.org/beliefs-and-teachings/ecumenical-and-interreligious/jewish/upload/Catholic-Teaching-on-the-Shoah-Implementing-the-Holy-See-s-We-Remember-2001.pdf/.

of a peace accord that would do justice to the need for security for both peoples.[14] One can expect further controversies between the Church and the Jewish people, revolving around both the State of Israel and the *Shoah* in future years, as in the past and up to the present. This, of course, is the inevitable legacy and challenge of the past two millennia of Christian anti-Jewish teaching and persecution of Jews.

One such continuing challenge is the disposition of the case of the Society of Saint Pius X (SSPX), a dissident group of Catholics who went into schism because they rejected key teachings of the Second Vatican Council. One of the chief teachings of the Council rejected by SSPX, along with the statements on religious liberty and ecumenism, was *Nostra Aetate*. SSPX did not and seemingly does not want to relinquish the ancient teaching of contempt, which holds the Jews collectively guilty of the death of Jesus, and which holds that Christianity has superseded Judaism in God's favor, such that the "irrevocable" covenant, to use the term of Saint Paul in Romans 9–11, which the Council repeated in its declaration, was broken to be replaced by a new covenant between God and the followers of Christ. *Nostra Aetate* very clearly rejected this ancient false teaching. To argue, as SSPX does, that God changed his mind and rejected the Jews because of their alleged sins, of course, is to argue that the word of God in the Hebrew Scriptures and the New Testament was false. One cannot say that one believes in God as the author of Truth and say, as SSPX does, that God spoke falsely to the Jews. If God can abandon the divine promises to the Jews because of their sins, we Christians likely are not in covenant with God ourselves, for we sin no less than did the Jews. Part of the reason for the obduracy and, indeed, anti-Semitism of so many of the members of SSPX would seem to be its history. It originated as a group with the French clerics who collaborated with the Nazis during the occupation of France by Germany in World War II, internalizing Nazi anti-Semitism, and it seems (at least many of its members seem) to be incapable of letting go of its less-than-honorable past.

Most recently, the Holy See has issued an ultimatum of sorts to the SSPX, requiring it to officially acknowledge the authority of the Second Vatican Council and all its teachings, including those, such as *Nostra*

14. On the theological and practical issues involved, see Richard C. Lux, *The Jewish People, the Holy Land, and the State of Israel: A Catholic View* (New York: Paulist, 2010); and Eugene Fisher and Leon Klenicki, eds., *A Challenge Long Delayed: The Diplomatic Exchange between the Holy See and the State of Israel* (New York: Anti-Defamation League, 1996).

Aetate, with which it is unhappy. This has yet to be resolved, and there may still be some drama before it is. It will likely be on the agenda for the new pope to resolve so that the Church as a whole can move on.

Another issue that will need further development in official Catholic teaching is that of mission. In brief, does the Church have a mission to convert the Jews to Christianity, or a mission with the Jews to witness to the Name of the One God of Israel to the world, and to work together to alleviate hunger, disease, and poverty in the world? The latter, of course, is the agenda of the Hebrew prophets and of Jesus (for example in the Sermon on the Mount, which affirms and carries forward the teaching of the prophets in terms of the central significance of serving those in need as the core of God's Torah for Jews and Christians alike).

The 1985 Vatican *Notes* provide a solid basis for such a rethinking of the mission of the Church in terms of God's People, the Jews, as of course did *Nostra Aetate* when it cites Saint Paul in Romans 11, foreseeing that the Jews will rightly remain faithful to God's will for them as expressed in their Bible, the Hebrew Scriptures, until the end time, when the "fullness of the Gentiles" will come to Jesus, and then "all Israel will be saved." Paul does not say, as he does with the Gentiles, that the Jews will be saved if they convert to Christianity, only that they will in the end be saved. Paul, and Catholic teaching, quite rightly leaves the relationship between God and the People of God, the Jews, in the hands of God to determine.

In its 1985 *Notes on the Correct Way to Present the Jews and Judaism in Preaching and Catechesis in the Roman Catholic Church*,[15] the Holy See's Commission for Religious Relations with the Jews set a solid foundation for further theological development, in strong words which will also serve to conclude the present essay. The Pontifical Commission stated:

"In underlying the eschatological dimension of Christianity, we shall reach a greater awareness that the people of God of the Old and the New Testament are tending towards a like end in the future: the coming or return of the Messiah—even if they start from two different points of view. It is more clearly understood that the person of the Messiah is not only a point of division for the people of God but also a point of convergence (cf. the Ecumenical Guidelines of the diocese of Rome, no. 140). Thus, it can be said that Jews and Christians meet in a comparable hope, founded on the same promise made to Abraham (cf. Gen 12:1–3; Heb 6:13–18).

15. http://www.vatican.va/roman_curia/pontifical_councils/chrstuni/relations-jews-docs/rc_pc_chrstuni_doc_19820306_jews-judaism_en.html/.

"Attentive to the same God who has spoken, hanging on the same word, we have to witness to one same memory and one common hope in Him who is the master of history. We must also accept our responsibility to prepare the world for the coming of the Messiah by working together for social justice, respect for the rights of persons and nations, and for social and international reconciliation. To this we are driven, Jews and Christians, by the command to love our neighbor, by a common hope for the Reign of God and by the great heritage of the prophets" (nos. 10 and 11).

PART 5

Symposium: How *Nostra Aetate* Affected Me

19

A Rabbi Teaches at Catholic
and Protestant Colleges

Barry Cytron

ALONG WITH MANY OF my rabbinical school classmates at New York's Jewish Theological Seminary, I taught in an afternoon congregational school. On Tuesday, November 9, 1965, I walked out of the suburban New Jersey synagogue where I had just finished classes, and hopped the bus back to George Washington Bridge terminal. As we neared the western entrance of that majestic span, the bus driver blurted out something like: "Look at *that*! The city is pitch black."

Manhattan, and much of the Northeast, had been plunged into that renowned '65 blackout darkness. By the early morning hours the next morning, power was pretty much restored. Good news, of course, for all those millions whose lives had been so suddenly interrupted. And especially good news for Union Theological Seminary, one of America's premier religious institutions in those years, and the just-across-Broadway neighbor from our seminary. For on that Wednesday, the administration of Union was set to make history, as it welcomed a Jewish faculty member to its ranks, our own seminary's premier theologian, Professor Abraham Joshua Heschel.

To the great relief of many, the long-anticipated event went off just as scheduled, and those in attendance heard Dr. Heschel deliver this astonishing opening:

> I speak as a member of a congregation whose founder was Abraham, and the name of my rabbi is Moses. I speak as a person who was able to leave Warsaw, the city in which I was born, just six weeks before the disaster began. My destination was New York, it would have been Auschwitz or Treblinka. I am a brand plucked from the fire, in which my people was burned to death.[1]

With those powerful cadences echoing through that hall, Heschel began his tenure as the Harry Emerson Fosdick Visiting Professor, and affirmed his singular place as a preeminent Jewish voice in interfaith affairs. It was early on in those rousing, halcyon days of interreligious rapprochement.[2] The ink was barely dry on the groundbreaking Catholic document *Nostra Aetate*, which Heschel had played such a pivotal advisory role in shaping during the debate of the Vatican Council.[3] Altogether fitting then that his Union Seminary talk, when published, would bear the title "No Religion Is an Island," a quite memorable phrase from his text and an evident paean to John Donne's immortal poem.

Heschel's address that evening, and his continuing involvement in the world beyond our seminary's walls, profoundly affected my own understanding of what it would mean to be an American rabbi. Soon thereafter, I would enroll in one of the first jointly taught courses between faculty of the two seminaries: a history survey taught by church historian

---

1. Abraham Joshua Heschel, "No Religion Is an Island," *Union Theological Seminary Quarterly Review* 21/2 (January 1966) 1. The article is more readily accessible in Harold Kasimow and Byron L. Sherwin, eds., *No Religion Is an Island: Abraham Joshua Heschel and Interreligious Dialogue* (Maryknoll, NY: Orbis, 1991), 3. Page numbers herein refer to that latter edition.

2. Heschel's invocation of Auschwitz and Treblinka in his opening remarks may not seem, to our contemporary ears, especially noteworthy. But in that era, it would have made a much more intense impact. As Peter Novick has demonstrated (though with some dissent) in Novick, *The Holocaust in American Life* (Boston: Houghton, Mifflin, 1999), citing the *Shoah* in either moral or religious discourse was decidedly uncommon before the early 1960s.

3. Harold Kasimow, "Heschel's View of Religious Diversity," in Stanisław Krajewski and Adam Lipszyc, eds., *Abraham Joshua Heschel: Philosophy, Theology and Interreligious Dialogue* (Wiesbaden: Harrassowitz, 2009), 196–97.

Robert Handy and the then-dean of historians of Conservative Judaism, Moshe Davis, who was in residence that year at our seminary.

After graduation, personal circumstances uprooted our little family from comfortable New York environs and led my wife and me back toward our Midwestern roots. As a novice rabbi, I wound up in Des Moines, and almost instantly realized that in that town, where the Jewish population is relatively miniscule, interfaith conversation would be almost as central to my working days as many intrafaith experiences.

In thinking back to having begun my rabbinic education in that same 1965 autumn term, it seems especially fortuitous that my earliest rabbinical student days coincided with one of the most notable American moments in Jewish-Christian relations. During the years that have followed, first in Iowa and now for more than three decades in Minnesota's Twin Cities, interreligious activity has been a remarkably stable feature of my rabbinate. In the beginning, from welcoming church and student groups to pulpit exchanges to joint communal activity spearheaded by representative religious voices, my smaller-town placements were not so very different from those of many other rabbis who serve the congregational communities away from the Eastern Seaboard and other large cities. But midway through my career, I received an unusual invitation, and once having accepted it, my experience veered considerably from those more informal interreligious interactions common to so many of my colleagues. For then, the interfaith dimension would come to totally dominate my vocational experiences.

Almost twenty years ago, I was induced to leave congregational life and take up full-time work at two Catholic universities, teaching in their respective theology departments, and directing a public-lecture series held in various locales across Minnesota. In 1983, a dozen years before that invitation was extended me, a remarkable Minneapolis rabbi, Max Shapiro, the celebrated leader of Temple Israel, had created a thriving program of lectures and classes aimed at bringing Jews and Christians into serious study and enrichment. That center for interreligious learning was based at the University of St. Thomas, a large diocesean undergraduate college and graduate school located in St. Paul.

Rabbi Shapiro had known that I not only had a special interest in the field but had completed a PhD dissertation on the topic at Iowa State University. That credential prompted him to recommend me early on for a faculty post at the school. Ultimately, in order to reach beyond the urban settings of Minneapolis and St. Paul, the original funders convinced the St. Thomas administration to join that community-oriented program to a more strictly academic position in Jewish studies based at St. John's University, a prestigious Benedictine Abbey and set of educational institutions in the central part of the state. It was that combined Catholic program that I was privileged to direct for well over a decade.

Teaching both undergraduate and graduate students, as well as many preparing for the priesthood and religious education, formed the central thrust of the work. Alongside those classroom responsibilities, there were countless public lectures that drew leading scholars and foundational leaders in Jewish-Christian affairs to both campuses. In time, Luther Seminary, the largest Lutheran training ground in the country, would become a quasi-partner, and I would take up teaching responsibilities there, too.

It was hardly the full-time work my fellow rabbinical school classmates could have imagined any of us would be doing when, as students, we spoke with one another of Professor Heschel and his path-breaking lecture at Union. Nor, truth be told, was it the sort of work that my European-born parents could have ever envisaged—that any Jew, and a rabbi, much less their son, would be encouraged to teach at a Christian university and seminary.

By the time I moved into this role, the central messages of *Nostra Aetate* had profoundly altered the religious landscape. Whenever, for example, the question of putative Jewish responsibility for Jesus's crucifixion would be raised, students would express surprise, even disbelief, that such a charge could be leveled at my faith community. "But we were taught," so many would say, "a much different understanding. That we, that our sinful acts, and the world's, that all three carry culpability for that crime." A very few, to be sure, might chime in that they could remember an aged grandparent revisiting the ancient canard about Jewish guilt.

For nearly all those young college students, then, and the generations that have followed, a single, powerful Catholic document had upended a two-thousand-year-old justification for acrimony and devastation. In large measure, our post–Vatican II world can finally boast that the charge of Jewish deicide is a monumental historical tragedy, but not a continuing calumny.

If I happened to use the terms "Jew" or "Jews" in a lecture, more than one student might whisper to me at class end: "But, rabbi, we have been taught always to say 'Jewish person,' never 'Jew.'" After that occurred a couple times, I asked one of my Catholic colleagues about it. "Well,

Barry, maybe it's just a Midwestern thing, but we are really working hard in the Church at escaping any semblance of the sort of anti-Semitism associated with economics and the old-fashioned Shylock slander. We consciously tell our students to always say 'Jewish person,' just to make certain of our good-faith efforts at eradicating long-held biases."

Among the many memorable experiences I had during those years, three especially stand out. Once, during the opening class in a jointly taught history course at Saint Paul Seminary, my colleague and I asked the seminarians to introduce themselves and say a word or two about why they had enrolled in our elective offering. One of those students, who is surely a parish priest now, looked up at us and admitted quite bravely: "Truth is, when I first read the words of *Nostra Aetate* last year in our history class, I realized something terrible about myself. That not so secretly, I disliked Judaism and the Jewish people. Today I understand that doing so is a sin, a very grave one. I am here to make amends. I am here to learn."

Then there was the time a distinguished Bible scholar at Luther Seminary and I were teaching a continuing-education course for pastors and their congregants. As the semester came to a close, we decided to study the 1994 Declaration of the Evangelical Lutheran Church in America to the Jewish community, which courageously acknowledges the hateful teachings of their namesake, Martin Luther, and asks forgiveness and the opportunity to build a new relationship.[4] When one of those present cautiously raised the question of the importance of evangelism aimed especially at us Jews, my Lutheran co-teacher stepped forward and interrupted: "There is no need to bring the Jews to God. They are already with God. *Our* Bible teaches us that they are God's people!"

Finally, there is a moment that remains forever inscribed in my heart. Those who helped sponsor the joint Catholic-university programs were unfathomably generous philanthropists. One family annually supported our chartering a plane for a daylong, round-trip flight to our nation's capital and to the United States Holocaust Memorial Museum. Leaving at 5:30 a.m., and returning often at close to 11:00 p.m., we routinely escorted some 150 undergraduate and graduate students for a daylong visit there, a journey that included talks, the exhibitions, and some time for joint reflection.

After one such excursion, it turned out that we had class the next morning at Saint John's. I asked the students to go around the room and

4. The 1994 Declaration, and other interfaith documents of the ELCA. may be found at http://www.elca.org/en/Faith/Ecumenical-and-Inter-Religious-Relations/Inter-Religious-Relations/Jewish-Relations/.

share what they had found most moving or decisive about the trip. What one young woman uttered still tears at me. She said it this way: "We entered this large exhibit room, and I noticed that there were people standing around a table, peering down at something. I immediately walked over, and saw that the display had been designed in such a way as to shield the very young who might be visiting the museum from being able to easily see what was on view on the table.

"There were grainy, black and white photographs—photographs of a dozen or so of the incarcerated, and what those so-called Nazi doctors had done to them. And as I walked past the photos, one after another, I kept going back, again and again, to one picture in particular. One that I couldn't rip myself away from.

"It was a snapshot of about a dozen Jewish women, with a couple of those Nazi experimenters standing at either end. Those men were showing off their gruesome handiwork, the bodily wreckage they had wrought on these blameless women. I stared at the faces of those German officers, wondered who they were and how they could have done what they did. I glared at the evil they had wrought, and I was never so ashamed to be a human being.

"Then my eyes were drawn to the faces of those forlorn women. I gazed at their faces, at their aloneness, their innocence. As I did, I tried to peer within, to envision their inner strength, their integrity, despite all that had been done to them. Contemplating them and what they had endured, beholding these women who had born the unfathomable, never have I been so proud to be a human being."

My years spent with eloquent students like that young woman have forever blessed me. Her experience at the museum, and so many similar to that during these past decades, are a powerful reminder of the prodigiously constructive consequences that began with Pope John XXIII and those who rallied to support his profound gesture of reconciliation. Today, perhaps, that pioneering deed may be taken for granted and the sheen on this critical religious and communal transformation may no longer seem so bright. Other exigencies and priorities, sadly, have seemed to intervene. In many ways, interfaith activity is far removed from the center of focus it occupied in that earlier era.

Nonetheless, I keep looking back and hoping—hoping that the lofty call of Abraham Joshua Heschel for interfaith education will not be abandoned, hoping that his final words on that November 1965 evening will continue to bear fruit:

What is urgently needed are ways of helping one another in the terrible predicament of here and now by the courage to believe that the word of the Lord endures forever, as well as in the here and now; to cooperate in trying to bring about a resurrection of sensitivity, a revival of conscience; to keep alive the divine sparks in our souls; to nurture openness to the spirit of the Psalms, reverence for the words of the prophets, and faithfulness to the Living God.[5]

5. Heschel, "No Religion Is an Island," 22.

20

An Unlikely Path

Reflections on Catholic-Jewish Collaboration

Lawrence Frizzell

How did an ordinary education focused on the basics in remote areas of western Canada provide a foundation for a lifetime dedication to teaching about Christian-Jewish relations? As I look back over the decades, the background for this work seems unlikely. Rural farming and lumbering settings in Alberta and northern British Columbia were home to few Catholics and virtually no Jews. Ours was a devout Catholic home, and after my father became crippled with arthritis, my mother returned to the classroom. We moved frequently, looking for a better teaching situation, i.e., twenty-three children instead of forty spread over eight grades in a one-room school.

The idea of Christian ecumenism had not reached northern Alberta. In 1952 we moved to a small town where the neighbors would wait until my parents were away shopping and then come to inform us children that Catholics are destined for hell. In another place we received tracts with photographs of the Basilica of Our Lady of Guadalupe; the caption read, "Women worshipping at a pagan shrine."

When I finished high school (three grades to a room), I considered to prepare for teaching or the priesthood and soon chose the latter. Then after I had studied philosophy, the archbishop of Edmonton sent me to the University of Ottawa to obtain a degree in theology. Because I had worked with a painting crew of evangelicals from the Prairie Bible Institute (Three Hills, Alberta) and had been told that Catholics are ignorant of Sacred Scripture, I decided to specialize in biblical studies. My thesis for the License in Sacred Theology was on the Hebrew terms relating to poverty in the Jewish Scriptures.

The archbishop's policy was that a person must prove his ability to teach before being sent for advanced studies. So a priest was sent to study Canon Law, and I succeeded him for two years. Then the 1917 Code contained 2,414 canons; compared with the 613 commandments of the Torah, teaching this seemed to be a challenge! I also taught Liturgy, beginning a longtime interest in the use of the Bible in worship.

In June 1964 the opportunity to prepare for biblical studies in Rome led me to Jerusalem where I spent six months in Ulpan Etzion. For the first time I encountered Jews who migrated to Israel from Romania, northern Europe, Arab countries, the United States, and South Africa. From Jerusalem I went to Athens for six months and, on another passport, visited Cyprus, Lebanon, Syria, and Jordan before returning to Israel in June 1965, the day after Martin Buber's death.

Rome in the autumn of 1965 was abuzz with the excitement of the fourth and final session of the Second Vatican Council! Students in the Pontifical Biblical Institute were asked to pray for the assembled hierarchs as they voted on the Declaration on the Church's Relation to Non-Christian Religions (*Nostra Aetate*) and the Constitution on divine Revelation (*Dei Verbum*).

In the last days of October I showed an American friend from the Ulpan and four Israelis around Rome. I obtained tickets for us to be present when Pope Paul VI promulgated the Declaration *Nostra Aetate* on October 28, 1965. Gary Abrams understood that this was a momentous occasion as we stood beneath the statue of Veronica in the area of Saint Peter's Basilica near the altar. I pointed out to them that a Jewish woman as a benign influence was represented among those giant figures linked to the Passion of Jesus.

To implement the work required by *Nostra Aetate* Cardinal Bea asked the Sisters of Sion, an international congregation with headquarters in Rome and Paris, to create a documentation center for Catholic-Jewish relations. Mother Edward Berkeley from England was in charge of this task, assisted by Sister Joan Poulin from Saskatchewan. I became a volunteer in late 1965 and was introduced to Father Cornelius Rijk, who in 1966 was called from a seminary in Holland to become the first officer of the Holy See for relations with the Jewish people. The first issue of the *SIDIC Review* was published in the spring of 1967, and it became an important vehicle of education, with Jewish and Christian contributors on themes of common interest in biblical and theological questions as well as a record of interfaith activities throughout the world.

In July 1967 I attended an international Jewish-Catholic conference in Strasbourg, France. There I met Msgr. John Oesterreicher, Father Edward Flannery, Sister Katherine Hargrove, RSCJ, and several European scholars. Rabbi André Neher was still living in France at the time, and he gave a memorable lecture on God's Word and silence.

Two years of specialized studies in the Bible gave students detailed exposure to a few chapters of Exodus, Ezekiel, Mark, and Romans, along with an introduction to textual criticism, geography, Johannine theology and archeology. The following September would find me teaching all the Torah, Psalms, Gospels and Paul to seminarians in Edmonton, Alberta. Feeling that I was ill-prepared, I consulted with an American Jesuit, Fr. Francis McCool. "Yes," he said "the Biblicum provides a great foundation for a Jesuit who will have fifteen years to perfect the methods of study!" He gave me a list of books to read so that I could "cover the matter." When the new Lectionary with a three-year cycle of Sunday readings, including a selection from the Jewish Scriptures, was introduced, seminarians had a new incentive to study the Word of God in its entirety. Unfortunately, these were years of upheaval in seminaries, so I was pleased with new developments for Catholic higher education in Alberta. Saint Joseph's Seminary became a degree-granting institution under the title Newman Theological College. The archbishop's devotion to John Henry Cardinal Newman led to his choice prevailing over the idea of naming the college in honor of Augustin Cardinal Bea.

In the summer of 1968 I attended a Catholic-Jewish meeting in Memphis, Tennessee. Among the speakers were Dr. Michael Wyschogrod and Msgr. Edward Synan, a Seton Hall collaborator with John Oesterreicher, who in 1959 had moved to the Pontifical Institute of Medieval Studies in Toronto. Both scholars would continue to work with the Institute of Judaeo-Christian Studies over the decades.

The first Menorah Institute, a ten-day course in Catholic-Jewish relations, took place at Seton Hall University in July 1969. I took part in this program and met Sister Rose Thering, OP, and Dr. Joseph Lichten of the Anti-Defamation League, who later would move to Rome in an active retirement.

In August 1968 the International Conference of Christians and Jews held its annual meeting in Toronto. The Reverend James Parkes was honored for his valiant work during the Nazi period and for his research and publications. The major Jewish leaders from the United States were there: Rabbis Marc Tenebaum, Balfour Brickner, Jordan Pearlson of Toronto , and others impressed us ordinary participants!

The highlight of these years was the invitation to be the Canadian representative at a meeting called by Father Rijk to prepare a *schema* (draft) for a document to implement *Nostra Aetate*. Twenty-one people from fourteen countries met at the Motherhouse of the Sisters of Sion in April 1969. Perhaps because the text included reference to the State of Israel, the document was promulgated only on December 1, 1974. By that time the Holy See gave all matters relating to the State of Israel to the Secretary of State, and Pope Paul VI founded the Commission for Religious Relations with the Jews to be housed within the Secretariat (Pontifical Council) for Promoting Christian Unity. This location for the new Commission, rather than in the context of wider interfaith dialogue, showed the importance of the Jewish people for understanding the challenges of Christian ecumenism. Grave issues debated in the sixteenth century can at times be solved by referring back to the Second Temple period.

During the postconciliar years in Edmonton, I had opportunities to collaborate with Saint Stephen's College (United Church of Canada) and the Conservative congregation in Edmonton for events in Christian-Jewish relations.

A friend from my stay in Jerusalem was at the University of Oxford, studying with Dr. Geza Vermes, the Reader in Jewish Studies who succeeded Cecil Roth in 1965. After a visit to meet Dr. Vermes on my return from the meeting in Rome, I applied for a Canada Council grant to pursue studies of the Qumran scrolls and related Jewish literature. This led to four years (1970–1974) of involvement with the work fostered by the Sisters of Sion in London, including many memorable meetings and lectures by people like Rabbis Louis Jacobs, Lionel Blue, and the Reverend William Simpson, founder of the National Conference of Christians and Jews in England.

The work of Professor Kurt Schubert in Austria from the late 1940s attracted a number of students who became great scholars of Judaism and Jewish-Christian relations. After years in the Vienna area, Father Clemens Thoma, SVD, founded the Institute of Jewish-Christian Studies at the University of Lucerne in Switzerland. Msgr. Oesterreicher invited me to join him for a conference on "The People of God" in Lucerne in 1972. There he told me of the plan to develop a master's program in Jewish-Christian studies. Months later he invited Rabbi Asher Finkel and me to give lectures for the celebration of the twentieth anniversary of the Institute at Seton Hall. This was within the context of the Yom Kippur War, the second time in six years when Israel faced grave danger.

On completion of my doctorate with a dissertation on the ecclesiology of the Qumran (Dead Sea) documents available in the early 1970s, I received permission from the archbishop of Edmonton to accept an academic position at Seton Hall University. Archbishop McNeil stated that a context wherein I could continue research in the field of Jewish-Christian studies could be beneficial. The arrival of the Scholasticate of the Oblates of Mary Immaculate (OMI) in Edmonton brought a professor qualified to teach Sacred Scripture, so I was able to enter a creative relationship with Rabbi Asher Finkel, a man of great erudition in rabbinics and with a doctorate from the University of Tübingen in comparative religion. His dissertation, which became *The Pharisees and the Teacher of Nazareth*, provided an indication of his capacity to teach the Gospels with a great sensitivity with regard to their Jewish matrix.

With thirteen students, six Jewish, six Catholic and one Protestant, the faculty of two full-time and three adjunct professors began to offer the MA program in the fall of 1975. Among the adjuncts was young Joseph Sievers, a graduate of Professor Schubert's Judaica program in Vienna. He was completing the doctorate at Columbia University and later became Professor of Second Temple literature in the Pontifical Biblical Institute. In coming years, Finkel and I team-taught innovative courses: Fall of Jerusalem: Jewish and Christian Interpretations, Eschatology in the two traditions, and Jewish Philosophy of Education. We also covered various areas in biblical and postbiblical Judaism and the early church.

We gave papers in the annual meetings of the Society of Biblical Literature, the American Academy of Religion, the International Congress on Medieval Studies, the Catholic Biblical Association, the National Jewish-Christian Workshop, and other venues, including the World Congress of Jewish Studies and meetings of the Catholic-Jewish International

Liaison Committee in Prague (1990), Manhattan (2001), Paris (2011), and Madrid (2013). In early 1975 I was invited to a meeting at the Motherhouse of the Sisters of Sion in Rome for a discussion with Rabbi Adin Steinsaltz and other Jewish leaders.

The Institute of Judaeo-Christian Studies was represented on the Advisory Committee on Catholic-Jewish Relations to the United States Conference of Catholic Bishops by Msgr. Oesterreicher and later by myself. Recognition of the Institute's work over the decades came in 2008 when Pope Benedict XVI appointed me for a five-year term as consultor in the Pontifical Council's Commission for Religious Relations with the Jews.

The fortieth anniversary of the Institute was celebrated in March 1993, with the last presentation by Msgr. Oesterreicher, who died at the age of eighty-nine on April 18, 1993.

The work of the Institute and the MA program continue with a series of celebrations for its sixtieth anniversary in 2013. Rabbi Finkel retired from the classroom in June 2013, and steps are being undertaken to find a successor. Seton Hall University has been very supportive of this work, and with the greatest gratitude to our major donor, Ms. H. Suzanne Jobert, we hope to continue into the next generation of a process of building bridges of understanding and amity between Christians and Jews.

Lifelong learning is guaranteed for anyone who is dedicated to Jewish-Christian studies!

21

On Modern Miracles

Eugene Korn

IN JUNE 2013 I had an extraordinary experience in the land of miracles—
the State of Israel. I spent four days with seventy-five Christians and
fifteen Jews from Milan who ascended to the Holy Land to honor the
life of Cardinal Carlo Maria Martini. As the former archbishop of Milan
who rose to a high position in the Vatican, Cardinal Martini loved both
Israel and the Jewish people. After retiring from his work in Italy, he realized his fondest wish to live in the land he loved. The cardinal moved
to Jerusalem and resided there for six years before returning to Italy for
treatment for advanced Parkinson's disease. Cardinal Martini ultimately
passed away in August 2012, and before he was buried the former chief
rabbi of Milan, Rabbi Giuseppe (Yosef) Laras, honored the cardinal's last
request by inserting soil from the land of Israel into his friend's coffin.

During our pilgrimage, rabbis and priests as well as Catholic and
Jewish laypersons recited psalms at Jerusalem's Western Wall, ate Shabbat
meals, and sang Shabbat songs together in a spirit of warm friendship. On
Sunday we planted seedlings in a Jewish National Fund (JNF) clearing in
the Galilee, the first trees of what will ultimately be a five-thousand-tree
forest in Cardinal Martini's name. These were modern miracles, events

that only two generations ago my Eastern European Jewish grandfather could never have imagined.

None of this would have been possible without the "*Nostra Aetate* revolution."[1] The document was formally accepted at the Second Vatican Council in 1965, and it began the dramatic transformation in Church teachings about Jews and Judaism. Early on, Rabbi Gilbert Rosenthal correctly compared the Catholic doctrinal change to the shift from Ptolemaic geocentrism to Copernican heliocentrism that fundamentally revised our conception of the universe. *Nostra Aetate* revised the Church's understanding of Jews and Judaism in a fundamental way and in the process established the foundation for new relations between the Church and the Jewish people. Though ratified in 1965, *Nostra Aetate* was the necessary theological step for the Vatican to recognize the Jewish State twenty-nine years later in 1993, and for the subsequent friendly visits of Popes John Paul II (2000) and Benedict XVI (2009) and for the visit of Francis to Israel in May 2014.[2]

Nostra Aetate also provided the theological ground for the important post-conciliar documents, *Guidelines and Suggestions for Implementing the Conciliar Declarations "Nostra Aetate"* (1974), *Notes on the Correct Way to Present Jews and Judaism in Preaching and Catechesis in the Roman Catholic Church* (1985), *We Remember: A Reflection on the Shoah* (1998), and *The Jewish People and Their Sacred Scriptures in the Christian Bible* (2002), which taken together enabled Catholic-Jewish relations to evolve with more nuance and understanding. Sister Mary Boys succinctly articulated the groundbreaking results of this "revolution" as "the six *R*'s":

1. Understandably, some Catholic officials avoid terms like *revolution* or even *change* when referring to official doctrine. Recently, I had an amusing but telling interchange with a high Vatican official. When I casually mentioned the changes in Church teachings initiated by *Nostra Aetate*, he looked at me with a broad knowing smile, and responded, "We do not speak of changes here, but 'developments.'"

2. To see the monumental changes that *Nostra Aetate* initiated, one need only compare Pope Paul VI's pre–*Nostra Aetate* visit to Israel to the more recent visit of John Paul II. The purpose of Paul VI's 1964 visit was to promote Christian unity. He spent only eleven hours in Israel, avoided Israeli Jerusalem, refused to meet with Israel's chief rabbi, and forced Israeli President Shazar and Prime Minister Eshkol to travel to the remote town of Megiddo to greet him in a short ceremony. In his thank-you letter to Shazar, the pope left out the title *president* and erroneously but pointedly addressed it to Tel Aviv, not Jerusalem, Israel's capital. In 2000, Pope John Paul II made an official visit to Israel, met in public ceremonies with the Israel's president, prime minister, and chief rabbis in Jerusalem, and prayed at Jerusalem's Western Wall for the welfare of the Jewish people as his elder brothers who remain the people of God's covenant.

(1) repudiation of anti-Semitism, (2) rejection of the charge of deicide, (3) repentance after the *Shoah*, (4) recognition of Israel, (5) review of teaching about Jews and Judaism, and (6) rethinking of proselytizing Jews.[3] Nor has this fifty-year process ended. Cardinal Walter Kasper, former president of the Commission for Religious Relations with the Jews, recently proclaimed, "We stand only at the beginning of a new beginning."[4]

The impact of *Nostra Aetate* on the Catholic Church and its faithful thus far has been bountifully documented.[5] But how, if at all, has it affected Jews, and what is *Nostra Aetate's* potential for changing Jewish hopes, theology, and future experiences?

I see two broad areas of critical impact on the Jewish people that the *Nostra Aetate* revolution has had and should continue to exercise on our people. The first is psychological and cultural; the second is theological—and both are of historic moment.

There is no doubt that the *Shoah* was the catalyst for *Nostra Aetate*. Reflecting on the unimaginable evil of the Holocaust became the seed for Christian reappraisal of its tortured history and theology regarding Jews. Something in Christendom had gone undeniably wrong, and Christian thinkers recoiled from what had been wrought. In order for Christianity to regain its moral credibility after the *Shoah*, many Church leaders from Pope John XXIII down understood that the Church had to rethink its doctrine about Jews and Judaism.

For the Jewish people the *Shoah* had more existential consequences. Nearly destroyed, we emerged from the grisly Final Solution traumatized, frightened and alone. The trust that Jews had put in the European Enlightenment was shattered, and after the *Shoah* the best chances for Jewish survival lay in the sovereign State of Israel, where Jews sought to free themselves of dependence on the Gentile world. Even today in America where Jews have gained unprecedented success, deep insecurity surfaces palpably not only among historically oriented traditional Jews but in the most affluent and Americanized of our people. We live with

3. Mary C. Boys, *Has God Only One Blessing? Judaism as a Source of Christian Self-Understanding* (New York: Paulist, 2000), 248; see also 247–66.

4. Foreword to Phillip A. Cunningham et al., *Christ Jesus and the Jewish People Today: New Explorations of Theological Interrelationships* (Grand Rapids: Eerdmans, 2011), xiv.

5. Among many studies, see Boys, *Has God Only One Blessing?*; and *Milestones in Modern Catholic-Jewish Relations*, compiled by Sister Lucy Thorson, NDS, and Murray Watson, found at http://www.scarboromissions.ca/JC_Relations/catholic_jewish_relations.php/.

an ethic of suspicion as the memories, wounds, and lessons of the *Shoah* refuse to fade in our souls. Can we ever learn to trust others again?

Nor has Israel worked out the way Zionist ideologues and idealists hoped. The presence of Israel in the middle of *Dar al Islam* has fanned hatred of Jews among Israel's neighbors. And the Jewish State's continuing unresolved conflict with the Arab world deepens the insecurity Israelis and Jews around the world feel. In Europe, anti-Semitism is now becoming more common, less than sixty years after Nazism, even as European Jewish life dwindles and becomes increasingly precarious.

In such a political and cultural climate, the Catholic Church's frequent public condemnation of "hatred, persecutions, displays of anti-Semitism, directed against Jews at any time and by anyone" (words of *Nostra Aetate* and repeated in nearly every Vatican statement dealing with Catholic-Jewish relations) is an important element in the fight against Jew hatred. We participants in interfaith activity have intimate knowledge of the *Nostra Aetate* revolution, but most Jews are still unaware of the extent of the dramatic salutary transformation of Christian teachings about Jews and Judaism. It is exceedingly difficult to overcome the memory of nearly two thousand years of Christian enmity against Jews and the theological duel to the death that the Church forced upon us, yet we refrain from doing so at our own peril. The Holocaust taught Jews the terrible danger of being alone in the world where anti-Semitism remains and radical evil has proven real. And any serious Jew understands today that the Jewish people is still vulnerable, that it needs friends in an increasingly violent world, and that the Israeli Defense Forces alone cannot guarantee the continued survival of Israel and the Jewish people. The Church's firm rejection of anti-Semitism helps us emerge from our *Shoah* trauma, helps convince Jews that we are no longer alone, and buttresses our hope that the future for the Jewish people need not be the same as our tragic past.

For me and for many of my Jewish colleagues engaged in interfaith dialogue, experiencing the new respect of Catholic clergy and laity for Jews and Judaism as we review together our tortured history, navigate our complex current relationships, and dedicate ourselves to building a more understanding future sows seeds of trust and hope. It lightens our Jewish sense of alienation and aloneness in the world. Political and religious support for Jewish survival from more than one billion Catholics around the world is significant both strategically and psychologically for Jews committed to creating a safer world for our grandchildren and the entire human family. In the religious sphere, this friendship fortifies our commitment to Judaism's covenantal vision for the Jewish people to play a central role in human culture by interacting with humanity, being an instrument of "blessing to all the families of the earth" and "a light unto the nations."

In dialogue, Jews witness the Church's newfound respect for Judaism as it recognizes Judaism as the spiritual patrimony of Christianity. This can easily lead to a renewed Jewish appreciation of our own heritage. A strengthening of our faith has been an unexpected blessing for me and many of my Jewish interfaith colleagues. This is another reason why it is critical to educate more Jews about *Nostra Aetate* and the Church's sincere attempts to forge friendship with her "elder brothers." So for practical and religious reasons, widespread education about *Nostra Aetate* and the teachings it has spawned is a vital objective for Christians and Jews alike.

Second, the Christian doctrinal revolution toward Jews and Judaism has momentous implications for *Jewish* theology. Now that the Church has rejected its hostile replacement theology and the Church no longer threatens Jews and their heritage, we need not feel defensive about scouring Jewish tradition to uncover rabbinic attitudes and religious texts that view Christianity favorably. Armed with such precedents, we can develop a healthy theological orientation toward Christianity and Christians— one that is built on authentic religious grounds and that fosters constructive, warm relations.[6]

Throughout all the pre–*Nostra Aetate* eras of Jewish-Christian history, Jews had little incentive to view their spiritual and physical enemies sympathetically. Jewish texts and precedents for positive understandings of Christian doctrine and Christians were relegated to the back rows of our libraries and deep recesses of our collective memory—if they appeared all. Even among Jewish scholars, few are aware of the words of the Rabbi Moses Rivkes in seventeenth-century Lithuania:

> The gentiles in whose shadow Jews live . . . believe in *creatio ex nihilo* and the Exodus from Egypt and the main principles of

---

6. I have attempted to begin this dimension of Jewish theology in Korn, "Rethinking Christianity: Rabbinic Positions and Possibilities," in Alon Goshen-Gottstein and Eugene B. Korn, eds., *Jewish Theology and World Religions* (Oxford: Littman Library of Jewish Civilization, 2012), 189–215; and Korn, "The People Israel, Christianity and the Responsibility to History," in Robert W. Jenson and Eugene B. Korn, eds., *Covenant and Hope: Christian and Jewish Reflections* (Grand Rapids: Eerdmans, 2012), 145–72.

faith. Their intention is to the Creator of Heaven and Earth and we are obligated to pray for their welfare.[7]

And Rabbi Jacob Emden wrote in eighteenth-century Germany:

> Jesus brought a double goodness to the world . . . Christians eradicated idolatry, removed idols [from the nations] and obligated them in the seven commandments of Noah so that they would not behave like animals of the field, and instilled them firmly with moral traits . . . Christians and Moslems are congregations that [work] for the sake of heaven—(people) who are destined to endure, whose intent is for the sake of heaven and whose reward will not denied.[8]

> We should consider Christians as instruments for the fulfillment of the prophecy that the knowledge of God will one day spread throughout the earth . . . the rise of Christianity and Islam spread among the nations . . . the knowledge that there is One God who rules the world, who rewards and punishes and reveals Himself to man.[9]

And Rabbi Samson Raphael Hirsch wrote in nineteenth-century Germany:

> Before Israel set out on its long journey through the ages and the nations, . . . it produced an offshoot [Christianity] that had to become estranged from it in great measure, in order to bring to the world—sunk in idol worship, violence, immorality and the degradation of man—at least the tidings of the One Alone, of the brotherhood of all men, and of man's superiority over the beast . . . It represented a major step in bringing the world closer to the goal of all history.[10]

These traditional rabbis planted the seeds for a historic transformation of Jewish attitudes toward Christianity and positive relations with Christian believers. Yet it took the Church's *Nostra Aetate* revolution for Jews to begin to water those seeds, care for them, and guide their growth. Will the two-thousand-year-old Christian-Jewish enmity end? Does a better future await us? Can Jews and Christians become, for the first time

---

7. Gloss on *Shulhan Arukh, Hoshen Mishpat*, Section 425:5.

8. *Seder Olam Rabbah* 35–37; *Sefer ha-Shimush* 15–17.

9. *Commentary on Ethics of the Fathers* 4:11.

10. Samson Raphael Hirsch. *The Nineteen Letters on Judaism* (New York: Feldheim, 1969), 63 (Letter 9).

in history, partners in *tikkun olam*—repair of our broken world—and work together toward the biblical messianic ideal for sacred history?

For too long both Jews and Christians understood their relationship to each other as a permanent, even ontological, conflict. Its religious archetype was the hatred between Esau and Jacob, siblings locked in mortal eternal warfare. The initiator of the *Nostra Aetate* revolution, Pope John XXIII, changed that paradigm when he announced to the Jewish people, "I am Joseph, your brother."[11] These words transformed the ideal of Jewish-Christian relations from conflict to reconciliation. On the Jewish side, more than a half century before John XXIII, Rabbi Naftali Zvi Yehudah Berliner (known by his name's acronym, "Netziv") also dreamed of reconciliation. Commenting on the reunion of Esau and Jacob described in Gen 32:4, he wrote, "In future generations when the descendents of Esau [i.e. Christians] are stirred by a pure spirit to recognize the descendents of Jacob, we also will be moved to recognize that Esau is our brother."[12] Netziv lived in Lithuania at a difficult time between Jews and Christians, when Tsars Nicholas and Alexander aggressively attempted to force Russian Christian identity on the Jewish community. Netziv could only wistfully imagine some time, far in the distant future, when Christians might recognize the integrity of the Jewish people and the validity of their faith.

Our generation is blessed to live in the time when Netziv's dream is unfolding before our eyes. *Nostra Aetate* is its genesis, but as Cardinal Kasper observed, more work remains for both Catholics and Jews. Each of us needs to continue nurturing this vision, ensuring that it becomes unshakably and permanently rooted. Building the brotherhood between Christians and Jews that Netziv visualized is holy work for both communities. Under the enduring influence of *Nostra Aetate*, Jews and Christians are uniquely privileged today to be the recipients, the shapers, and the transmitters of this divine blessing.

---

11. This alludes to the relationship between the biblical Joseph and his brothers, whose reconciliation the Bible records in poignant detail—in contrast to the irreconcilable strife between Jacob and Esau.

12. *Commentary* on the Pentateuch, *Ha'ameq Davar*, ad loc.

22

Being a Child of Vatican II

Shira L. Lander

I AM A CHILD of Vatican II. Not in the way Catholics make that claim, to be sure, but in the sense that all of my encounters with Catholics, and to a certain extent all Christians, were filtered through and measured by that watershed council. I was three years old when the council promulgated *Nostra Aetate.* Growing up in a household where interfaith dialogue was deeply integrated into our family ethic made me keenly aware of the document's import for as long as I can remember. It seemed as though the Jewish world divided Catholics into two types: those who supported *Nostra Aetate,* and those who didn't. I wouldn't question whether this Manichaean dualism aligned with pro- or anti-Jewish sentiments until I was much older.

My father, a rabbinic chaplain at an all-women's college, welcomed his closest colleague, Sister Judith O'Connell, into our home, and she reciprocated by inviting us to her priory around Christmas. For many years she was the only female spiritual leader I knew. She, and the many other Irish and Polish Catholic neighbors who inhabited the small New England town where I grew up, seemed to embody the spirit of *Nostra Aetate* in our encounters. Our conversations about religion were always mutually respectful and curious, and beneath it all there hovered what I sensed to be a deep ground of trust and caring. No one ever laughed at anyone else's expense; no one ever felt denigrated or dismissed. I'll never forget when my friend Molly informed me that my bubbie's *pierogi*, prepared for the holiday of Shavuot, was not a Jewish dish, but a Polish one that *her* grandmother made for Christmas! *Nostra Aetate* allowed the two of us to sit side by side, doing our catechism and Hebrew-school homework, each occasionally helping the other with an answer or asking about a question from the other's tradition. In many ways we had more in common with each other than either of us did with our Protestant schoolmates, for whom religion seemed taken for granted, something that rarely seemed to impinge on their lives. My Catholic friends struggled with religious restrictions and strictures in much the same way that I did. We both had to deal with the kind of embarrassment of difference that comes from wearing ash on your forehead throughout the school day or eating a matzah sandwich in the lunchroom.

America provided a unique and fruitful laboratory for how *Nostra Aetate* would play out or be instantiated, since here Catholics and Jews shared a common immigrant history, a common political agenda, a common social ethic (excepting the issue of women's reproductive rights), and a common place in the once-dominant Protestant society. Not until I was in college in 1983 did I realize the full impact of the document referred to by its opening two Latin words, *Nostra Aetate*, "In our time," more formally the *Declaration on the Relation of the Church to Non-Christian Religions*. I read the complete document for the first time in a seminar on American religion in the 1950s and '60s. The class discussed the import of statements like "God holds the Jews most dear for the sake of their Fathers; He does not repent of the gifts He makes or of the calls He issues—such is the witness of the Apostle"; and, "His passion cannot be charged against all the Jews, without distinction, then alive, nor against the Jews of today. Although the Church is the new people of God, the Jews should not be presented as rejected or accursed by God, as if this followed from the Holy Scriptures." Although I had never personally experienced anti-Semitism, and if my parents had they kept it to themselves, I had learned my people's history and knew all too well why "the Church" felt the need to "decr[y] hatred, persecutions, displays of anti-Semitism, directed against Jews at any time and by anyone." Inspired by my father's involvement in interfaith dialogue as part of the National Institute of Campus Ministries and leadership in the National

Association of College and University Chaplains, and wanting to go beyond the conversations I enjoyed both in and out of the classroom, I joined the interfaith-dialogue group on my own campus. Once again I found that my Catholic counterparts shared many of the same attitudes toward their religion and feelings about their place in what was then, culturally speaking, still a predominately Protestant university. Here was a safe place, however, to discuss theology, to fulfill what *Nostra Aetate* had requested by recommending that Jews and Christians engage in "biblical and theological studies as well as . . . fraternal dialogues." This was no tea-and-cakes Kumbaya fluff; these gatherings exposed deeply held principles, and forced us to consider how we would make room for the other in our religious worldviews. What made those dialogues so fruitful was that there was no predetermined outcome or prescribed answers. We were guided by some basic ground rules, like respect and honesty. Valuable life lessons.

Nostra Aetate was implemented at the seminary level with programs that brought seminarians and religious educators together for a weekend retreat of study and dialogue. The professional camaraderie cut across religious boundaries; we shared many similar goals and concerns. I enjoyed these so much that I expanded my work with the archdiocese of Cincinnati on a number of interfaith projects. Whether interacting with clergy or lay folks, I always felt that we both left the encounter with a deeper understanding of and sensitivity toward the other. I had begun to study Greek and patristic literature, which broadened my understanding and appreciation of the Catholic heritage of exegetical and homiletical tradition.

Another course, this one in rabbinical school with Jacob Petuchowski, would enrich my gratitude for *Nostra Aetate* in the broader context of Jewish-Christian relations. Similar documents had been issued by other Christian denominations. Some even predated Vatican II. Aside from representing the largest Christian body internationally, this document was particularly significant because of the history of Jewish-Catholic relations, as Petuchowski impressed upon us. My appreciation was growing.

The twenty-fifth anniversary of *Nostra Aetate* arrived while I was the Jewish scholar at the Institute for Jewish and Christian Studies (ICJS) and teaching at the Ecumenical Institute of Saint Mary's Seminary in Baltimore. The two institutions collaborated to put on a conference that both celebrated the document's accomplishments and challenged its audience to push further. It was there that I first had the honor and privilege of meeting Dr. Eugene Fisher. I have the highest regard for his lifetime of work in behalf of Jewish-Catholic relations up to and since that time, and value the collegial trust that I came to rely on as a fellow professional in the field. He has been a tireless champion of *Nostra Aetate* and its related implementation documents.

Three other powerful witnesses to *Nostra Aetate* who shaped my understanding of Catholics and Catholicism have been women friends and colleagues: Dr. Rosann Catalano, with whom I worked at the ICJS, Dr. Mary Boys, SNJM, and Dr. Celia Deutsch, NDS, with whom I have worked on various projects over the years. Our frank, funny, and iconoclastic discussions about religion, family, institutional politics, and everything else that matters; our work with various groups of Catholics and Jews—lay, clerical, and educational leaders—have all been supported, either explicitly or implicitly, by Church approval in *Nostra Aetate*. Rosann and Mary have broken bread at my table, and all of us have shared late-night drinks in far-flung cities across the globe: necessary ingredients in laying the foundation for sustained, honest, and open dialogue, and for building the kind of lifelong friendships that you can pick up where you left off whenever and wherever you happen to see each other.

When I found myself in graduate school once again, this time studying ancient Christianity in addition to formative Judaism, I needed to learn Latin. Since I was commuting from Baltimore to Philadelphia, and since language study required more time than my commuting schedule permitted, I sought out a local teacher. A college friend recommended his high-school Latin teacher, who happened to then teach at Saint Mary's Seminary, where I was still teaching. I joined his first-year seminary ecclesiastical Latin class and learned along with "the boys," as Fr. James Conn liked to call them. I learned more than just Latin. Fr. Jim welcomed me into the fold and treated me no differently than the other students. When the class concluded, I invited him to join my family at our house for dinner. As he sat at the kitchen counter while I prepared dinner, we wandered into the topic of *kashrut*. He asked why we/I kept kosher. I had not been asked that question since I was in college, and thinking about it in the context of the years that had passed and in the presence of my Catholic Latin teacher and now friend caused me to reformulate my answer. I replied, "I think it gives me something to do, some way to maintain my connection to the divine even when I don't feel like it." He smiled a knowing smile and said something to the effect of, "I believe that's something we share. Rituals that bind us to our God and our community even when the head and heart fail us." It was a *Nostra Aetate* moment.

Public institutional documents tend to function in one of two ways. Either they can be prophetic, pushing their constituents to move beyond where they currently are, somewhat begrudgingly, toward moral progress; or they can give voice to a tide that is in motion, coalescing and naming a movement already underway. *Nostra Aetate*, because it addressed a Church that was so diverse, did both. For some, *Nostra Aetate* served a visionary role, carving out a space that was unsettling. For many, like those with whom I had the pleasure of working over the years, it served the latter function. I appreciate that *Nostra Aetate* gave courage and support to those Catholics who have attempted to heal the theological wounds between Jews and Catholics that festered for nearly two millennia, and to think more creatively about the Jewish-Catholic relationship. *Nostra Aetate* has given me the opportunity to explore what the Christian event might mean in Jewish providential history and to consider what Jews might learn by listening in on Catholic conversations in dialogue with institutionally supported Catholic partners. For that I am sincerely grateful.

23

A Catholic Priest Goes to the Jewish Theological Seminary

Guy A. Massie

MY NAME IS GUY Massie. I was ordained a Catholic priest in 1983, and I have been serving the people of the Roman Catholic Diocese of Brooklyn for thirty years. In 1993, I was granted the honor and distinction of being selected to study at the Jewish Theological Seminary (JTS) in New York City in order to help facilitate Catholic-Jewish dialogue in the Diocese of Brooklyn. In 1997 I graduated with a Master's Degree in Judaic studies, and I would like to tell you about this opportunity and my extraordinary experiences at JTS.

My degree is in Judaic studies was interdisciplinary; this means that I was exposed to a well-rounded exposition of many fields of Jewish study and Jewish life. I studied Judaism as Jews study Judaism. I studied with Jewish students who were seriously committed to Judaism. I learned as Jews learn. While the academic work was important, the Jewish environment, the Jewish feel, the Jewish-school atmosphere—all were equally important. For me, a non-Jew, it was a privileged and a gifted time. The result of the time spend at Jewish Theological Seminary gave me not only the knowledge of Judaism; it gave me the ethos of Jewish life. It created in my heart certain identification with the Jewish people, which is difficult to explain. I feel I can appreciate what hurts them and what their dreams are as a people. Because of my studies and my relationships with the Jewish people I feel they have a special place forever in my heart. It is because of this identification that I find myself speaking out against all forms of anti-Jewish behavior or anti-Semitic activities, while explaining the importance of the land of Israel and promoting dialogue.

I found the environment at Jewish Theological Seminary to be welcoming. I was never made to feel different or excluded from activities. I was invited to the homes of classmates or to the dorms of fellow students for Shabbat. I was always invited to dinner for Jewish holidays. Family, food, and friends are part of being Jewish. While I did not hide the fact that I was not Jewish or that I was a priest, I did not advertise it either. I did not want other students to feel ill at ease or that I was out to convert anyone. In fact, as people discovered my background, great dialogue and conversation often ensued. We were all students without distinction, and in the classroom, as in study groups, we were all part of the group. This meant we studied together, complained together, ate together and sometimes prayed together. These study groups were a source of great help and support to me and have yielded me many lifelong friends.

I found my classes interesting, challenging, and difficult at times but always fulfilling.

I studied in four major areas: Jewish History, Jewish Literature, Bible, and Talmud.

In Jewish History, I elected to study ancient Jewish history, which covered the period from 200 BCE to 400 CE. This covered the period during which time Christianity was coming into being. For me, this was important study. We spoke about ancient Christianity from a Jewish perspective. Such discussions opened up a new viewpoint on the Pharisees and Sadducees, and on Jewish social and political life at the time of the emergence of the Christian movement. Such information has expanded my view and resulted in my ability to share my learning with others. I could now look at my own tradition from a broader perspective. I am now able to present a more informed historical view of early Christianity. In my preaching, teaching, and leadership roles in the Catholic community, I am apt to quote from Jewish sources and Jewish authors. This has resulted in a fuller understanding of both current and historical events.

The Holocaust was my next history class. If anyone wishes to understand modern Jewish experience, the study of this tragic time is essential. Discussion in this class explored the history of anti-Semitism, the paralyzing fear that terrorized the Jewish community of Europe, and the heroism and bravery of many who, at peril to their own live, saved many Jews. I think that modern Jewish theological inquiry was born as a result of the Holocaust.

Against the backdrop of the Holocaust, I registered for a class on the Modern History of the Land of Israel (Eretz Yisrael.) I think learning about the founding of Israel and Zionism is essential for understanding modern Judaism. As a result of my visiting Israel, seeing it in the flesh, studying about it, I was led to realize that this land, while struggling to survive, is an oasis of hope and safety for the Jewish people throughout the world. Recognizing that from the Jewish theological point of view Eretz Yisrael is the land of promise, it is important for Catholic-Jewish dialogue to create a language that will adequately express the intrinsic nature of the land of Israel for the Jewish people, as well as the secular and theological nature of the land of Israel for Catholicism.

Learning Hebrew was an adventure for me. The structure of the language and its literature taught me how the Jewish people communicated and ordered their reality. This ancient and modern language was used to tell the narrative of the Jewish people throughout the centuries. This was at first a difficult subject for me. I studied Hebrew for the five years (including summers). I must say, I received a great deal of help and understanding from my classmates and teachers who were most kind to me.

Today, I can follow the liturgy in the synagogue, read some biblical passages, and even read some of the headlines in Hebrew newspapers. Hebrew opened the doors to Jewish literature for me. Being able to look at biblical texts in their original language was a great experience (even though I was not a great Hebrew scholar). And the ability to recite the *Shema* in the synagogue, made me happy and somewhat fulfilled.

To learn about a people it is necessary to read their literature. Jewish literature is expansive. Truly I understand why the Jewish people are people of the word of the book.

From reading the Bible as literature or as a religious tract, to Midrash to Talmud to Maimonides to Rashi to Kafka to Oz to Ozack to Bialik to Babel to Agnon and beyond—Jewish literature gave me an insight into the Jewish mind and Jewish worldviews. It was in this discipline of literature that I truly came to appreciate, in depth, Jewish sentiments and wisdom. Reading coupled with discussions and questions made the literary heritage of the Jewish people come to life for me. It seems that the vibrancy of Jewish life appeared to be on every page, as well as around me living in the people with whom I was studying.

In 1993, I came to the Jewish Theological Seminary for my entering interview. Rabbi Steven Garfinkel met with me. After explaining the classes I would take, he asked me a profound question. He reminded me that JTS is a religious school. He than said to me, "I need for you to answer a question which is personal but is required."

"Yes," I replied. "What might that be?"

He responded: "Do you believe in God?"

I answered: "What do you mean by God?"

He responded, "Please, it is a one-word answer: yes or no."

I responded, "Seeing that I am dressed as a priest, yes I do believe in God because who else could have possibly orchestrated my time to study at JTS? Imagine: I, a Catholic priest, studying Judaic studies at a rabbinical School! Who else but God could do such a thing!"

I will be forever grateful to the Roman Catholic Diocese of Brooklyn for allowing me to have such a great Jewish education. Very few priests, if any, have had this wonderful experience and this great opportunity to learn. To learn is a *mitzvah.*

Thank you to the faculty and community of the Jewish Theological Seminary for embracing me with kindness, warmth, and understanding. When I graduated, a fellow student said to me: "You will never forget that for five years of your life you studied with us, you lived with us, and you were part of us. We are part of you, Father, and you are part of all who studied with you." True words and true feelings were never more truly spoken.

All of this was made possible because of the Second Vatican Council and its historic document, *Nostra Aetate.*

24

Raised in a World of Dialogue

David Sandmel

I WAS NINE YEARS old in 1965 when *Nostra Aetate* was promulgated. It had a profound effect on my family and me. Being around Roman Catholics, especially priests and nuns, was simply part of my childhood. It is only in retrospect that I have come to appreciate that I witnessed, and to an extent participated in, a transformative time in Jewish-Christian relations.

My father, Samuel Sandmel (1911–1979), was professor of Bible and Hellenistic Literature (the latter was a term that included New Testament) at the Hebrew Union College—Jewish Institute of Religion in Cincinnati, Ohio, and a pioneer in the world of post–World War II Jewish-Christian dialogue. He had joined the faculty of HUC-JIR in 1952, having previously held a chair in Jewish studies at Vanderbilt University, in its day one of the few chairs in Jewish studies at a Christian institution.

By 1965, my father had published well-received, dare I say groundbreaking, books on Philo, the New Testament, and Paul,[1] and was a

---

1. Samuel Sandmel, *Philo's Place in Judaism: A Study on Conceptions of Abraham in Jewish Literature* (Cincinnati: Hebrew Union College Press, 1956); Sandmel, *A Jewish Understanding of the New Testament* (Cincinnati: Hebrew Union College Press, 1957); and Sandmel, *The Genius of Paul* (New York: Farrar, Straus & Cudahy, 1958).

sought-after lecturer at Protestant churches and seminaries. While he had some limited contact with Catholic scholars, the release of *Nostra Aetate*, changed everything. Michael Signer (1945–2009), who was my father's student and one of my teachers and mentors, once related to me that my father told him that before *Nostra Aetate* he had never been invited to a Roman Catholic institution. After its release, "it was as if the floodgates had opened," and he was immediately in great demand at Catholic institutions as well. That is a telling comment about American Catholicism in the 1960s and its openness to the changes heralded by the Second Vatican Council. The influence of the American Church on that Council has been well documented.[2]

The effect on our family was immediate. While Protestant ministers and scholars had long been fixtures at our Sabbath and Passover tables, now priests and nuns—usually in collars and habits—suddenly, it seemed, became regular guests. I remember that for several years, my mother, Frances Fox Sandmel (1917–1989), who had, in 1959, published a children's novel about interreligious relations,[3] put on a "model seder" for the sisters at a convent in our neighborhood, and I tagged along to help and to chant the Four Questions. I have vivid memories of those *sedarim* to this day and of the attention showered on me by the sisters.

While all this may seem quaint today, in its time it was still new and fresh. As a child just beginning to understand religious differences, I was unaware of its novelty, or that I was participating in something that just a few decades earlier would have been inconceivable.

Once, when my grandfather came to visit us in Cincinnati, my father picked him up at the train station. On the way home, my father said, "I've got some tickets to see a production of *Tevye and His Daughters*; would you like to go?" (*Tevye and His Daughters* is the collection of short stories by the great Yiddish author Sholem Aleichem that was eventually turned into the 1964 musical *Fiddler on the Roof*.) My grandfather was a great fan of Sholem Aleichem and was excited to go. What my father neglected to tell him was that the play was being produced at Edgecliff College, a small Roman Catholic women's college in Cincinnati that was renowned for its drama program (it merged with Xavier University in 1980). When my father and grandfather arrived at the theater on campus, my grandfather

2. See, for example, A. James Rudin, *Cushing, Spellman, O'Connor: The Surprising Story of How Three American Cardinals Transformed Catholic-Jewish Relations* (Grand Rapids: Eerdmans, 2011).

3. Frances Fox Sandmel, *All on the Team* (New York: Abingdon, 1959).

looked around the foyer and saw all these men in collars and women in habit—priests and nuns—and his instinctive reaction was fear. He associated Christian clergy with the pogroms that had driven him from Tsarist Russia and said to my father, "What did you bring me here for? Let's go." Before they could leave, however, a number of those priests and nuns came and surrounded them and greeted my father, their friend, warmly. My grandfather ended up staying and enjoyed the production immensely.

My experience has been very different from those of my father or grandfather. Christians, especially in clerical garb, terrified my grandfather. My father, who as a child avoided the local Catholic school on his way home, lest he and his friends be beaten and called "Christ-killers," came to be close friends with priests and Catholic scholars and received honorary degrees from Xavier University in Cincinnati and Rosary College (now Dominican University) in Illinois. As a scholar and a dialogian, he explored hitherto uncharted territory.

By the time I attended rabbinical school, it was a given that one of the tasks of Reform rabbis (at least) was to represent the Jewish community to the Christian world and to seek out relations with our Christian counterparts in the communities where we would serve. At HUC-JIR, I studied New Testament with one of my father's students, Michael Cook. When I began my doctoral program in Judaism and Christianity in the Greco-Roman world, a rabbi studying Christianity was no longer unique; indeed, there were two other rabbis in the program with me.

Nostra Aetate does not deserve all the credit for ushering in a new era in Jewish-Christian relations. Protestant scholars and denominations have contributed significantly to the positive shift in Jewish-Christian relations, both before and after *Nostra Aetate*. Nonetheless, it is because of the size of the Roman Catholic Church, the international prestige of the papacy, and the significance of the entire Second Vatican Council, of which *Nostra Aetate* is but a small part, that *Nostra Aetate* has come to represent the transformation of Jewish-Christian relations since the *Shoah*.

In 1998, I accepted a position as the Jewish Scholar at the Institute for Christian & Jewish Studies (ICJS) in Baltimore, managing the ICJS's Jewish Scholar's Project, which led to the publication of "*Dabru Emet*: A Jewish Statement on Christians and Christianity" in September 2000. "*Dabru Emet*" was, and remains, unique. It is only the document written and endorsed by Jews representing a broad spectrum of the Jewish community (it was endorsed by Reform, Reconstructionist, Conservative and Orthodox rabbis and scholars) to address the changes in Christianity represented by *Nostra Aetate*. Indeed, it has been called the Jewish *Nostra Aetate*—an understandable, if not entirely apt, appellation. Like *Nostra Aetate*, *Dabru Emet* grabbed the attention of the Jewish and Christian world. The crucial difference between the two statements is that *Nostra Aetate* is an authoritative document of the Roman Catholic Church, while *Dabru Emet* has no institutional authority; as the document itself makes clear, it represents only the opinion of its authors and those who endorsed it. Yet in public perception, the two often seen as complementary—the Jewish and the Christian statements of the new age of dialogue and relationship.

In 2003, I joined the faculty of the Catholic Theological Union, as the Crown-Ryan Chair in Jewish Studies, cofounded by a Jew and a Catholic. CTU, the largest Catholic graduate seminary in the country, was founded in 1968, and the spirit of *Nostra Aetate* has infused it since the very beginning. Rabbi Hayim Goren Perlmuter served on the faculty from CTU's inception until his death in 2001; Fr. John Pawlikowski, a leading scholar and advocate of Jewish-Christian relations, has also been on the faculty since the beginning. Joseph Cardinal Bernardin of Chicago, who helped shape the American Catholic Church in the vision of the Second Vatican Council and was considered a good friend of the Jewish community, also heavily influenced CTU.

It has been my privilege to represent the Central Conference of American Rabbis in a number of interfaith settings, including on the National Council of Synagogues and the International Jewish Committee on Interreligious Consultations, and through these organizations I have had substantial contact with the U.S. Conference of Catholic Bishops and the Holy See. There have been times when the Church's commitment to *Nostra Aetate* has seemed to waiver or has been called into question (the Good Friday prayer and the reaction to Mel Gibson's movie *The Passion of the Christ* are two examples). In each of these instances, the commitment to the *Nostra Aetate* that I have encountered on the part of Church officials has provided a framework for working through the difficulties that have arisen, and that inevitably will arise.

Finally, I think it essential to remember that the Church has released a number of documents that extend and deepen the understanding of *Nostra Aetate*—among them *Notes on the Correct Ways to Present Jews and Judaism in Catholic Teaching and Catechesis* (1985), *We Remember: A Reflection of the Shoah* (1998), and *The Jewish People and Their Sacred*

Scriptures in the Christian Bible (2001). Thus, the Church has continued to develop its formal theology of the relationship to Jews and Judaism far beyond any other denomination. Popes have demonstrated in word and action that *Nostra Aetate* is firmly imbedded in the Church.

The Catholic Church after *Nostra Aetate* is the Church that I have known, and my understanding of Christianity and my relationships with Christians, especially Catholic Christians, have been profoundly shaped by it.

25

Nostra Aetate

A Reflection

Byron L. Sherwin

TIMES HAVE CHANGED SINCE *Nostra Aetate* (*In Our Time*). And, we have changed since then as well. In interfaith relations, especially in Catholic-Jewish relations, much has changed; and little has changed because of and since *Nostra Aetate*. It all depends upon where you look.

The agendas, priorities, and demographics of both the Catholic and Jewish communities have changed since Vatican II. The communities that encounter one another today are not who they were then, not only in the United States, but elsewhere as well. For example, rabbis and priests have the same titles as they did then, but they often differ from what was then the case in terms of education, training, background, ethnicity, and even (for the rabbis) gender. Put another way, even the players now differ from those, like myself, who greeted *Nostra Aetate* with enthusiasm decades ago, and committed themselves to change what was to what might be.

From a theological and historical perspective, *Nostra Aetate* (and the subsequent notes for its implementation) was a game changer in the relationship between Catholics and Jews. One of the most radical features of Vatican II, it provided Jews and Catholics engaged in improving Catholic-Jewish relations with a justification—a support and a proof-text for advancing an agenda we probably would have pursued even without it. Jews could point to these documents as evidence that longtime barriers between Catholics and Jews, and between Catholicism and Judaism, were being lowered, that Judaism had finally been recognized as a faith with its own religious integrity, that the supersessionist doctrine was in decline, that theologically rooted anti-Semitism was being uprooted, that the dangerous teaching that Jews were "Christ-killers" was in retreat, that the Church teaching of "mission to the Jews" was going into remission. Catholics could now point to the inclusion of these views in the official teachings of the Church, binding upon all Catholics. Initially conceived by the popular Pope John XXIII, with his impeccable record of having helped to save Jews during the Holocaust, *Nostra Aetate* served as the foundation for future popes, especially John Paul II, to propel Catholic-Jewish relations to a fraternal level almost inconceivable in the mid-1960s when *Nostra Aetate* was first issued, and when I began to be involved in Catholic-Jewish relations. (John Paul II, it should be remembered, was the first pope since the first pope, Peter, to have grown up and lived among Jews.) For this miracle alone, these two popes deserve canonization.

The significance of *Nostra Aetate* is eminently clear to those who, like myself, have been personally committed to and professionally engaged in improving Catholic-Jewish relations. We carefully studied the relevant documents, painstakingly reviewed relevant statements of popes and of Vatican commissions, proclamations of national episcopates, and of leading Catholic prelates like Joseph Cardinal Bernardin, archbishop of Chicago. However, truth be told, our activities in this area have often been—to our dismay—marginal in our respective faith communities. Indeed, sometimes they have been resisted or ignored by powerful forces within our own faith communities. Often, we labored despite, rather than because of, support from our own faith community.

Within the Jewish community, the implications of *Nostra Aetate* and related documents seem unknown, negligible or greeted with disbelief or even ridicule. For example, in the 1990s, Edward Cardinal Cassidy, then president of the Holy See's Commission on Religious Relations with the Jews, observed how startled he was at how little awareness of current Catholic teaching on Jews and Judaism contemporary Jews had whom he met throughout the world, and how he found Jewish understanding of Catholicism to reflect archaic, pre–Vatican II, if not medieval, realities. Until today, many Jews, with some justification, believe the Church has no intention of discontinuing its missionary activities vis-à-vis Jews, that supersessionist theology has not really been repudiated. The long history of Christian anti-Semitism is difficult for Jews to forgive and to forget, despite current Church teaching that "anti-Semitism is a sin against God."

Though in large American cities (such as Chicago) with substantial Jewish populations, Catholic-Jewish relations have been highly developed theologically and socially, largely because of support by local archbishops, there are still many places in the United States and certainly elsewhere throughout the world, where recent Church and papal teachings on Jews and Judaism remain unknown or ignored both by Catholics and Jews. Even in places where Jewish-Catholic relations have flourished, they are no longer the "front-burner" issue that they were not so long ago. For some, this is because Catholic-Jewish relations have become normalized and have been successful. For others, it is because they have failed. And, for still others, it is simply because there are other currently more press-ing issues. In places around the globe like Africa and Asia, with miniscule Jewish communities, the implications of these documents seem socially irrelevant. In most of Europe, where secularization advances, and where the remnants of Jewish communities destroyed during the Holocaust wither further, while European Islam proliferates, and where anti-Jewish and anti-Israel sentiments escalate, Catholic-Jewish relations seem to have been supplanted by other, more pressing concerns and agendas. For those of us who have been committed to and engaged in Catholic-Jewish relations since *Nostra Aetate,* it sometimes seems that all our efforts have been for naught, that the locomotive that once steamed forward is now moving in reverse.

As a Jewish theologian, I have found my interests and activities in interreligious dialogue either condemned or stifled both by Ortho-dox and secular forces within the American Jewish community. Jewish Orthodoxy, for various social and religious reasons, largely repudiates theologically based interreligious dialogue, often removing theological discourse from the agenda. Secular Jewish advocacy organizations also tend to remove discussions of faith from the interfaith agenda. Yet, as my mentor, Abraham Heschel, put it, "the premise of interfaith is faith." It is not surprising that Catholic participants in dialogue find it strange that theological issues are often excommunicated from the agenda of inter-religious dialogue by their Jewish dialogic partners. I, and other Jewish theologians, find it strange as well. Sometimes dialogue seems like two simultaneous monologues.

The secular Jewish advocacy groups that in recent decades have dominated Jewish involvement in interreligious dialogue have marginalized issues of faith, seeking instead to further their institutionally based sociopolitical agendas. Often their fundraising ploys and their justification for interreligious dialogue are related to their sociopolitical goals, with real inter*faith* dialogue considered an irrelevancy or an unaffordable luxury. As Cardinal Cassidy and others have pointed out, we are not two social service agencies or two political action committees but two faith communities. Whereas Heschel and other Jewish theologians have refused to engage in interreligious dialogue as long as "mission to the Jews" remains part of the Christian agenda, Jewish advocacy agencies often attempt a kind of proselytizing of their own, in that they aim at "converting" Christians to affirm certain Jewish communal policies regarding the State of Israel, stimulated by evoking Christian guilt for a history of anti-Semitism culminating in the Holocaust. The strategy of many Jewish advocacy organizations in interreligious dialogue is neither religious, theological, nor authentic, but is rather an effort to enlist Christian support for the Jewish communal agenda.

In my almost fifty years of involvement in Catholic-Jewish dialogue, *Nostra Aetate* has primarily served as a backstop or as a backstory. In my experience, more significant than the documents relating to *Nostra Aetate* have been the efforts of courageous and committed individuals on each side of the Catholic-Jewish hyphen. More than anything else in this endeavor, I value many of the personal, individual relationships forged in my work in Catholic-Jewish relations. As a Jewish theologian who is part of a Jewish community that either is uninterested in Jewish theology or affirms its nonexistence or both, I find Christians whom I have met through interfaith dialogue, who take theology and spirituality seriously, among the few I can speak to and learn from about issues of faith and spirituality. As a Jewish bioethicist, I realize that Catholic and Jewish teachings on issues of bioethical concern often radically differ. But bioethics is not a priority on the Jewish communal agenda. I therefore greatly appreciate the efforts of Catholic ethicists in playing a major role in forging the field of bioethics in America, who, by their continued preoccupation with this vital field, have made our work together in this field both significant and fulfilling. We have much to say to one another and much to contribute together to the public square.

In recent years, it seems that, for a variety of reasons, mostly benign, Catholic-Jewish dialogue has been put on the "back burner" in both the Jewish and Catholic communities. I therefore fear a retrenchment on both sides and a return to undesirable conditions that already have been overcome through many years of sustained effort, including my own. Yet, I have hope that the pontificate of Francis I will build on past achievements and will inspire Catholic-Jewish relations to new heights. As an Argentinean, the pope knows all too well that it takes two to tango.

Afterword

IN MUSIC WE HAVE a term, *leitmotif*. It means that there are certain dominant themes that recur in a composition—an opera or a symphony or concerto—and that they symbolize a specific person or situation or idea. What are the salient leitmotifs in this volume containing the views of twenty-five diverse contributors from five nations and different religious traditions? I have carefully reviewed each piece several times and have culled the dominant themes.

The most obvious theme all concur is that we have witnessed a theological revolution in Christian thinking and a radical transformation of the Roman Catholic magisterium ever since Vatican II and the publication of *Nostra Aetate* as well as the several other relevant documents that emerged in the wake of that historical conclave. The terms "revolution," "change," and "transformation" reappear countless times in the essays of the contributors to this volume. Moreover, many indicate that this radical transformation was undoubtedly sparked by the tragedy of the *Shoah* that wiped out six million, one-third of world Jewry, in Christian Europe, and that signified a dismal failure of Christianity and Christians. After all, Western Europe has been Christian since Emperor Constantine in the fourth century, and the rest of Europe followed suit roughly a thousand years ago. How could this tragedy have occurred in the lands of Christianity? This questions gnaws at the contributors as they seek to heal the wounds between the two faiths.

The contributors affirm that the covenant between God and the Jewish people has never been revoked, and that (tellingly) the documents that discuss this issue use the present tense of the verb: the Jewish people *remains in the covenant with the Divine*—despite centuries of teachings to the contrary. Thus, the ancient doctrine of supersessionism, which insisted that Christianity had superseded or displaced Israel as God's people is no longer valid; that mutual respect and trust must displace that notion once and for all time. In the end of time, in God's own plan known only to Him but a mystery to flesh and blood, Israel will unite with the Gentile Christian world (Paul, Romans 9–11). Consequently, the Jewish people are granted salvation and need not convert to Christianity to achieve that end. Hence, proselytizing Jews is no longer valid or needed, and indeed the Vatican no longer maintains an office for the conversion of the Jews.

There is clearly a growing awareness and acknowledgment that we share many common values: that there is a spiritual bond between Judaism and Christianity and a new relationship of trust. This has led to a reorientation of Christian views of Judaism and a fundamental link to the message of Jesus that had been broken or distorted for many centuries. This reorientation has reiterated the Jewishness of Jesus and his disciples—a fact much ignored or distorted for centuries. Current scholarship indicates that Jesus was much closer in his thinking to the much-maligned Pharisees than to any other sect of his day. He certainly did not intend to found a new church or a new religion, and the separation between the two faiths took at least several centuries.

All agree that *Nostra Aetate* repudiated the odious "deicide" charge that caused so much death and mayhem in Jewish communities around the world. The document also went far in terminating the "teaching of contempt" that had had for so many centuries poisoned relations between the two faiths. It engendered the principle, formulated unambiguously by Pope John Paul II, that anti-Semitism is a sin against God and humanity. These new positions have fostered revision of the liturgy as well as new educational themes and emphases.

Nostra Aetate has given life to a new appreciation of the Hebrew Bible, no longer referred to pejoratively as the Old Testament. No longer is it regarded as merely prelude to the superior New Testament; no longer is its text viewed through the lens of the New Testament or the often jaundiced perspective of the Church Fathers. It is today regarded as a positive resource for Christian theology, and the faith of Israel is intrinsic to Christianity that continues to draw nourishment from the ancient olive tree.

This newfound respect for the Hebrew Bible has stimulated a greater respect for the Jewish interpretations of the Scriptures and the legitimacy of its messianic hopes. Judaism did not—despite many of the Church

Fathers, Christian theologians, and scholars of the last two centuries—end with the death of Jesus and the destruction of the Temple in Jerusalem in 70 CE. A creative and fertile civilization has carried on and flourished in dozens of lands on several continents, fashioning some masterpieces of the spirit as well as cultural, scientific, technological, and artistic creations that have impacted our civilization. Thus, despite all the centuries of denigration, Judaism continues to flourish and foliate and enrich the world.

True to the summons of *Nostra Aetate*, dialogue and cooperation between Jews and Christians of various denominations have become the norm We have become partners in a "culture of healthy dialogues." We have created institutes and departments at various colleges and universities as well as programs in other realms for Jewish-Christian learning. Moreover, ever since *Nostra Aetate*, Jews, Catholics, Protestant and Eastern Orthodox have developed warm personal friendships; we have gotten to know one another as never before; we have shared meals and social occasions; we have visited in each other's homes; we have entered various houses of worship and observed the diverse religious occasions and rituals; we have become colleagues and true friends.

Nostra Aetate has spawned a resurgence of interest among Jews in the New Testament and in the early relationship between Judaism and nascent Christianity. In the past, Jews generally shunned such an enterprise. Today there is an ever-increasing number of Jewish scholars whose field is Jewish-Christian relations.

Nostra Aetate paved the way for the elimination of theological arguments against the rebirth of the State of Israel and the return of the Jewish people to its ancient homeland. Having discarded the ancient patristic view that Israel lost its Temple and homeland as punishment for having rejected Jesus, it became possible for the Vatican to recognize Israel and open diplomatic relations as well as schedule papal visits.

In a broader sense, *Nostra Aetate* as well as the other documents issued by Vatican II such as *Lumen Gentium*, expressed a willingness to recognize the dignity, validity, and integrity of other religious faiths and their right to religious freedom. The old notion that "error has no rights" gave way at long last to the idea that each legitimate faith tradition possesses a modicum of truth and a ray of divine enlightenment.

Finally, *Nostra Aetate* served as an impetus or catalyst for other faith groups to reexamine their relationship to Judaism and to reevaluate their theology, their teachings, their preaching and their liturgy, and how they portray Jews and Judaism. This has been abundantly evident in the Protestant world, among Eastern Orthodox, and in evangelical circles.

All of these accomplishments and developments were unthinkable fifty short years ago. Remarkably, all of this resulted from a short document of a mere eight paragraphs. But I remind the reader that the Ten Commandments consist of only 172 Hebrew words, and Lincoln's Gettysburg address took only two minutes to deliver. Brevity is not necessarily a vice even as verbosity is not necessarily a virtue.

There is the tendency in certain Jewish quarters to minimize these accomplishments and to complain that it is too little or too late; that progress is slow and attitudes have not totally changed. I remind such skeptics of the old Jewish proverb that "all beginnings are hard." Nineteen centuries of teaching and preaching cannot be overturned in a mere fifty years or so. Of course, all agree that further education on all levels is needed. Teaching, educational materials, curricula, preaching, and religious and educational guidelines that embody the principles laid down at Vatican II must be introduced in all Catholic dioceses. We might recall that approximately 40 percent of world Catholics reside in Central and South America. Have the teachings of Vatican II and *Nostra Aetate* been adequately disseminated there? With the advent of Pope Francis I from Argentina, I believe there are good prospects to achieve that goal. Then, of course, there are millions of Catholics in Asia and Africa, not to mention Europe, where these new principles have perhaps not yet been sufficiently absorbed. Therein lies a challenge to the Roman Catholic faith. But equally important is the need for the Protestants and Eastern Orthodox to confront the past honestly and courageously and set a new course based on the Catholic pattern.

As I reflect on all that has occurred these past fifty years, and as I reread the essays in this volume, I wonder: Maybe our reconciliation with the Christian world can spark other faith groups to make shalom between them. Maybe the Muslim world will end its antipathy to Christians, who are severely persecuted these days. Maybe Shiites and Sunnis—all Muslims—will cease their murderous attacks on one another. Maybe Jews will no longer be the target of anti-Semites. Maybe the Hindus and Buddhists and other faiths will follow the benevolent path blazed at Vatican II. The eminent Roman Catholic theologian Hans Küng observed that there must be peace between the religions if there is to be peace between the nations. *Nostra Aetate* pointed the way to the right road we must all take if we are to witness the fulfillment of the messianic dream (Mic 4:4): "And each person will sit beneath his or her vine and fig tree with none to make them afraid."

Appendix I

DECLARATION ON
THE RELATION OF THE CHURCH TO NON-
CHRISTIAN RELIGIONS
NOSTRA AETATE
PROCLAIMED BY HIS HOLINESS
POPE PAUL VI
ON OCTOBER 28, 1965

4. As the sacred synod searches into the mystery of the Church, it remembers the bond that spiritually ties the people of the New Covenant
to Abraham's stock.

Thus the Church of Christ acknowledges that, according to God's saving
design, the beginnings of her faith and her election are found already
among the Patriarchs, Moses and the prophets. She professes that all who
believe in Christ—Abraham's sons according to faith[6]—are included in
the same Patriarch's call, and likewise that the salvation of the Church is
mysteriously foreshadowed by the chosen people's exodus from the land
of bondage. The Church, therefore, cannot forget that she received the
revelation of the Old Testament through the people with whom God in
His inexpressible mercy concluded the Ancient Covenant. Nor can she
forget that she draws sustenance from the root of that well-cultivated

olive tree onto which have been grafted the wild shoots, the Gentiles.[7] Indeed, the Church believes that by His cross Christ, Our Peace, reconciled Jews and Gentiles. making both one in Himself.[8]

The Church keeps ever in mind the words of the Apostle about his kinsmen: "theirs is the sonship and the glory and the covenants and the law and the worship and the promises; theirs are the fathers and from them is the Christ according to the flesh" (Rom. 9:4-5), the Son of the Virgin Mary. She also recalls that the Apostles, the Church's main-stay and pillars, as well as most of the early disciples who proclaimed Christ's Gospel to the world, sprang from the Jewish people.

As Holy Scripture testifies, Jerusalem did not recognize the time of her visitation,[9] nor did the Jews in large number, accept the Gospel; indeed not a few opposed its spreading.[10] Nevertheless, God holds the Jews most dear for the sake of their Fathers; He does not repent of the gifts He makes or of the calls He issues—such is the witness of the Apostle.[11] In company with the Prophets and the same Apostle, the Church awaits that day, known to God alone, on which all peoples will address the Lord in a single voice and "serve him shoulder to shoulder" (Zeph. 3:9).[12]

Since the spiritual patrimony common to Christians and Jews is thus so great, this sacred synod wants to foster and recommend that mutual understanding and respect which is the fruit, above all, of biblical and theological studies as well as of fraternal dialogues.

True, the Jewish authorities and those who followed their lead pressed for the death of Christ;[13] still, what happened in His passion cannot be charged against all the Jews, without distinction, then alive, nor against the Jews of today. Although the Church is the new people of God, the Jews should not be presented as rejected or accursed by God, as if this followed from the Holy Scriptures. All should see to it, then, that in catechetical work or in the preaching of the word of God they do not teach anything that does not conform to the truth of the Gospel and the spirit of Christ.

Furthermore, in her rejection of every persecution against any man, the Church, mindful of the patrimony she shares with the Jews and moved not by political reasons but by the Gospel's spiritual love, decries hatred, persecutions, displays of anti-Semitism, directed against Jews at any time and by anyone.

Besides, as the Church has always held and holds now, Christ underwent His passion and death freely, because of the sins of men and out of infinite love, in order that all may reach salvation. It is, therefore, the burden of the Church's preaching to proclaim the cross of Christ as the sign of God's all-embracing love and as the fountain from which every grace flows.

NOTES

6. Cf. *Gal.* 3:7

7. Cf. *Rom.* 11:17-24

8. Cf. *Eph.* 2:14-16

9. Cf. *Lk.* 19:44

10. Cf. *Rom.* 11:28

11. Cf. *Rom.* 11:28-29; cf. dogmatic Constitution, *Lumen Gentium* (Light of nations) AAS, 57 (1965) pag. 20

12. Cf. *Is.* 66:23; *Ps.* 65:4; *Rom.* 11:11-32

13. Cf. *John* 19:6

Appendix II

From Pope Francis's apostolic exhortation
Evangelii Gaudium [On the Proclamation of the
Gospel In Today's World], issued November 24, 2013

Relations with Judaism

247. We hold the Jewish people in special regard because their covenant with God has never been revoked, for "the gifts and the call of God are irrevocable" (*Rom* 11:29). The Church, which shares with Jews an important part of the sacred Scriptures, looks upon the people of the covenant and their faith as one of the sacred roots of her own Christian identity (cf. *Rom* 11:16-18). As Christians, we cannot consider Judaism as a foreign religion; nor do we include the Jews among those called to turn from idols and to serve the true God (cf. *1 Thes* 1:9). With them, we believe in the one God who acts in history, and with them we accept his revealed word.

248. Dialogue and friendship with the children of Israel are part of the life of Jesus' disciples. The friendship which has grown between us makes us bitterly and sincerely regret the terrible persecutions which they have endured, and continue to endure, especially those that have involved Christians.

249. God continues to work among the people of the Old Covenant and to bring forth treasures of wisdom which flow from their encounter

with his word. For this reason, the Church also is enriched when she receives the values of Judaism. While it is true that certain Christian beliefs are unacceptable to Judaism, and that the Church cannot refrain from proclaiming Jesus as Lord and Messiah, there exists as well a rich complementarity which allows us to read the texts of the Hebrew Scriptures together and to help one another to mine the riches of God's word. We can also share many ethical convictions and a common concern for justice and the development of peoples.

Interreligious dialogue

250. An attitude of openness in truth and in love must characterize the dialogue with the followers of non-Christian religions, in spite of various obstacles and difficulties, especially forms of fundamentalism on both sides. Interreligious dialogue is a necessary condition for peace in the world, and so it is a duty for Christians as well as other religious communities. This dialogue is in first place a conversation about human existence or simply, as the bishops of India have put it, a matter of "being open to them, sharing their joys and sorrows".[194] In this way we learn to accept others and their different ways of living, thinking and speaking. We can then join one another in taking up the duty of serving justice and peace, which should become a basic principle of all our exchanges. A dialogue which seeks social peace and justice is in itself, beyond all merely practical considerations, an ethical commitment which brings about a new social situation. Efforts made in dealing with a specific theme can become a process in which, by mutual listening, both parts can be purified and enriched. These efforts, therefore, can also express love for truth.

251. In this dialogue, ever friendly and sincere, attention must always be paid to the essential bond between dialogue and proclamation, which leads the Church to maintain and intensify her relationship with non-Christians.[195] A facile syncretism would ultimately be a totalitarian gesture on the part of those who would ignore greater values of which they are not the masters. True openness involves remaining steadfast in one's deepest convictions, clear and joyful in one's own identity, while at the same time being "open to understanding those of the other party" and "knowing that dialogue can enrich each side".[196] What is not helpful is a diplomatic openness which says "yes" to everything in order to avoid problems, for this would be a way of deceiving others and denying them the good which we have been given to share generously with others.

Evangelization and interreligious dialogue, far from being opposed, mutually support and nourish one another.[197]

252. Our relationship with the followers of Islam has taken on great importance, since they are now significantly present in many traditionally Christian countries, where they can freely worship and become fully a part of society. We must never forget that they "profess to hold the faith of Abraham, and together with us they adore the one, merciful God, who will judge humanity on the last day".[198] The sacred writings of Islam have retained some Christian teachings; Jesus and Mary receive profound veneration and it is admirable to see how Muslims both young and old, men and women, make time for daily prayer and faithfully take part in religious services. Many of them also have a deep conviction that their life, in its entirety, is from God and for God. They also acknowledge the need to respond to God with an ethical commitment and with mercy towards those most in need.

253. In order to sustain dialogue with Islam, suitable training is essential for all involved, not only so that they can be solidly and joyfully grounded in their own identity, but so that they can also acknowledge the values of others, appreciate the concerns underlying their demands and shed light on shared beliefs. We Christians should embrace with affection and respect Muslim immigrants to our countries in the same way that we hope and ask to be received and respected in countries of Islamic tradition. I ask and I humbly entreat those countries to grant Christians freedom to worship and to practice their faith, in light of the freedom which followers of Islam enjoy in Western countries! Faced with disconcerting episodes of violent fundamentalism, our respect for true followers of Islam should lead us to avoid hateful generalisations, for authentic Islam and the proper reading of the Koran are opposed to every form of violence.

254. Non-Christians, by God's gracious initiative, when they are faithful to their own consciences, can live "justified by the grace of God",[199] and thus be "associated to the paschal mystery of Jesus Christ".[200] But due to the sacramental dimension of sanctifying grace, God's working in them tends to produce signs and rites, sacred expressions which in turn bring others to a communitarian experience of journeying towards God.[201] While these lack the meaning and efficacy of the sacraments instituted by Christ, they can be channels which the Holy Spirit raises up in order to liberate non-Christians from atheistic immanentism or from purely

individual religious experiences. The same Spirit everywhere brings forth various forms of practical wisdom which help people to bear suffering and to live in greater peace and harmony. As Christians, we can also benefit from these treasures built up over many centuries, which can help us better to live our own beliefs.

FOOTNOTES CORRESPONDING TO THE ABOVE TEXT:

[194] Indian Bishops' Conference, Final Declaration of the XXX Assembly: *The Role of the Church for a Better India* (8 March 2013), 8.9.

[195] Cf. *Propositio* 53.

[196] John Paul II, Encyclical Letter *Redemptoris Missio* (7 December 1990), 56: AAS 83 (1991), 304.

[197] Cf. Benedict XVI, Address to the Roman Curia (21 December 2012): AAS 105 (2006), 51; Second Vatican Ecumenical Council, Decree on the Missionary Activity of the Church *Ad Gentes*, 9; *Catechism of the Catholic Church*, 856.

[198] Second Vatican Ecumenical Council, Dogmatic Constitution on the Church *Lumen Gentium*, 16.

[199] International Theological Commission, *Christianity and the World Religions* (1996), 72: *Enchiridion Vaticanum* 15, No. 1061.

[200] Ibid.

[201] Cf. ibid., 81-87: *Enchiridion Vaticanum* 15, Nos. 1070-1076.

Contributors

Rabbi Dr. DAVID BERGER is Ruth and I. Lewis Gordon Professor of Jewish History and Dean of the Graduate School of Yeshiva University in New York City. Previously he was Professor of Jewish Studies at Brooklyn College and has written several volumes and essays on medieval Jewish-Christian relations.

Rabbi Dr. MICHAEL COOK is Sol and Arlene Bronstein Professor of Jewish-Christian Studies and Intertestamental and Early Christian Literature at the Hebrew Union College-Jewish Institute of Religion in Cincinnati. He has authored books and essays on Jewish-Christian relations.

Dr. PHILIP A. CUNNINGHAM is Professor of Theology and Director of the Institute for Jewish-Catholic Relations at St. Joseph's University in Philadelphia. Previously he headed the Institute for Christian-Jewish Learning at Boston College and he has authored essays and volumes on interreligious affairs.

Rabbi Dr. BARRY CYTRON is Professor of Jewish Studies and Jewish Chaplain at Macalester College in St. Paul, Minnesota, and formerly directed the Jay Phillips Center in Interfaith Education at St. John's University and the University of St. Thomas in Minneapolis-St. Paul.

Dr. EUGENE FISHER is Distinguished Professor of Theology at St. Leo's University in Florida. He served for many years as the director of Catholic-Jewish relations for the US Conference of Catholic Bishops and as a *Consultor* to the Holy See. He authored numerous books and essays on Jewish-Catholic relations.

Fr. Dr. LAWRENCE E. FRIZZELL, S.T.L., is Director of the Institute of Judeo-Christian Studies and program director of the M.A. program and Professor of Judeo-Christian Studies at Seton Hall University in South Orange, New Jersey.

Rabbi Dr. IRVING GREENBERG served as Executive Director of the President's Commission on the Holocaust and Chairman of the U.S. Holocaust Museum Memorial Council and was a Professor of Jewish Studies at the City University of New York. He has authored books and essays on Jewish theology.

Dr. SUSANNAH HESCHEL is the Eli Black Professor of Jewish Studies at Dartmouth College in New Hampshire and has taught at Princeton University, the University of Capetown, the University of Edinburgh, and the University of Frankfurt and authored works on German-Jewish thought.

Rev. Dr. ALAN F. JOHNSON is Emeritus Professor of New Testament and Christian Ethics, Wheaton College, Illinois, Adjunct Professor of Christian Ethics, Wheaton Graduate School, and Emeritus Director of the Center for Applied Christian Ethics at Wheaton College.

Dr. EDWARD KESSLER, M.B.E., is the founder and Executive Director of the Woolf Institute and a fellow of St. Edmunds College, Cambridge, Great Britain. He has authored several volumes and numerous papers on interreligious affairs. He received the M.B.E. award from Queen Elizabeth II.

Rev. Dr. ANTONIOS KIREOPOULOS is Associate General Secretary for Faith and Order and Interfaith Relations at the National Council of Churches USA. Previously he was Executive Director of Religions for Peace USA and Special Assistant to the Greek Orthodox Archbishop of America.

Rabbi Dr. EUGENE KORN is the American Director of the Center for Jewish-Christian Understanding and Cooperation in Israel and author and editor of books and articles in the field of Jewish thought and ethics.

Rabbi Dr. RON KRONISH is founder and Director of the Interreligious Coordinating Council in Israel where has lived since 1979. He served as lecturer in education at Tel Aviv University and Hebrew University and has produced the film, "I Am Joseph Your Brother."

Rabbi Dr. SHIRA LANDER is Professor of Practice and Director of Jewish Studies at Southern Methodist University in Dallas, Texas. Formerly Professor of Jewish Studies at Rice University, she also taught at St. Mary's Seminary in Baltimore and authored the commentary on I Corinthians for the *Oxford Jewish Annotated New Testament*.

Msgr. GUY A. MASSIE is Pastor of Sacred Hearts/St. Stephen Parish in Brooklyn. He served as Catholic Chaplain at Brooklyn College and is Diocesan Ecumenical and Interfaith Chairman for the Diocese of Brooklyn and Queens.

Fr. Dr. JOHN T. PAWLIKOWSKI, O.S.M., is Professor of Social Ethics and Director of the Catholic-Jewish Studies Program at the Catholic Theological Union in Chicago. Author of numerous articles and books on Catholic-Jewish relations, he served as President of the International Council of Christians and Jews.

Dr. ELENA G. PROCARIO-FOLEY is Chairperson of the Religious Studies Department, Driscoll Professor of Jewish-Catholic Studies and Associate Professor of Religious Studies at Iona College in New Rochelle, New York. She is currently Associate Editor of *Horizons: The Journal of the College Theology Society*.

Rabbi Dr. DAVID ROSEN is the International Director of Interreligious Affairs of the American Jewish Committee and past President of the International Council of Christians and Jews. He was made a Knight Commander by Pope Benedict XVI and a Commander of the British Empire by Queen Elizabeth II.

Rabbi Dr. GILBERT S. ROSENTHAL is Director of the National Council of Synagogues. He served as a congregational rabbi for 33 years and Executive Vice President of the New York Board of Rabbis for 10 years. He has authored and edited 12 books and numerous articles on Jewish ideas and doctrines.

Rabbi Dr. DAVID SANDMEL is Director of Interfaith Affairs for the Anti-Defamation League. Previously, he held the Crown-Ryan Chair of Jewish Studies at the Catholic Theological Union in Chicago and was Rabbi-Educator at Temple Sholom in Chicago.

Rabbi Dr. BYRON SHERWIN is Distinguished Service Professor and Vice President Emeritus at the Spertus Institute for Jewish Studies in Chicago and author and editor of numerous books and essays on Jewish theology. He was decorated by the Republic of Poland for his work in Christian-Jewish dialogue.

Rev. Dr. JOSEPH D. SMALL served as Director of the Office of Theology and Worship of the Presbyterian Church (USA) from 1989–2011. Currently he is Adjunct Professor at the University of Dubuque Theological Seminary and consultant on church relations to the Presbyterian Foundation.

Fr. Dr. LIAM TRACEY, O.S.M., S.L.D., is Professor of Liturgy and Director of Post-Graduate Studies at St. Patrick's College in Maynooth, Ireland. Currently, he serves as Review Editor of the *Irish Theological Quarterly*.

Dr. MICHAEL R. TRICE is Assistant Dean of Ecumenical and Interreligious Dialogue and Assistant Professor of Theology at Seattle University School of Theology and Ministry. He served as Associate Executive Director of Ecumenical and Interreligious Relations for the Evangelical Lutheran Church.

Fr. Dr. MURRAY WATSON is the cofounder of the Centre for Jewish-Catholic-Muslim Learning at King's University College, London, Ontario, and is a member of the Canadian Catholic-Jewish Consultation Commission. He is Academic Director of the Bat Kol Institute for Jewish Studies of the Sisters of Sion.

Dr. DEBORAH WEISSMAN settled in Israel in 1972 and has taught at the Hebrew University in Jerusalem and directed a teachers training institute for Israeli high schools. She is the first woman President of the International Council of Christians and Jews.